GUARDIAN Hearts

1

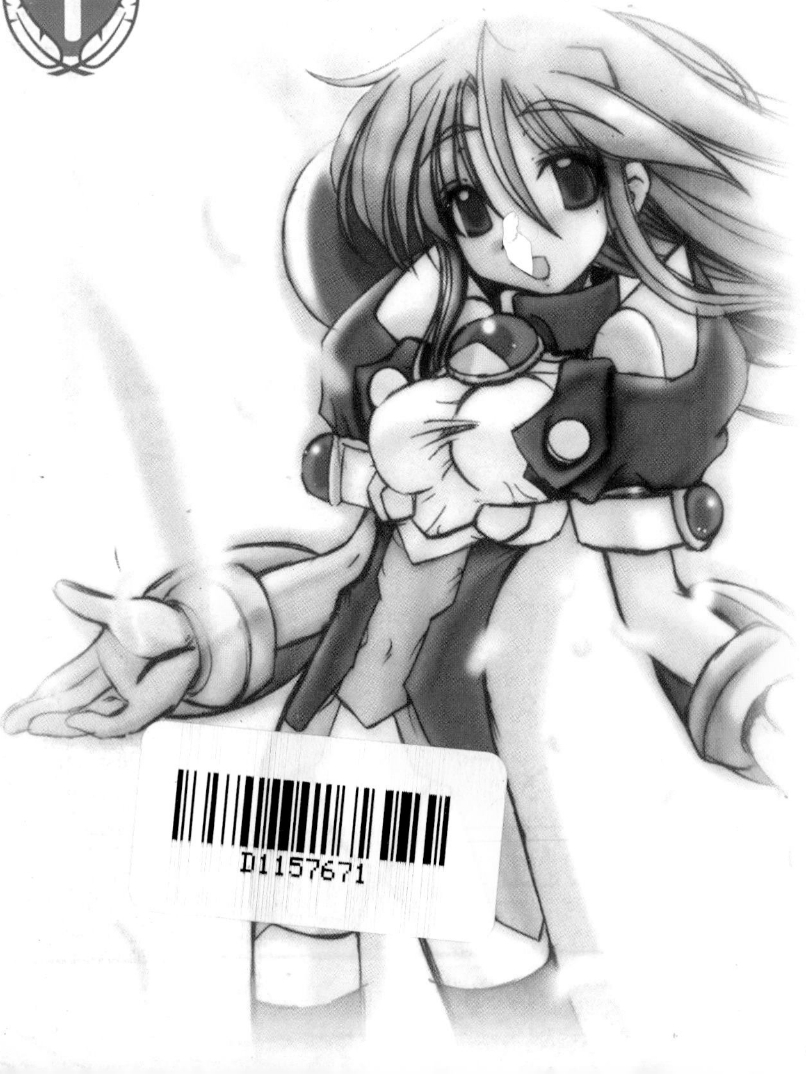

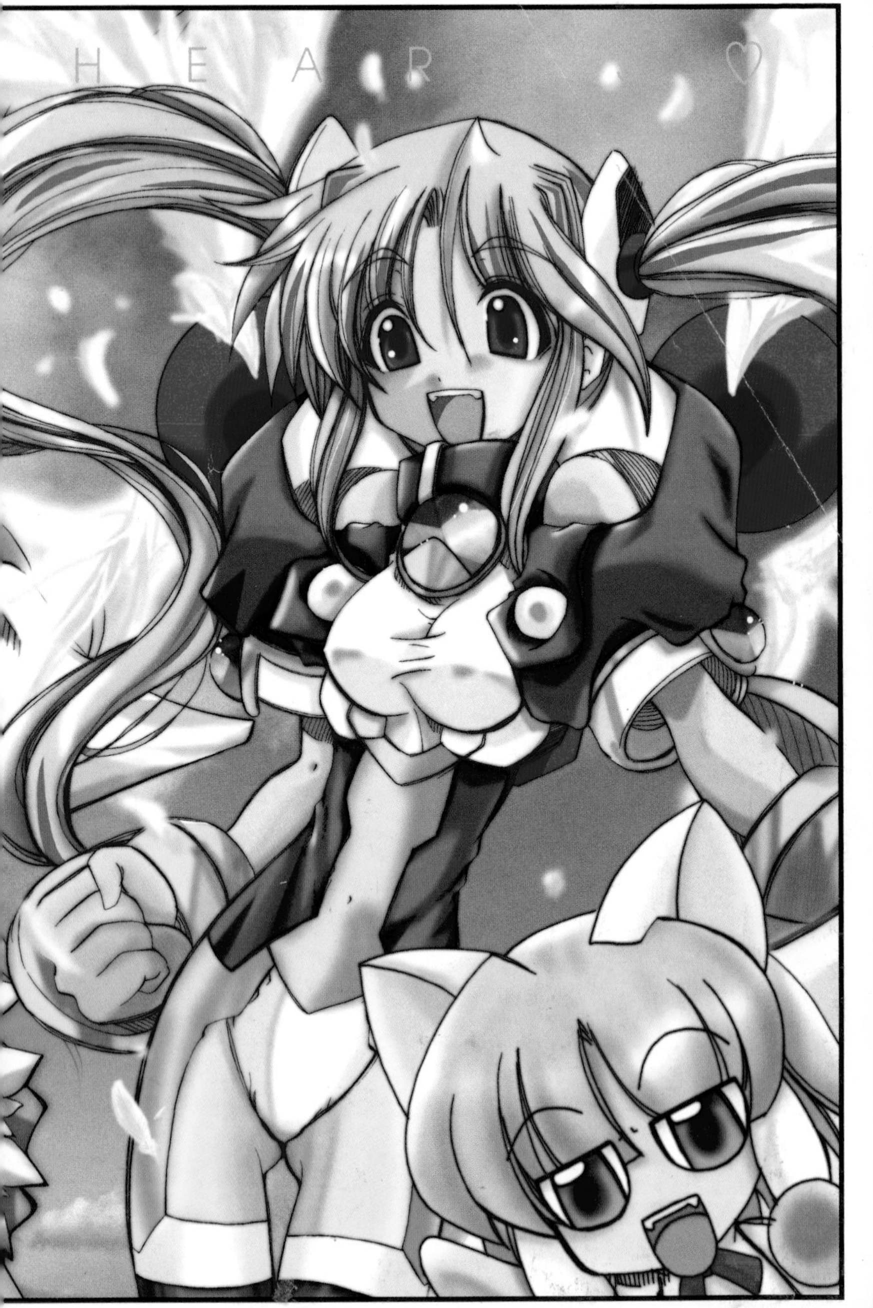
H E A R T ♡

GUARDIAN Hearts

Created by
Sae Amatsu

HAMBURG // LONDON // LOS ANGELES // TOKYO

Guardian Hearts Vol.1
Created by Sae Amatsu

Translation - Monica Seya Chin
English Adaptation - Erin M. Blakemore
Copy Editor - Jessica Chavez
Retouch and Lettering - Star Print Brokers
Production Artist - Jennifer M. Sanchez
Cover Design - Al-Insan Lashley

Editor - Bryce P. Coleman
Digital Imaging Manager - Chris Buford
Pre-Production Supervisor - Lucas Rivera
Production Manager - Elisabeth Brizzi
Managing Editor - Vy Nguyen
Creative Director - Anne Marie Horne
Editor-in-Chief - Rob Tokar
Publisher - Mike Kiley
President and C.O.O. - John Parker
C.E.O. and Chief Creative Officer - Stu Levy

A  Manga

TOKYOPOP and  are trademarks or registered trademarks of TOKYOPOP Inc.

TOKYOPOP Inc.
5900 Wilshire Blvd. Suite 2000
Los Angeles, CA 90036

E-mail: info@TOKYOPOP.com
Come visit us online at www.TOKYOPOP.com

GUARDIAN HEARTS Volume 1
© SAE AMATSU 2001
First published in Japan in 2001 by KADOKAWA SHOTEN
PUBLISHING CO., LTD., Tokyo.
English translation rights arranged with KADOKAWA SHOTEN
PUBLISHING CO., LTD., Tokyo
through TUTTLE–MORI AGENCY, INC., Tokyo.
English text copyright © 2008 TOKYOPOP Inc.

ISBN: 978-1-4278-0947-6

First TOKYOPOP printing: July 2008

10 9 8 7 6 5 4 3 2 1

Printed in the USA

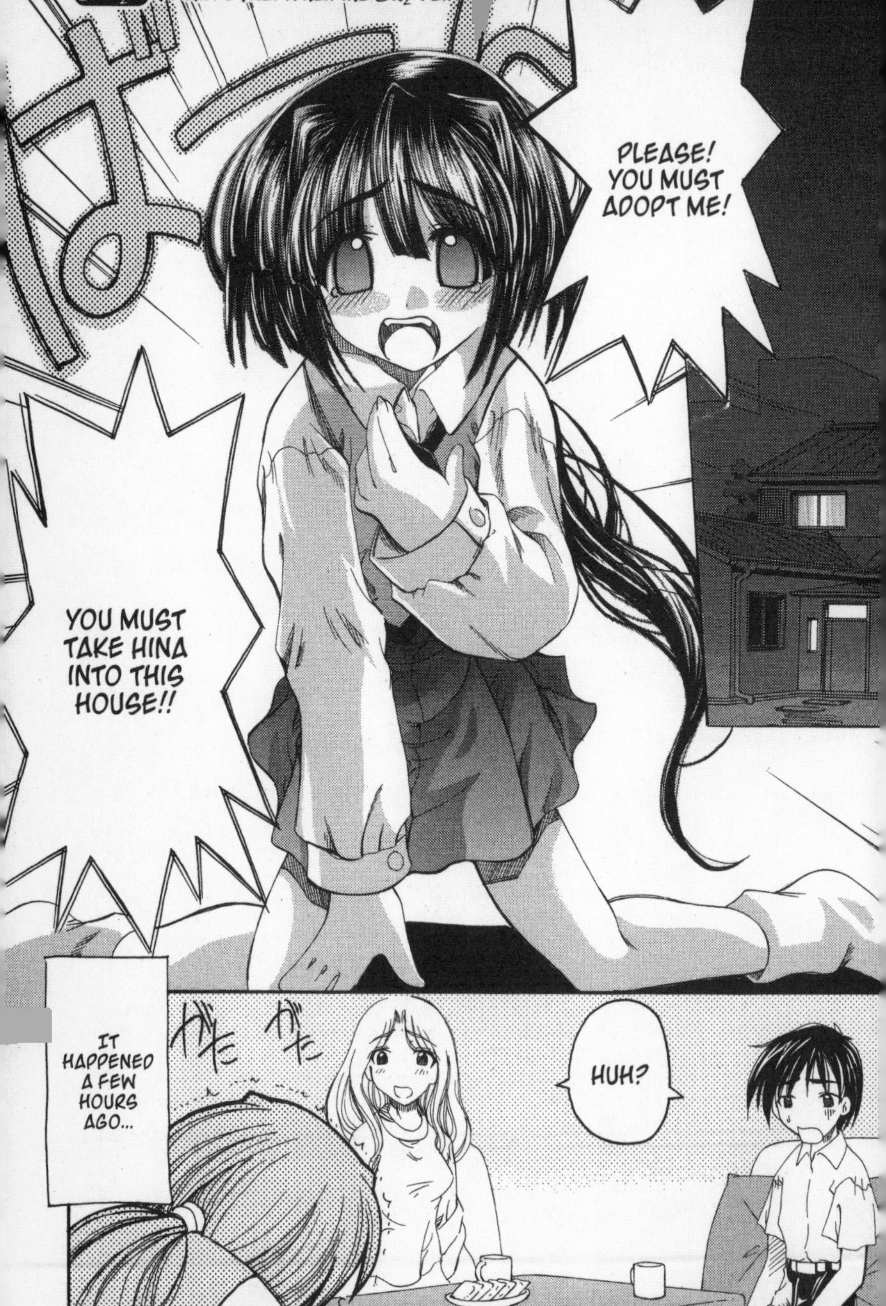
PLEASE! YOU MUST ADOPT ME!
YOU MUST TAKE HINA INTO THIS HOUSE!!
HUH?
IT HAPPENED A FEW HOURS AGO...

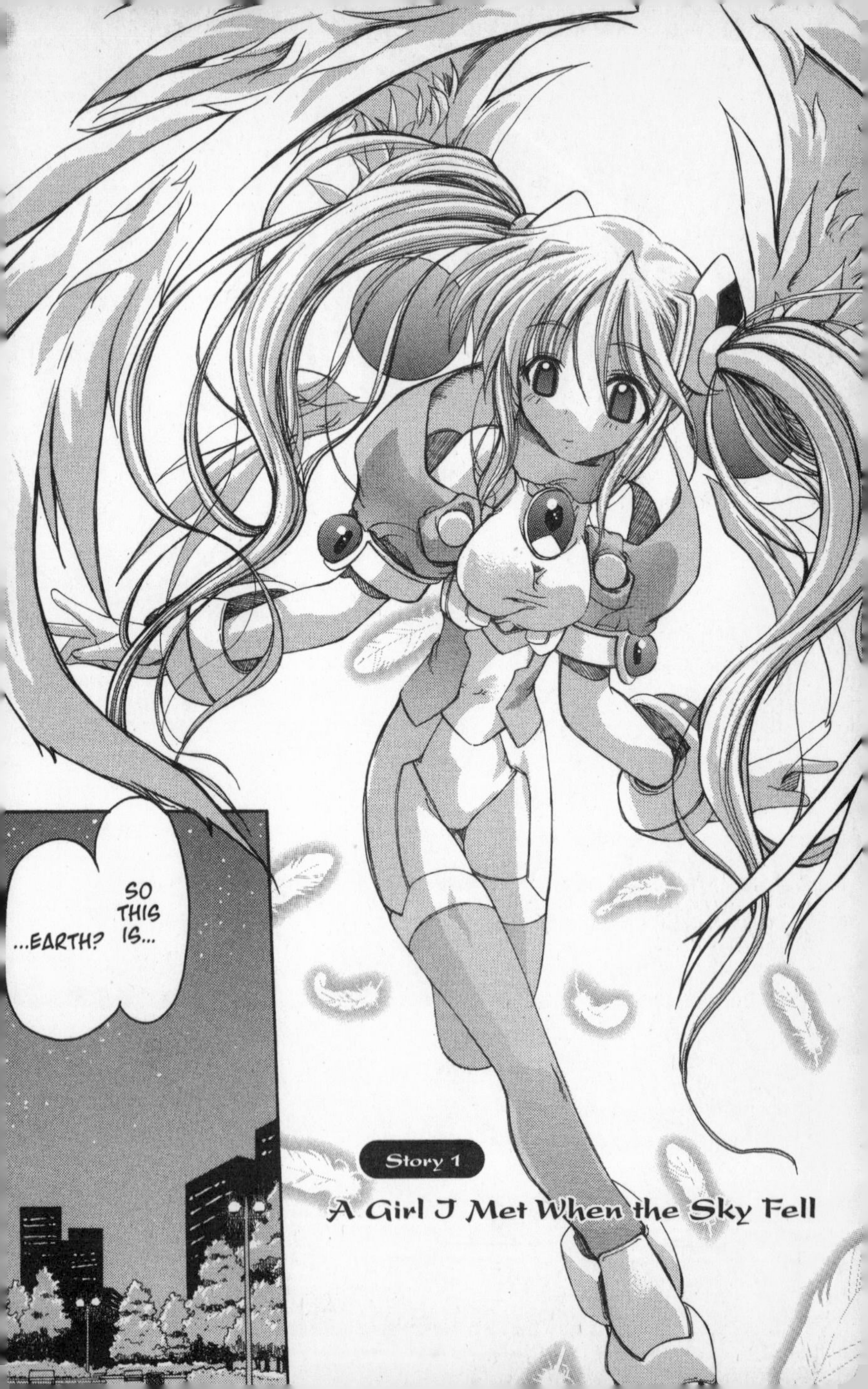
SO THIS IS...
...EARTH?
Story 1
A Girl I Met When the Sky Fell

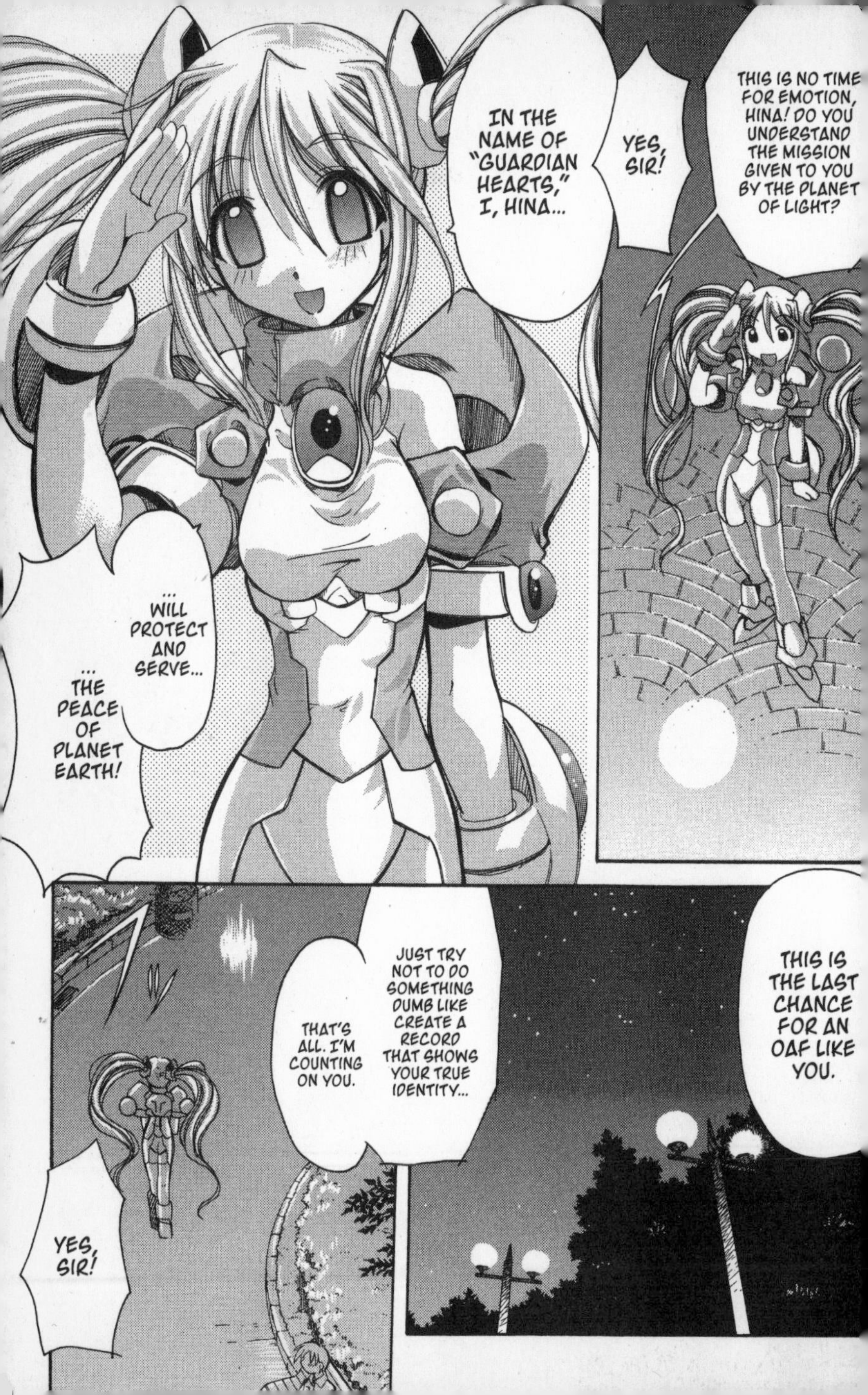
THIS IS NO TIME FOR EMOTION, HINA! DO YOU UNDERSTAND THE MISSION GIVEN TO YOU BY THE PLANET OF LIGHT?
YES, SIR!
IN THE NAME OF "GUARDIAN HEARTS," I, HINA...
... WILL PROTECT AND SERVE...
... THE PEACE OF PLANET EARTH!
THIS IS THE LAST CHANCE FOR AN OAF LIKE YOU.
JUST TRY NOT TO DO SOMETHING DUMB LIKE CREATE A RECORD THAT SHOWS YOUR TRUE IDENTITY...
THAT'S ALL. I'M COUNTING ON YOU.
YES, SIR!

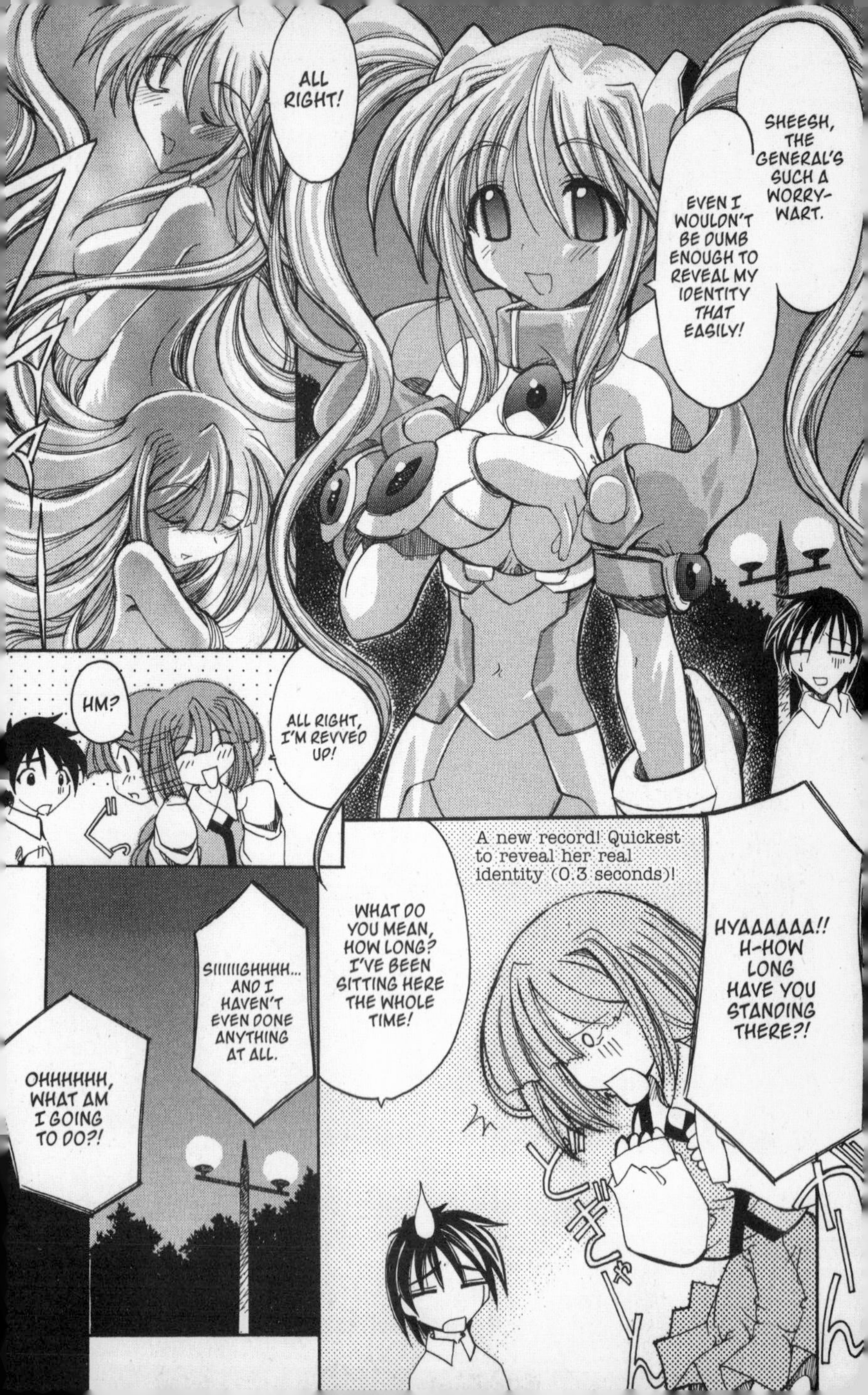
SHEESH, THE GENERAL'S SUCH A WORRY-WART.
EVEN I WOULDN'T BE DUMB ENOUGH TO REVEAL MY IDENTITY THAT EASILY!
ALL RIGHT!
ALL RIGHT, I'M REVVED UP!
HM?
A new record! Quickest to reveal her real identity (0.3 seconds)!
HYAAAAAA!! H-HOW LONG HAVE YOU STANDING THERE?!
WHAT DO YOU MEAN, HOW LONG? I'VE BEEN SITTING HERE THE WHOLE TIME!
SIIIIIGHHHH... AND I HAVEN'T EVEN DONE ANYTHING AT ALL.
OHHHHHH, WHAT AM I GOING TO DO?!

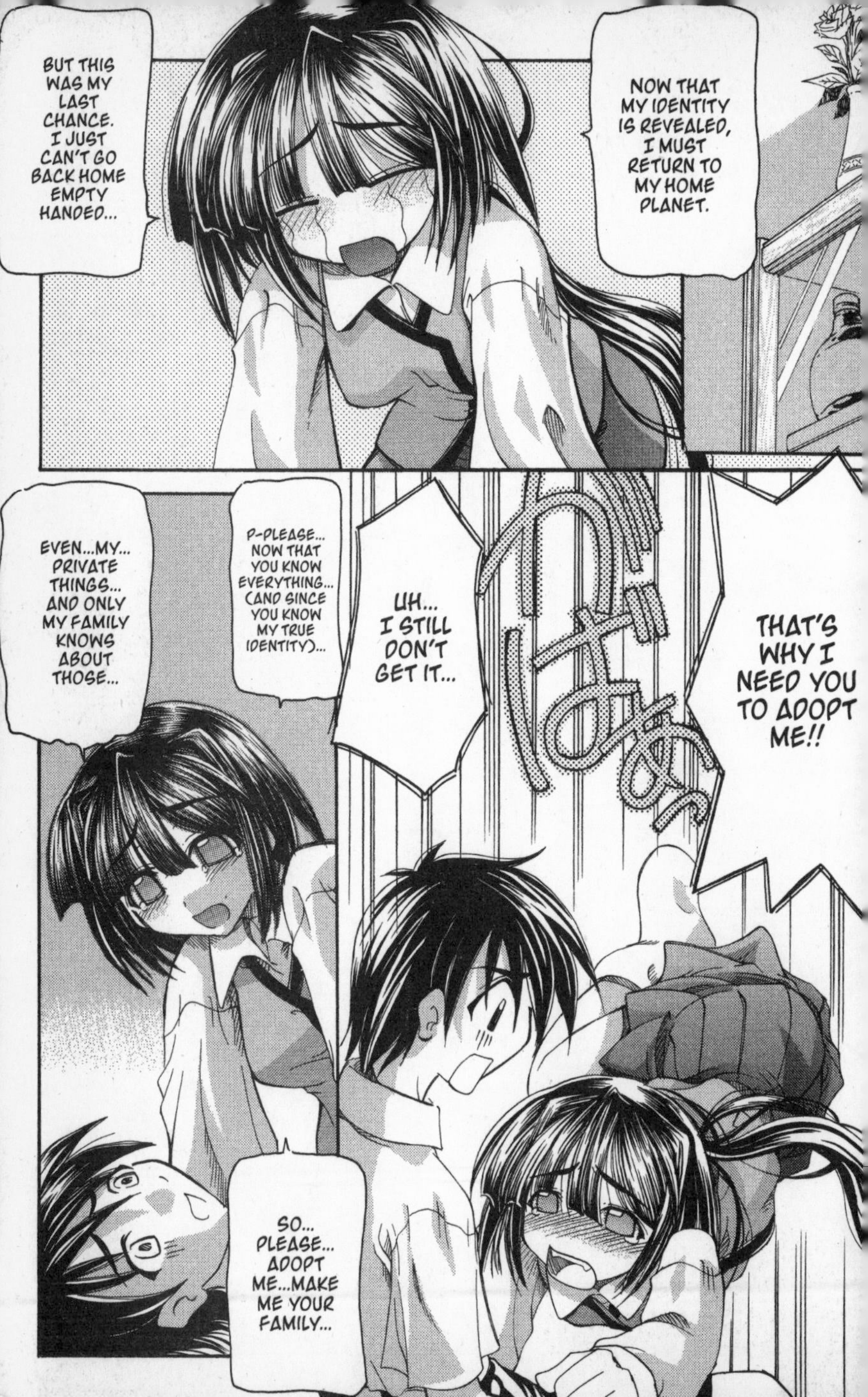
NOW THAT MY IDENTITY IS REVEALED, I MUST RETURN TO MY HOME PLANET.
BUT THIS WAS MY LAST CHANCE. I JUST CAN'T GO BACK HOME EMPTY HANDED...
THAT'S WHY I NEED YOU TO ADOPT ME!!
UH... I STILL DON'T GET IT...
P-PLEASE... NOW THAT YOU KNOW EVERYTHING... (AND SINCE YOU KNOW MY TRUE IDENTITY)...
EVEN...MY... PRIVATE THINGS... AND ONLY MY FAMILY KNOWS ABOUT THOSE...
SO... PLEASE... ADOPT ME...MAKE ME YOUR FAMILY...

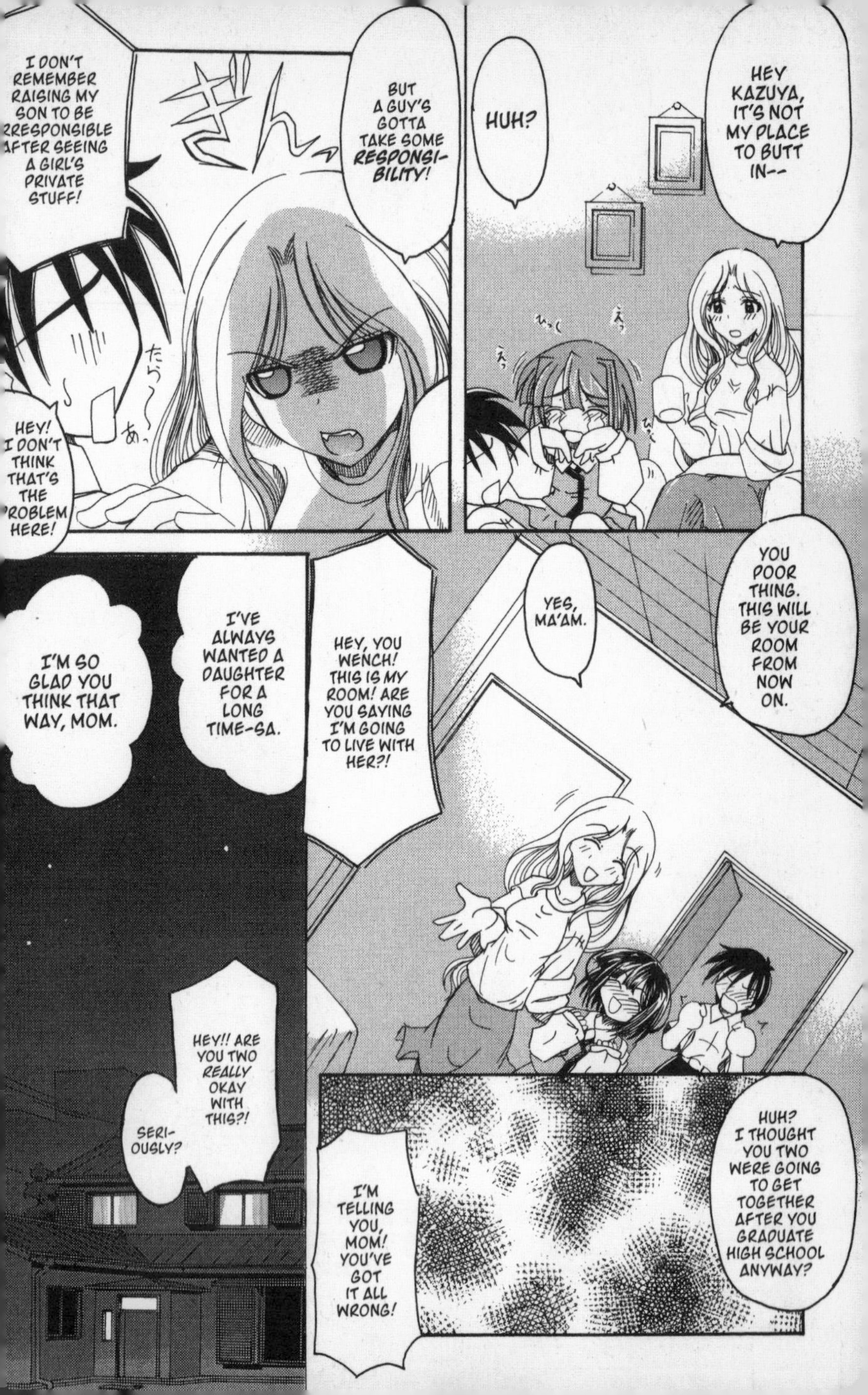

HEY KAZUYA, IT'S NOT MY PLACE TO BUTT IN--
HUH?
BUT A GUY'S GOTTA TAKE SOME RESPONSIBILITY!
ぎん
I DON'T REMEMBER RAISING MY SON TO BE IRRESPONSIBLE AFTER SEEING A GIRL'S PRIVATE STUFF!
HEY! I DON'T THINK THAT'S THE PROBLEM HERE!
YOU POOR THING. THIS WILL BE YOUR ROOM FROM NOW ON.
YES, MA'AM.
HEY, YOU WENCH! THIS IS MY ROOM! ARE YOU SAYING I'M GOING TO LIVE WITH HER?!
I'VE ALWAYS WANTED A DAUGHTER FOR A LONG TIME-SA.
I'M SO GLAD YOU THINK THAT WAY, MOM.
HUH? I THOUGHT YOU TWO WERE GOING TO GET TOGETHER AFTER YOU GRADUATE HIGH SCHOOL ANYWAY?
I'M TELLING YOU, MOM! YOU'VE GOT IT ALL WRONG!
HEY!! ARE YOU TWO REALLY OKAY WITH THIS?!
SERIOUSLY?

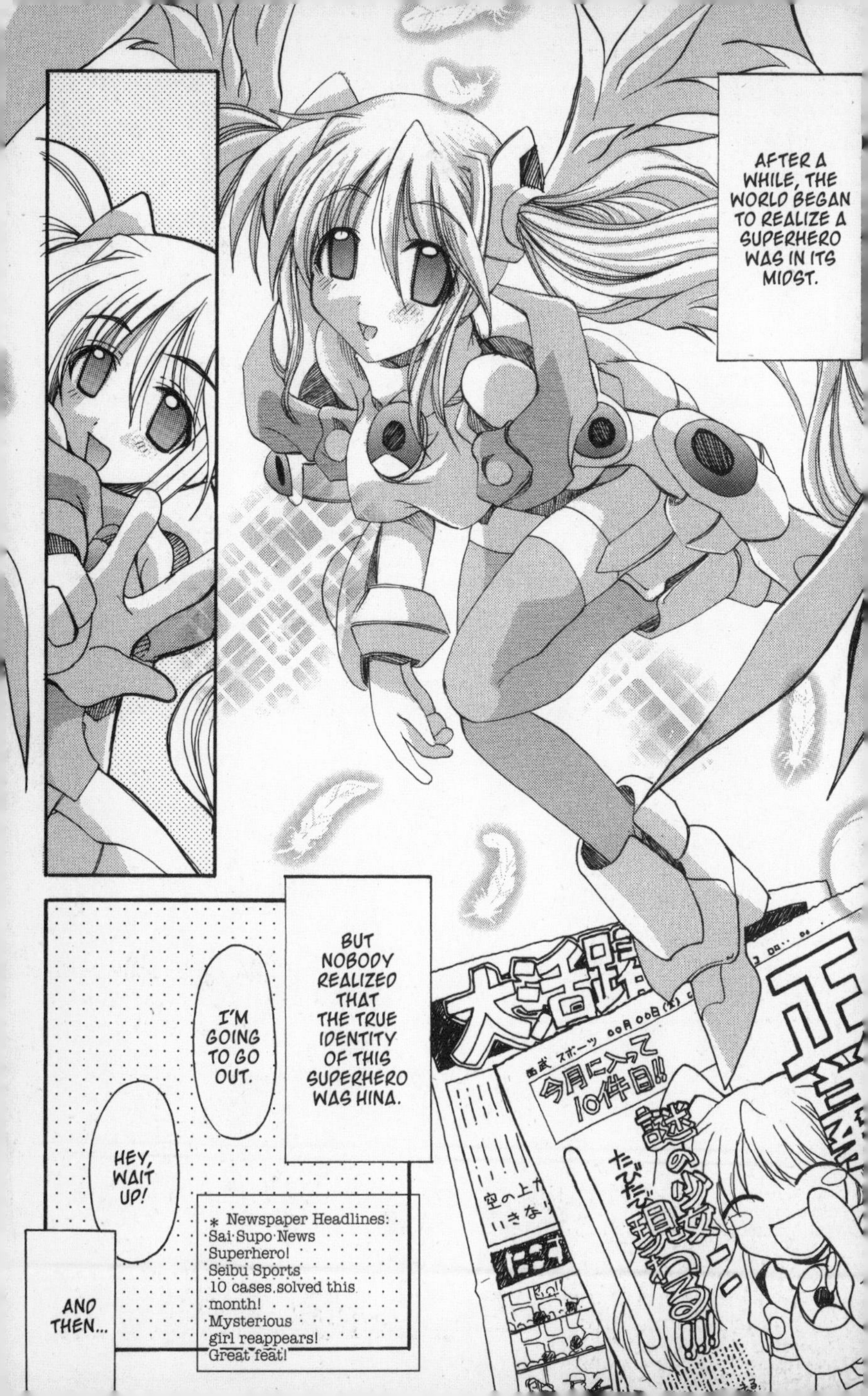

AFTER A WHILE, THE WORLD BEGAN TO REALIZE A SUPERHERO WAS IN ITS MIDST.
BUT NOBODY REALIZED THAT THE TRUE IDENTITY OF THIS SUPERHERO WAS HINA.
大活躍
西武スポーツ
今月に入って
10件目!!
謎の少女
ふたたび現わる!!
* Newspaper Headlines:
Sai·Supo·News
Superhero!
Seibu Sports
10 cases solved this month!
Mysterious girl reappears!
Great feat!
I'M GOING TO GO OUT.
HEY, WAIT UP!
AND THEN...

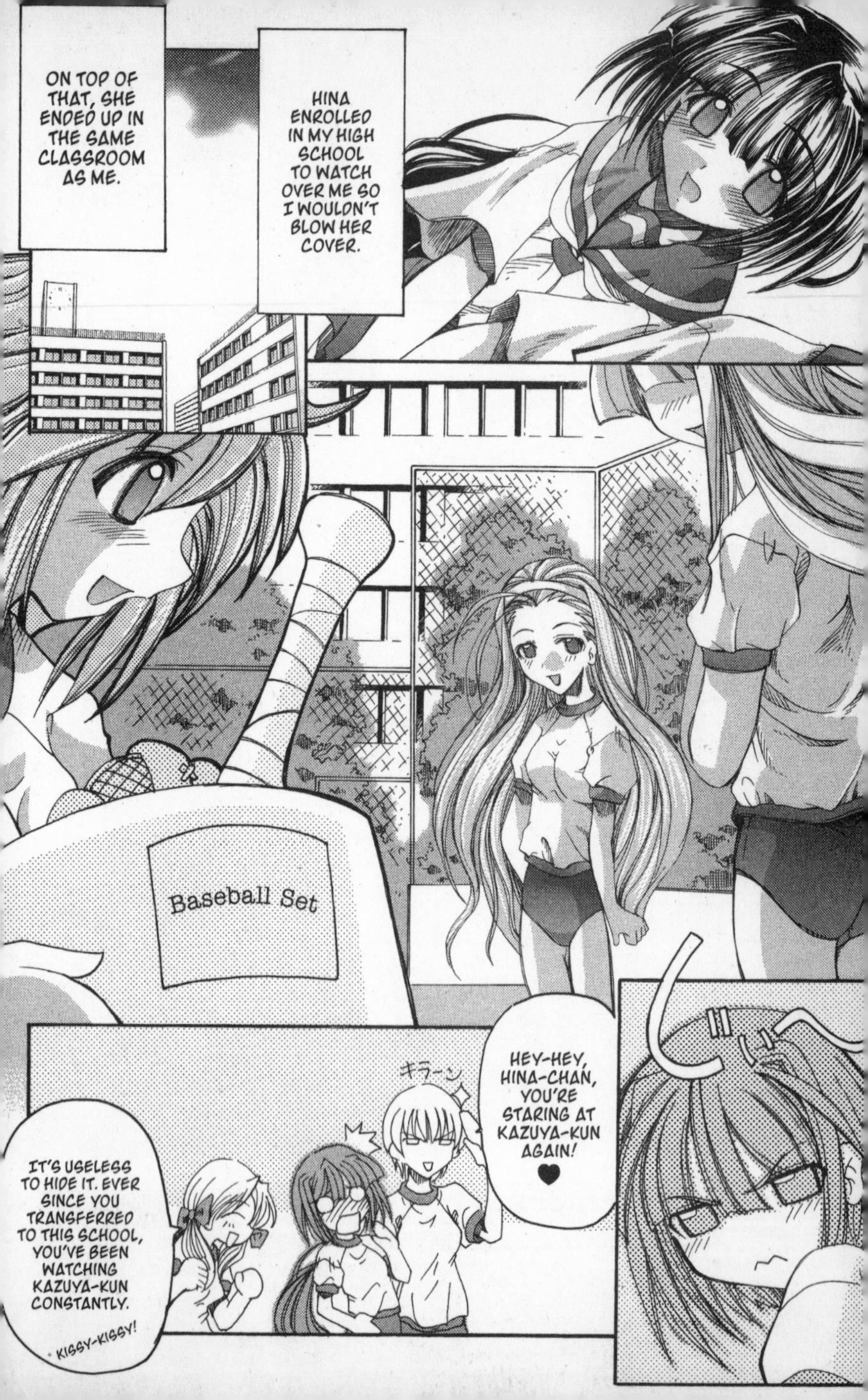
HINA ENROLLED IN MY HIGH SCHOOL TO WATCH OVER ME SO I WOULDN'T BLOW HER COVER.
ON TOP OF THAT, SHE ENDED UP IN THE SAME CLASSROOM AS ME.
Baseball Set
HEY-HEY, HINA-CHAN, YOU'RE STARING AT KAZUYA-KUN AGAIN! ♥
キラーン
IT'S USELESS TO HIDE IT. EVER SINCE YOU TRANSFERRED TO THIS SCHOOL, YOU'VE BEEN WATCHING KAZUYA-KUN CONSTANTLY.
KISSY-KISSY!

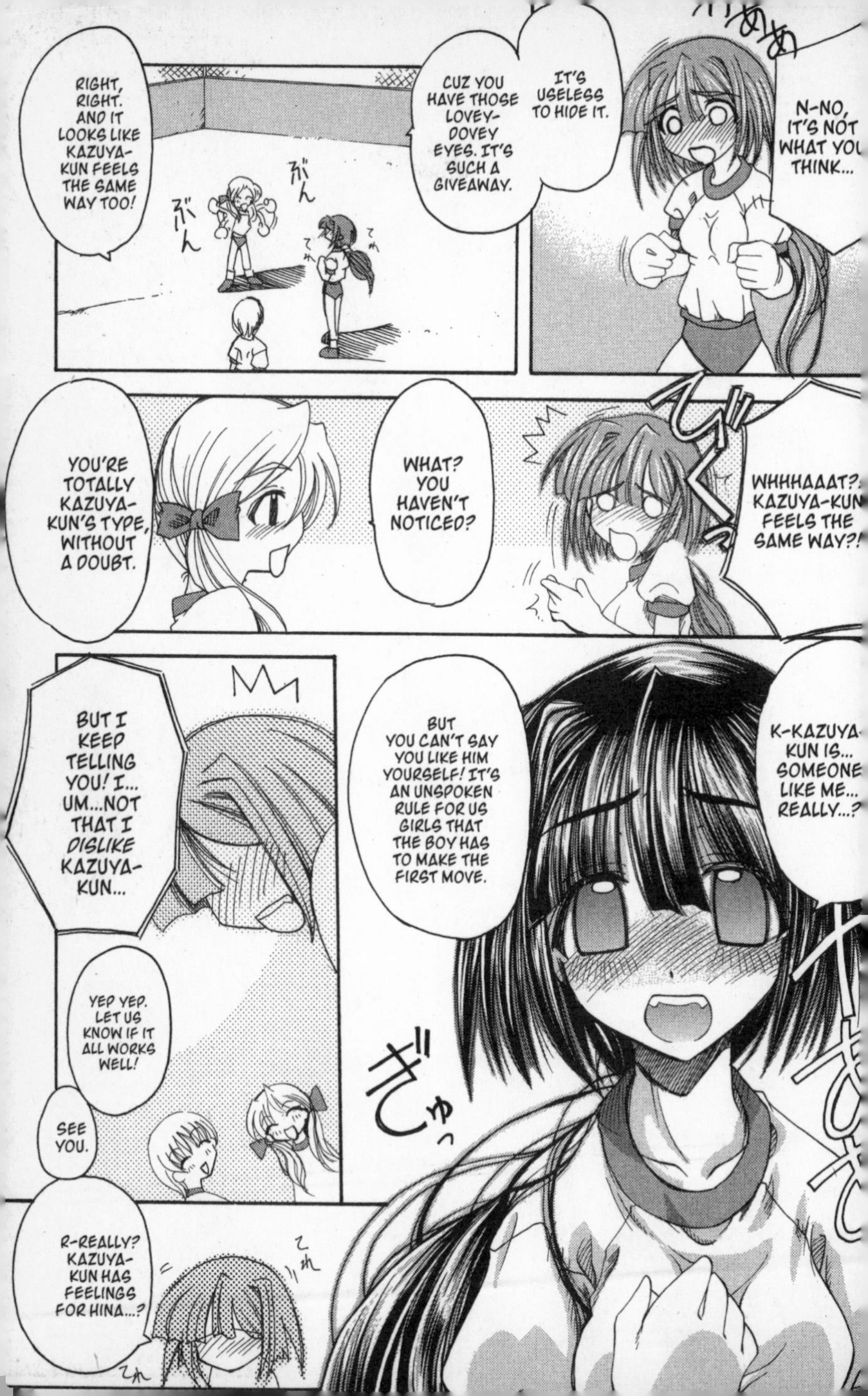
N-NO, IT'S NOT WHAT YOU THINK...
IT'S USELESS TO HIDE IT.
CUZ YOU HAVE THOSE LOVEY-DOVEY EYES. IT'S SUCH A GIVEAWAY.
ぶん
ぶん
てれ
てれ
RIGHT, RIGHT. AND IT LOOKS LIKE KAZUYA-KUN FEELS THE SAME WAY TOO!
WHHHAAAT?! KAZUYA-KUN FEELS THE SAME WAY?!
WHAT? YOU HAVEN'T NOTICED?
YOU'RE TOTALLY KAZUYA-KUN'S TYPE, WITHOUT A DOUBT.
K-KAZUYA-KUN IS... SOMEONE LIKE ME... REALLY...?
BUT YOU CAN'T SAY YOU LIKE HIM YOURSELF! IT'S AN UNSPOKEN RULE FOR US GIRLS THAT THE BOY HAS TO MAKE THE FIRST MOVE.
ぎゅっ
BUT I KEEP TELLING YOU! I... UM...NOT THAT I *DISLIKE* KAZUYA-KUN...
YEP YEP. LET US KNOW IF IT ALL WORKS WELL!
SEE YOU.
R-REALLY? KAZUYA-KUN HAS FEELINGS FOR HINA...?
てれ
てれ

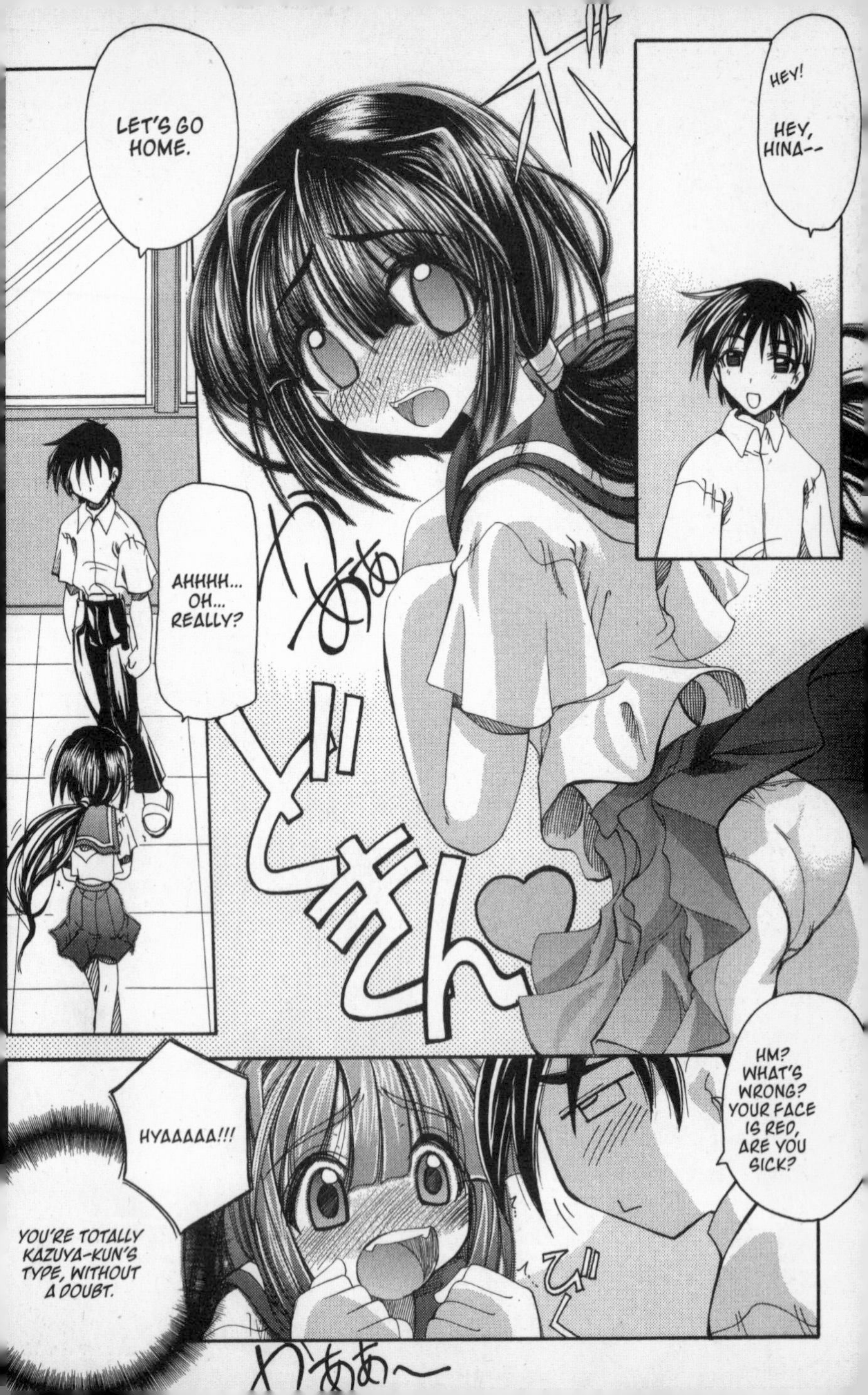
HEY!
HEY, HINA--
LET'S GO HOME.
AHHHH... OH... REALLY?
どきん
HM? WHAT'S WRONG? YOUR FACE IS RED, ARE YOU SICK?
HYAAAAA!!!
YOU'RE TOTALLY KAZUYA-KUN'S TYPE, WITHOUT A DOUBT.
わああ〜

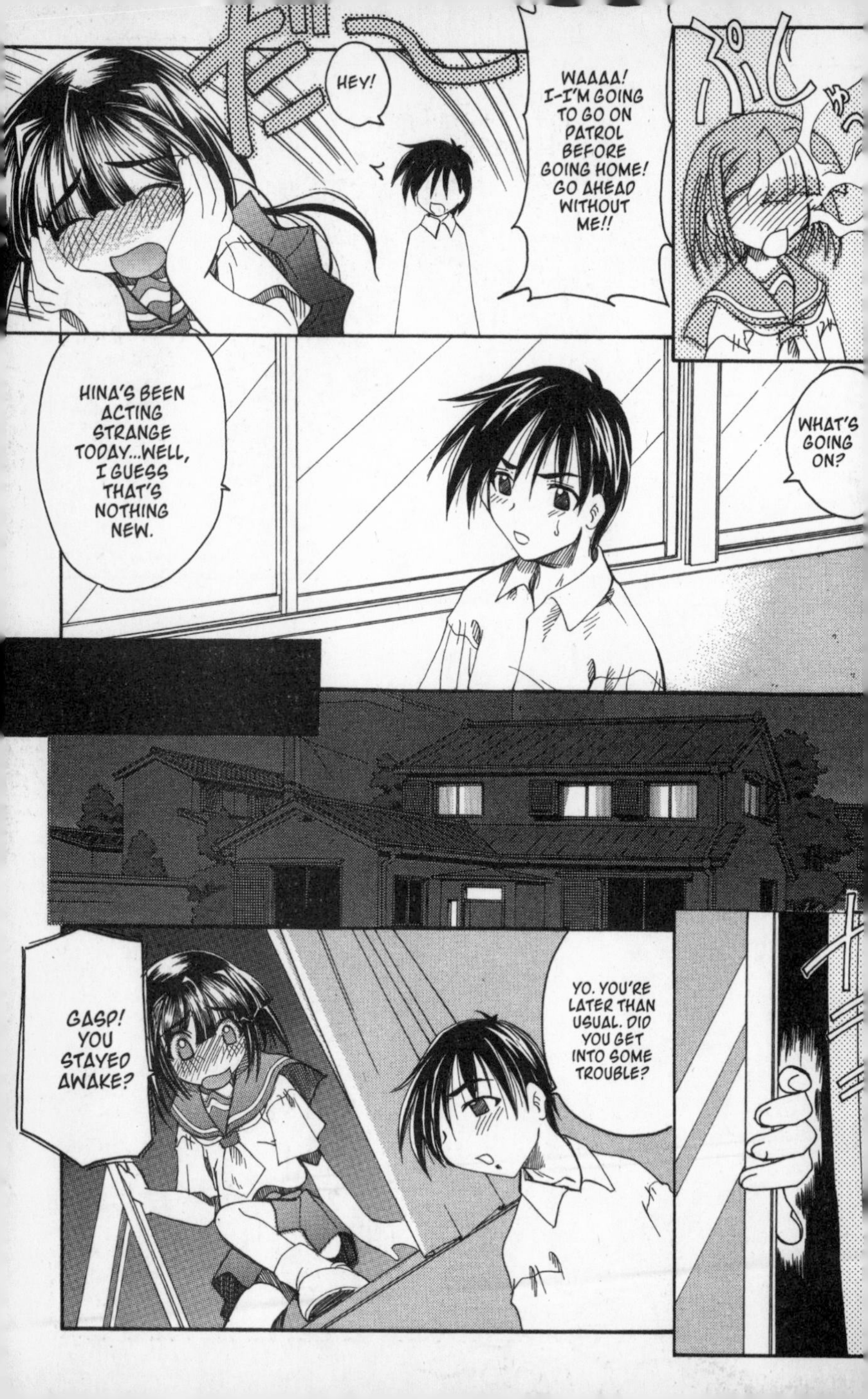
WAAAA! I-I'M GOING TO GO ON PATROL BEFORE GOING HOME! GO AHEAD WITHOUT ME!!
HEY!
WHAT'S GOING ON?
HINA'S BEEN ACTING STRANGE TODAY...WELL, I GUESS THAT'S NOTHING NEW.
YO. YOU'RE LATER THAN USUAL. DID YOU GET INTO SOME TROUBLE?
GASP! YOU STAYED AWAKE?

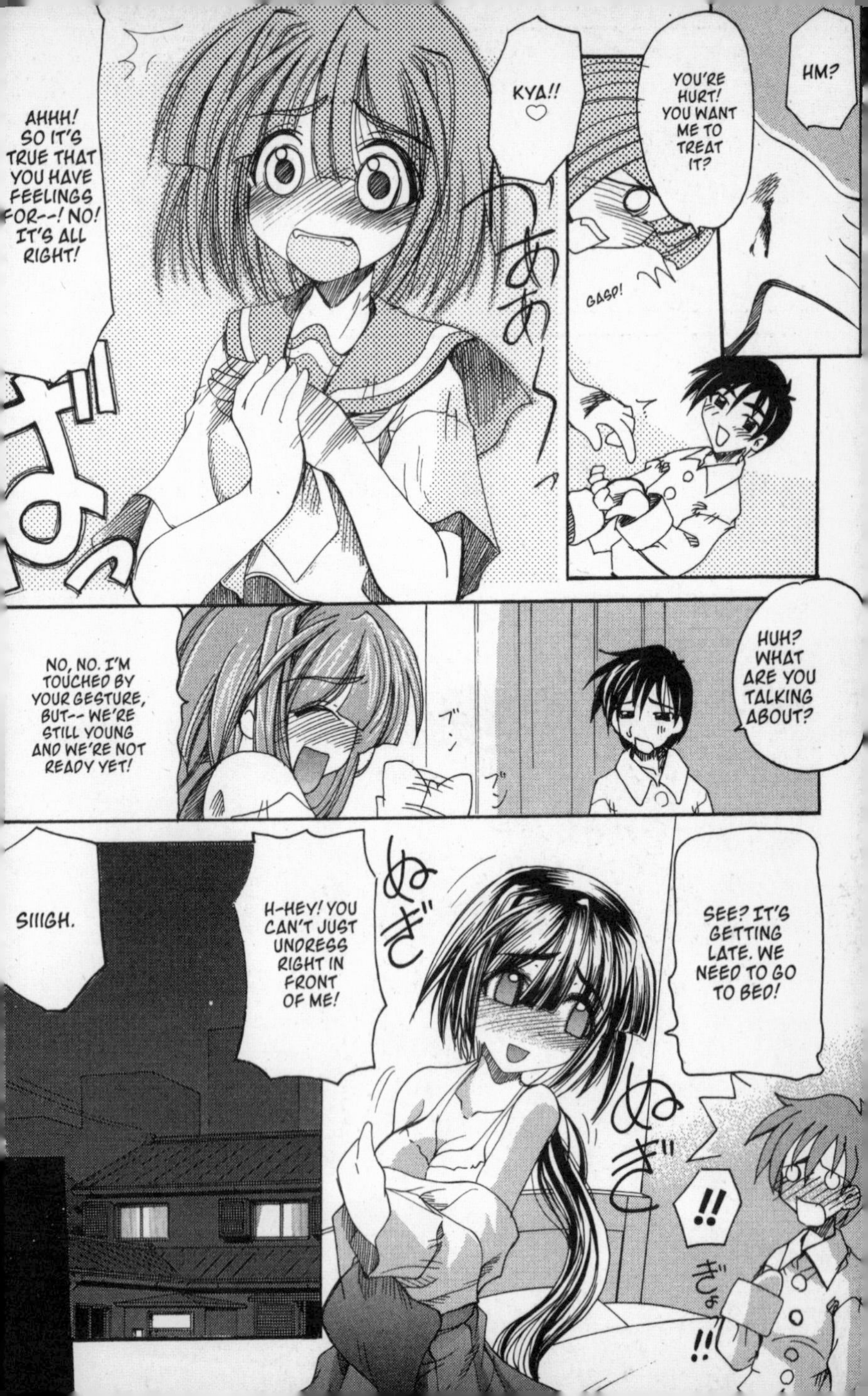
HM?
YOU'RE HURT! YOU WANT ME TO TREAT IT?
GASP!
KYA!! ♡
AHHH! SO IT'S TRUE THAT YOU HAVE FEELINGS FOR--! NO! IT'S ALL RIGHT!
ああ
HUH? WHAT ARE YOU TALKING ABOUT?
NO, NO. I'M TOUCHED BY YOUR GESTURE, BUT-- WE'RE STILL YOUNG AND WE'RE NOT READY YET!
ブン
ブン
SEE? IT'S GETTING LATE. WE NEED TO GO TO BED!
ぬぎ
ぬぎ
H-HEY! YOU CAN'T JUST UNDRESS RIGHT IN FRONT OF ME!
!!
ぎょ
!!
SIIIGH.

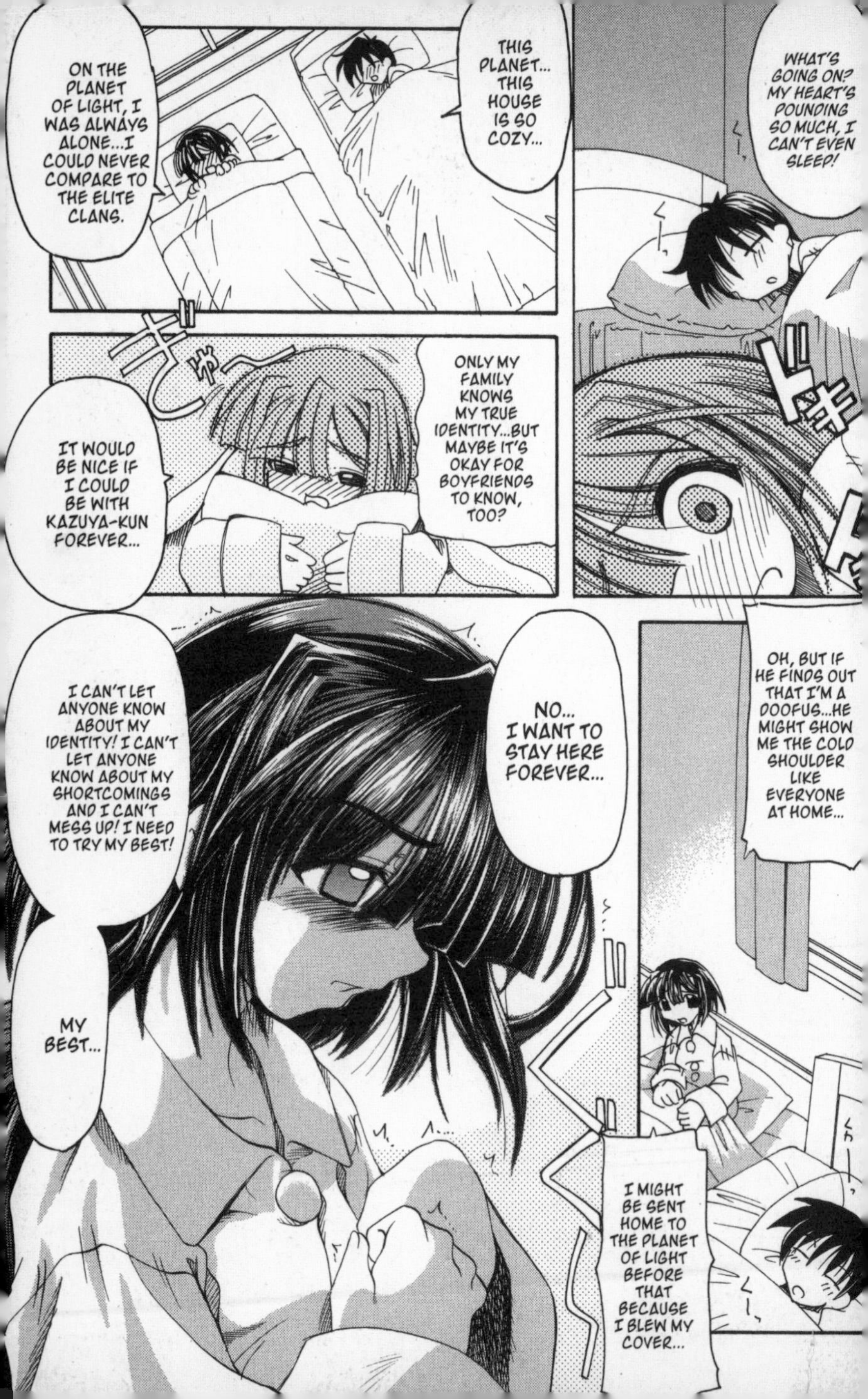
WHAT'S GOING ON? MY HEART'S POUNDING SO MUCH, I CAN'T EVEN SLEEP!
THIS PLANET... THIS HOUSE IS SO COZY...
ON THE PLANET OF LIGHT, I WAS ALWAYS ALONE...I COULD NEVER COMPARE TO THE ELITE CLANS.
ONLY MY FAMILY KNOWS MY TRUE IDENTITY...BUT MAYBE IT'S OKAY FOR BOYFRIENDS TO KNOW, TOO?
IT WOULD BE NICE IF I COULD BE WITH KAZUYA-KUN FOREVER...
OH, BUT IF HE FINDS OUT THAT I'M A DOOFUS...HE MIGHT SHOW ME THE COLD SHOULDER LIKE EVERYONE AT HOME...
I MIGHT BE SENT HOME TO THE PLANET OF LIGHT BEFORE THAT BECAUSE I BLEW MY COVER...
NO... I WANT TO STAY HERE FOREVER...
I CAN'T LET ANYONE KNOW ABOUT MY IDENTITY! I CAN'T LET ANYONE KNOW ABOUT MY SHORTCOMINGS AND I CAN'T MESS UP! I NEED TO TRY MY BEST!
MY BEST...

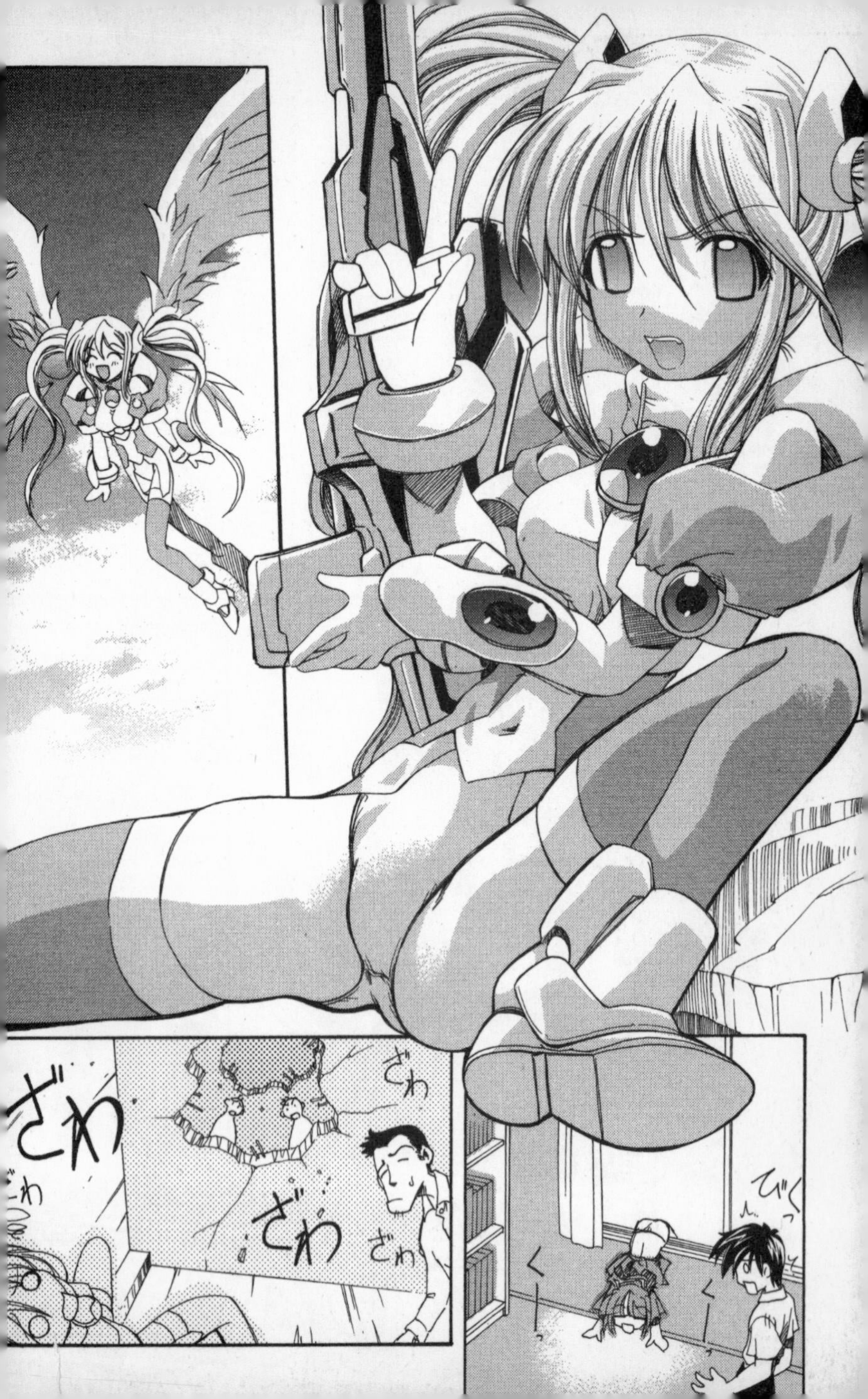
びくっ
ん‥
くーっ
ざわ
ざわ
ざわ
ざわ
ざわ

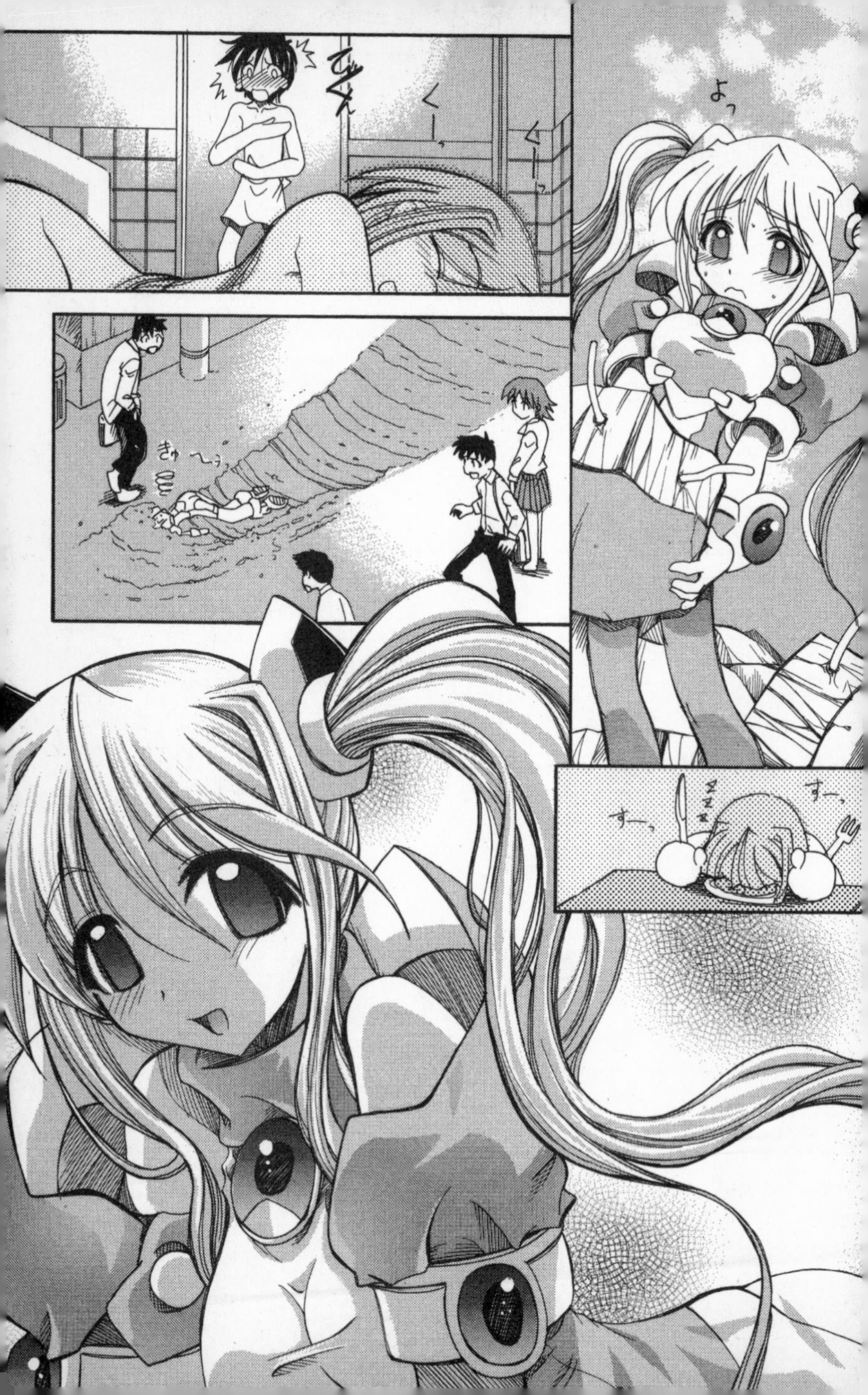
よっ
どくん
くーっ
くーっ
きゅ～っ
すーっ
ZZZ
すーっ

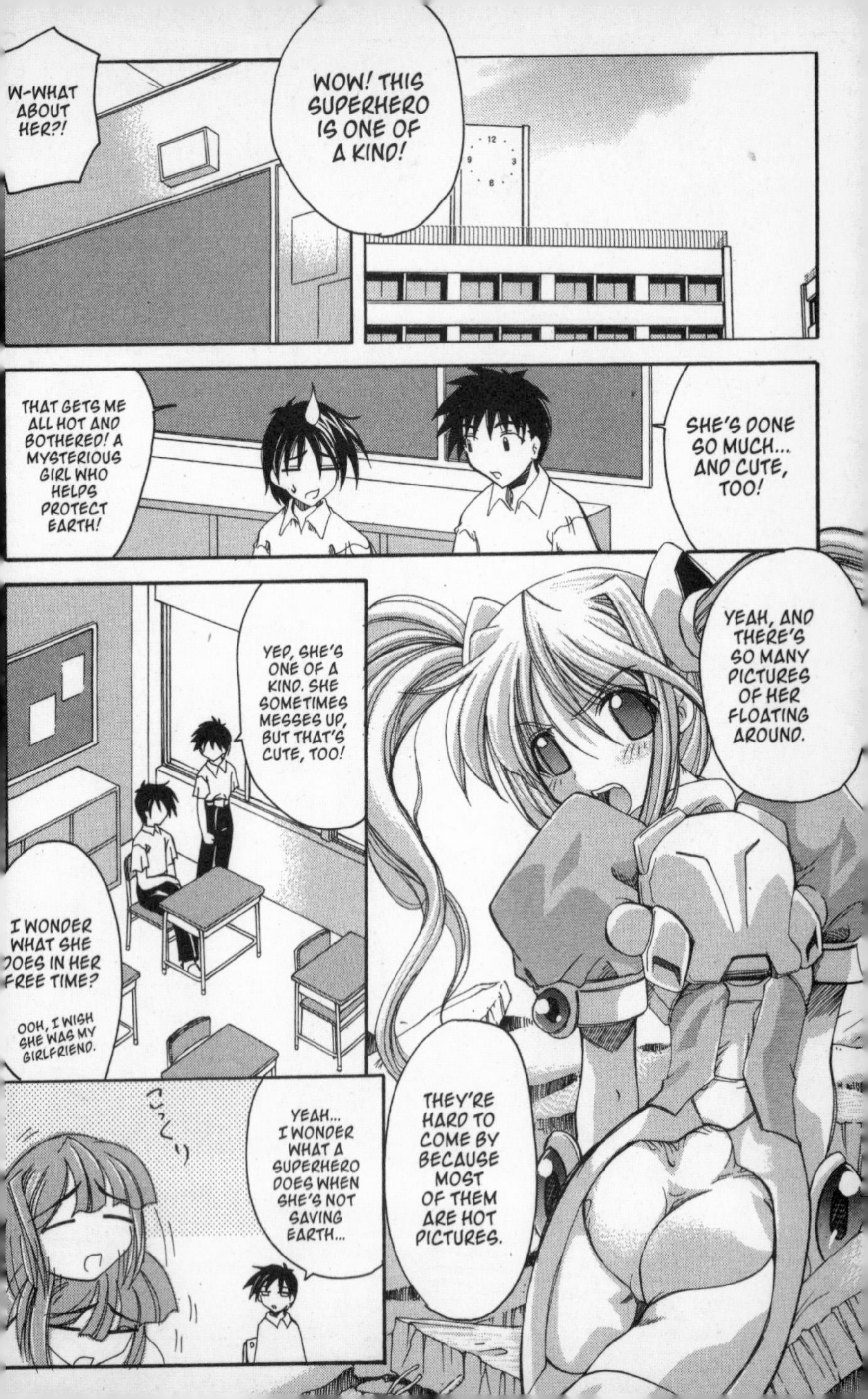
WOW! THIS SUPERHERO IS ONE OF A KIND!
W-WHAT ABOUT HER?!
SHE'S DONE SO MUCH... AND CUTE, TOO!
THAT GETS ME ALL HOT AND BOTHERED! A MYSTERIOUS GIRL WHO HELPS PROTECT EARTH!
YEAH, AND THERE'S SO MANY PICTURES OF HER FLOATING AROUND.
THEY'RE HARD TO COME BY BECAUSE MOST OF THEM ARE HOT PICTURES.
YEP, SHE'S ONE OF A KIND. SHE SOMETIMES MESSES UP, BUT THAT'S CUTE, TOO!
I WONDER WHAT SHE DOES IN HER FREE TIME?
OOH, I WISH SHE WAS MY GIRLFRIEND.
YEAH... I WONDER WHAT A SUPERHERO DOES WHEN SHE'S NOT SAVING EARTH...

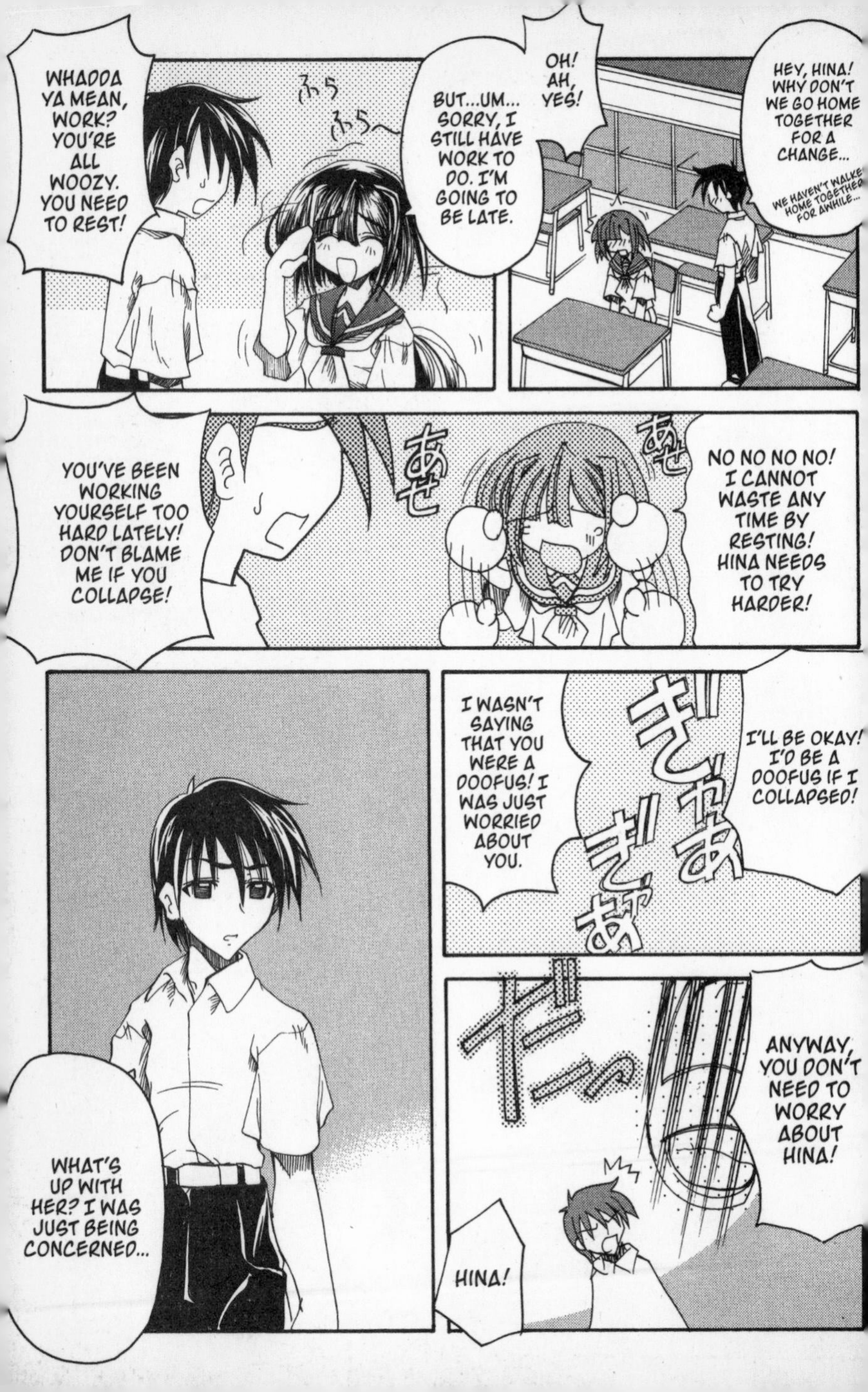
HEY, HINA! WHY DON'T WE GO HOME TOGETHER FOR A CHANGE...
WE HAVEN'T WALKE HOME TOGETHE FOR AWHILE...
OH! AH, YES!
BUT...UM... SORRY, I STILL HAVE WORK TO DO. I'M GOING TO BE LATE.
ふら ふら〜
WHADDA YA MEAN, WORK? YOU'RE ALL WOOZY. YOU NEED TO REST!
あせ あせ
NO NO NO NO! I CANNOT WASTE ANY TIME BY RESTING! HINA NEEDS TO TRY HARDER!
YOU'VE BEEN WORKING YOURSELF TOO HARD LATELY! DON'T BLAME ME IF YOU COLLAPSE!
I'LL BE OKAY! I'D BE A DOOFUS IF I COLLAPSED!
ぎゃあ ぎゃあ
I WASN'T SAYING THAT YOU WERE A DOOFUS! I WAS JUST WORRIED ABOUT YOU.
ANYWAY, YOU DON'T NEED TO WORRY ABOUT HINA!
ダーッ
HINA!
WHAT'S UP WITH HER? I WAS JUST BEING CONCERNED...

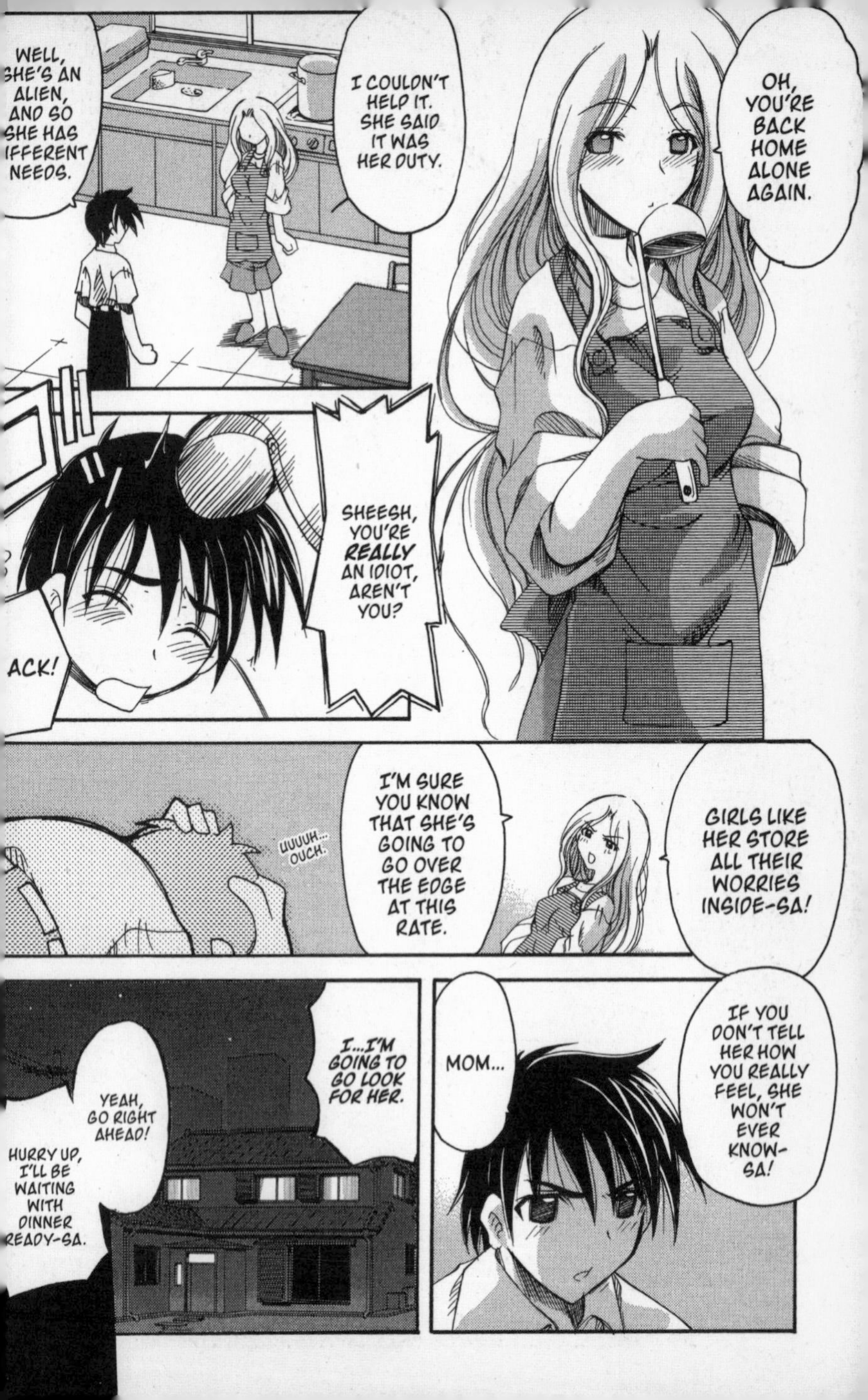
OH, YOU'RE BACK HOME ALONE AGAIN.
I COULDN'T HELP IT. SHE SAID IT WAS HER DUTY.
WELL, SHE'S AN ALIEN, AND SO SHE HAS IFFERENT NEEDS.
SHEESH, YOU'RE **REALLY** AN IDIOT, AREN'T YOU?
ACK!
GIRLS LIKE HER STORE ALL THEIR WORRIES INSIDE-SA!
I'M SURE YOU KNOW THAT SHE'S GOING TO GO OVER THE EDGE AT THIS RATE.
UUUUH... OUCH.
IF YOU DON'T TELL HER HOW YOU REALLY FEEL, SHE WON'T EVER KNOW-SA!
MOM...
I...I'M GOING TO GO LOOK FOR HER.
YEAH, GO RIGHT AHEAD!
HURRY UP, I'LL BE WAITING WITH DINNER READY-SA.

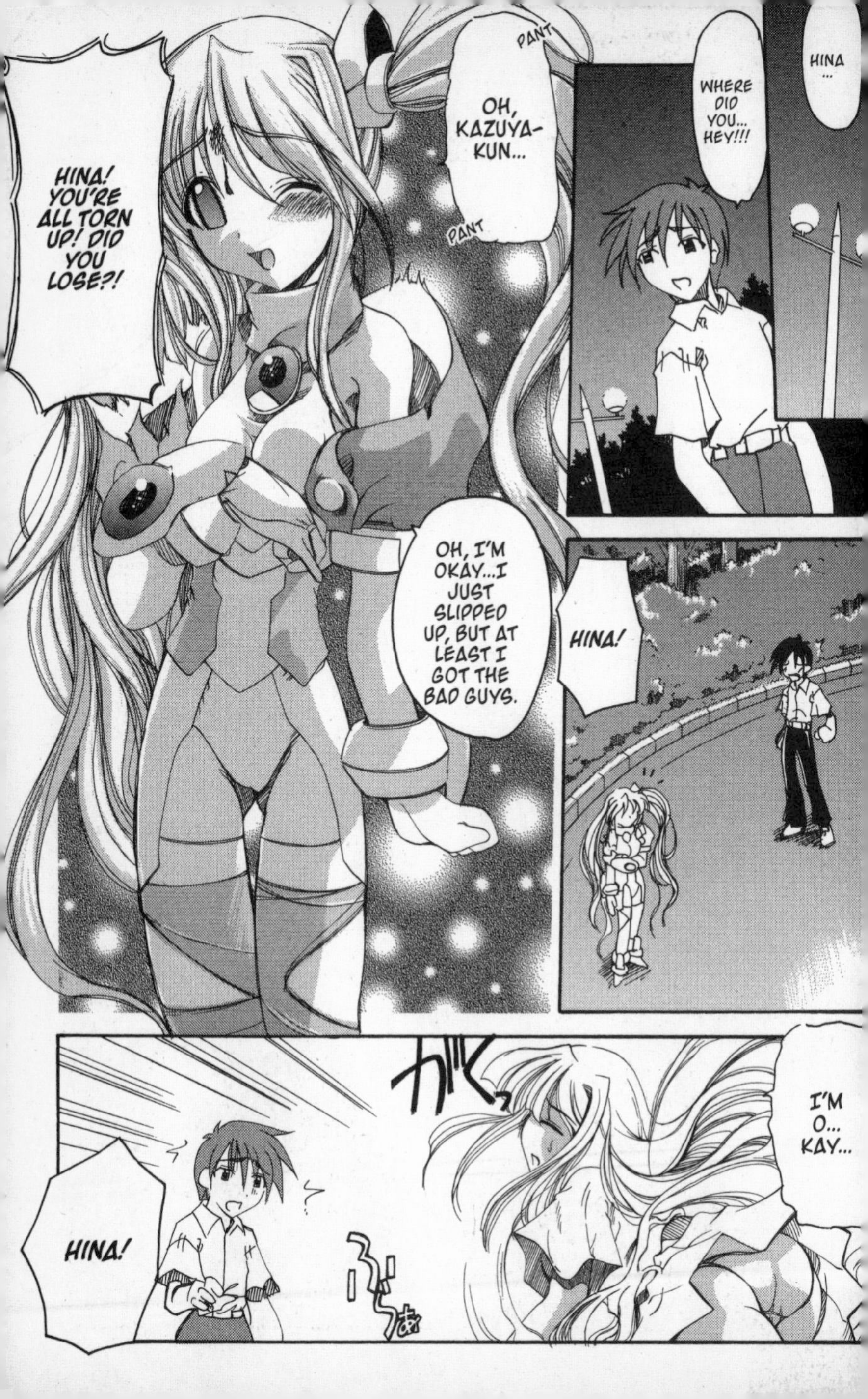
HINA...
WHERE DID YOU... HEY!!!
HINA!
PANT
OH, KAZUYA-KUN...
PANT
HINA! YOU'RE ALL TORN UP! DID YOU LOSE?!
OH, I'M OKAY...I JUST SLIPPED UP, BUT AT LEAST I GOT THE BAD GUYS.
I'M O... KAY...
HINA!

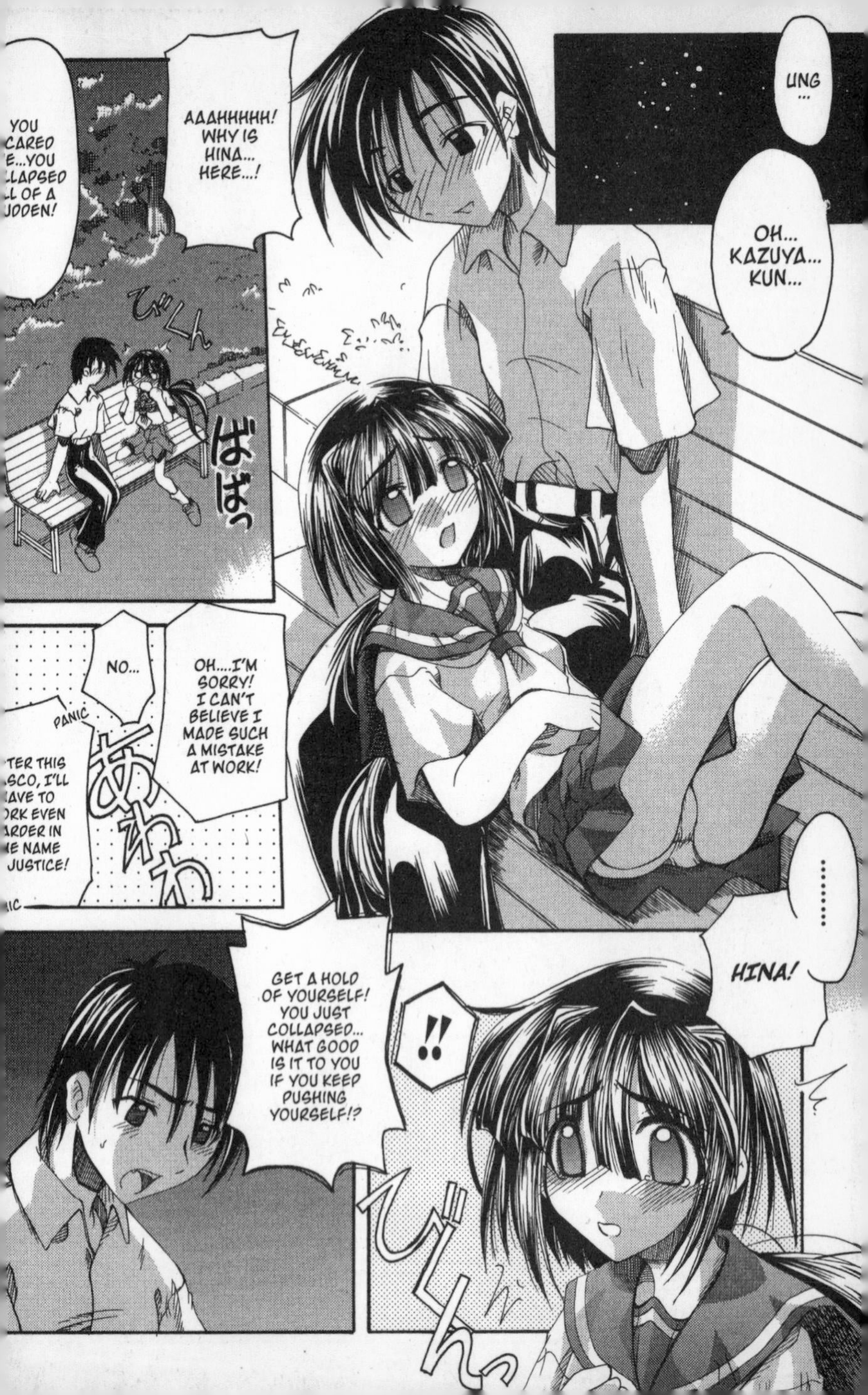
UNG...
OH... KAZUYA... KUN...
......
AAAHHHHH! WHY IS HINA... HERE...!
YOU CARED E...YOU LLAPSED LL OF A UDDEN!
びくん
ばばっ
OH....I'M SORRY! I CAN'T BELIEVE I MADE SUCH A MISTAKE AT WORK!
NO...
PANIC
あわわ
TER THIS SCO, I'LL AVE TO ORK EVEN ARDER IN E NAME JUSTICE!
NIC
HINA!
!!
びくんっ
GET A HOLD OF YOURSELF! YOU JUST COLLAPSED... WHAT GOOD IS IT TO YOU IF YOU KEEP PUSHING YOURSELF!?

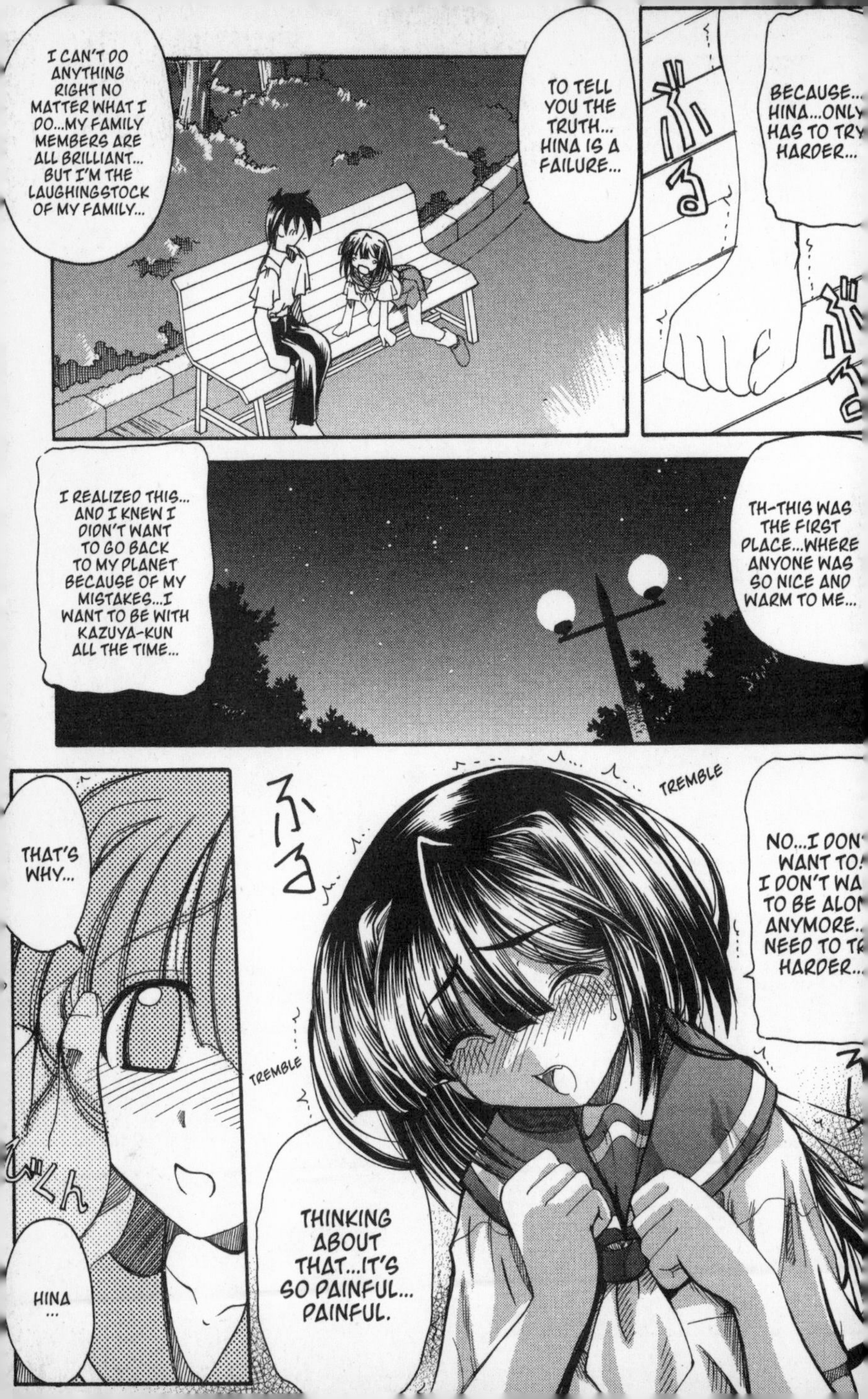
BECAUSE... HINA...ONLY HAS TO TRY HARDER...
ぶる
ぶる
TO TELL YOU THE TRUTH... HINA IS A FAILURE...
I CAN'T DO ANYTHING RIGHT NO MATTER WHAT I DO...MY FAMILY MEMBERS ARE ALL BRILLIANT... BUT I'M THE LAUGHINGSTOCK OF MY FAMILY...
TH-THIS WAS THE FIRST PLACE...WHERE ANYONE WAS SO NICE AND WARM TO ME...
I REALIZED THIS... AND I KNEW I DIDN'T WANT TO GO BACK TO MY PLANET BECAUSE OF MY MISTAKES...I WANT TO BE WITH KAZUYA-KUN ALL THE TIME...
NO...I DON WANT TO! I DON'T WA TO BE ALON ANYMORE.. NEED TO TR HARDER...
TREMBLE
ふる
TREMBLE
THINKING ABOUT THAT...IT'S SO PAINFUL... PAINFUL.
THAT'S WHY...
びくん
HINA ...

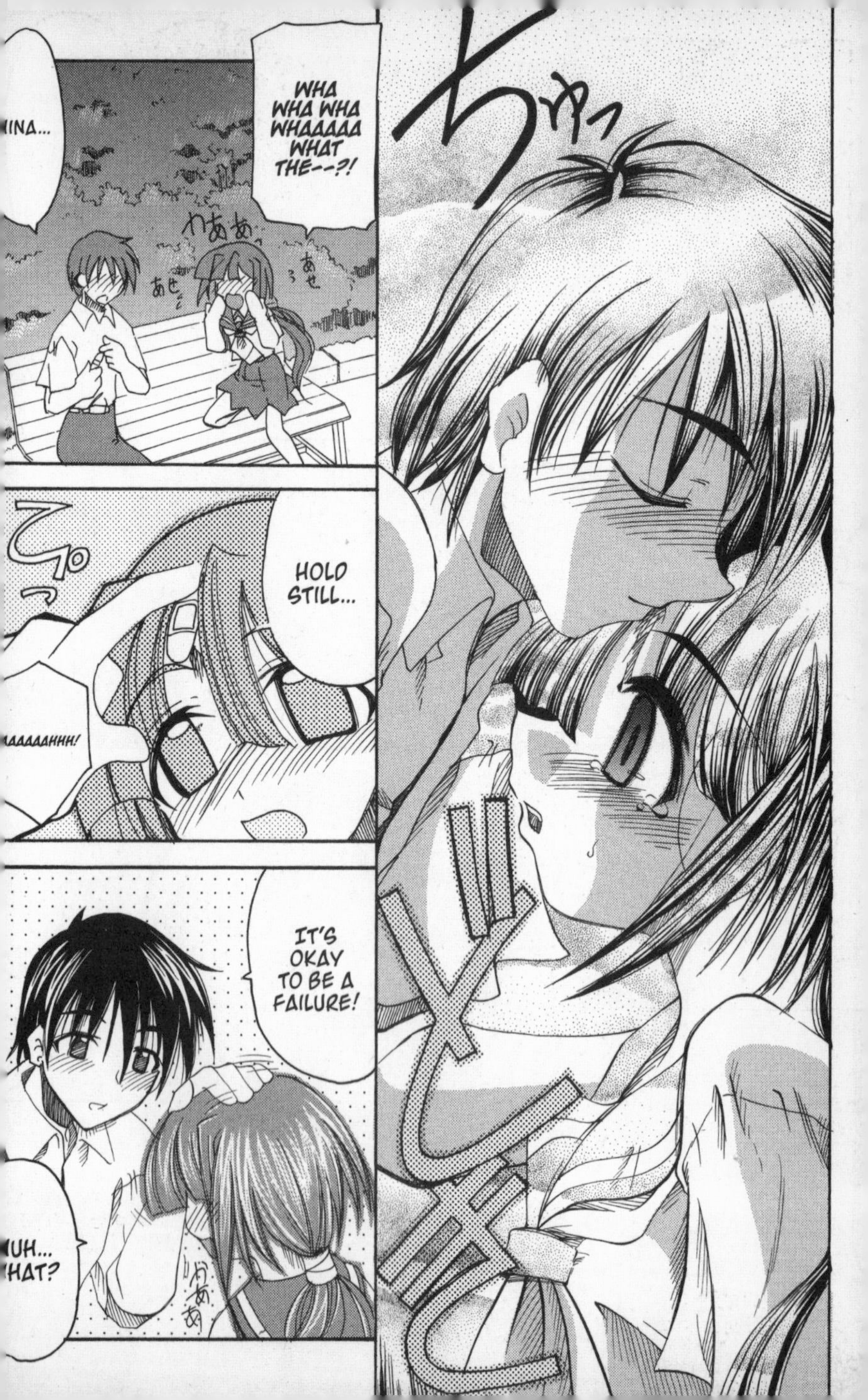
ちゅっ
WHA WHA WHA WHAAAAA WHAT THE--?!
INA...
わあぁ
あせ
あせ
HOLD STILL...
AAAAAAHHH!
IT'S OKAY TO BE A FAILURE!
HUH... WHAT?

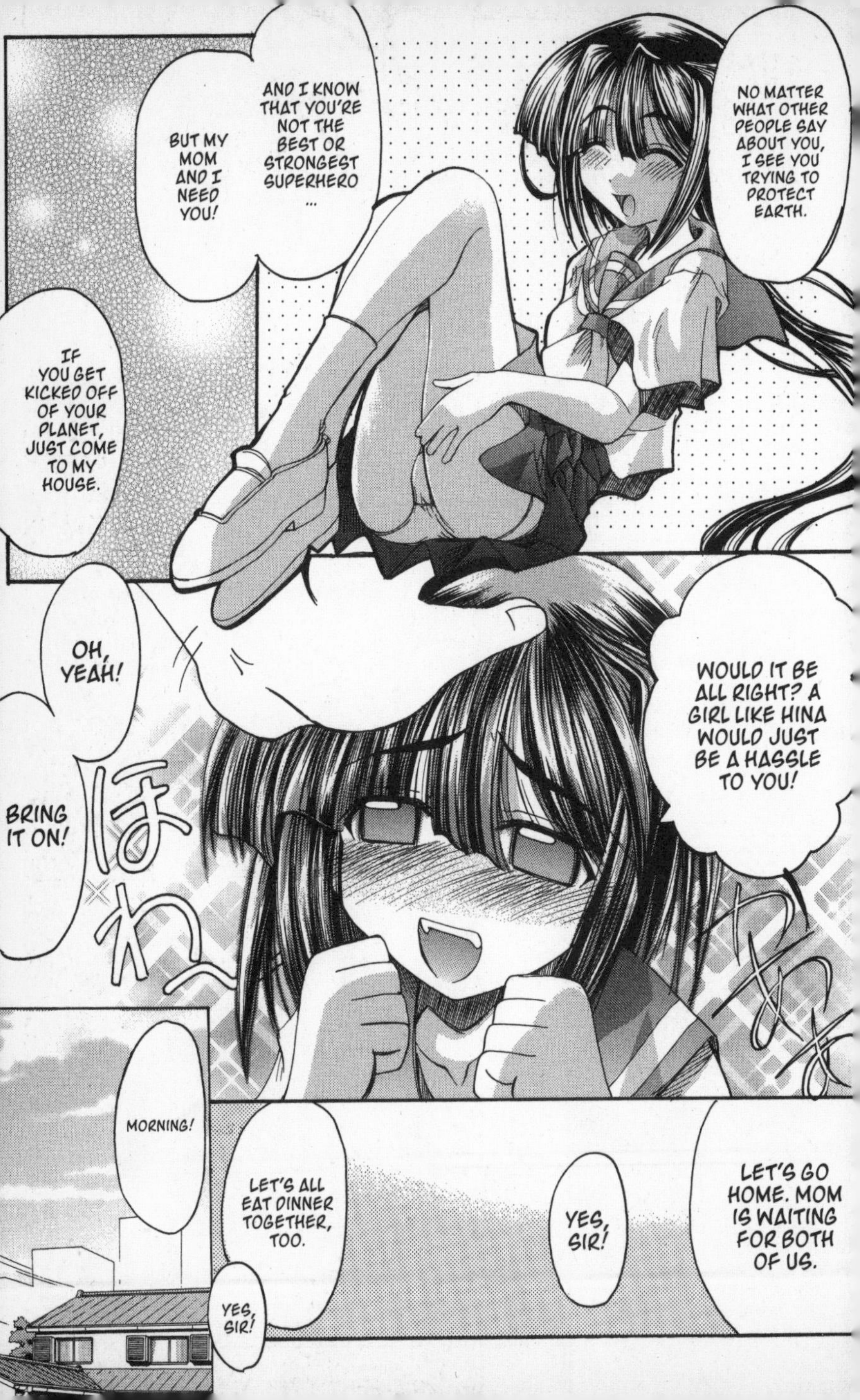
NO MATTER WHAT OTHER PEOPLE SAY ABOUT YOU, I SEE YOU TRYING TO PROTECT EARTH.
AND I KNOW THAT YOU'RE NOT THE BEST OR STRONGEST SUPERHERO ...
BUT MY MOM AND I NEED YOU!
IF YOU GET KICKED OFF OF YOUR PLANET, JUST COME TO MY HOUSE.
WOULD IT BE ALL RIGHT? A GIRL LIKE HINA WOULD JUST BE A HASSLE TO YOU!
OH, YEAH!
BRING IT ON!
ほわ～
LET'S GO HOME. MOM IS WAITING FOR BOTH OF US.
YES, SIR!
LET'S ALL EAT DINNER TOGETHER, TOO.
MORNING!
YES, SIR!

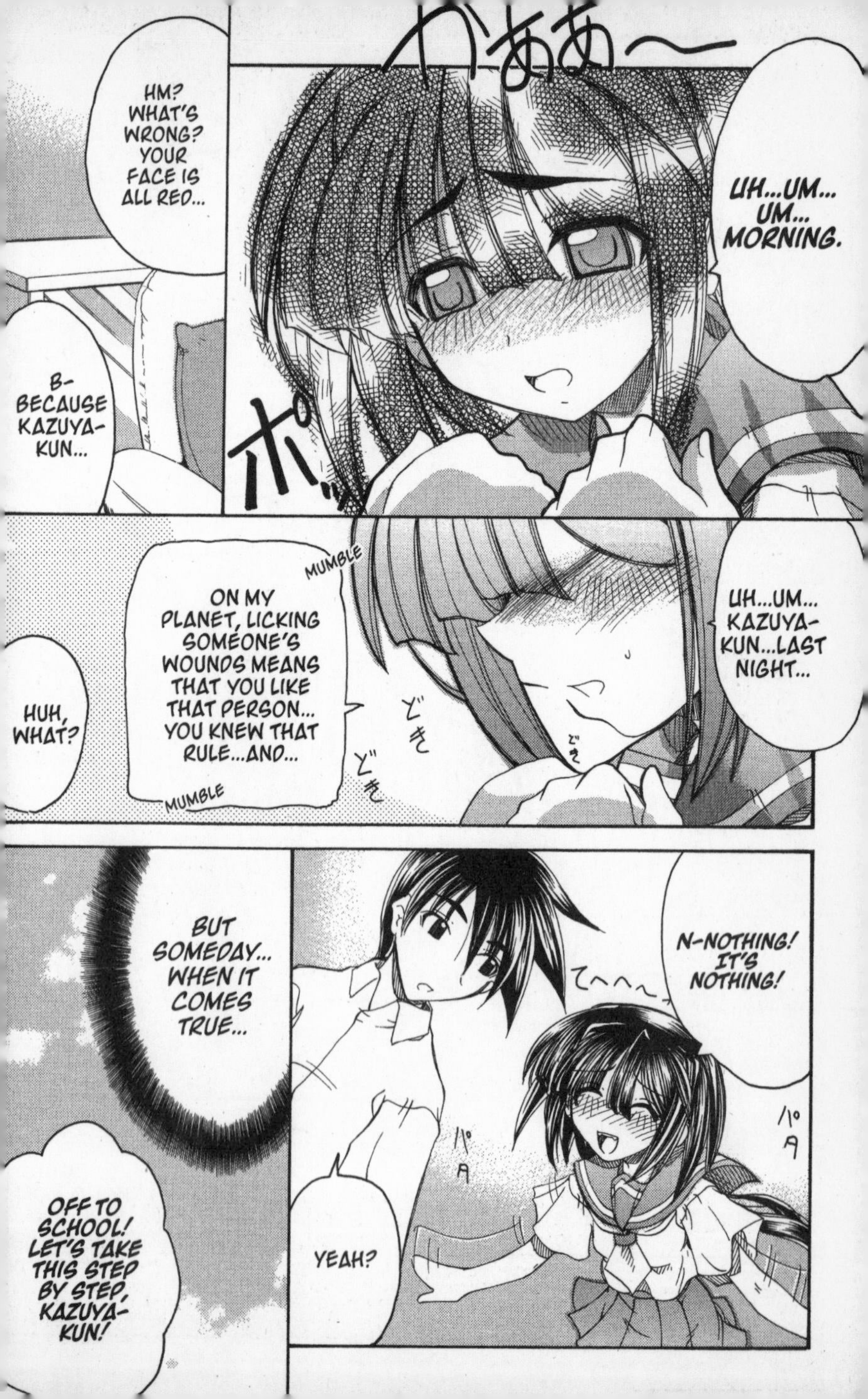
かあぁ～
UH...UM... UM... MORNING.
ポッ
HM? WHAT'S WRONG? YOUR FACE IS ALL RED...
B- BECAUSE KAZUYA-KUN...
UH...UM... KAZUYA-KUN...LAST NIGHT...
MUMBLE
ON MY PLANET, LICKING SOMEONE'S WOUNDS MEANS THAT YOU LIKE THAT PERSON... YOU KNEW THAT RULE...AND...
MUMBLE
どき
どき
どき
HUH, WHAT?
N-NOTHING! IT'S NOTHING!
てへへへ
パタ
パタ
YEAH?
BUT SOMEDAY... WHEN IT COMES TRUE...
OFF TO SCHOOL! LET'S TAKE THIS STEP BY STEP, KAZUYA-KUN!

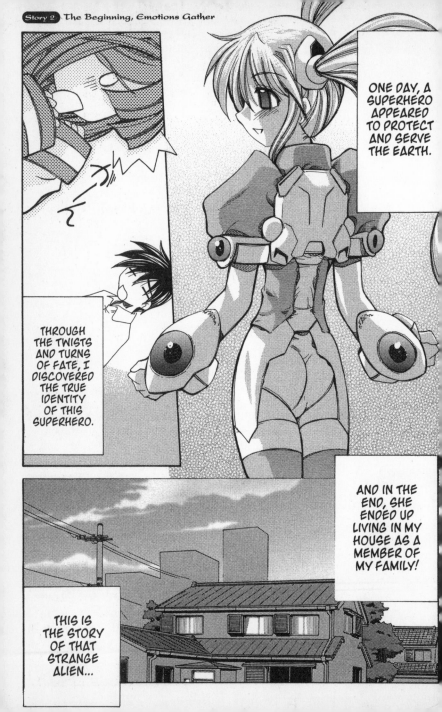

ONE DAY, A SUPERHERO APPEARED TO PROTECT AND SERVE THE EARTH.

THROUGH THE TWISTS AND TURNS OF FATE, I DISCOVERED THE TRUE IDENTITY OF THIS SUPERHERO.

AND IN THE END, SHE ENDED UP LIVING IN MY HOUSE AS A MEMBER OF MY FAMILY!

THIS IS THE STORY OF THAT STRANGE ALIEN...

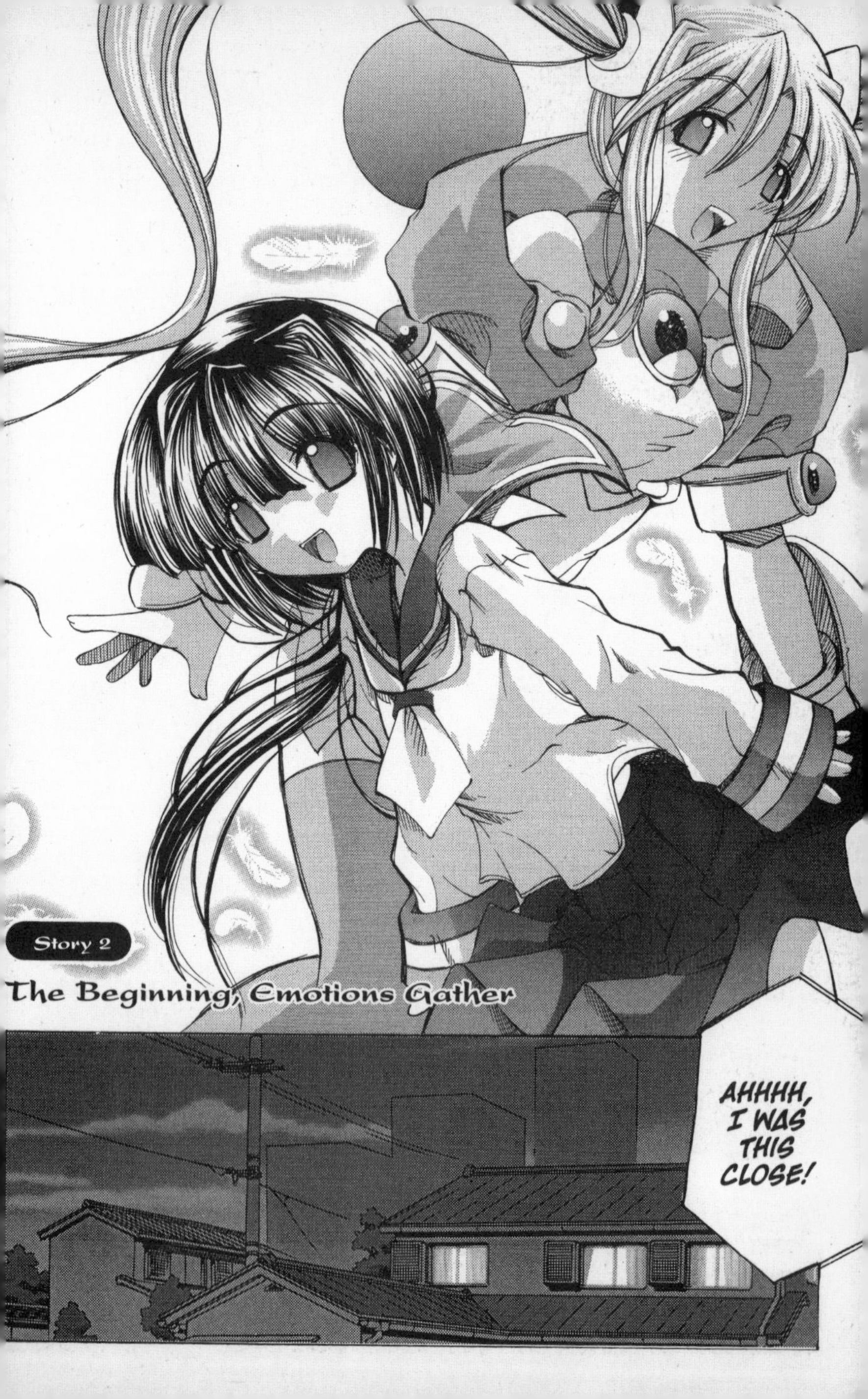
Story 2
The Beginning, Emotions Gather
AHHHH, I WAS THIS CLOSE!

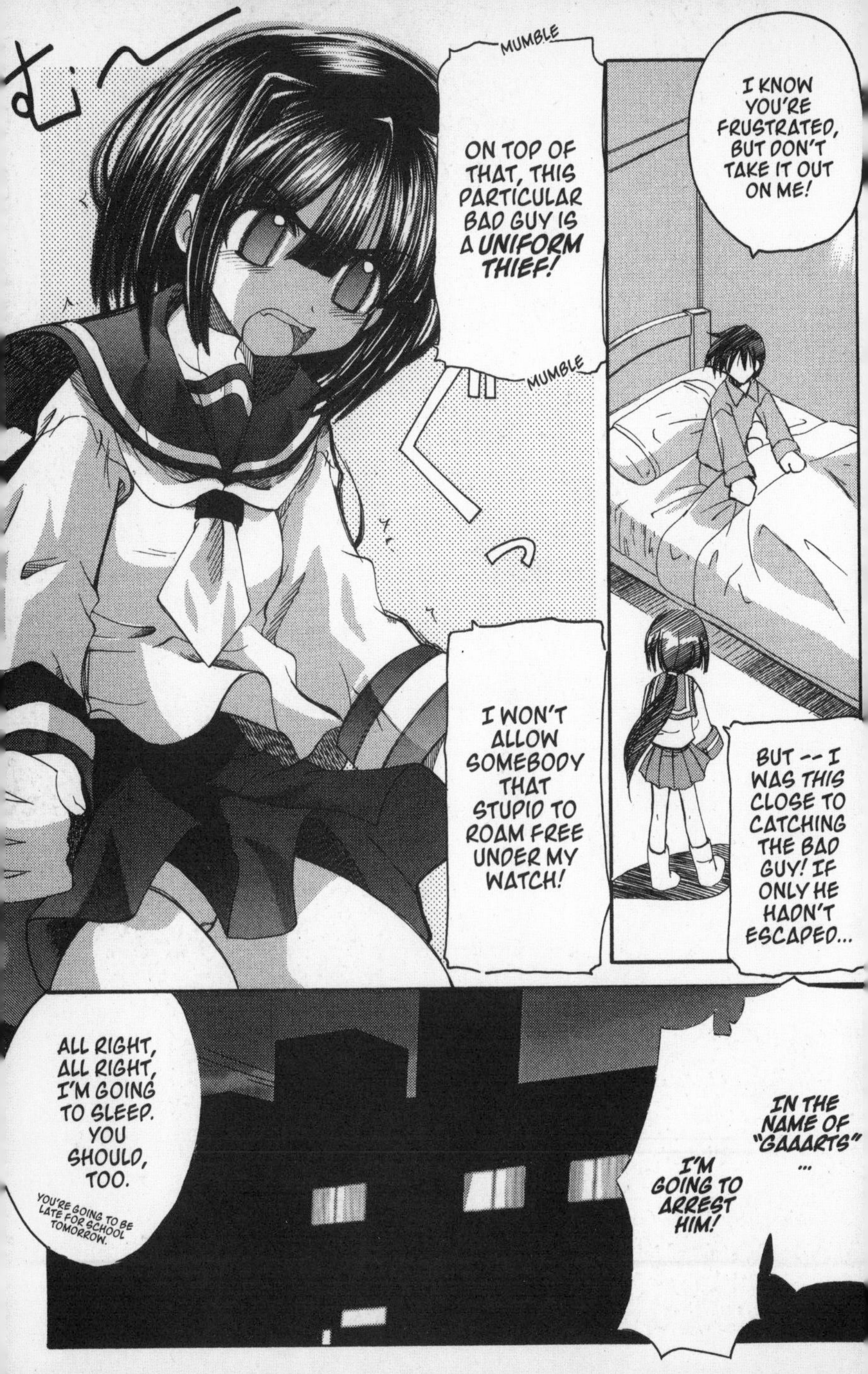
I KNOW YOU'RE FRUSTRATED, BUT DON'T TAKE IT OUT ON ME!
BUT -- I WAS THIS CLOSE TO CATCHING THE BAD GUY! IF ONLY HE HADN'T ESCAPED...
MUMBLE
ON TOP OF THAT, THIS PARTICULAR BAD GUY IS A ***UNIFORM THIEF!***
MUMBLE
I WON'T ALLOW SOMEBODY THAT STUPID TO ROAM FREE UNDER MY WATCH!
む〜
IN THE NAME OF "GAAARTS"...
I'M GOING TO ARREST HIM!
ALL RIGHT, ALL RIGHT, I'M GOING TO SLEEP. YOU SHOULD, TOO.
YOU'RE GOING TO BE LATE FOR SCHOOL TOMORROW.

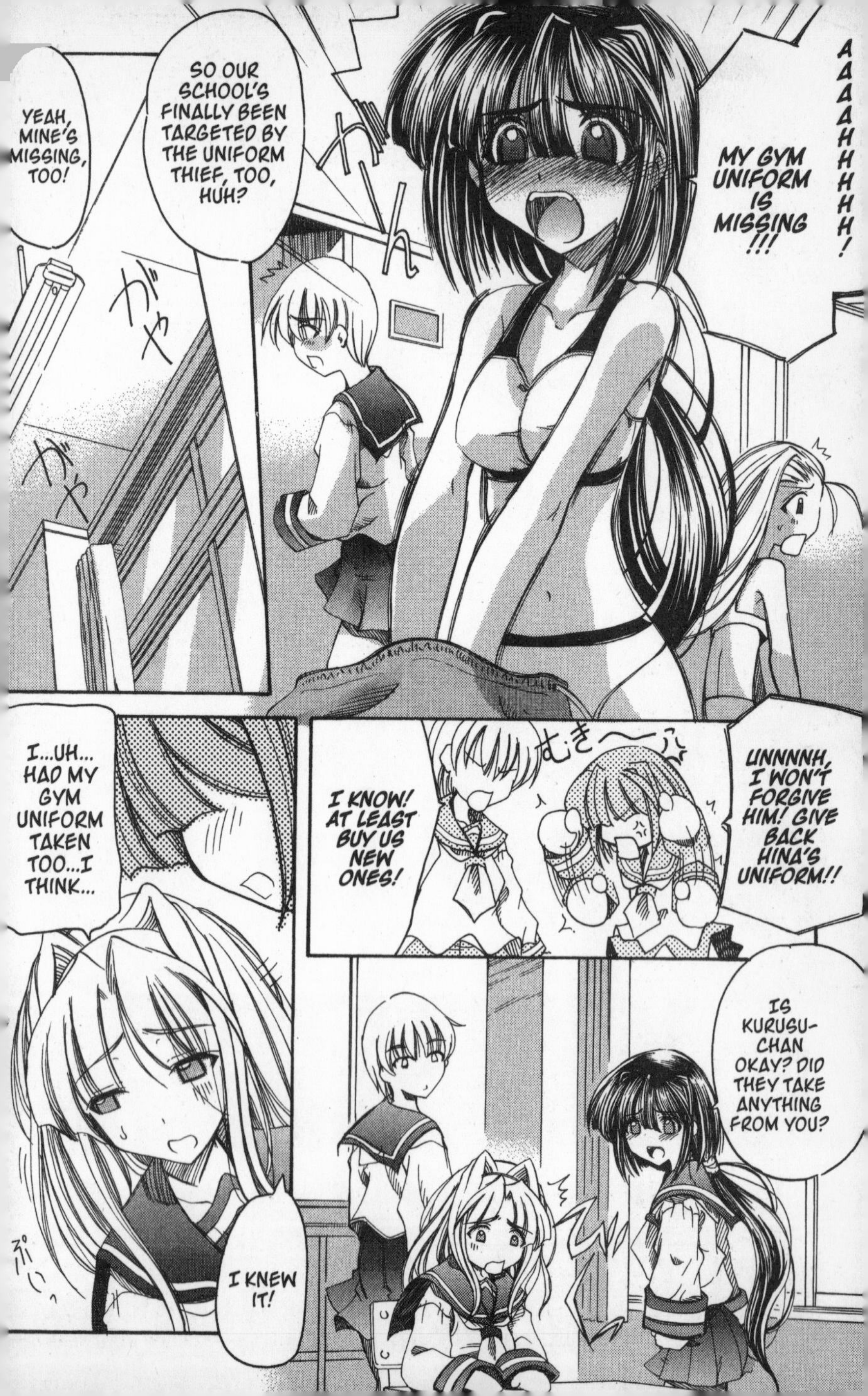
AAAAAHHHHHH!
MY GYM UNIFORM IS MISSING !!!
SO OUR SCHOOL'S FINALLY BEEN TARGETED BY THE UNIFORM THIEF, TOO, HUH?
YEAH, MINE'S MISSING, TOO!
がや
がや
UNNNNH, I WON'T FORGIVE HIM! GIVE BACK HINA'S UNIFORM!!
むき～っ
I KNOW! AT LEAST BUY US NEW ONES!
I...UH... HAD MY GYM UNIFORM TAKEN TOO...I THINK...
IS KURUSU-CHAN OKAY? DID THEY TAKE ANYTHING FROM YOU?
I KNEW IT!
ぷい

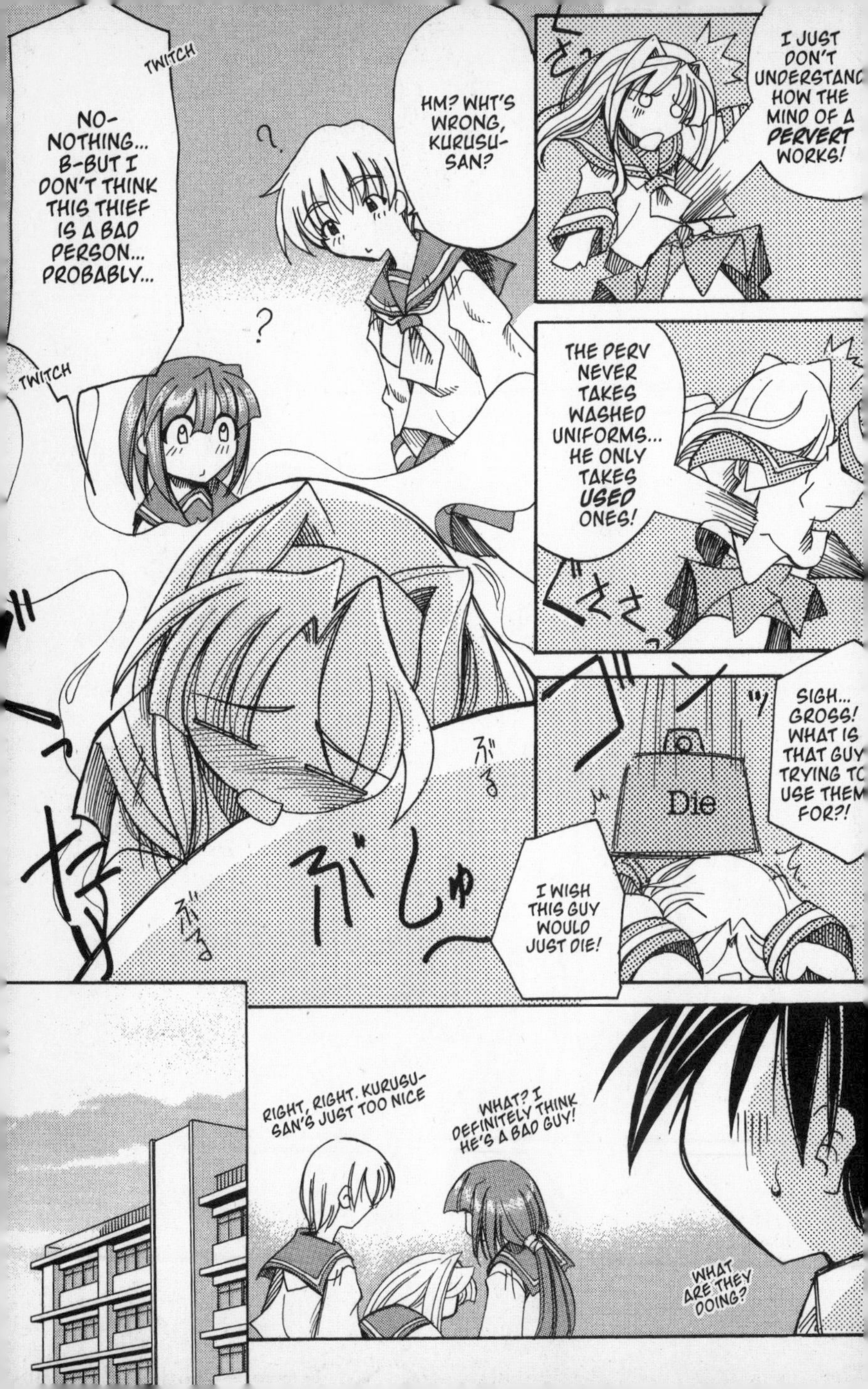
I JUST DON'T UNDERSTAND HOW THE MIND OF A PERVERT WORKS!
THE PERV NEVER TAKES WASHED UNIFORMS... HE ONLY TAKES USED ONES!
SIGH... GROSS! WHAT IS THAT GUY TRYING TO USE THEM FOR?!
Die
I WISH THIS GUY WOULD JUST DIE!
HM? WHT'S WRONG, KURUSU-SAN?
TWITCH
NO-NOTHING... B-BUT I DON'T THINK THIS THIEF IS A BAD PERSON... PROBABLY...
TWITCH
RIGHT, RIGHT. KURUSU-SAN'S JUST TOO NICE
WHAT? I DEFINITELY THINK HE'S A BAD GUY!
WHAT ARE THEY DOING?

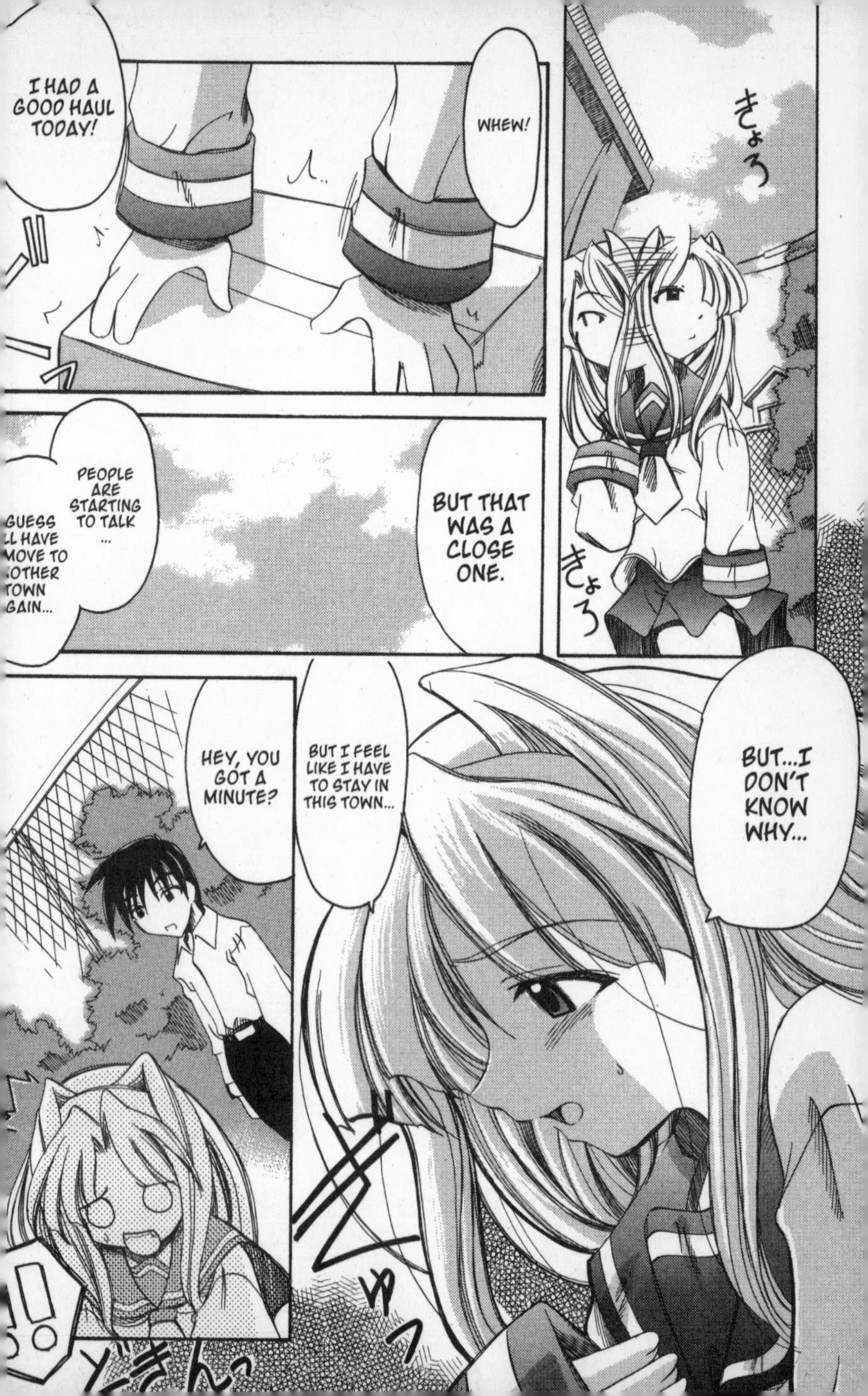
きょろ
きょろ
WHEW!
I HAD A GOOD HAUL TODAY!
BUT THAT WAS A CLOSE ONE.
PEOPLE ARE STARTING TO TALK ...
GUESS
LL HAVE
MOVE TO
OTHER
TOWN
GAIN...
BUT...I DON'T KNOW WHY...
BUT I FEEL LIKE I HAVE TO STAY IN THIS TOWN...
ゆっ
HEY, YOU GOT A MINUTE?
!
ぞきんっ

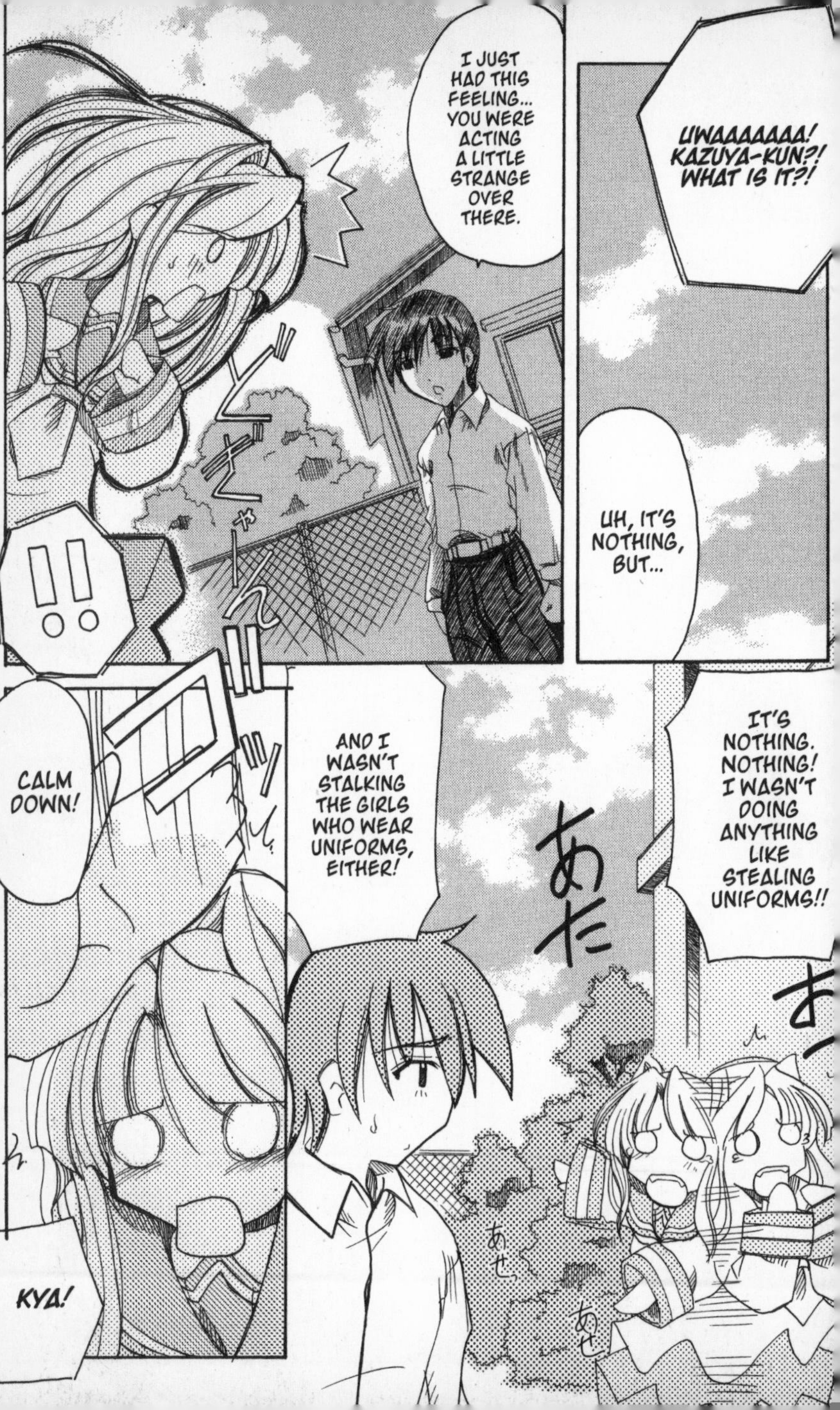
UWAAAAAAA! KAZUYA-KUN?! WHAT IS IT?!
UH, IT'S NOTHING, BUT...
I JUST HAD THIS FEELING... YOU WERE ACTING A LITTLE STRANGE OVER THERE.
!!
IT'S NOTHING. NOTHING! I WASN'T DOING ANYTHING LIKE STEALING UNIFORMS!!
AND I WASN'T STALKING THE GIRLS WHO WEAR UNIFORMS, EITHER!
CALM DOWN!
KYA!

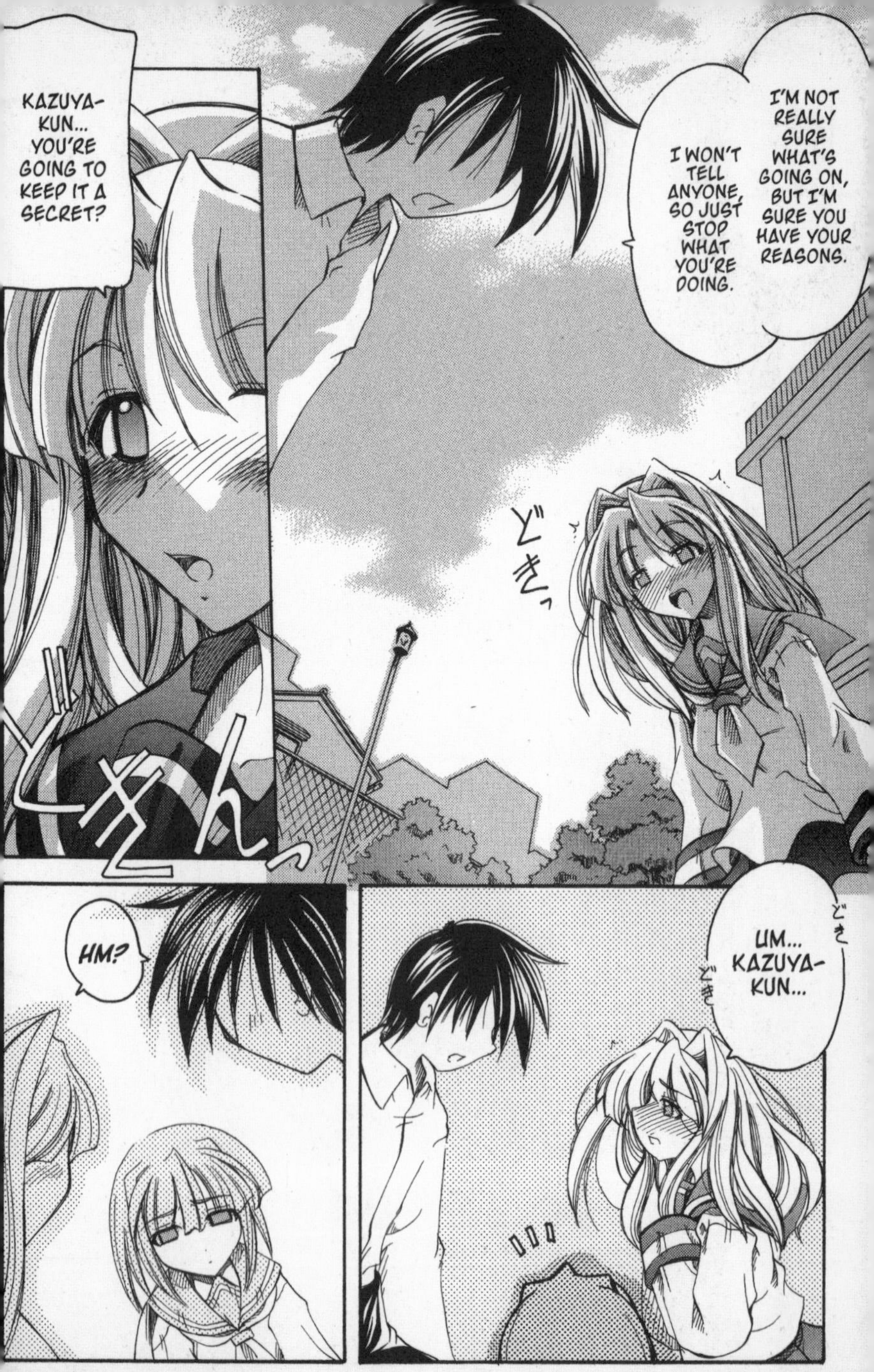
I'M NOT REALLY SURE WHAT'S GOING ON, BUT I'M SURE YOU HAVE YOUR REASONS.
I WON'T TELL ANYONE, SO JUST STOP WHAT YOU'RE DOING.
どきっ
KAZUYA-KUN... YOU'RE GOING TO KEEP IT A SECRET?
どきんっ
どき どき
UM... KAZUYA-KUN...
HM?

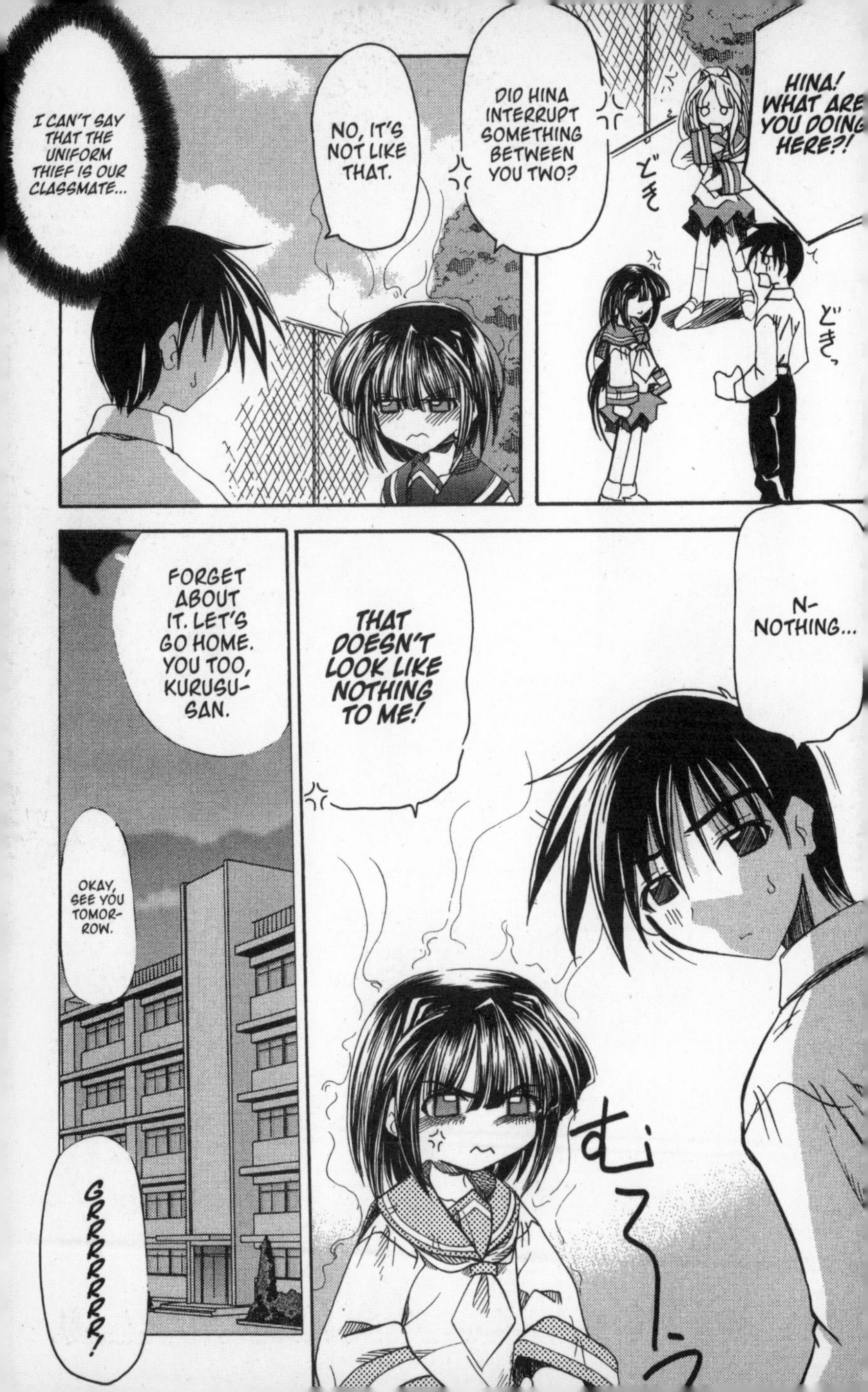
HINA! WHAT ARE YOU DOING HERE?!
どき
どきっ
DID HINA INTERRUPT SOMETHING BETWEEN YOU TWO?
NO, IT'S NOT LIKE THAT.
I CAN'T SAY THAT THE UNIFORM THIEF IS OUR CLASSMATE...
N-NOTHING...
THAT DOESN'T LOOK LIKE NOTHING TO ME!
むぅ〜っ
FORGET ABOUT IT. LET'S GO HOME. YOU TOO, KURUSU-SAN.
OKAY, SEE YOU TOMORROW.
GRRRRRRR!

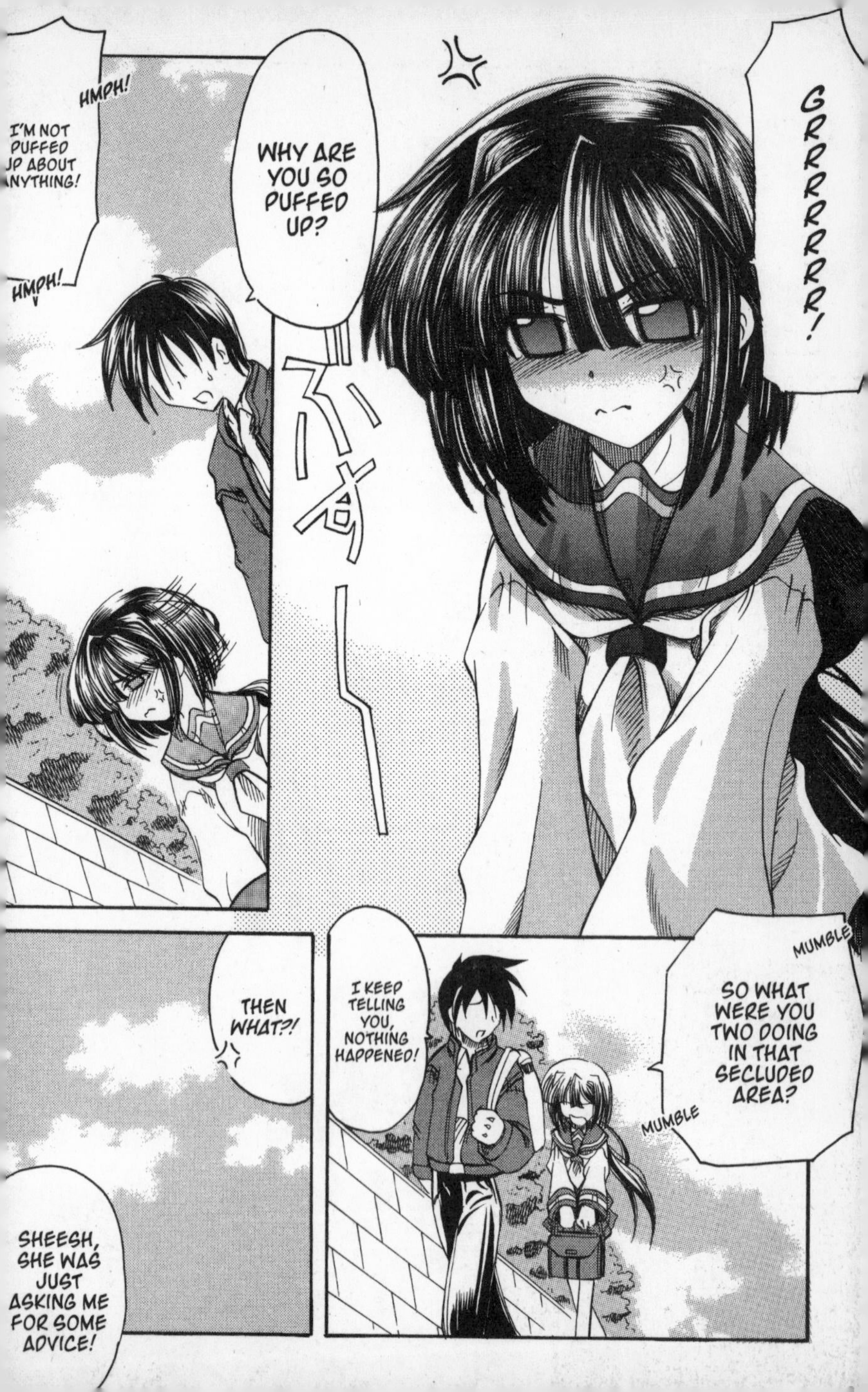
GRRRRRRR!
WHY ARE YOU SO PUFFED UP?
HMPH!
I'M NOT PUFFED JP ABOUT NYTHING!
HMPH!
MUMBLE
SO WHAT WERE YOU TWO DOING IN THAT SECLUDED AREA?
MUMBLE
I KEEP TELLING YOU, NOTHING HAPPENED!
THEN WHAT?!
SHEESH, SHE WAS JUST ASKING ME FOR SOME ADVICE!

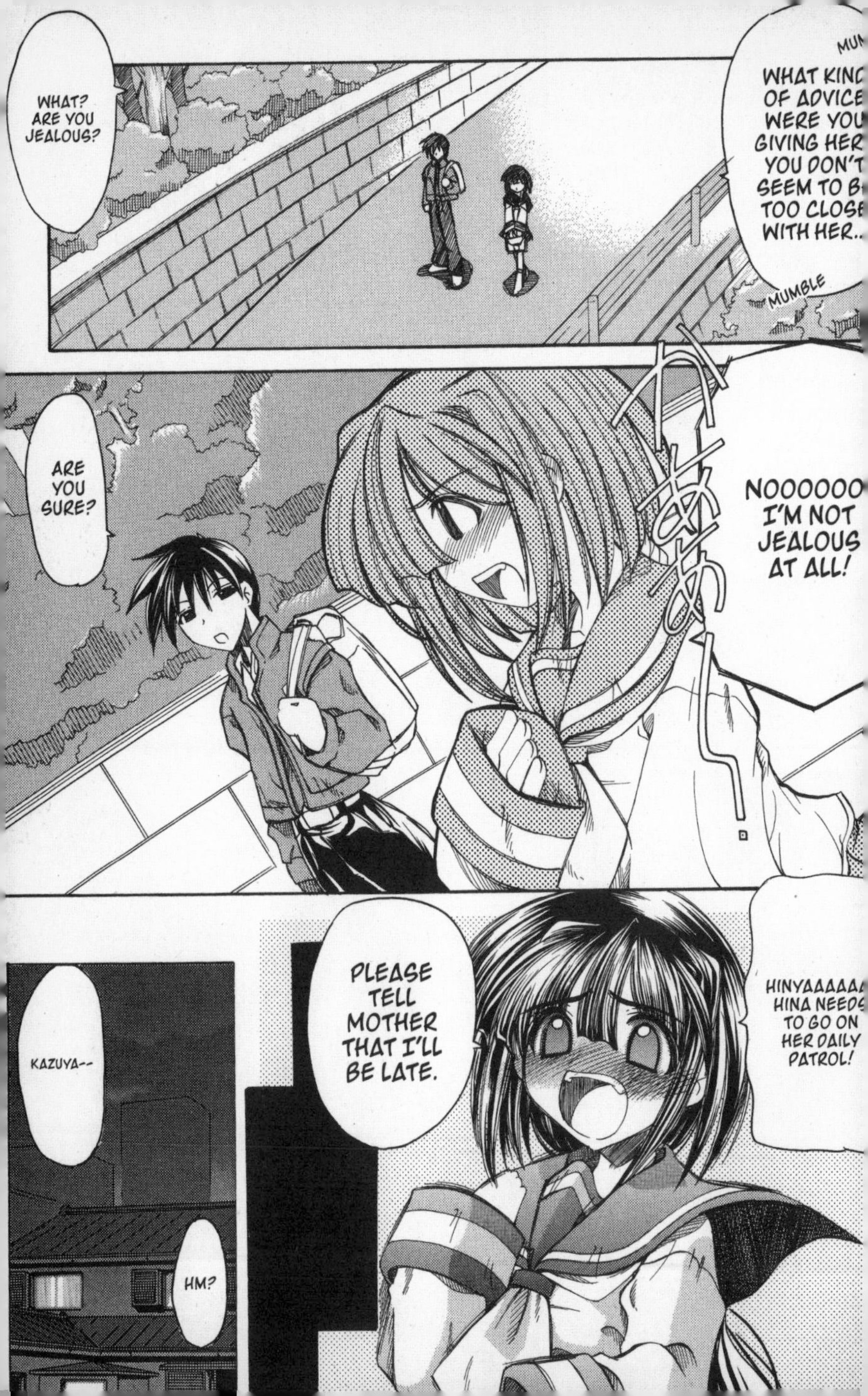
MUM
WHAT KIND OF ADVICE WERE YOU GIVING HER? YOU DON'T SEEM TO BE TOO CLOSE WITH HER...
MUMBLE
WHAT? ARE YOU JEALOUS?
NOOOOOO! I'M NOT JEALOUS AT ALL!
ARE YOU SURE?
HINYAAAAAA! HINA NEEDS TO GO ON HER DAILY PATROL!
PLEASE TELL MOTHER THAT I'LL BE LATE.
KAZUYA--
HM?

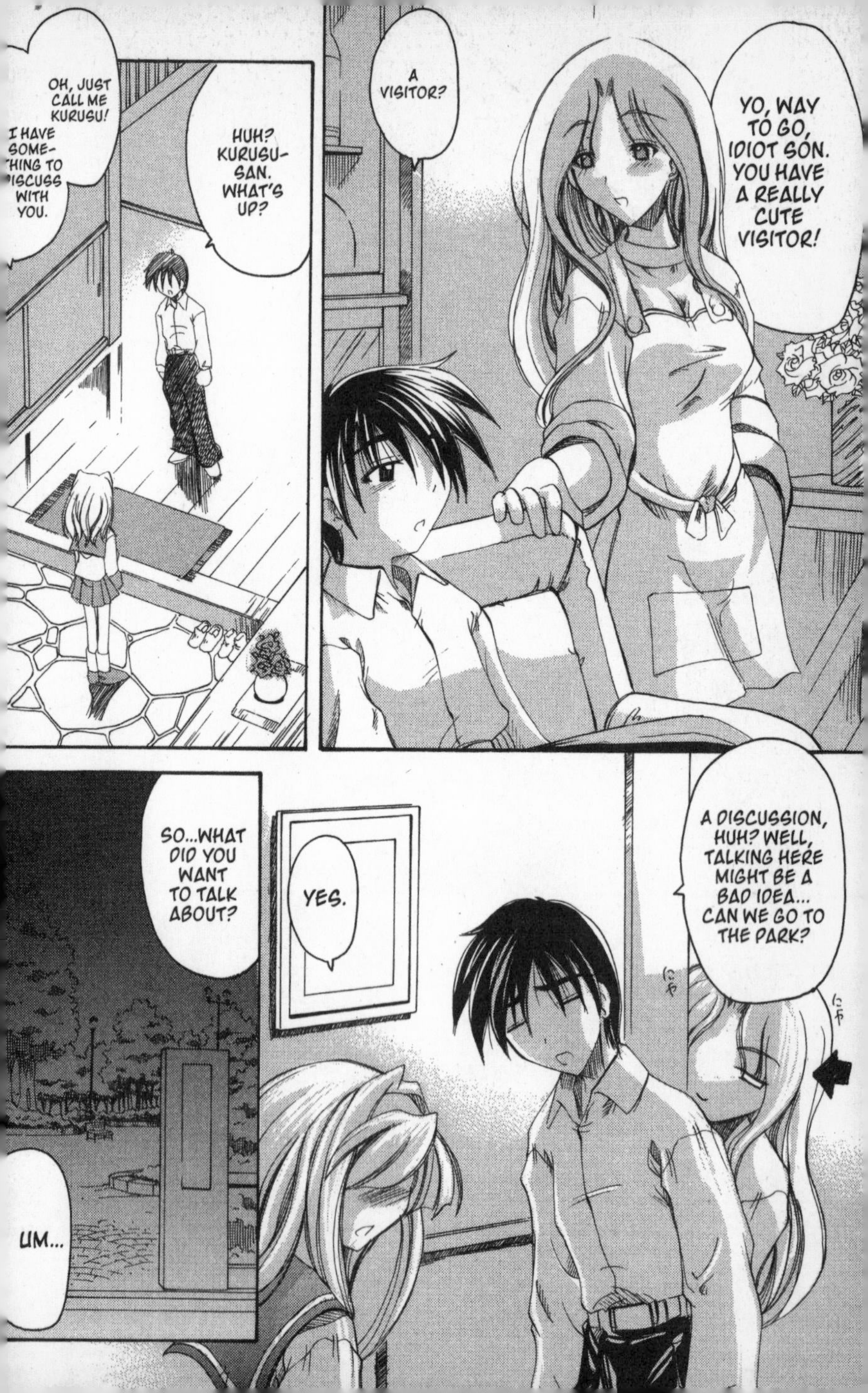
YO, WAY TO GO, IDIOT SON. YOU HAVE A REALLY CUTE VISITOR!
A VISITOR?
HUH? KURUSU-SAN. WHAT'S UP?
OH, JUST CALL ME KURUSU! I HAVE SOMETHING TO DISCUSS WITH YOU.
A DISCUSSION, HUH? WELL, TALKING HERE MIGHT BE A BAD IDEA... CAN WE GO TO THE PARK?
にや
にや
YES.
SO...WHAT DID YOU WANT TO TALK ABOUT?
UM...

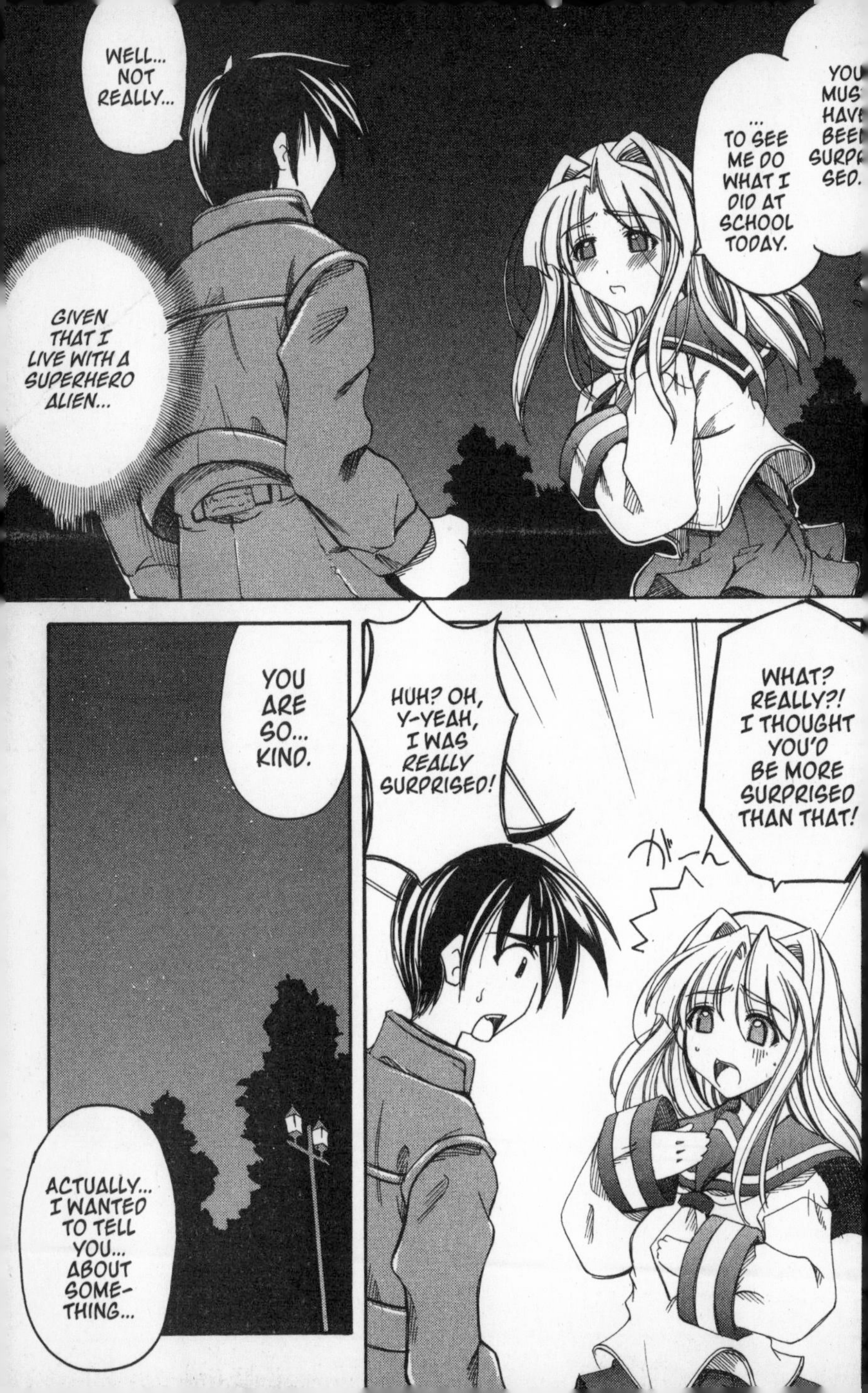
YOU MUS HAVE BEE SURPR SED.
... TO SEE ME DO WHAT I DID AT SCHOOL TODAY.
WELL... NOT REALLY...
GIVEN THAT I LIVE WITH A SUPERHERO ALIEN...
WHAT? REALLY?! I THOUGHT YOU'D BE MORE SURPRISED THAN THAT!
がーん
HUH? OH, Y-YEAH, I WAS REALLY SURPRISED!
YOU ARE SO... KIND.
ACTUALLY... I WANTED TO TELL YOU... ABOUT SOMETHING...

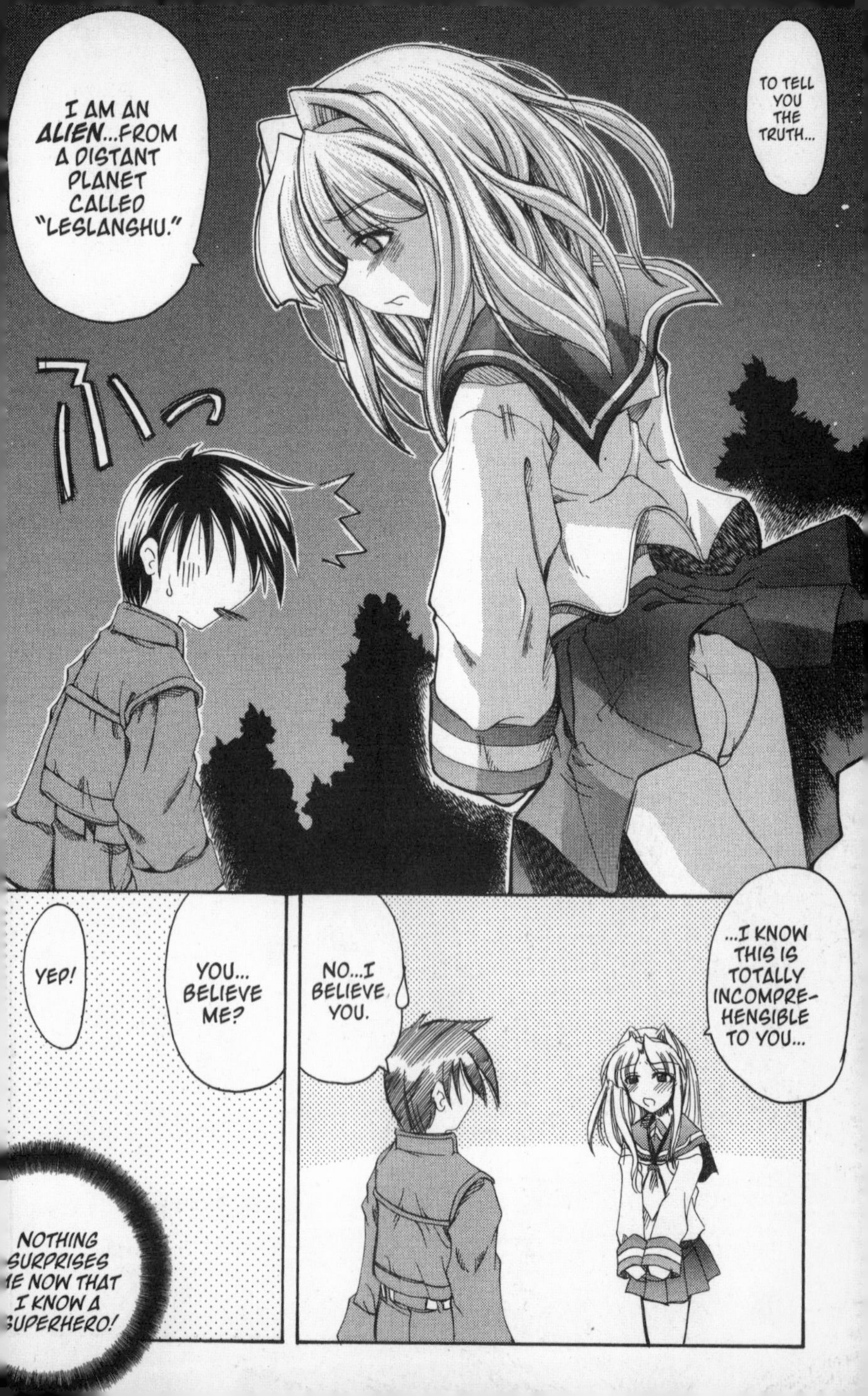

TO TELL YOU THE TRUTH...
I AM AN ALIEN...FROM A DISTANT PLANET CALLED "LESLANSHU."
ふっ
...I KNOW THIS IS TOTALLY INCOMPRE-HENSIBLE TO YOU...
NO...I BELIEVE YOU.
YOU... BELIEVE ME?
YEP!
NOTHING SURPRISES IE NOW THAT I KNOW A SUPERHERO!

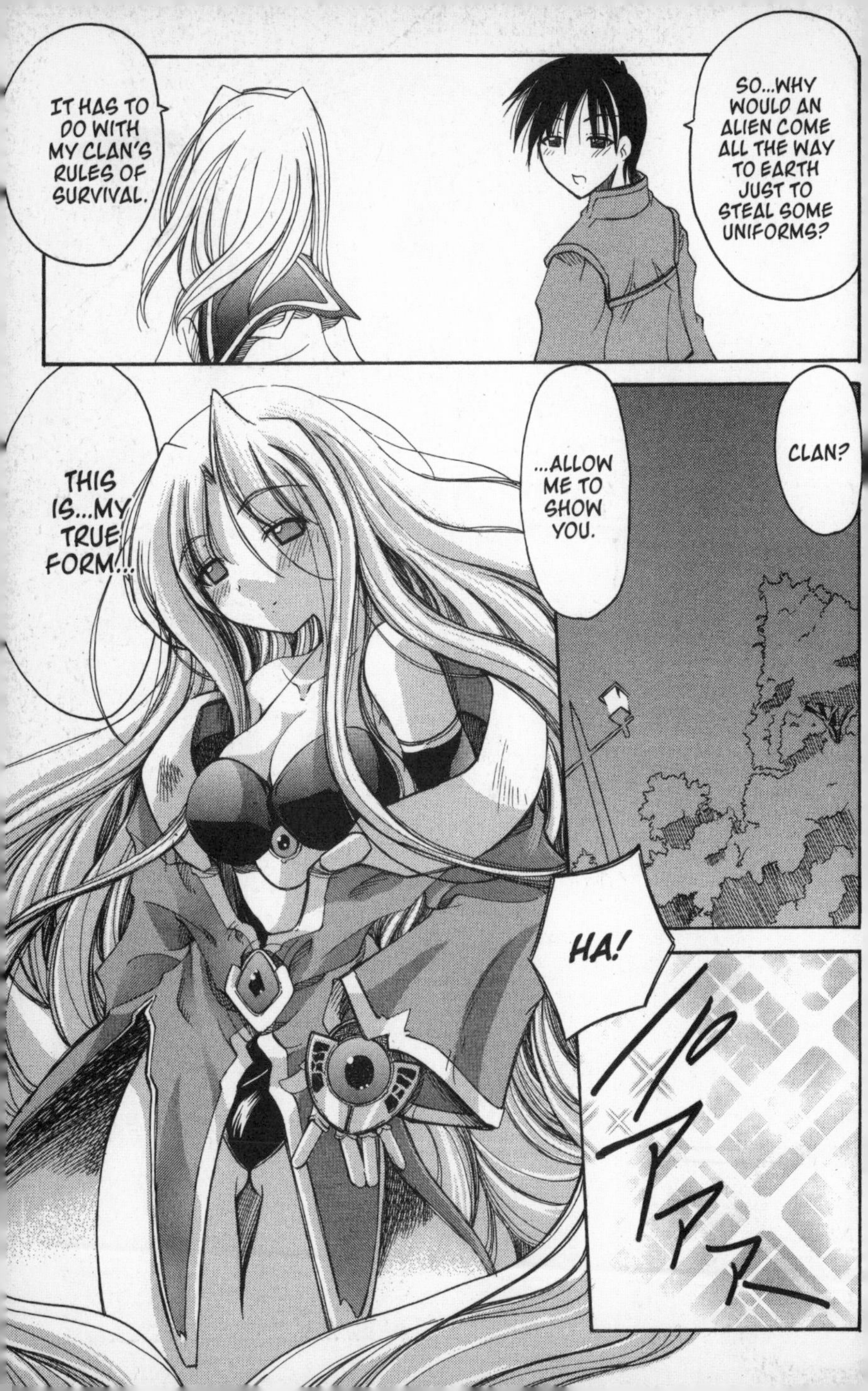
SO...WHY WOULD AN ALIEN COME ALL THE WAY TO EARTH JUST TO STEAL SOME UNIFORMS?
IT HAS TO DO WITH MY CLAN'S RULES OF SURVIVAL.
CLAN?
...ALLOW ME TO SHOW YOU.
HA!
THIS IS...MY TRUE FORM...

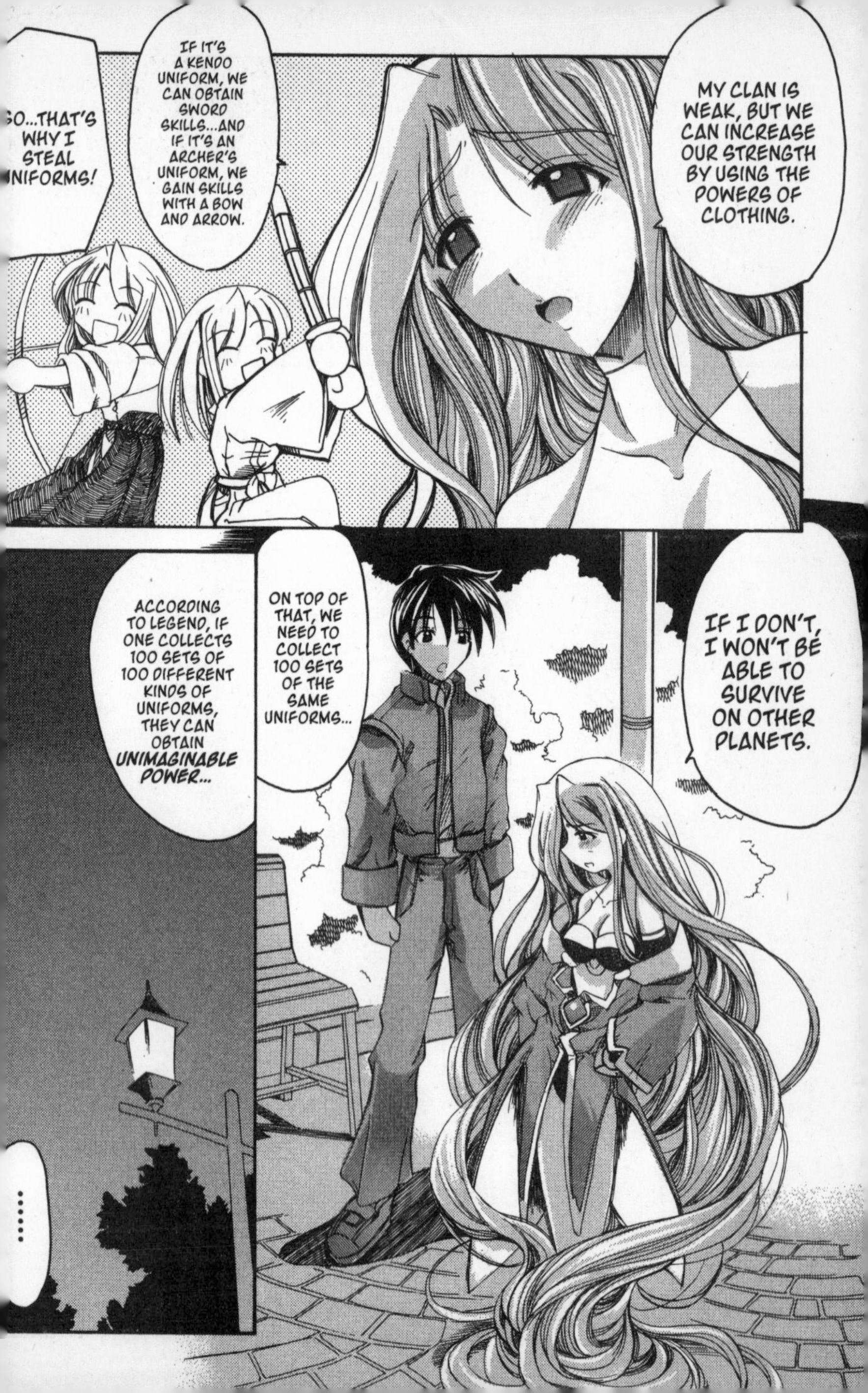

MY CLAN IS WEAK, BUT WE CAN INCREASE OUR STRENGTH BY USING THE POWERS OF CLOTHING.
IF IT'S A KENDO UNIFORM, WE CAN OBTAIN SWORD SKILLS...AND IF IT'S AN ARCHER'S UNIFORM, WE GAIN SKILLS WITH A BOW AND ARROW.
O...THAT'S WHY I STEAL NIFORMS!
IF I DON'T, I WON'T BE ABLE TO SURVIVE ON OTHER PLANETS.
ON TOP OF THAT, WE NEED TO COLLECT 100 SETS OF THE SAME UNIFORMS...
ACCORDING TO LEGEND, IF ONE COLLECTS 100 SETS OF 100 DIFFERENT KINDS OF UNIFORMS, THEY CAN OBTAIN *UNIMAGINABLE POWER...*
......

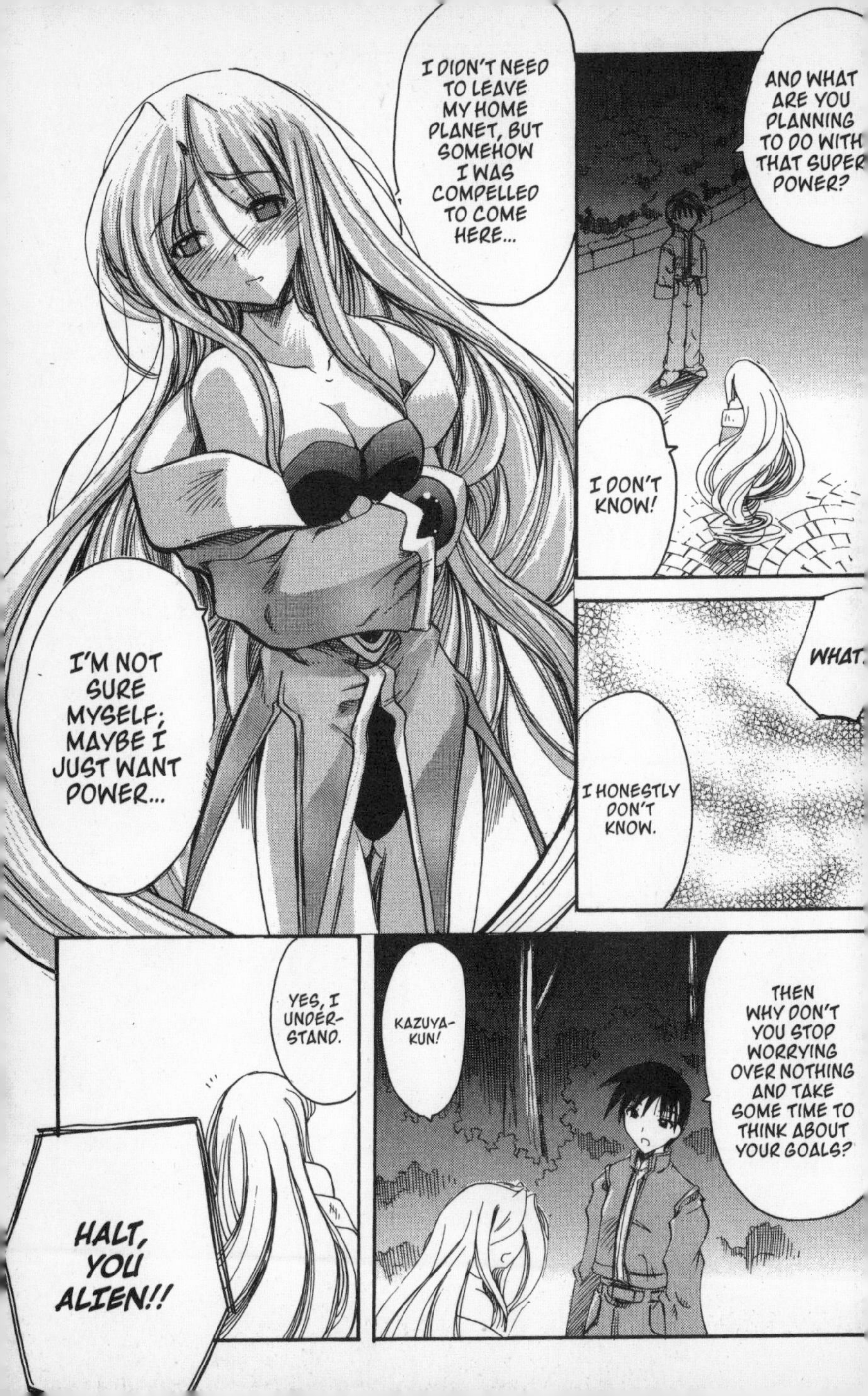
AND WHAT ARE YOU PLANNING TO DO WITH THAT SUPER POWER?
I DON'T KNOW!
WHAT.
I HONESTLY DON'T KNOW.
I DIDN'T NEED TO LEAVE MY HOME PLANET, BUT SOMEHOW I WAS COMPELLED TO COME HERE...
I'M NOT SURE MYSELF; MAYBE I JUST WANT POWER...
THEN WHY DON'T YOU STOP WORRYING OVER NOTHING AND TAKE SOME TIME TO THINK ABOUT YOUR GOALS?
KAZUYA-KUN!
YES, I UNDER-STAND.
HALT, YOU ALIEN!!

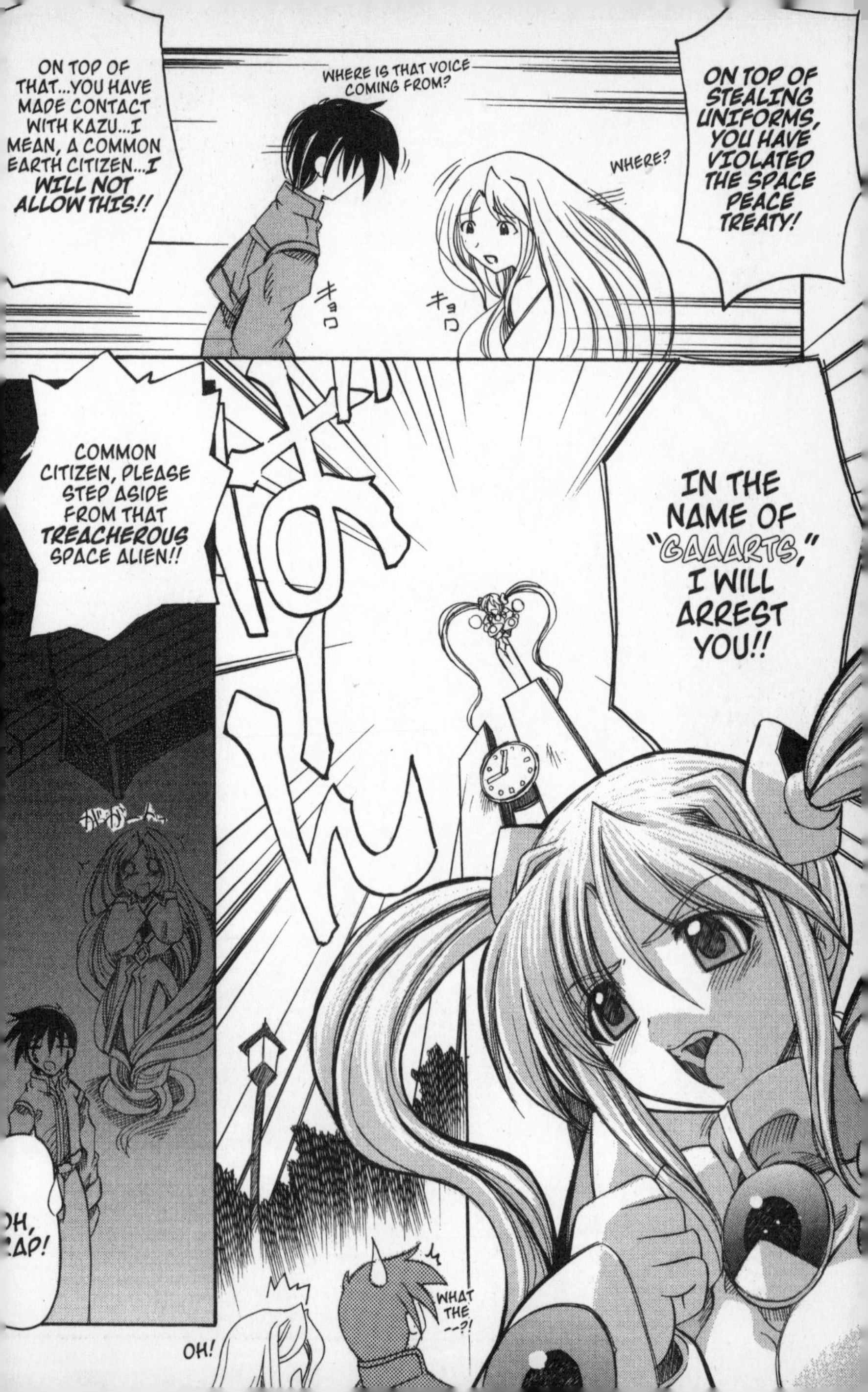
ON TOP OF STEALING UNIFORMS, YOU HAVE VIOLATED THE SPACE PEACE TREATY!
WHERE?
キョロ
WHERE IS THAT VOICE COMING FROM?
キョロ
ON TOP OF THAT...YOU HAVE MADE CONTACT WITH KAZU...I MEAN, A COMMON EARTH CITIZEN...I WILL NOT ALLOW THIS!!
IN THE NAME OF "GAAARTS," I WILL ARREST YOU!!
COMMON CITIZEN, PLEASE STEP ASIDE FROM THAT TREACHEROUS SPACE ALIEN!!
WHAT THE --?!
OH!

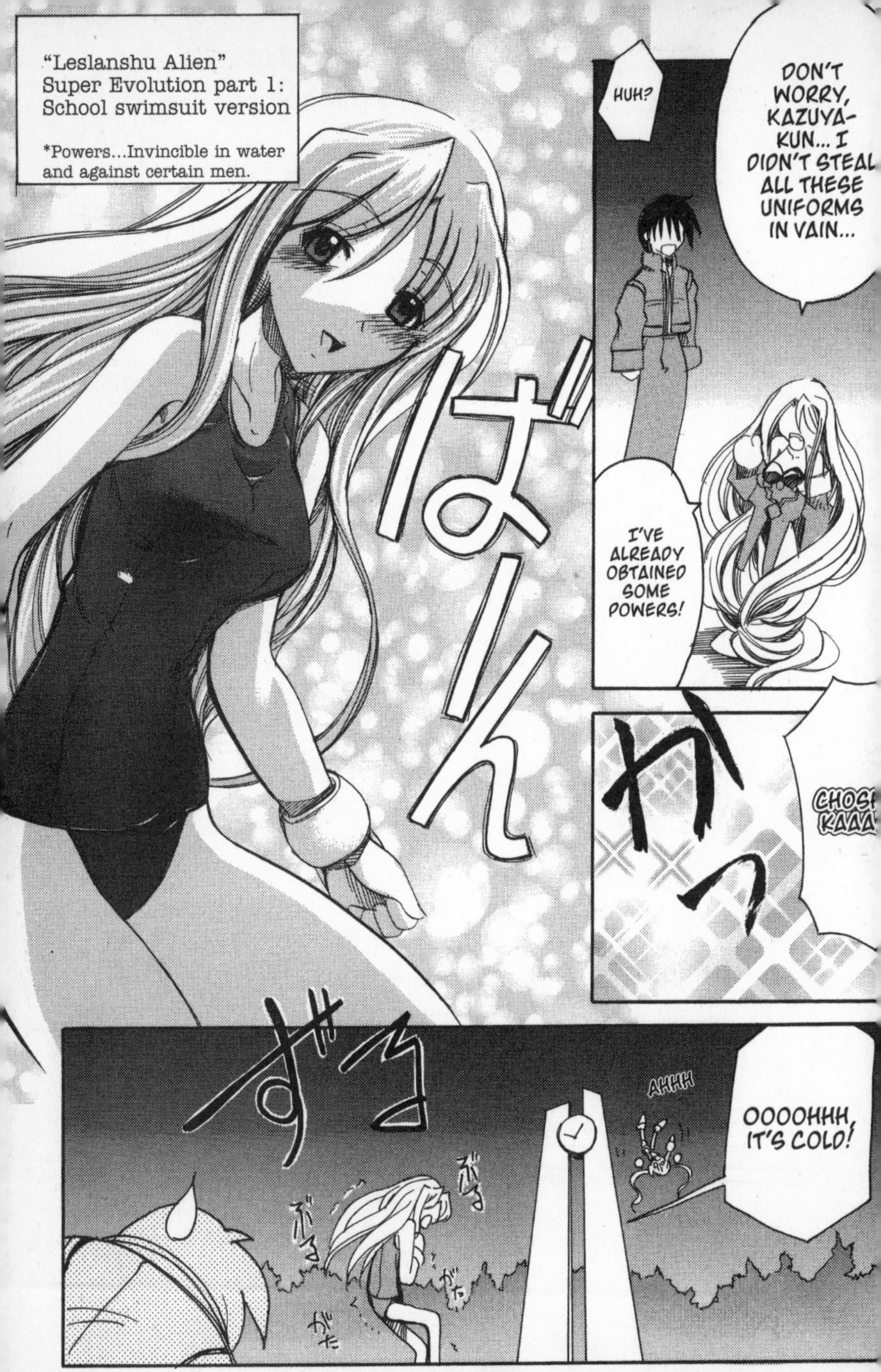

DON'T WORRY, KAZUYA-KUN... I DIDN'T STEAL ALL THESE UNIFORMS IN VAIN...
HUH?
I'VE ALREADY OBTAINED SOME POWERS!
CHOS KAAA
かっ
"Leslanshu Alien" Super Evolution part 1: School swimsuit version
*Powers...Invincible in water and against certain men.
ばーん
OOOOHHH, IT'S COLD!
AHHH
ぶる ぶる
がた がた

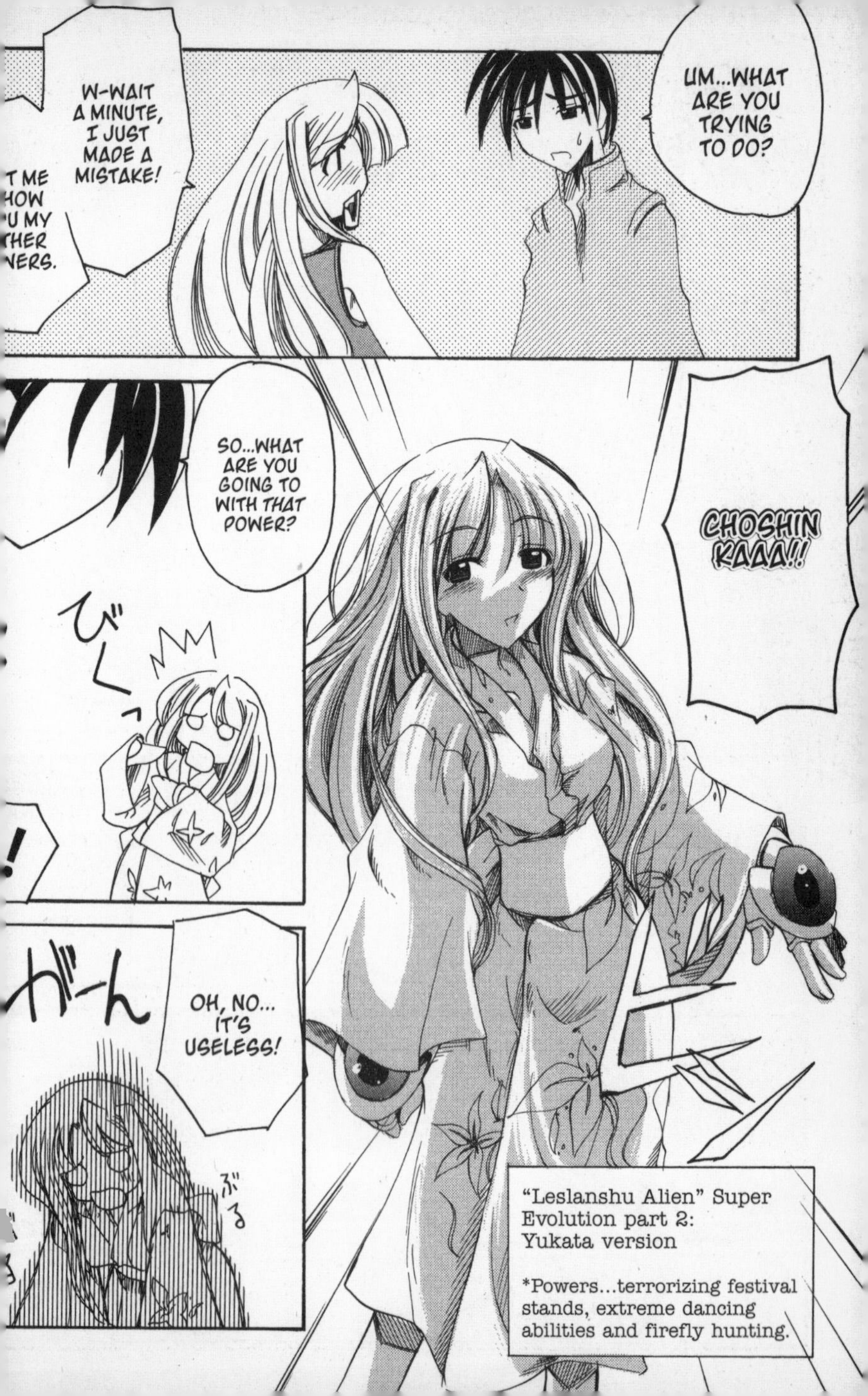
UM...WHAT ARE YOU TRYING TO DO?
W-WAIT A MINUTE, I JUST MADE A MISTAKE!
CHOSHIN KAAA!!
"Leslanshu Alien" Super Evolution part 2: Yukata version
*Powers...terrorizing festival stands, extreme dancing abilities and firefly hunting.
SO...WHAT ARE YOU GOING TO WITH THAT POWER?
びくっ
!
がーん
OH, NO... IT'S USELESS!
ぶる

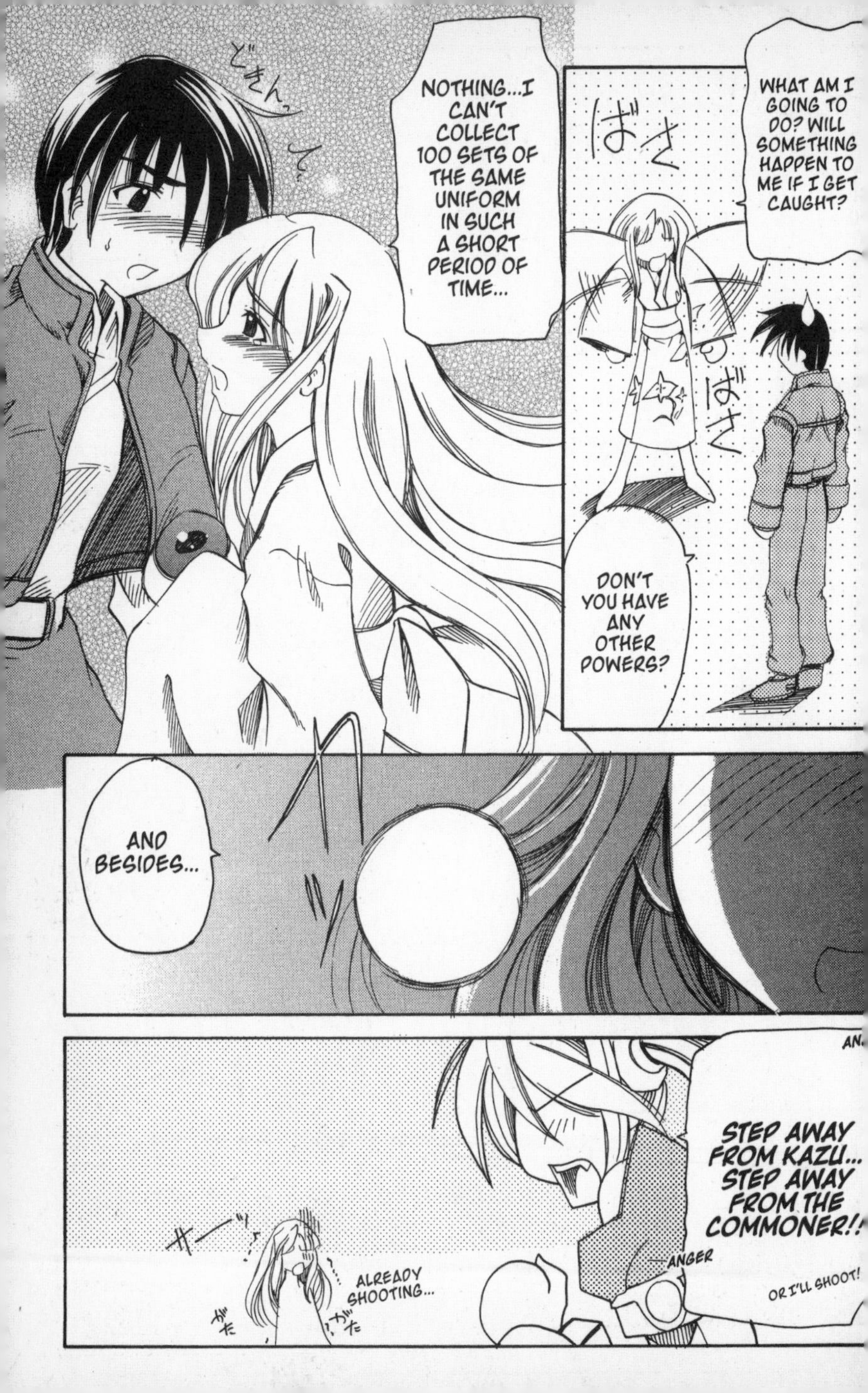

WHAT AM I GOING TO DO? WILL SOMETHING HAPPEN TO ME IF I GET CAUGHT?
ばき
ばき
DON'T YOU HAVE ANY OTHER POWERS?
どきん
NOTHING...I CAN'T COLLECT 100 SETS OF THE SAME UNIFORM IN SUCH A SHORT PERIOD OF TIME...
AND BESIDES...
STEP AWAY FROM KAZU... STEP AWAY FROM THE COMMONER!!
ANGER
OR I'LL SHOOT!
ALREADY SHOOTING...

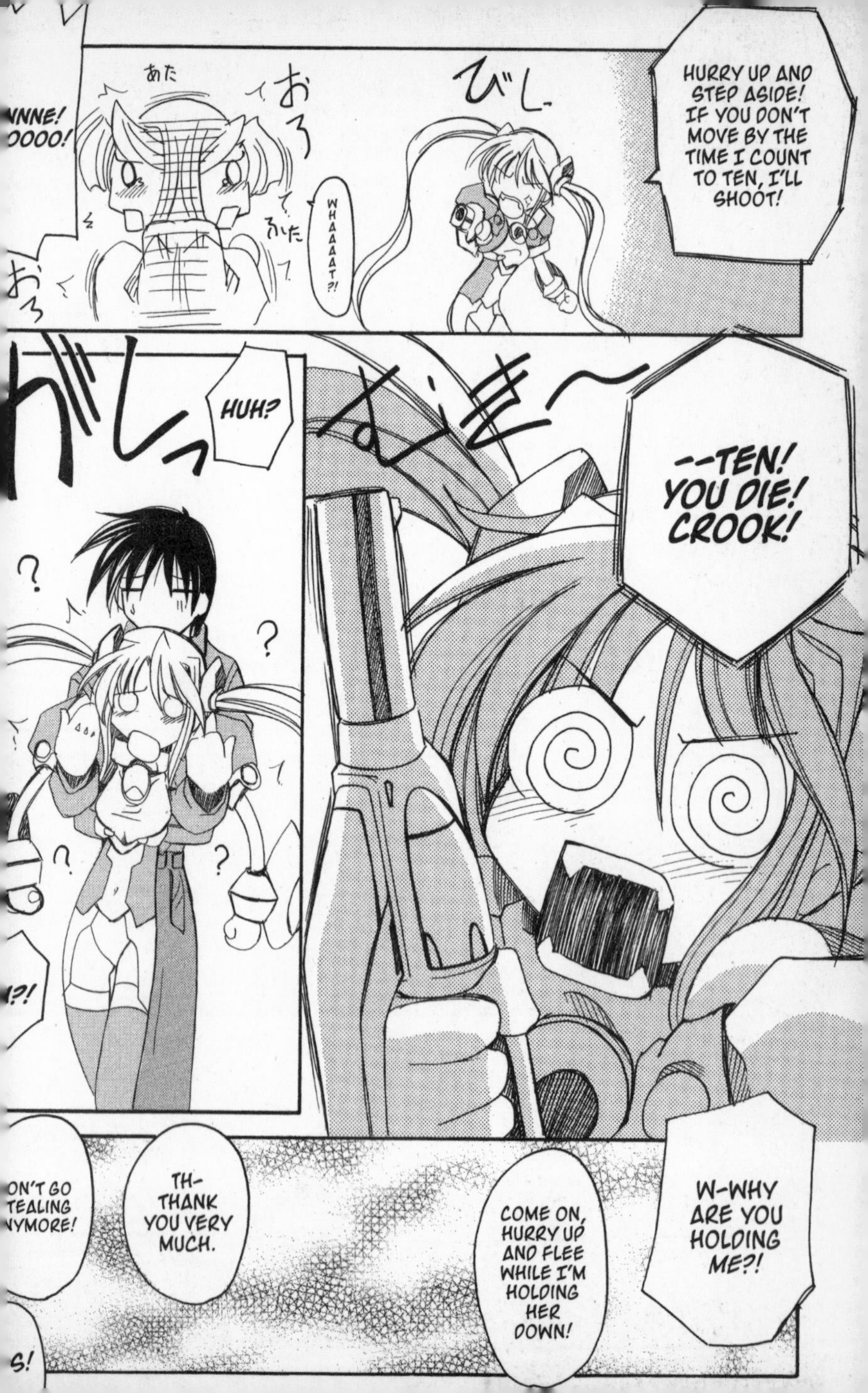
びし
HURRY UP AND STEP ASIDE! IF YOU DON'T MOVE BY THE TIME I COUNT TO TEN, I'LL SHOOT!
WHAAAAT?!
あた
おろ
おろ
--TEN! YOU DIE! CROOK!
がしっ
HUH?
W-WHY ARE YOU HOLDING ME?!
COME ON, HURRY UP AND FLEE WHILE I'M HOLDING HER DOWN!
TH-THANK YOU VERY MUCH.

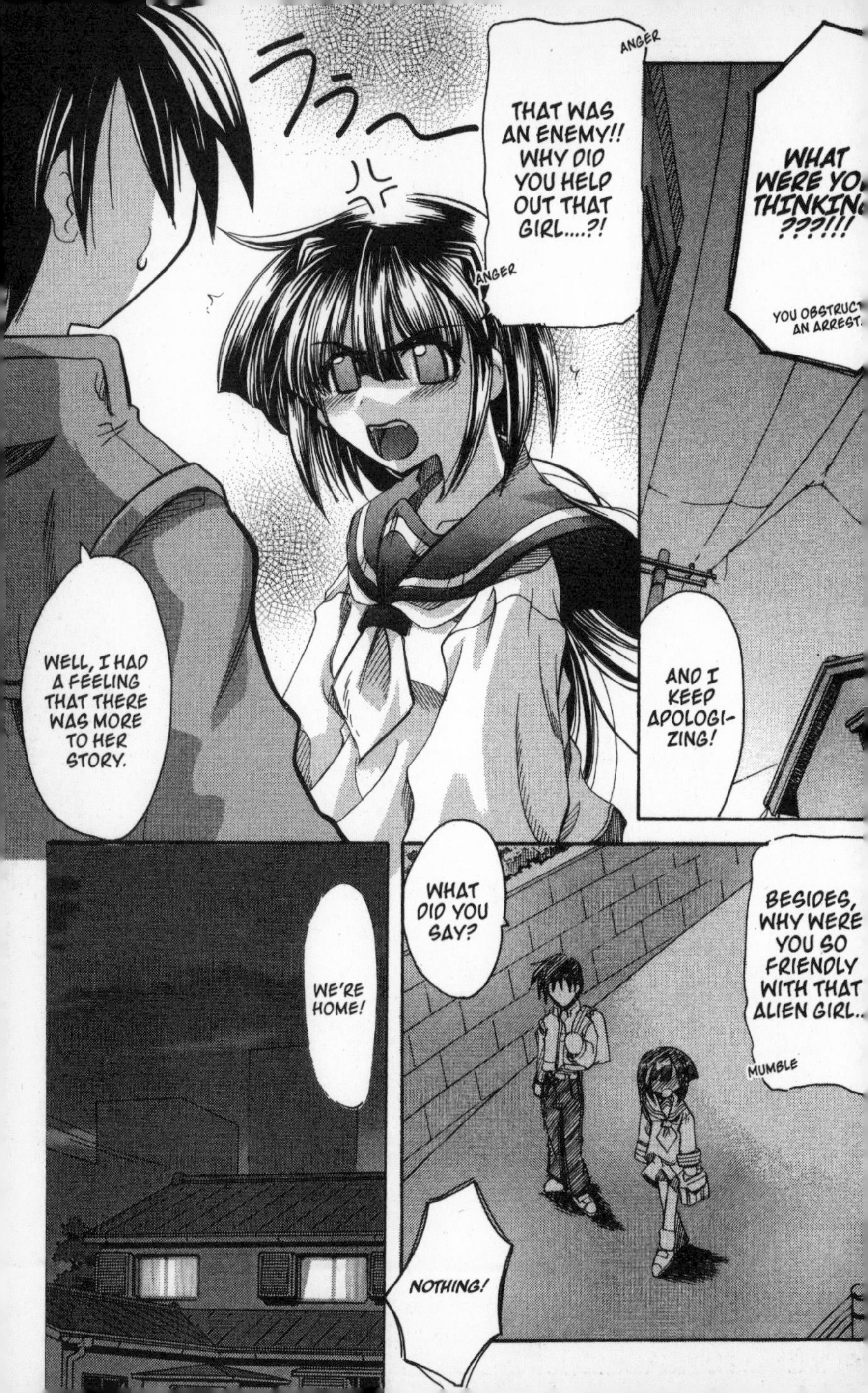
WHAT WERE YO THINKIN ???!!!
YOU OBSTRUCT AN ARREST
AND I KEEP APOLOGI-ZING!
ANGER
THAT WAS AN ENEMY!! WHY DID YOU HELP OUT THAT GIRL....?!
ANGER
うう〜
WELL, I HAD A FEELING THAT THERE WAS MORE TO HER STORY.
BESIDES, WHY WERE YOU SO FRIENDLY WITH THAT ALIEN GIRL..
MUMBLE
WHAT DID YOU SAY?
NOTHING!
WE'RE HOME!

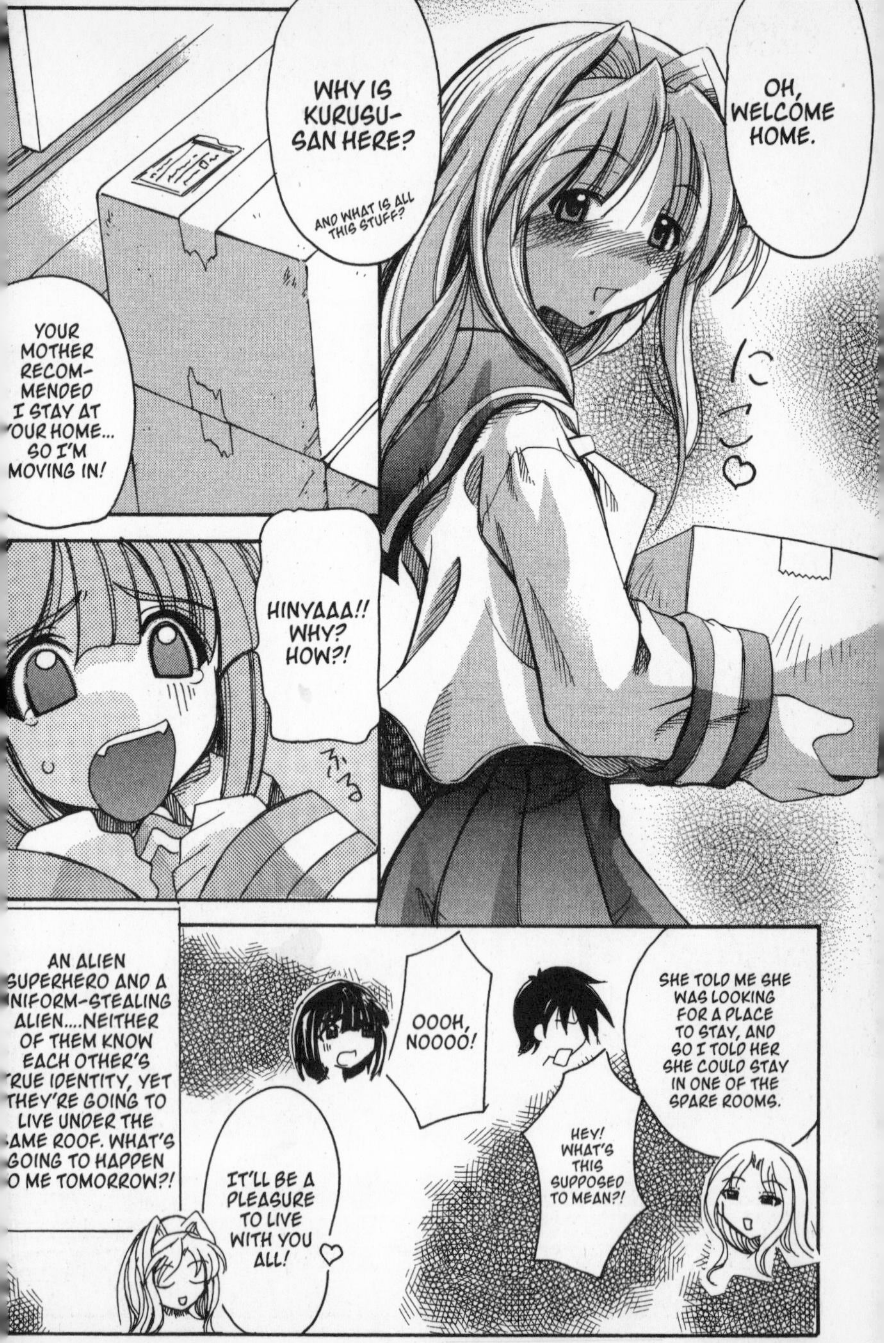
OH, WELCOME HOME.
WHY IS KURUSU-SAN HERE?
AND WHAT IS ALL THIS STUFF?
YOUR MOTHER RECOMMENDED I STAY AT OUR HOME... SO I'M MOVING IN!
HINYAAA!! WHY? HOW?!
SHE TOLD ME SHE WAS LOOKING FOR A PLACE TO STAY, AND SO I TOLD HER SHE COULD STAY IN ONE OF THE SPARE ROOMS.
HEY! WHAT'S THIS SUPPOSED TO MEAN?!
OOOH, NOOOO!
IT'LL BE A PLEASURE TO LIVE WITH YOU ALL!
AN ALIEN SUPERHERO AND A NIFORM-STEALING ALIEN....NEITHER OF THEM KNOW EACH OTHER'S RUE IDENTITY, YET THEY'RE GOING TO LIVE UNDER THE AME ROOF. WHAT'S GOING TO HAPPEN O ME TOMORROW?!

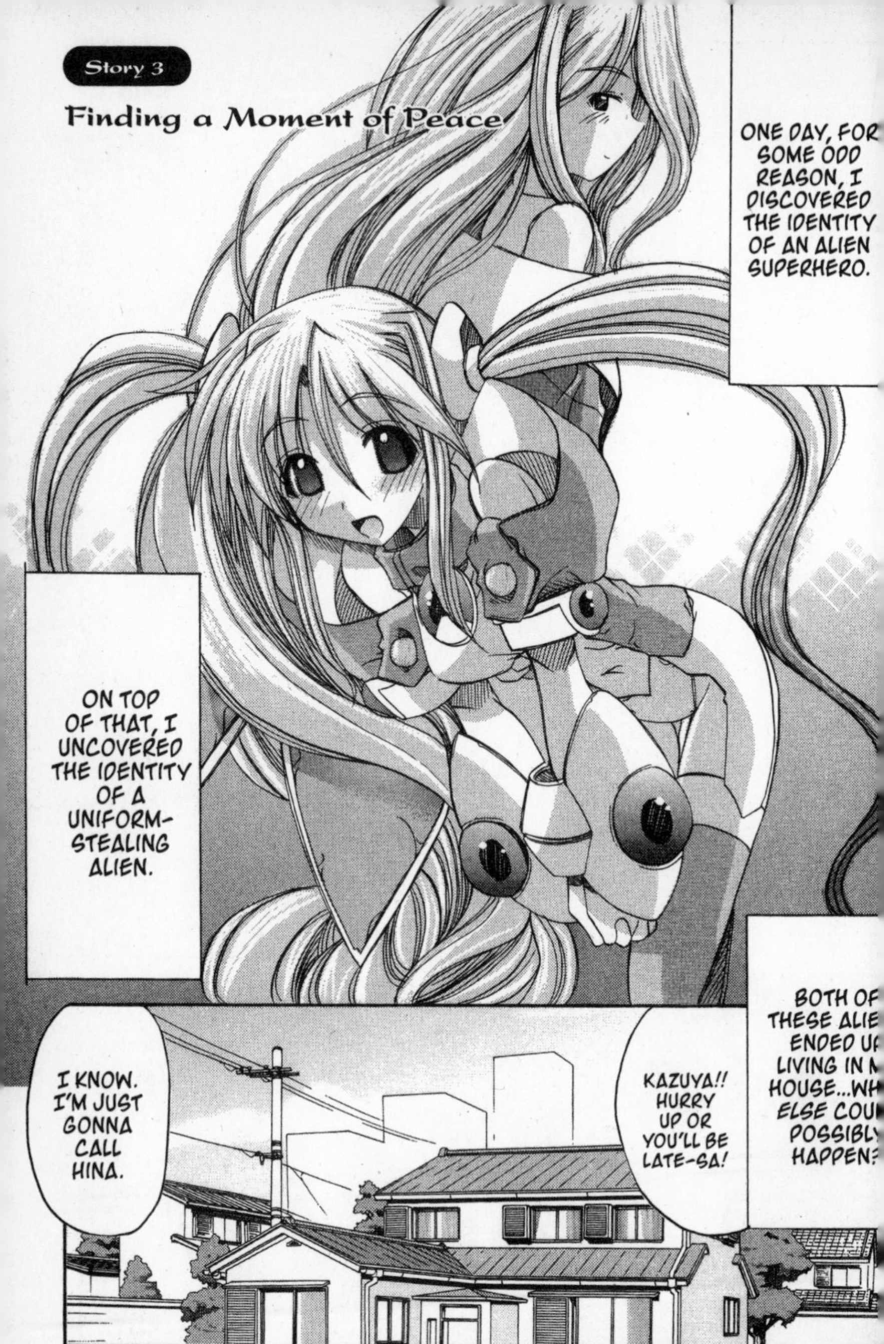
Story 3
Finding a Moment of Peace
ONE DAY, FOR SOME ODD REASON, I DISCOVERED THE IDENTITY OF AN ALIEN SUPERHERO.
ON TOP OF THAT, I UNCOVERED THE IDENTITY OF A UNIFORM-STEALING ALIEN.
BOTH OF THESE ALIE ENDED UP LIVING IN M HOUSE...WH ELSE COU POSSIBL HAPPEN?
KAZUYA!! HURRY UP OR YOU'LL BE LATE-SA!
I KNOW. I'M JUST GONNA CALL HINA.

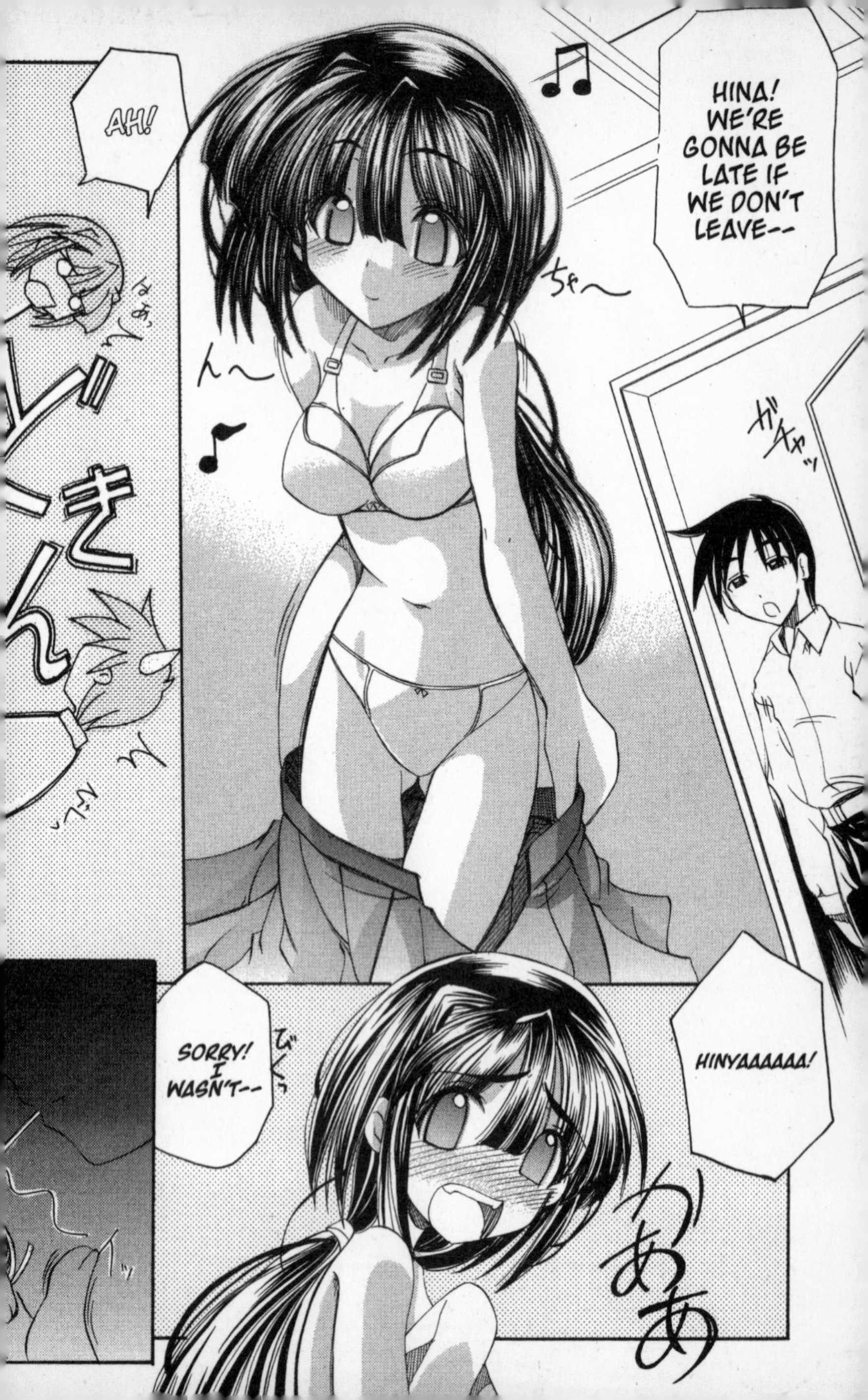
HINA! WE'RE GONNA BE LATE IF WE DON'T LEAVE--
ガチャッ
ちゃ~
ん~
AH!
HINYAAAAAAA!
びくっ
SORRY! I WASN'T--

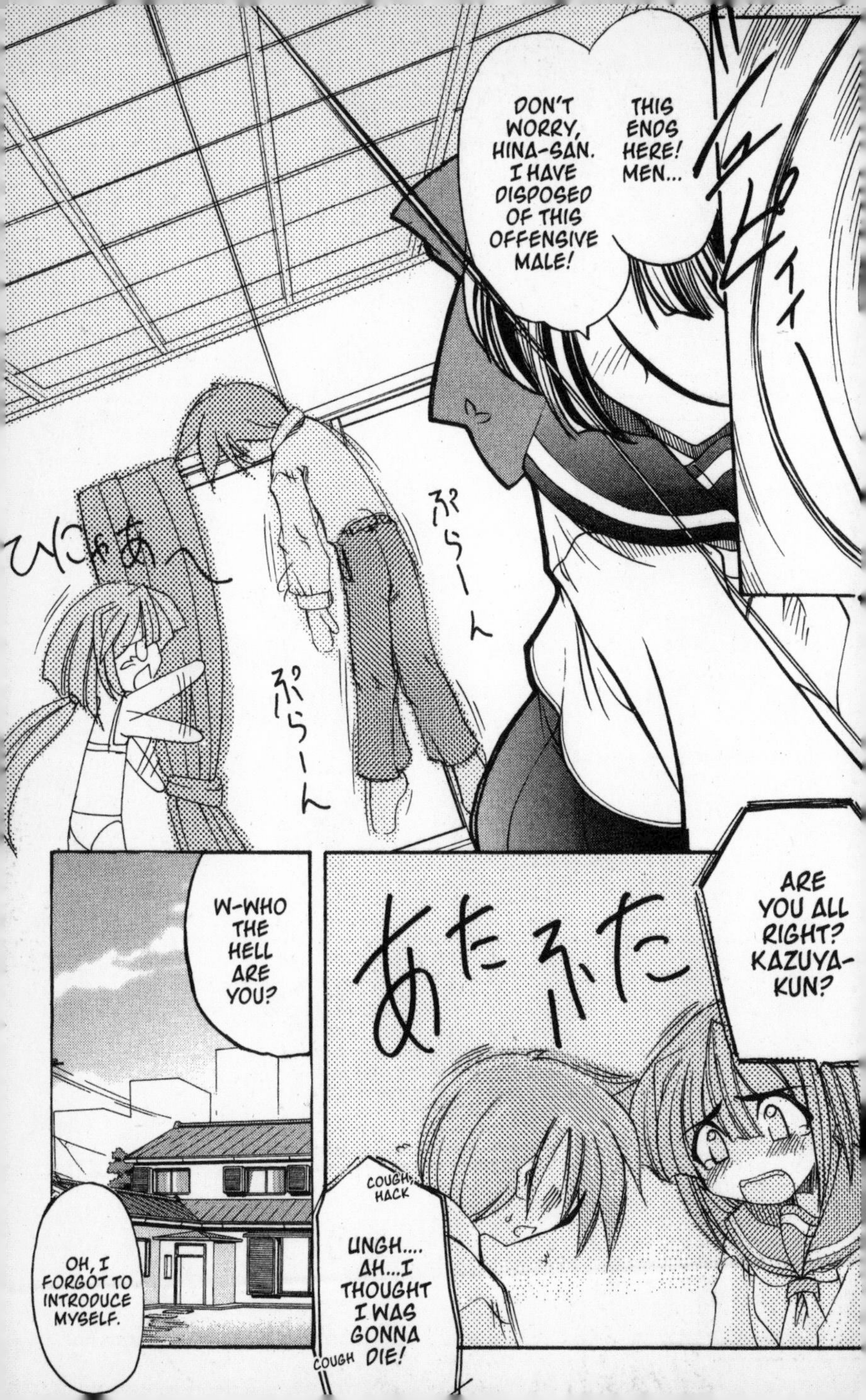
THIS ENDS HERE! MEN...
DON'T WORRY, HINA-SAN. I HAVE DISPOSED OF THIS OFFENSIVE MALE!
ぷらーん
ぷらーん
ひにゃあ〜
ARE YOU ALL RIGHT? KAZUYA-KUN?
あたふた
COUGH, HACK
UNGH.... AH...I THOUGHT I WAS GONNA DIE!
COUGH
W-WHO THE HELL ARE YOU?
OH, I FORGOT TO INTRODUCE MYSELF.

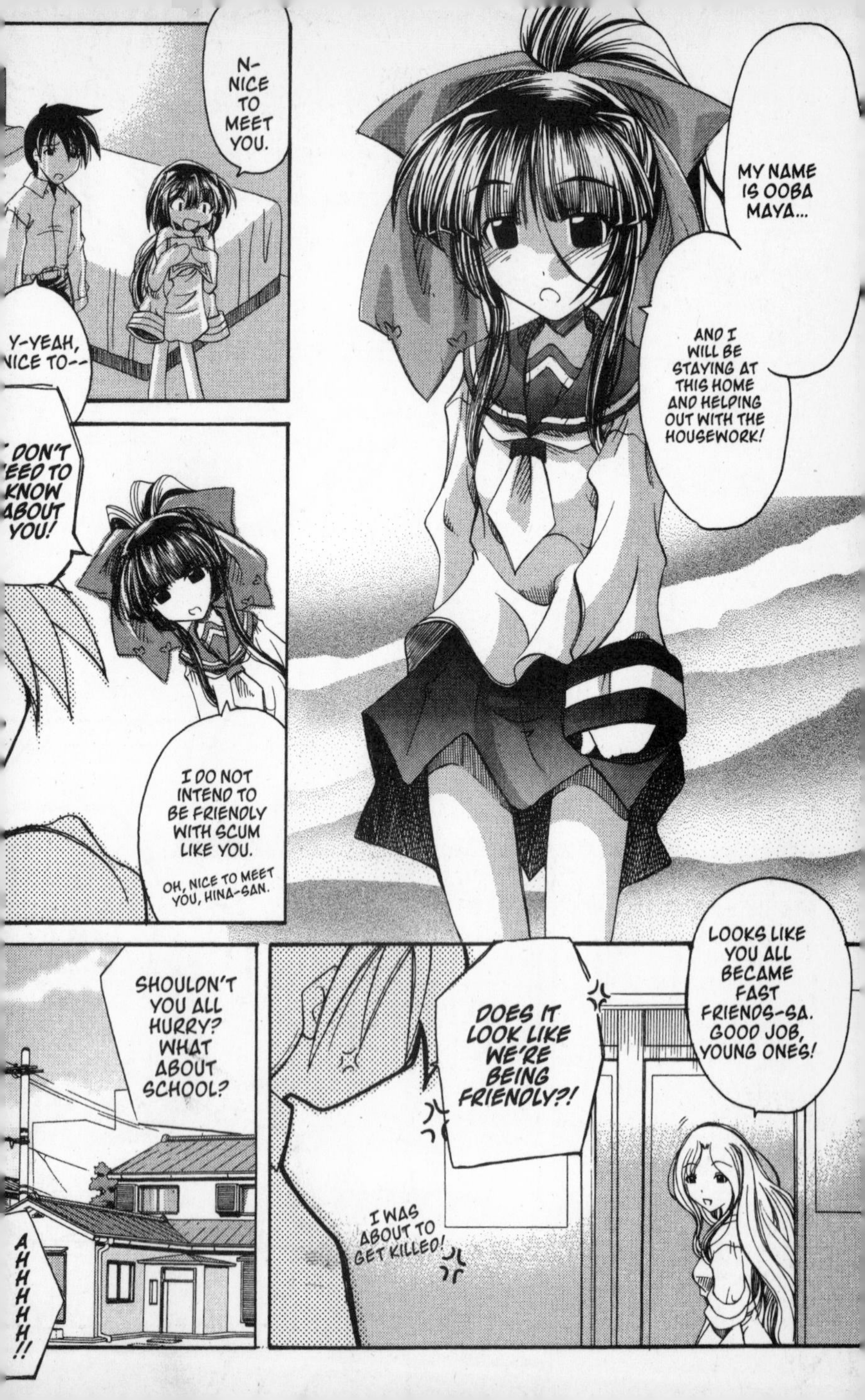
MY NAME IS OOBA MAYA...
AND I WILL BE STAYING AT THIS HOME AND HELPING OUT WITH THE HOUSEWORK!
N-NICE TO MEET YOU.
Y-YEAH, NICE TO--
DON'T EED TO KNOW ABOUT YOU!
I DO NOT INTEND TO BE FRIENDLY WITH SCUM LIKE YOU.
OH, NICE TO MEET YOU, HINA-SAN.
LOOKS LIKE YOU ALL BECAME FAST FRIENDS-SA. GOOD JOB, YOUNG ONES!
DOES IT LOOK LIKE WE'RE BEING FRIENDLY?!
I WAS ABOUT TO GET KILLED!
SHOULDN'T YOU ALL HURRY? WHAT ABOUT SCHOOL?
AHHHHHH!!

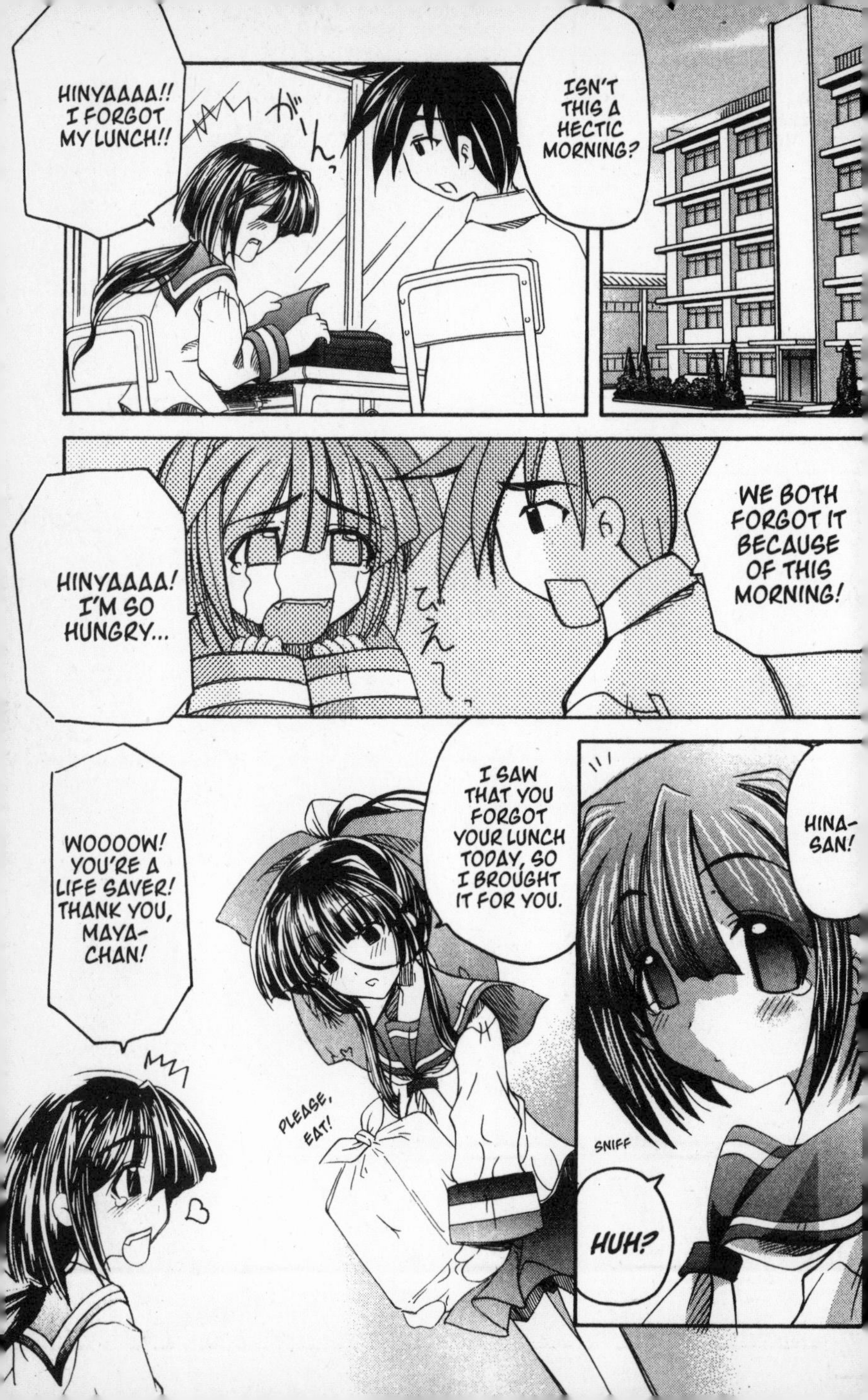
ISN'T THIS A HECTIC MORNING?
HINYAAAA!! I FORGOT MY LUNCH!!
WE BOTH FORGOT IT BECAUSE OF THIS MORNING!
HINYAAAA! I'M SO HUNGRY...
HINA-SAN!
SNIFF
HUH?
I SAW THAT YOU FORGOT YOUR LUNCH TODAY, SO I BROUGHT IT FOR YOU.
WOOOOW! YOU'RE A LIFE SAVER! THANK YOU, MAYA-CHAN!
PLEASE, EAT!

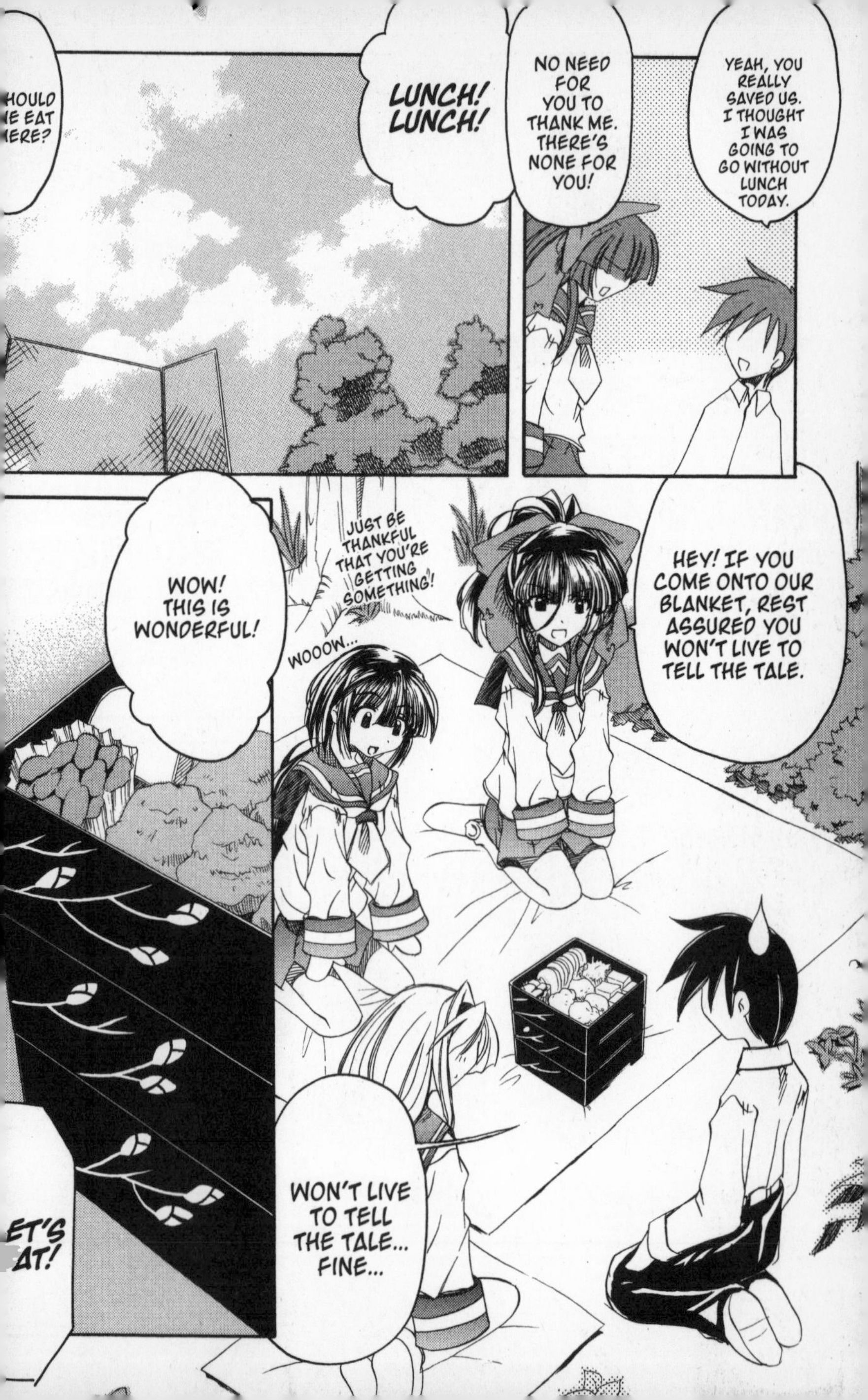
YEAH, YOU REALLY SAVED US. I THOUGHT I WAS GOING TO GO WITHOUT LUNCH TODAY.
NO NEED FOR YOU TO THANK ME. THERE'S NONE FOR YOU!
LUNCH! LUNCH!
HEY! IF YOU COME ONTO OUR BLANKET, REST ASSURED YOU WON'T LIVE TO TELL THE TALE.
JUST BE THANKFUL THAT YOU'RE GETTING SOMETHING!
WOOOW...
WON'T LIVE TO TELL THE TALE... FINE...
WOW! THIS IS WONDERFUL!

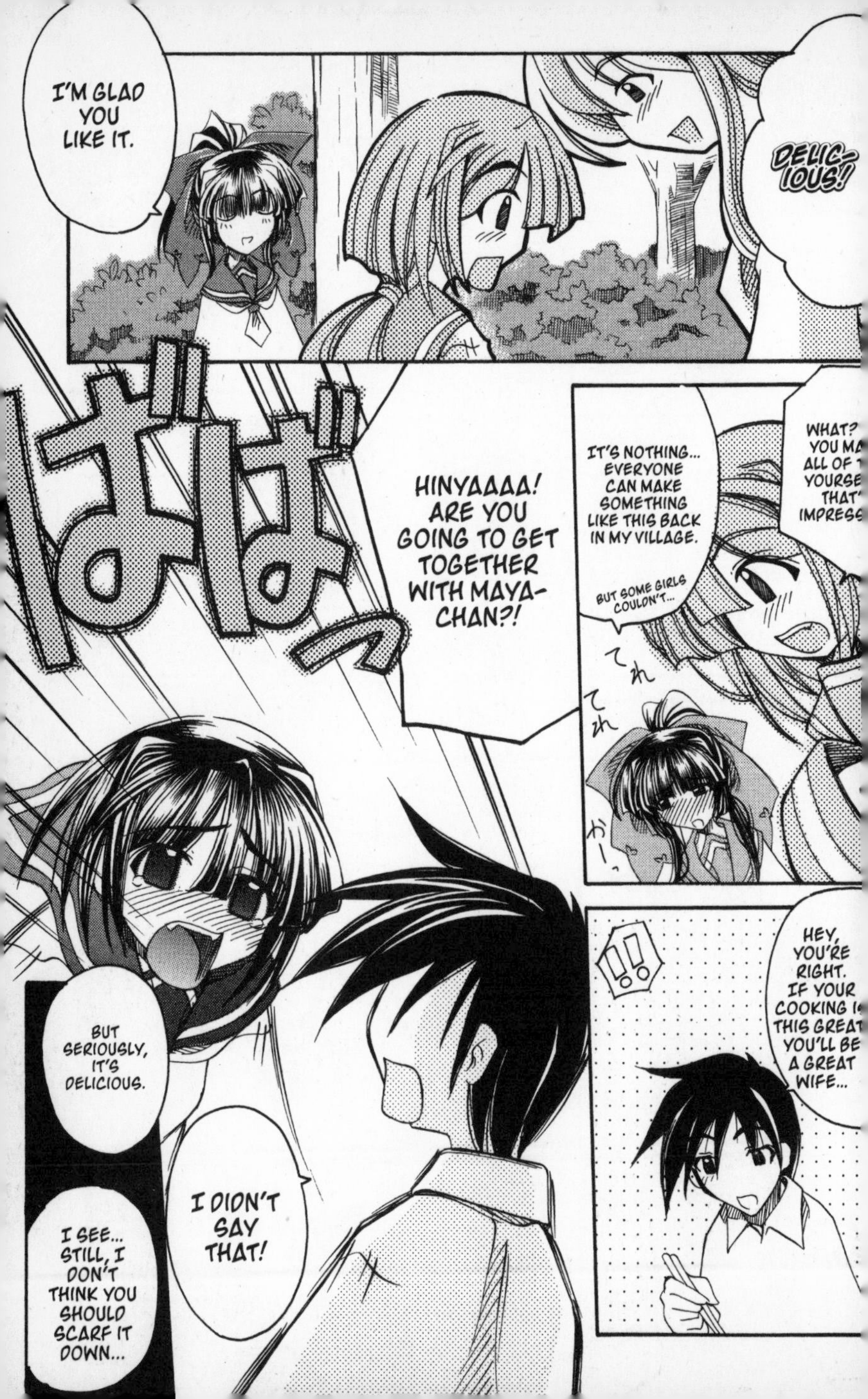
DELIC-IOUS!
I'M GLAD YOU LIKE IT.
WHAT? YOU MA ALL OF T YOURSE THAT' IMPRESS
IT'S NOTHING... EVERYONE CAN MAKE SOMETHING LIKE THIS BACK IN MY VILLAGE.
BUT SOME GIRLS COULDN'T...
てれ てれ
かーっ
!!
HEY, YOU'RE RIGHT. IF YOUR COOKING I THIS GREAT YOU'LL BE A GREAT WIFE...
ばばっ
HINYAAAA! ARE YOU GOING TO GET TOGETHER WITH MAYA-CHAN?!
I DIDN'T SAY THAT!
BUT SERIOUSLY, IT'S DELICIOUS.
I SEE... STILL, I DON'T THINK YOU SHOULD SCARF IT DOWN...

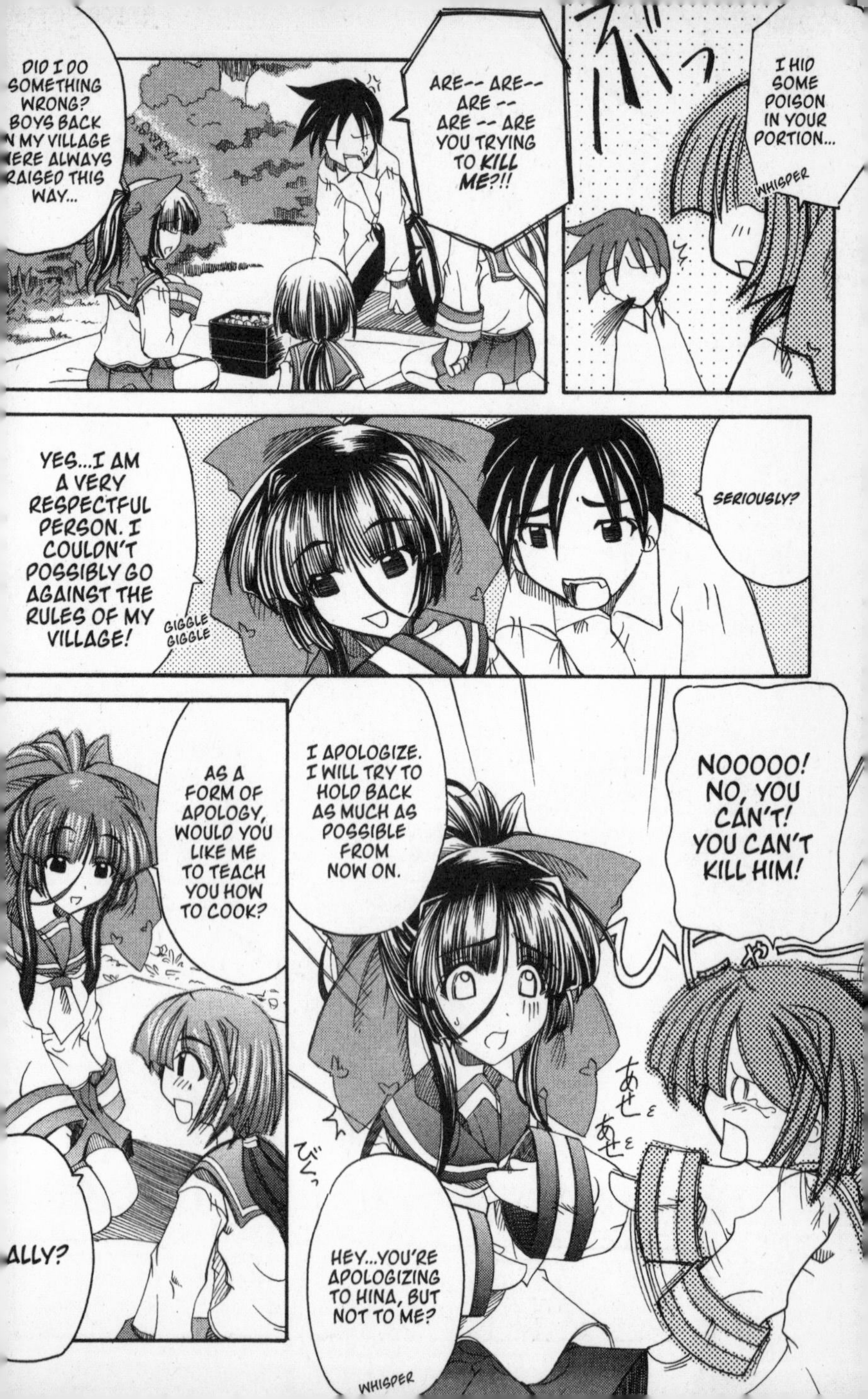
I HID SOME POISON IN YOUR PORTION...
WHISPER
ARE-- ARE-- ARE -- ARE -- ARE YOU TRYING TO KILL ME?!!
DID I DO SOMETHING WRONG? BOYS BACK N MY VILLAGE IERE ALWAYS RAISED THIS WAY...
SERIOUSLY?
YES...I AM A VERY RESPECTFUL PERSON. I COULDN'T POSSIBLY GO AGAINST THE RULES OF MY VILLAGE!
GIGGLE GIGGLE
NOOOOO! NO, YOU CAN'T! YOU CAN'T KILL HIM!
I APOLOGIZE. I WILL TRY TO HOLD BACK AS MUCH AS POSSIBLE FROM NOW ON.
あせ あせ
びくっ
HEY...YOU'RE APOLOGIZING TO HINA, BUT NOT TO ME?
WHISPER
AS A FORM OF APOLOGY, WOULD YOU LIKE ME TO TEACH YOU HOW TO COOK?
ALLY?

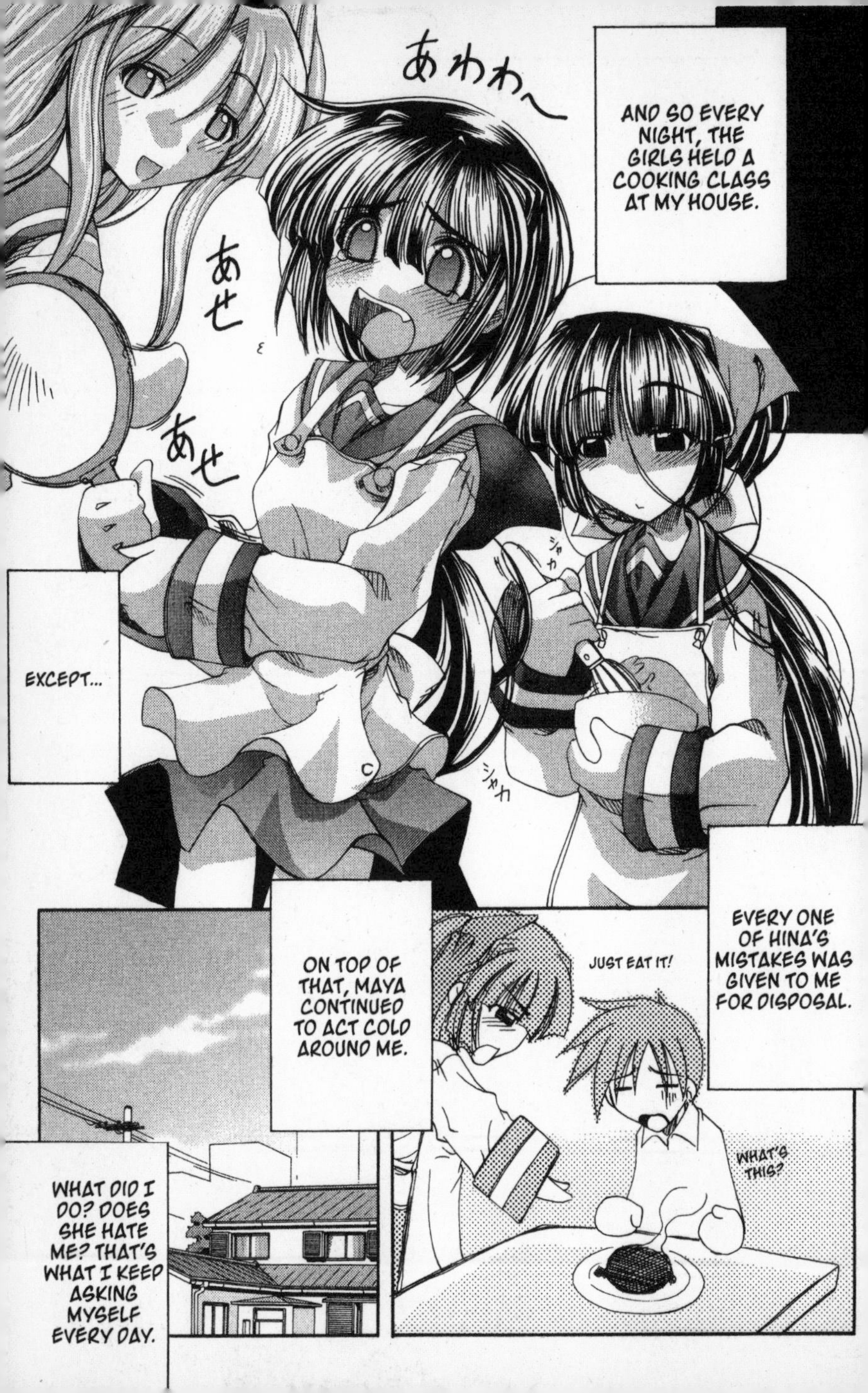
AND SO EVERY NIGHT, THE GIRLS HELD A COOKING CLASS AT MY HOUSE.
あわわ〜
あせ
あせ
シャカ
シャカ
EXCEPT...
EVERY ONE OF HINA'S MISTAKES WAS GIVEN TO ME FOR DISPOSAL.
JUST EAT IT!
WHAT'S THIS?
ON TOP OF THAT, MAYA CONTINUED TO ACT COLD AROUND ME.
WHAT DID I DO? DOES SHE HATE ME? THAT'S WHAT I KEEP ASKING MYSELF EVERY DAY.

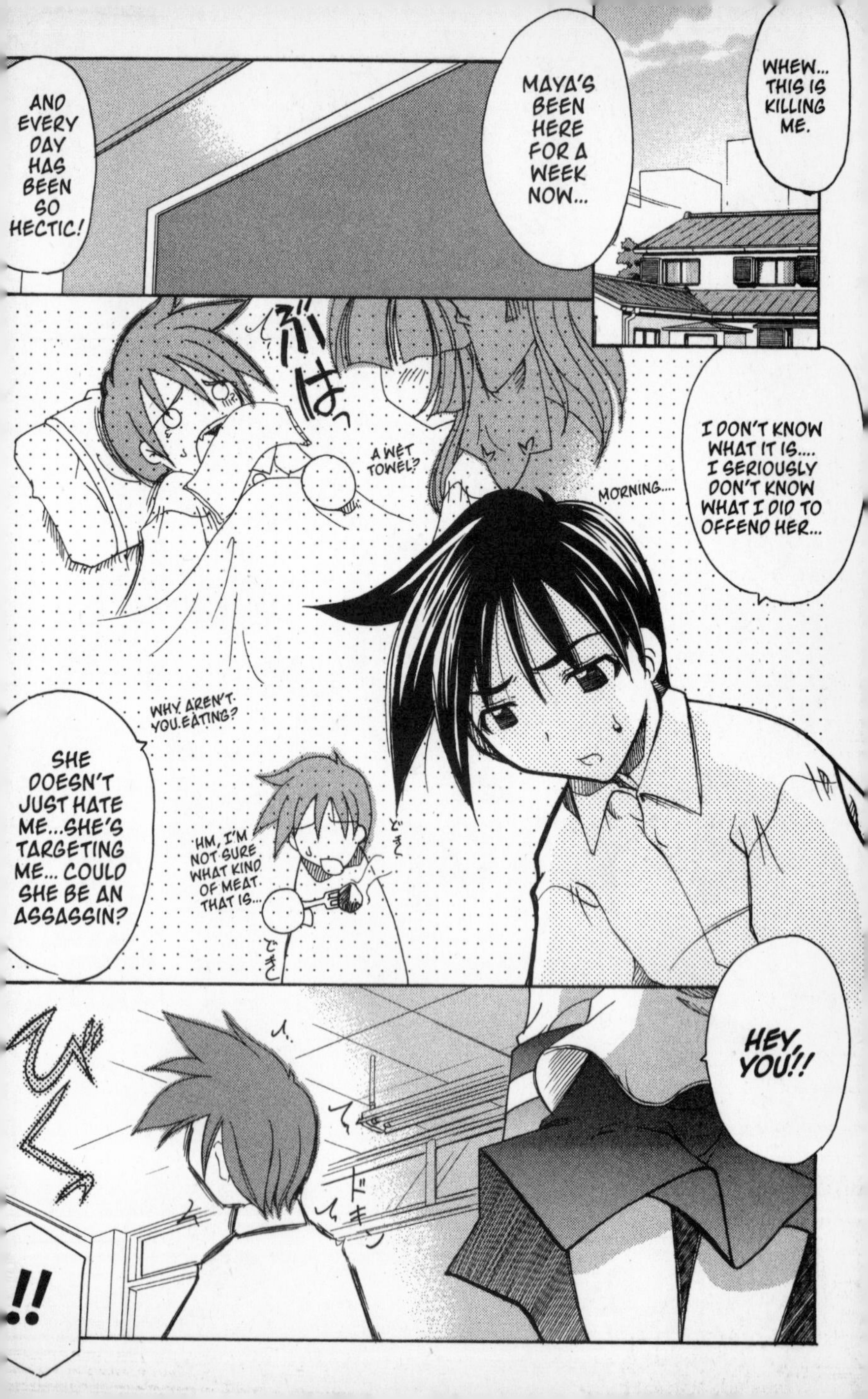
WHEW... THIS IS KILLING ME.
MAYA'S BEEN HERE FOR A WEEK NOW...
AND EVERY DAY HAS BEEN SO HECTIC!
I DON'T KNOW WHAT IT IS.... I SERIOUSLY DON'T KNOW WHAT I DID TO OFFEND HER...
MORNING....
ぶはっ
A WET TOWEL?
WHY AREN'T YOU EATING?
HM, I'M NOT SURE WHAT KIND OF MEAT THAT IS...
SHE DOESN'T JUST HATE ME...SHE'S TARGETING ME... COULD SHE BE AN ASSASSIN?
HEY YOU!!
!!

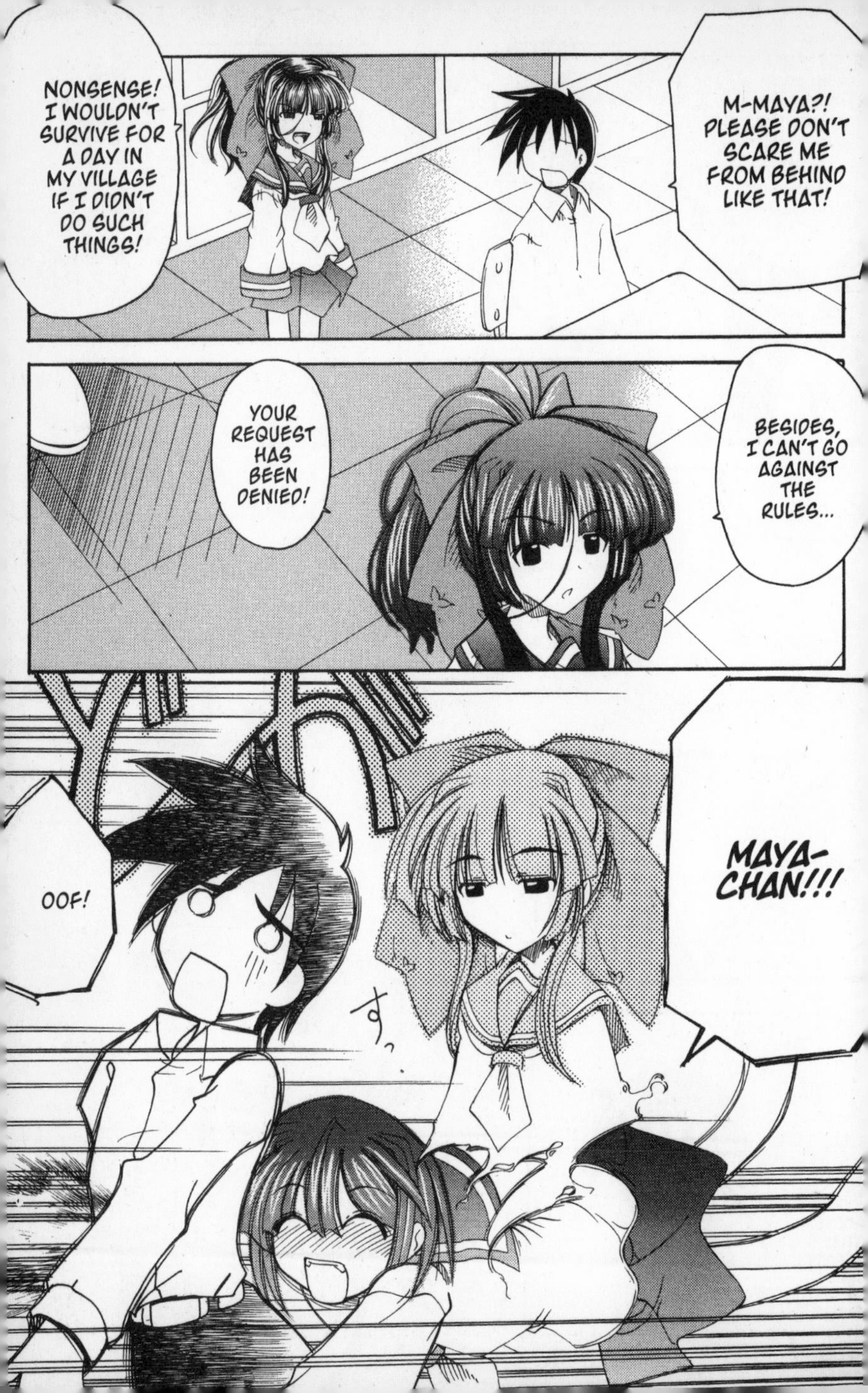
M-MAYA?! PLEASE DON'T SCARE ME FROM BEHIND LIKE THAT!
NONSENSE! I WOULDN'T SURVIVE FOR A DAY IN MY VILLAGE IF I DIDN'T DO SUCH THINGS!
BESIDES, I CAN'T GO AGAINST THE RULES...
YOUR REQUEST HAS BEEN DENIED!
MAYA-CHAN!!!
すっ
OOF!

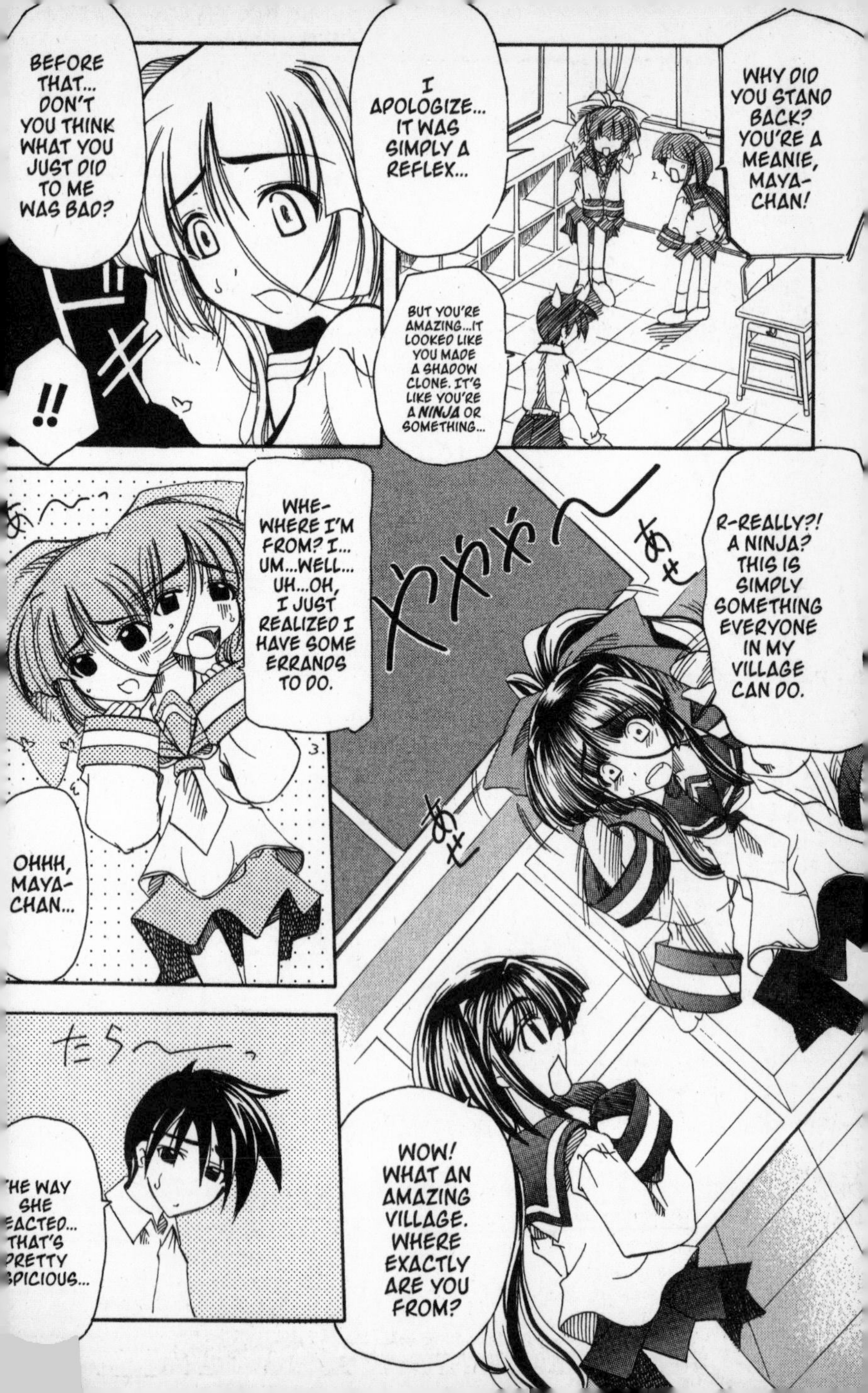
WHY DID YOU STAND BACK? YOU'RE A MEANIE, MAYA-CHAN!
I APOLOGIZE... IT WAS SIMPLY A REFLEX...
BUT YOU'RE AMAZING...IT LOOKED LIKE YOU MADE A SHADOW CLONE. IT'S LIKE YOU'RE A *NINJA* OR SOMETHING...
BEFORE THAT... DON'T YOU THINK WHAT YOU JUST DID TO ME WAS BAD?
!!
R-REALLY?! A NINJA? THIS IS SIMPLY SOMETHING EVERYONE IN MY VILLAGE CAN DO.
あせ
あせ
WOW! WHAT AN AMAZING VILLAGE. WHERE EXACTLY ARE YOU FROM?
WHE-WHERE I'M FROM? I... UM...WELL... UH...OH, I JUST REALIZED I HAVE SOME ERRANDS TO DO.
OHHH, MAYA-CHAN...
HE WAY SHE EACTED... THAT'S PRETTY SPICIOUS...

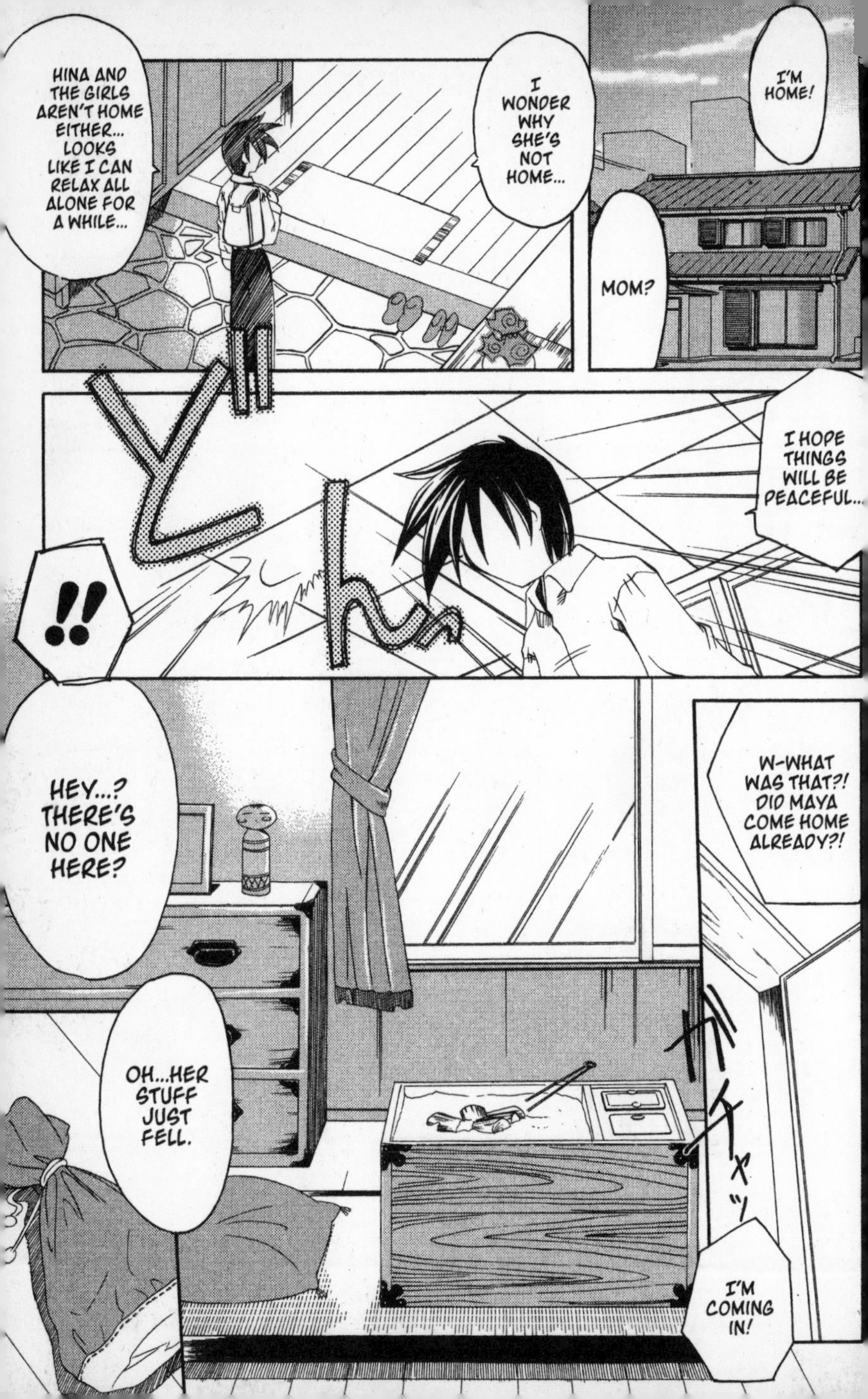
I'M HOME!
MOM?
I WONDER WHY SHE'S NOT HOME...
HINA AND THE GIRLS AREN'T HOME EITHER... LOOKS LIKE I CAN RELAX ALL ALONE FOR A WHILE...
I HOPE THINGS WILL BE PEACEFUL...
!!
W-WHAT WAS THAT?! DID MAYA COME HOME ALREADY?!
I'M COMING IN!
HEY...? THERE'S NO ONE HERE?
OH...HER STUFF JUST FELL.

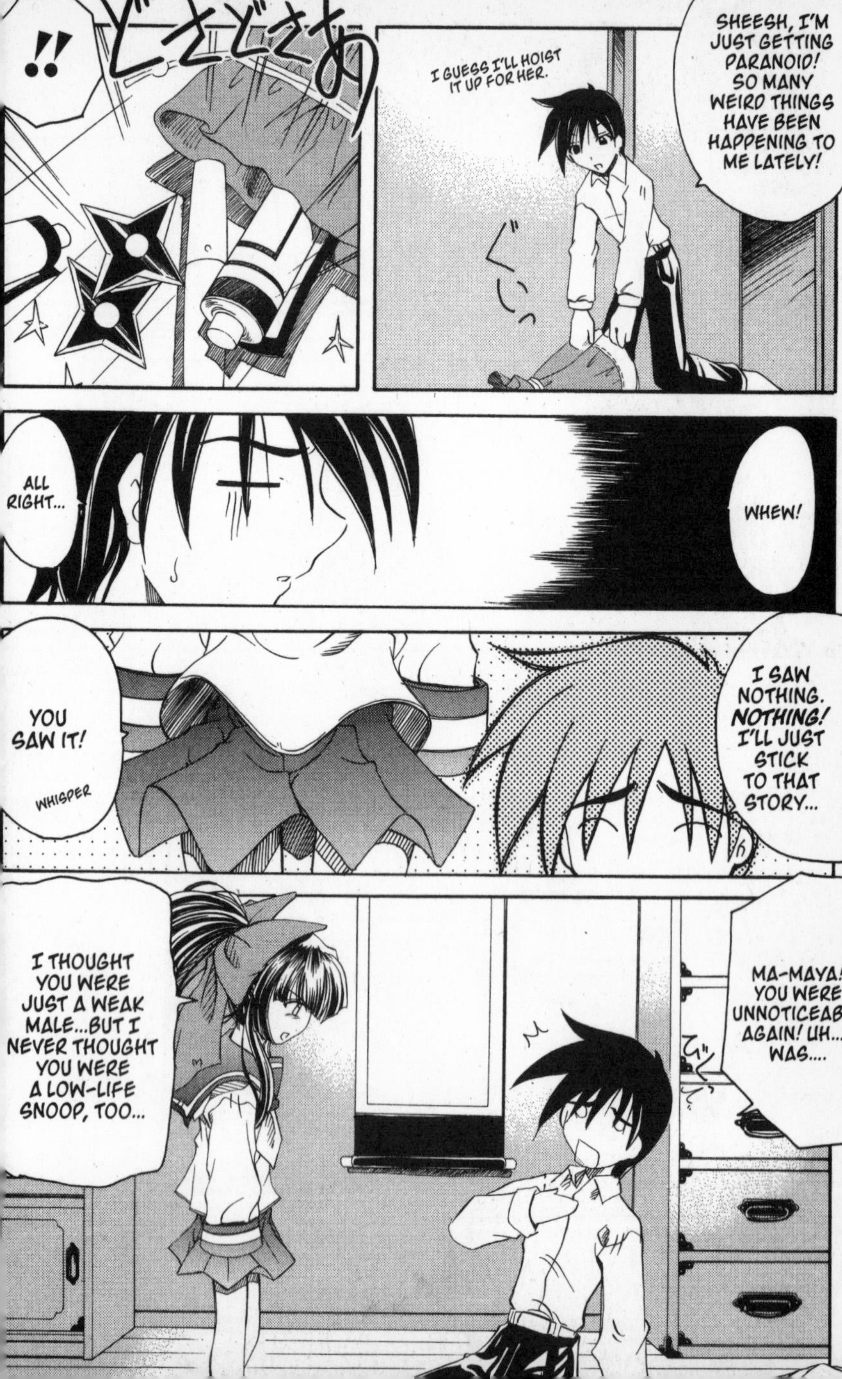
SHEESH, I'M JUST GETTING PARANOID! SO MANY WEIRD THINGS HAVE BEEN HAPPENING TO ME LATELY!
I GUESS I'LL HOIST IT UP FOR HER.
ぐいっ
!!
どさどさぁ
WHEW!
ALL RIGHT...
I SAW NOTHING. NOTHING! I'LL JUST STICK TO THAT STORY...
YOU SAW IT!
WHISPER
MA-MAYA! YOU WERE UNNOTICEABLE AGAIN! UH...I WAS....
I THOUGHT YOU WERE JUST A WEAK MALE...BUT I NEVER THOUGHT YOU WERE A LOW-LIFE SNOOP, TOO...

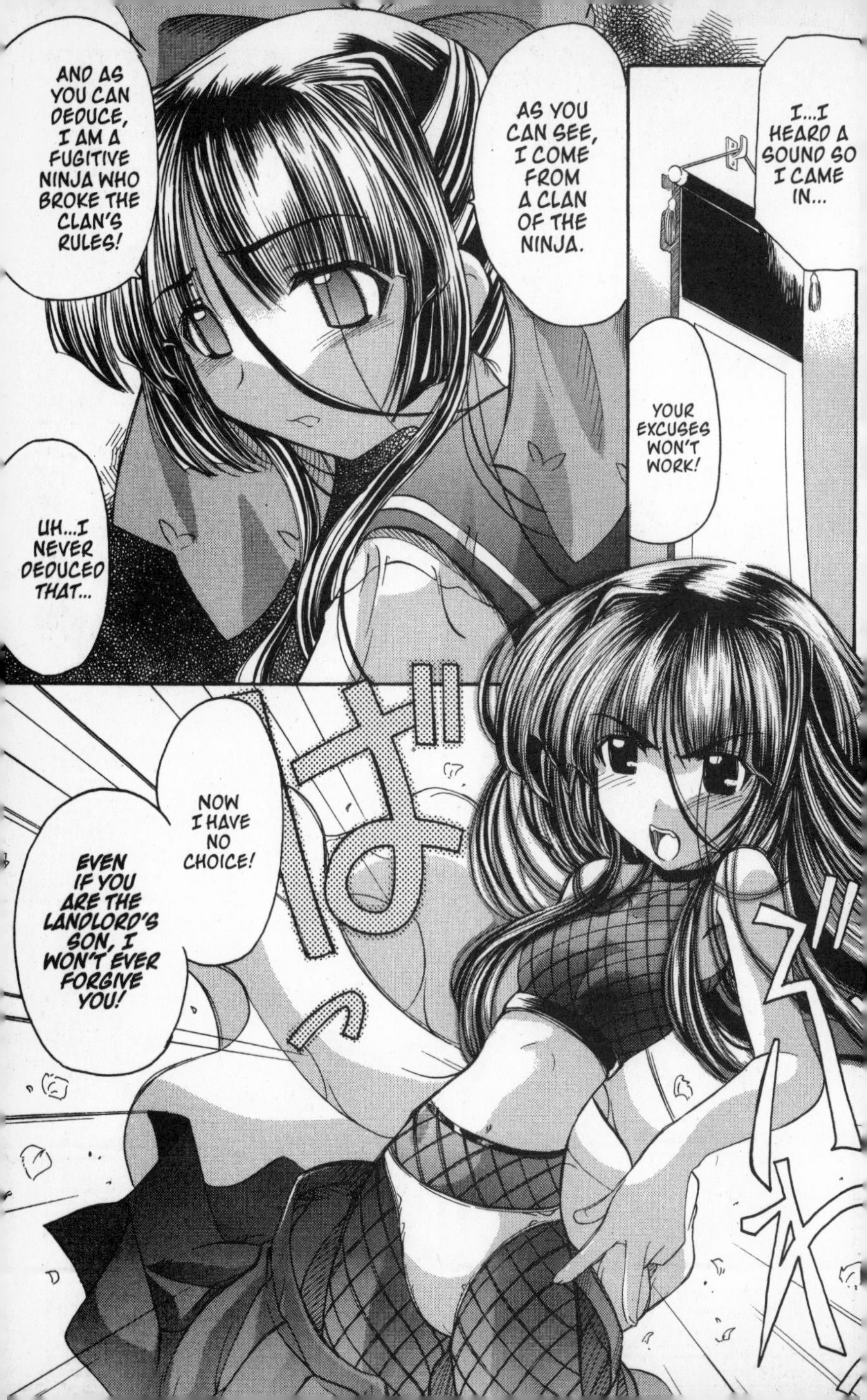
I...I HEARD A SOUND SO I CAME IN...
AS YOU CAN SEE, I COME FROM A CLAN OF THE NINJA.
AND AS YOU CAN DEDUCE, I AM A FUGITIVE NINJA WHO BROKE THE CLAN'S RULES!
YOUR EXCUSES WON'T WORK!
UH...I NEVER DEDUCED THAT...
NOW I HAVE NO CHOICE!
EVEN IF YOU ARE THE LANDLORD'S SON, I WON'T EVER FORGIVE YOU!

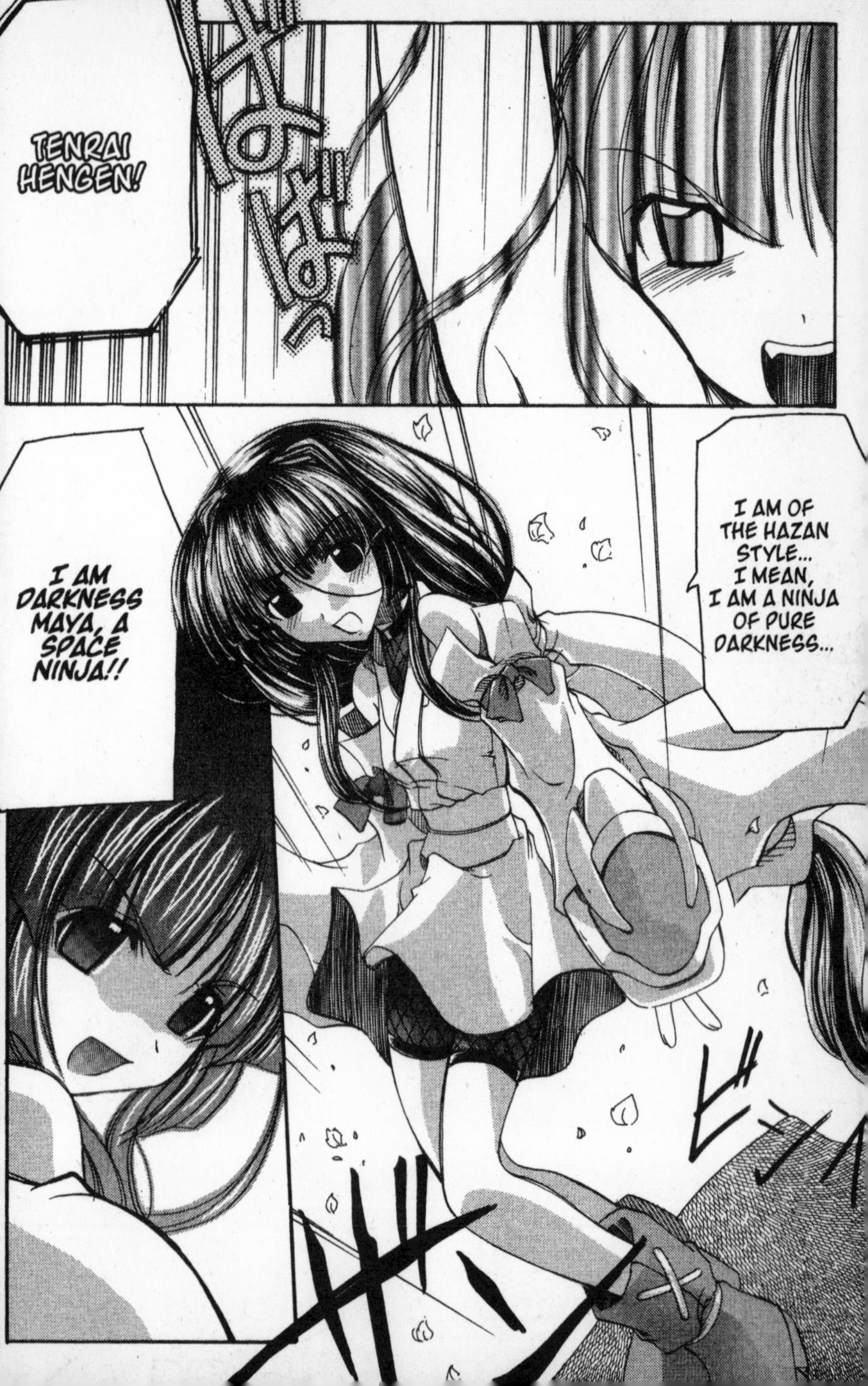
TENRAI HENGEN!
I AM OF THE HAZAN STYLE... I MEAN, I AM A NINJA OF PURE DARKNESS...
I AM DARKNESS MAYA, A SPACE NINJA!!

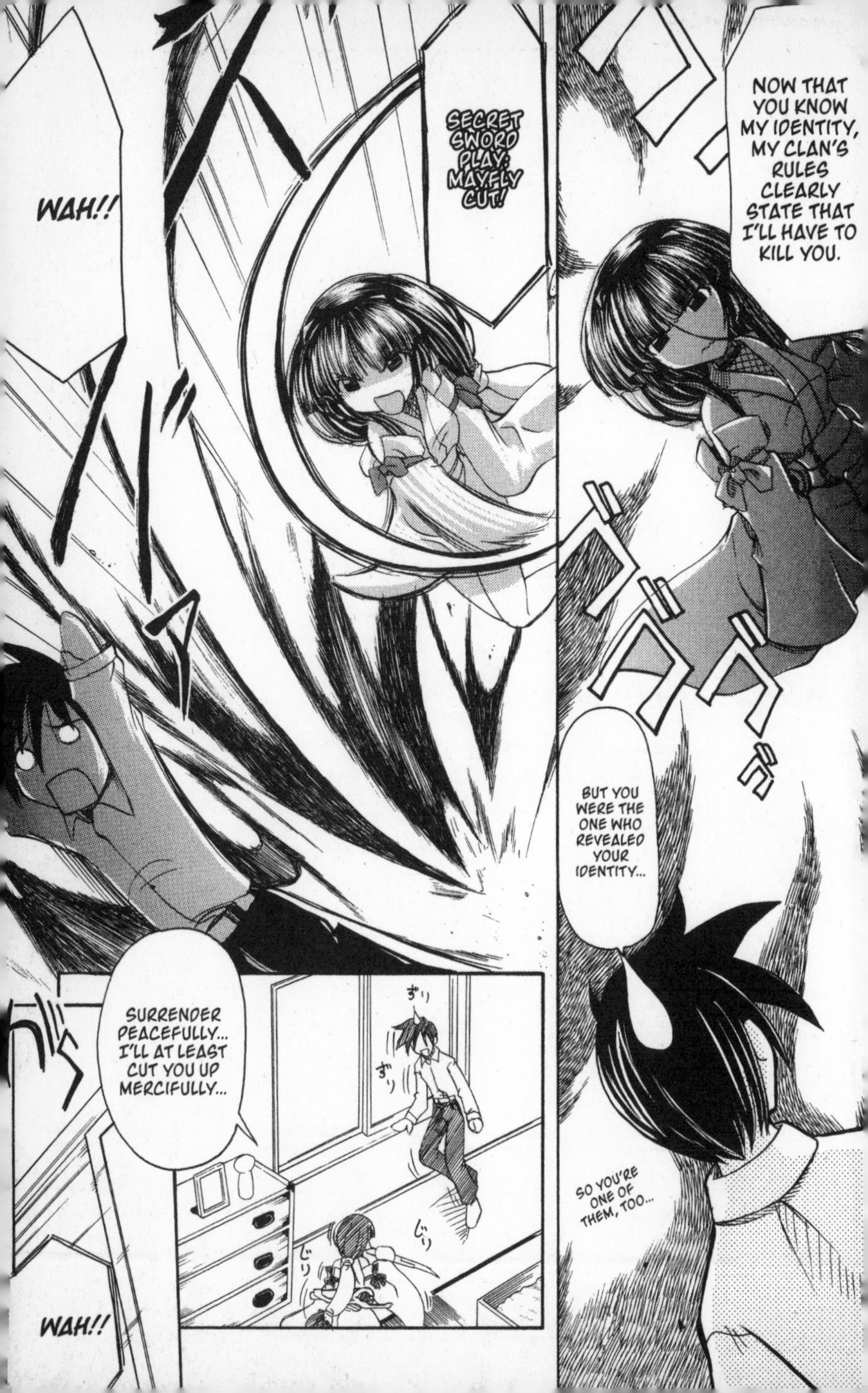
NOW THAT YOU KNOW MY IDENTITY, MY CLAN'S RULES CLEARLY STATE THAT I'LL HAVE TO KILL YOU.
BUT YOU WERE THE ONE WHO REVEALED YOUR IDENTITY...
SO YOU'RE ONE OF THEM, TOO...
SECRET SWORD PLAY: MAYFLY CUT!
WAH!!
SURRENDER PEACEFULLY... I'LL AT LEAST CUT YOU UP MERCIFULLY...
ずり
ずり
じり
じり
WAH!!

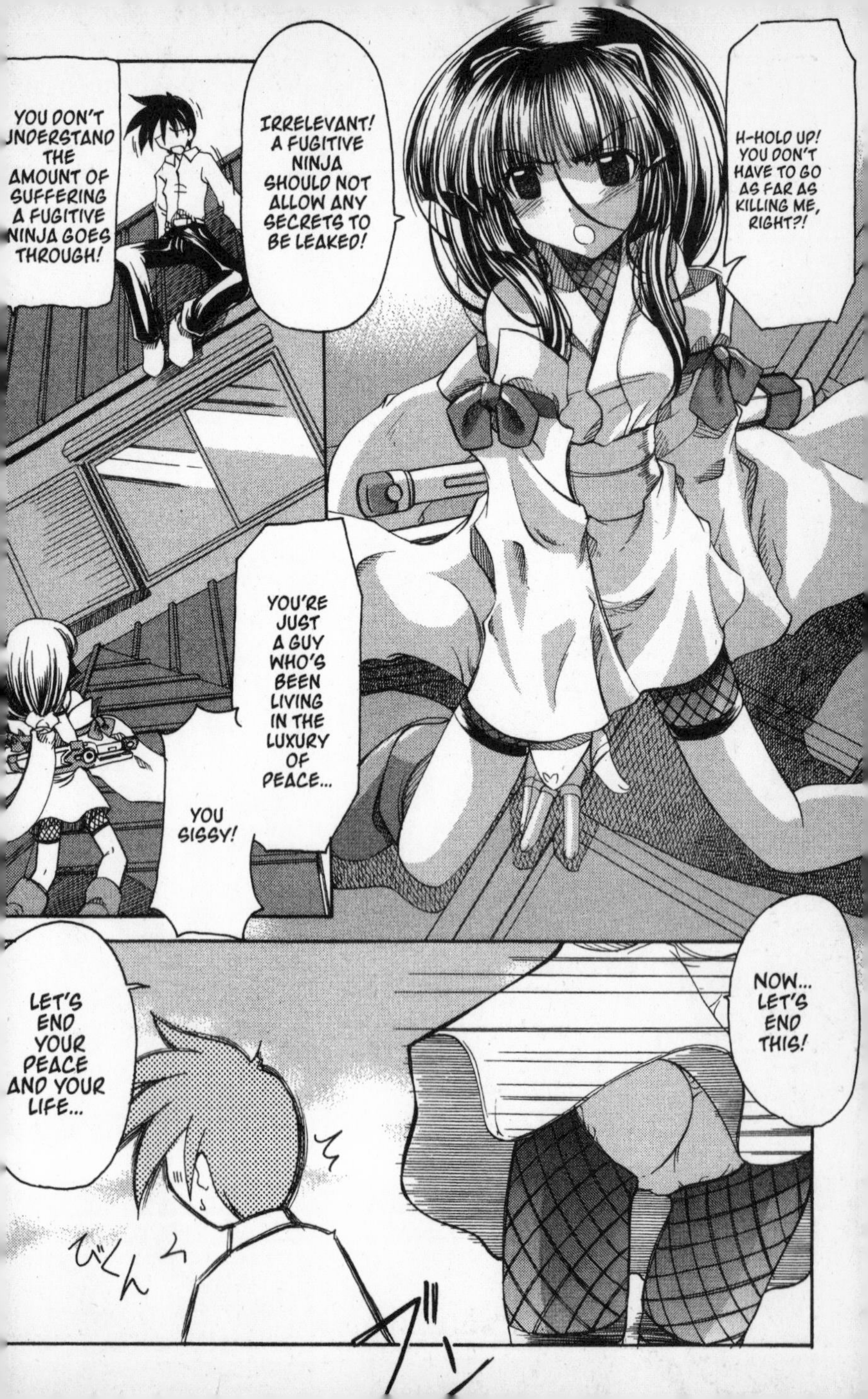

H-HOLD UP! YOU DON'T HAVE TO GO AS FAR AS KILLING ME, RIGHT?!
IRRELEVANT! A FUGITIVE NINJA SHOULD NOT ALLOW ANY SECRETS TO BE LEAKED!
YOU DON'T UNDERSTAND THE AMOUNT OF SUFFERING A FUGITIVE NINJA GOES THROUGH!
YOU'RE JUST A GUY WHO'S BEEN LIVING IN THE LUXURY OF PEACE...
YOU SISSY!
NOW... LET'S END THIS!
LET'S END YOUR PEACE AND YOUR LIFE...

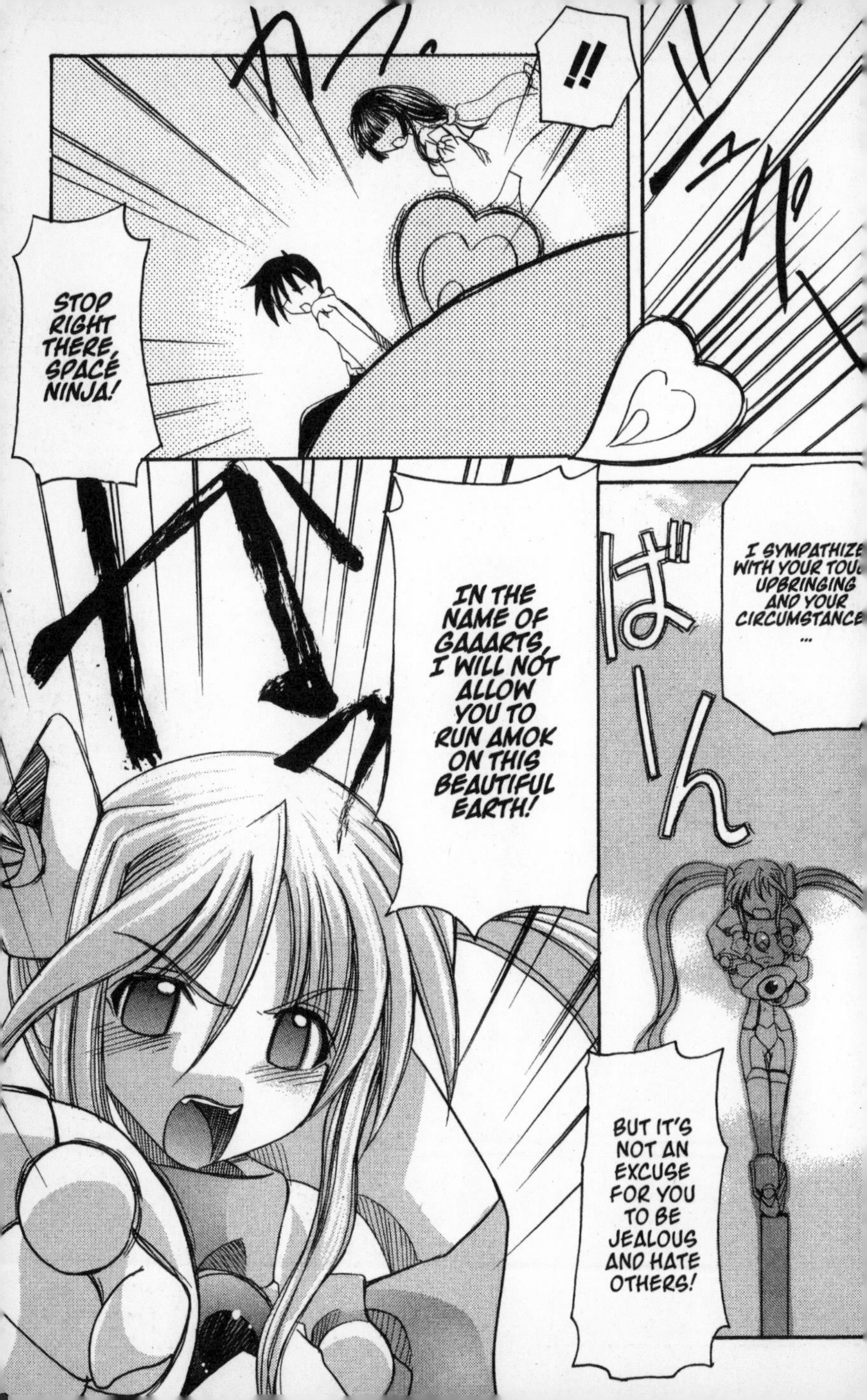
!!
STOP RIGHT THERE, SPACE NINJA!
I SYMPATHIZE WITH YOUR TOU UPBRINGING AND YOUR CIRCUMSTANCE ...
ばーん
BUT IT'S NOT AN EXCUSE FOR YOU TO BE JEALOUS AND HATE OTHERS!
IN THE NAME OF GAAARTS, I WILL NOT ALLOW YOU TO RUN AMOK ON THIS BEAUTIFUL EARTH!

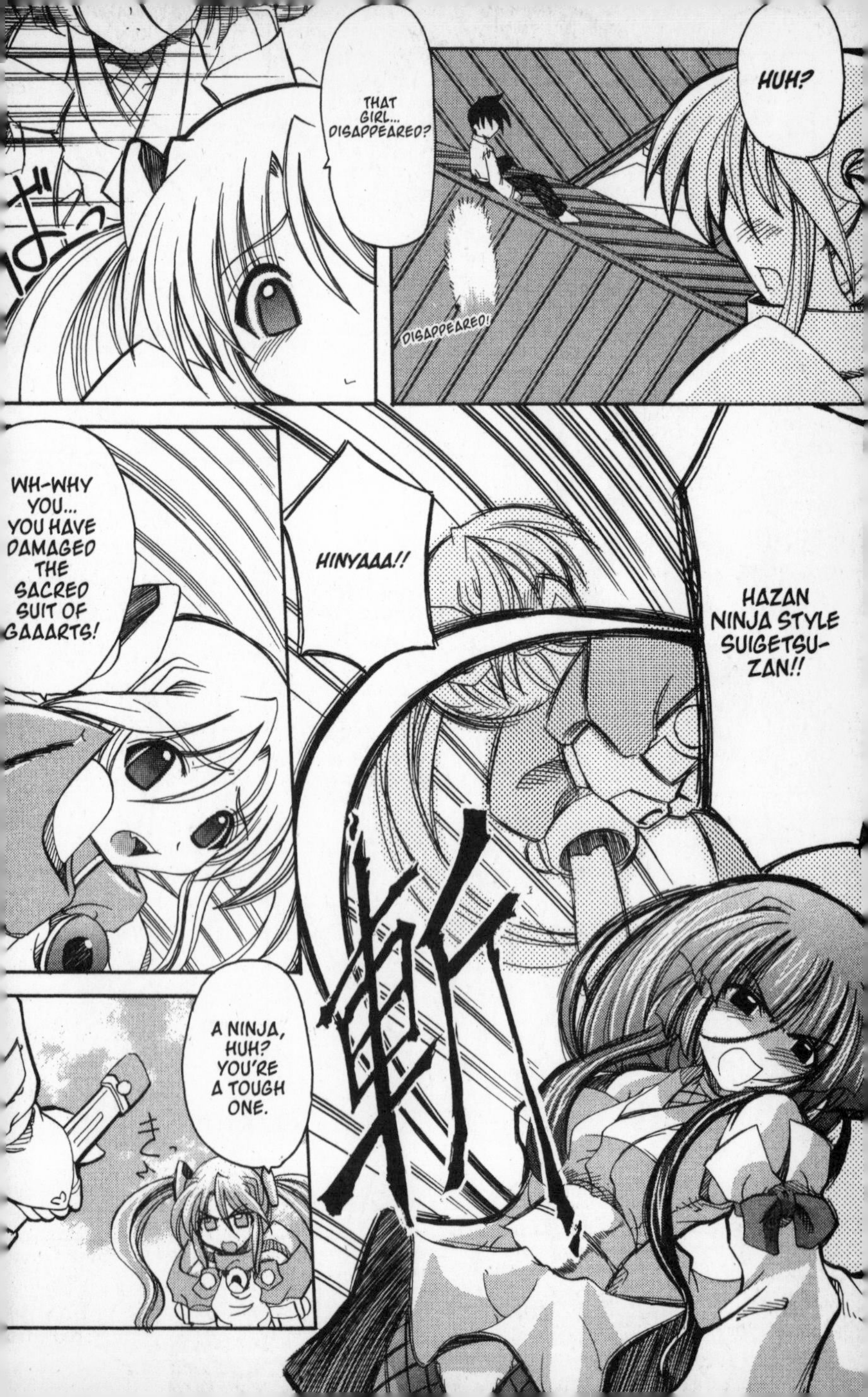
HUH?
THAT GIRL... DISAPPEARED?
DISAPPEARED!
ばっ
HAZAN NINJA STYLE SUIGETSU-ZAN!!
HINYAAA!!
斬
WH-WHY YOU... YOU HAVE DAMAGED THE SACRED SUIT OF GAAARTS!
A NINJA, HUH? YOU'RE A TOUGH ONE.
きっ

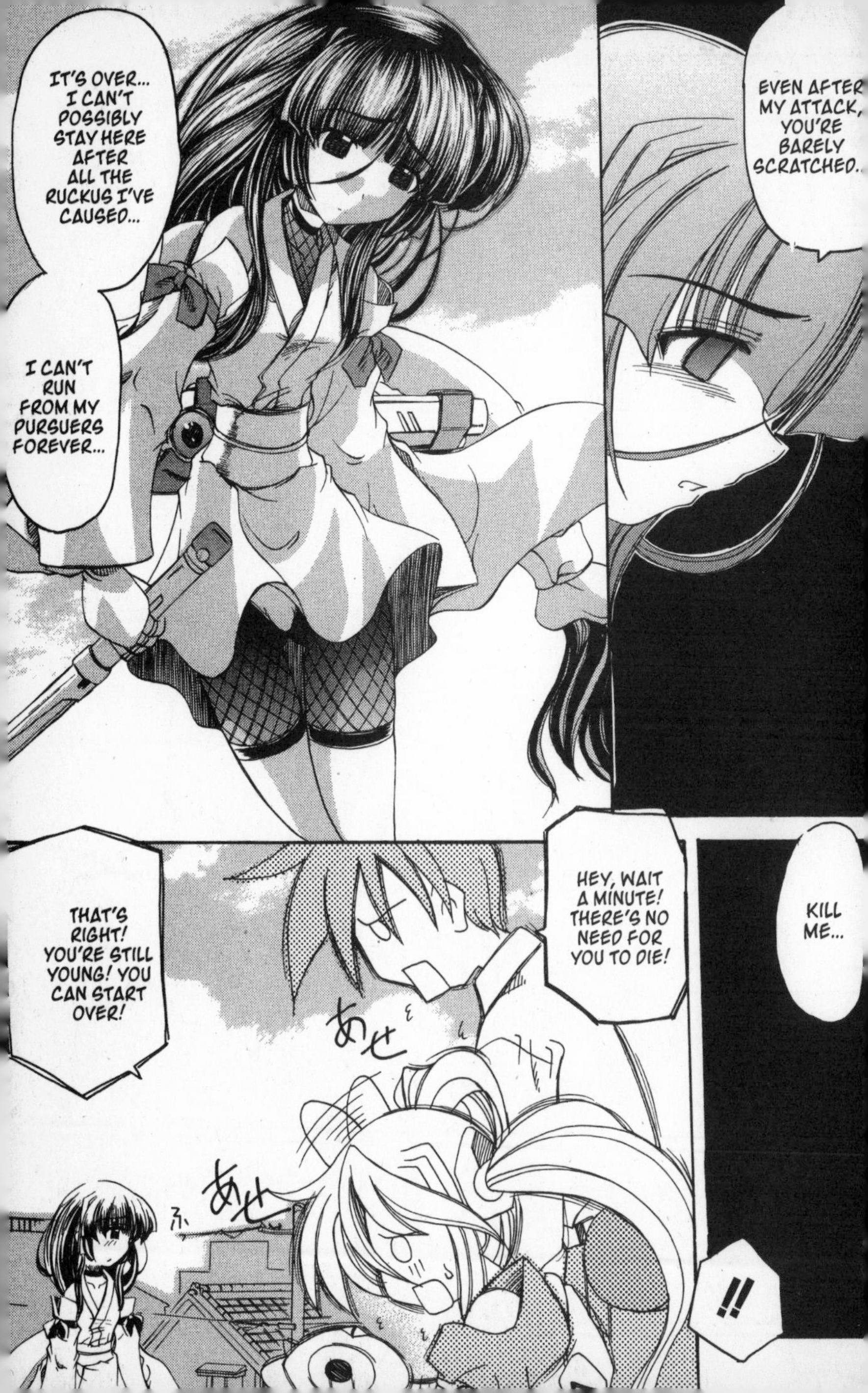
EVEN AFTER MY ATTACK, YOU'RE BARELY SCRATCHED...
IT'S OVER... I CAN'T POSSIBLY STAY HERE AFTER ALL THE RUCKUS I'VE CAUSED...
I CAN'T RUN FROM MY PURSUERS FOREVER...
KILL ME...
!!
HEY, WAIT A MINUTE! THERE'S NO NEED FOR YOU TO DIE!
THAT'S RIGHT! YOU'RE STILL YOUNG! YOU CAN START OVER!
あせ
あせ
ふ

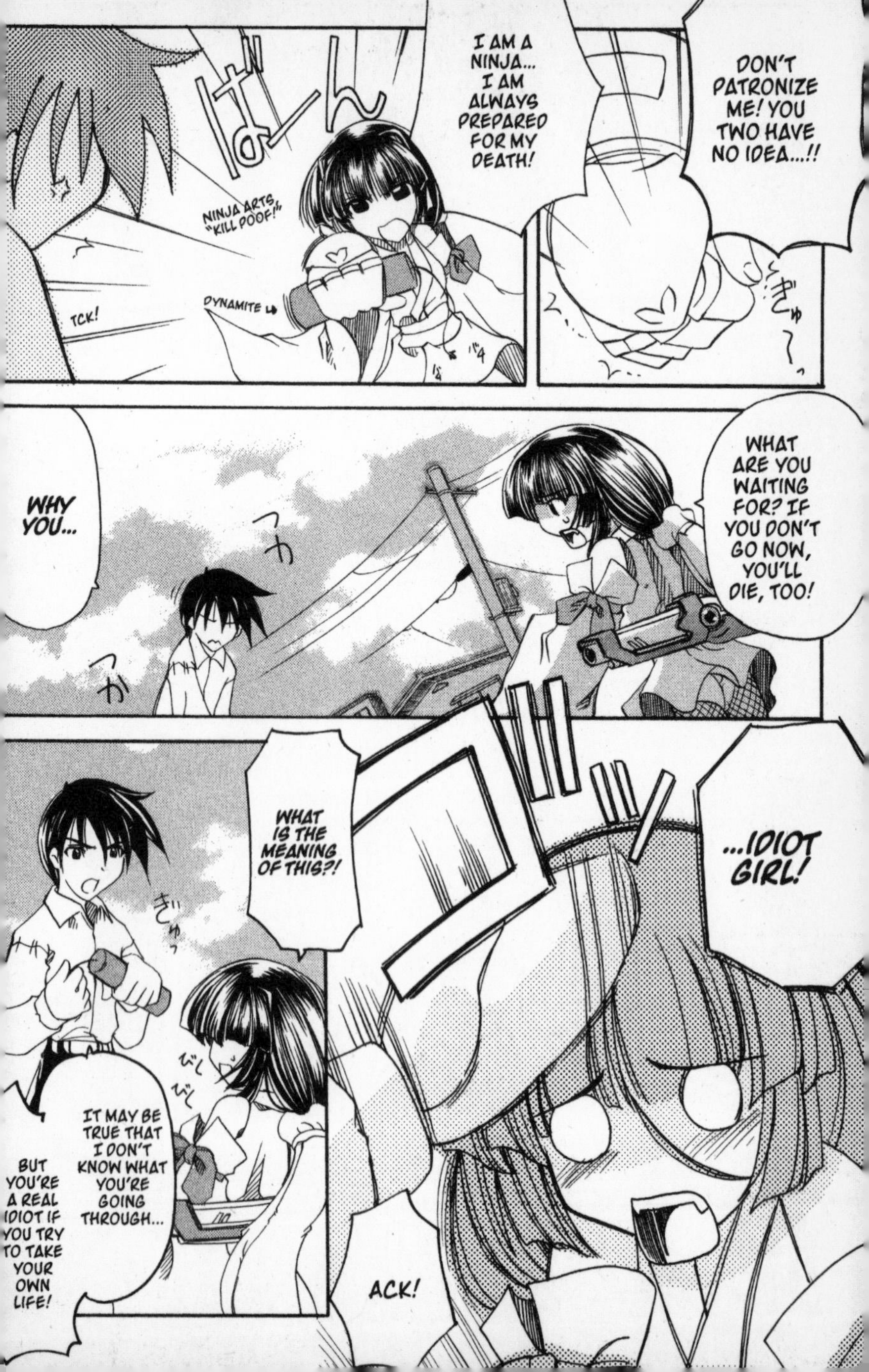
DON'T PATRONIZE ME! YOU TWO HAVE NO IDEA...!!
I AM A NINJA... I AM ALWAYS PREPARED FOR MY DEATH!
ばーん
NINJA ARTS, "KILL POOF!"
DYNAMITE
TCK!
WHAT ARE YOU WAITING FOR? IF YOU DON'T GO NOW, YOU'LL DIE, TOO!
WHY YOU...
つか
つか
...IDIOT GIRL!
ACK!
WHAT IS THE MEANING OF THIS?!
IT MAY BE TRUE THAT I DON'T KNOW WHAT YOU'RE GOING THROUGH...
BUT YOU'RE A REAL IDIOT IF YOU TRY TO TAKE YOUR OWN LIFE!

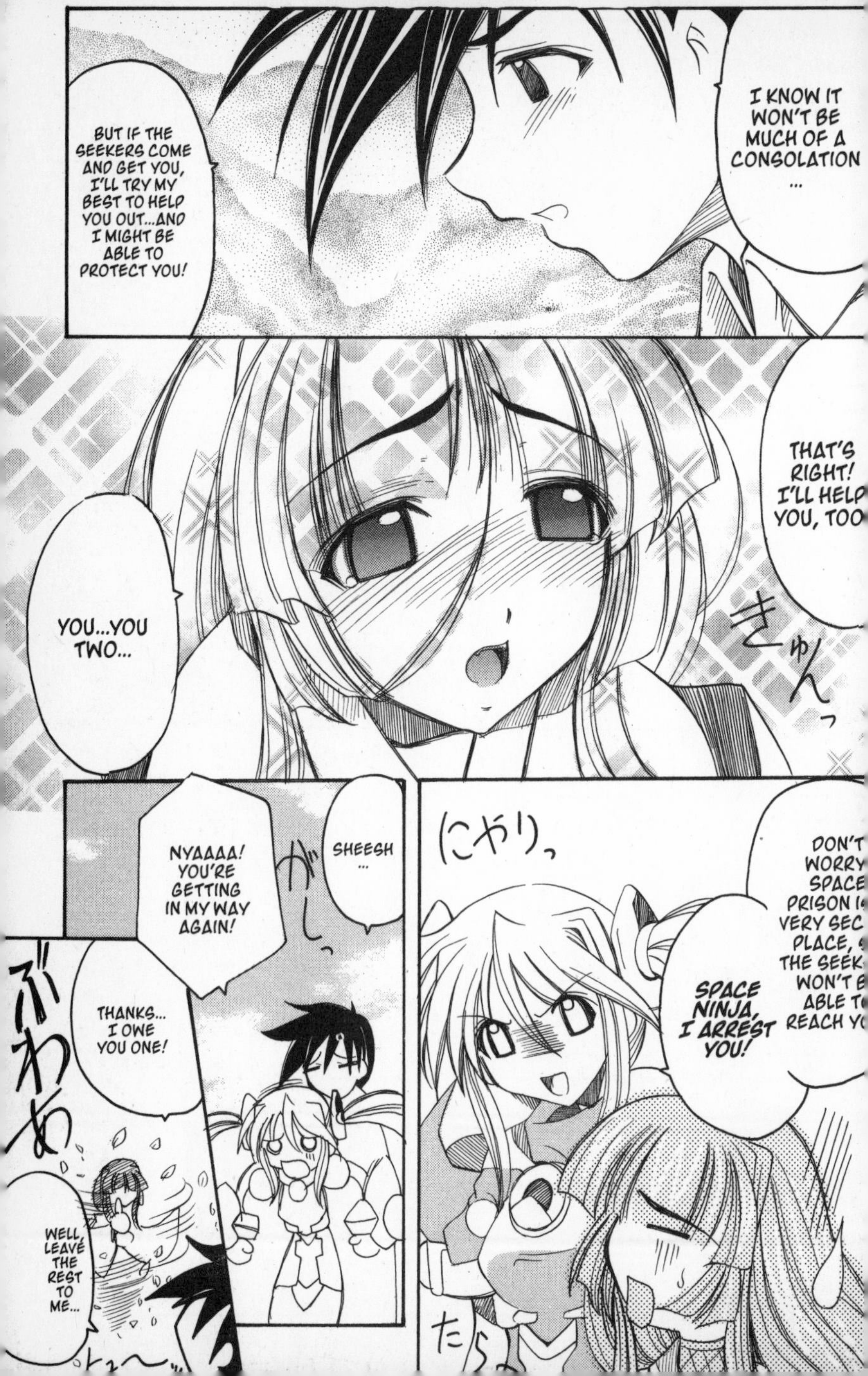

I KNOW IT WON'T BE MUCH OF A CONSOLATION ...
BUT IF THE SEEKERS COME AND GET YOU, I'LL TRY MY BEST TO HELP YOU OUT...AND I MIGHT BE ABLE TO PROTECT YOU!
THAT'S RIGHT! I'LL HELP YOU, TOO
きゅんっ
YOU...YOU TWO...
にやりっ
DON'T WORRY SPACE PRISON I VERY SEC PLACE, THE SEEK WON'T B ABLE T REACH YO
SPACE NINJA, I ARREST YOU!
たら
SHEESH ...
がしっ
NYAAAA! YOU'RE GETTING IN MY WAY AGAIN!
ぶわぁ
THANKS... I OWE YOU ONE!
WELL LEAVE THE REST TO ME...

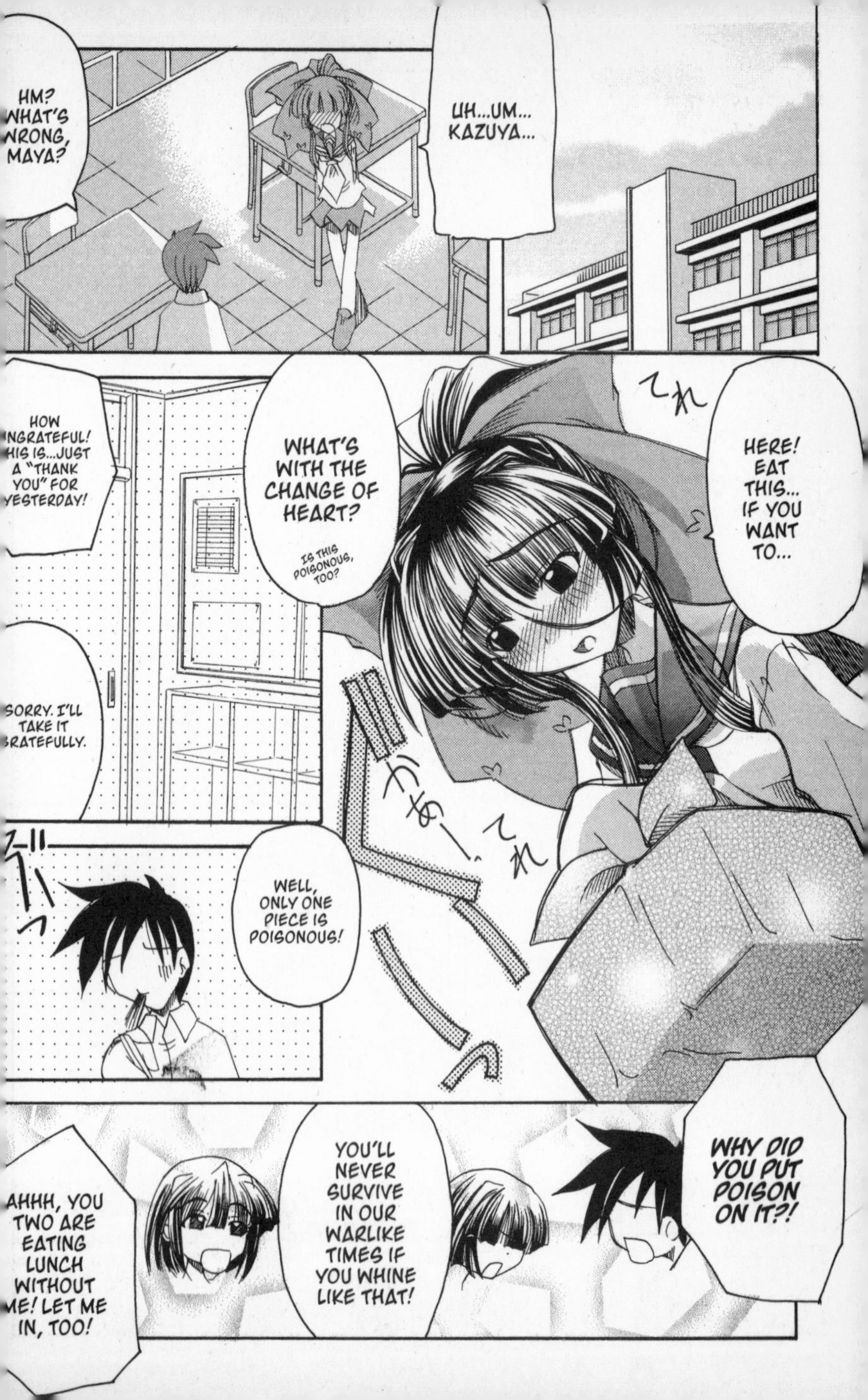
UH...UM... KAZUYA...
HM? WHAT'S WRONG, MAYA?
HERE! EAT THIS... IF YOU WANT TO...
WHAT'S WITH THE CHANGE OF HEART?
IS THIS POISONOUS, TOO?
HOW UNGRATEFUL! THIS IS...JUST A "THANK YOU" FOR YESTERDAY!
SORRY. I'LL TAKE IT GRATEFULLY.
WELL, ONLY ONE PIECE IS POISONOUS!
WHY DID YOU PUT POISON ON IT?!
YOU'LL NEVER SURVIVE IN OUR WARLIKE TIMES IF YOU WHINE LIKE THAT!
AHHH, YOU TWO ARE EATING LUNCH WITHOUT ME! LET ME IN, TOO!

Story 4

One Day, I'll Live in Your Town

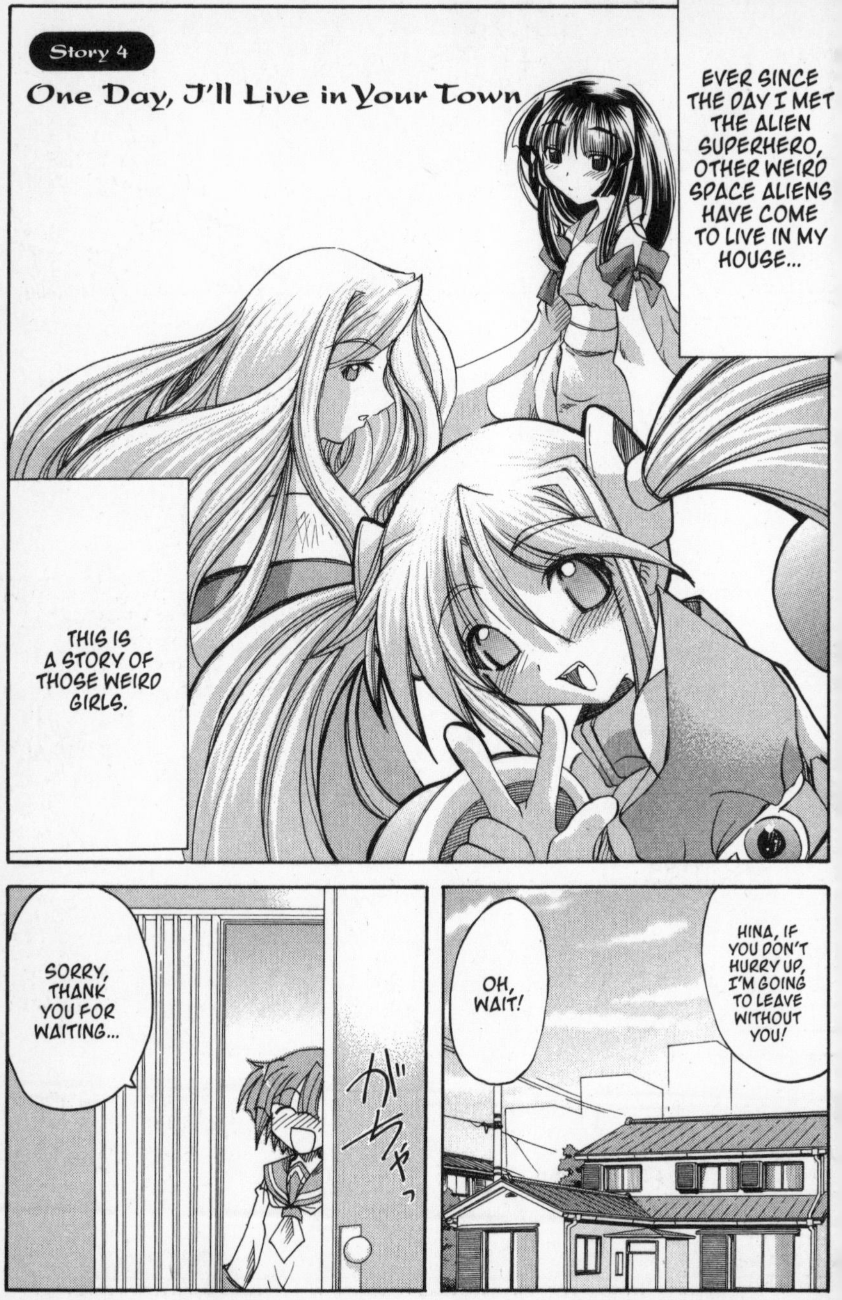
EVER SINCE THE DAY I MET THE ALIEN SUPERHERO, OTHER WEIRD SPACE ALIENS HAVE COME TO LIVE IN MY HOUSE...
THIS IS A STORY OF THOSE WEIRD GIRLS.
HINA, IF YOU DON'T HURRY UP, I'M GOING TO LEAVE WITHOUT YOU!
OH, WAIT!
SORRY, THANK YOU FOR WAITING...
がちゃっ

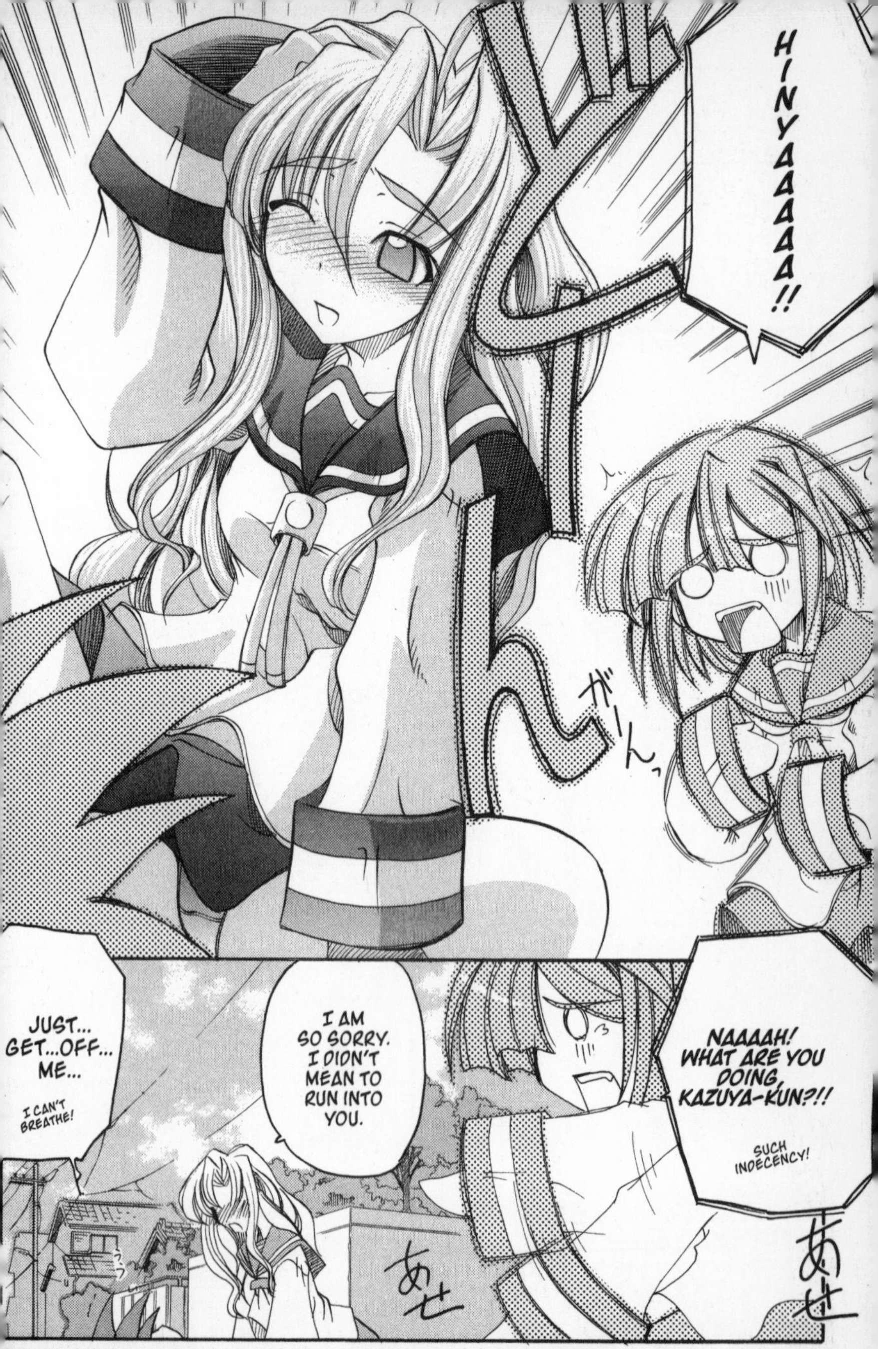
HINYAAAAAA!!
がーん
NAAAAH! WHAT ARE YOU DOING, KAZUYA-KUN?!!
SUCH INDECENCY!
あせ
I AM SO SORRY. I DIDN'T MEAN TO RUN INTO YOU.
あせ
JUST... GET...OFF... ME...
I CAN'T BREATHE!

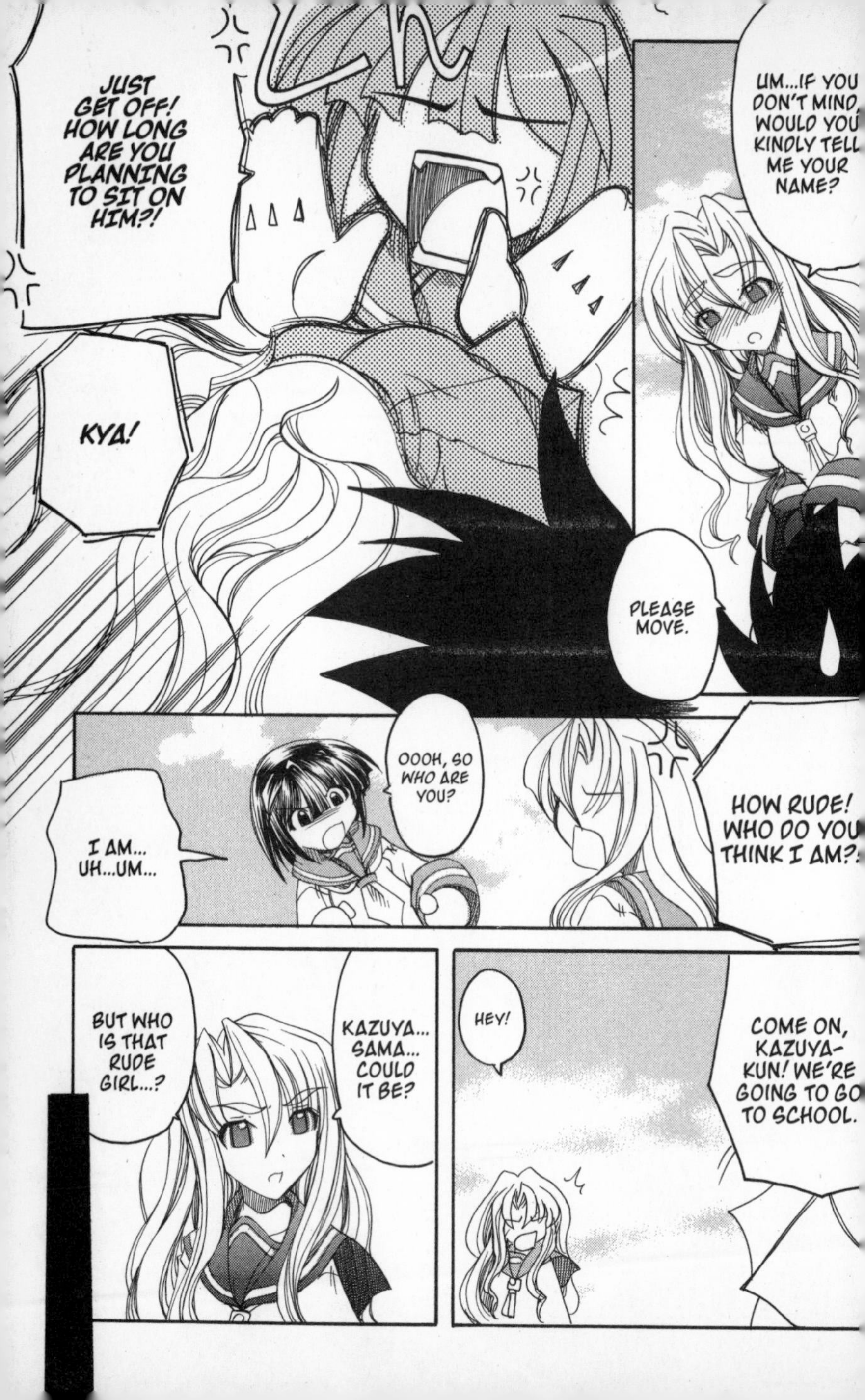
UM...IF YOU DON'T MIND, WOULD YOU KINDLY TELL ME YOUR NAME?
PLEASE MOVE.
JUST GET OFF! HOW LONG ARE YOU PLANNING TO SIT ON HIM?!
KYA!
HOW RUDE! WHO DO YOU THINK I AM?!
OOOH, SO WHO ARE YOU?
I AM... UH...UM...
COME ON, KAZUYA-KUN! WE'RE GOING TO GO TO SCHOOL.
HEY!
KAZUYA... SAMA... COULD IT BE?
BUT WHO IS THAT RUDE GIRL...?

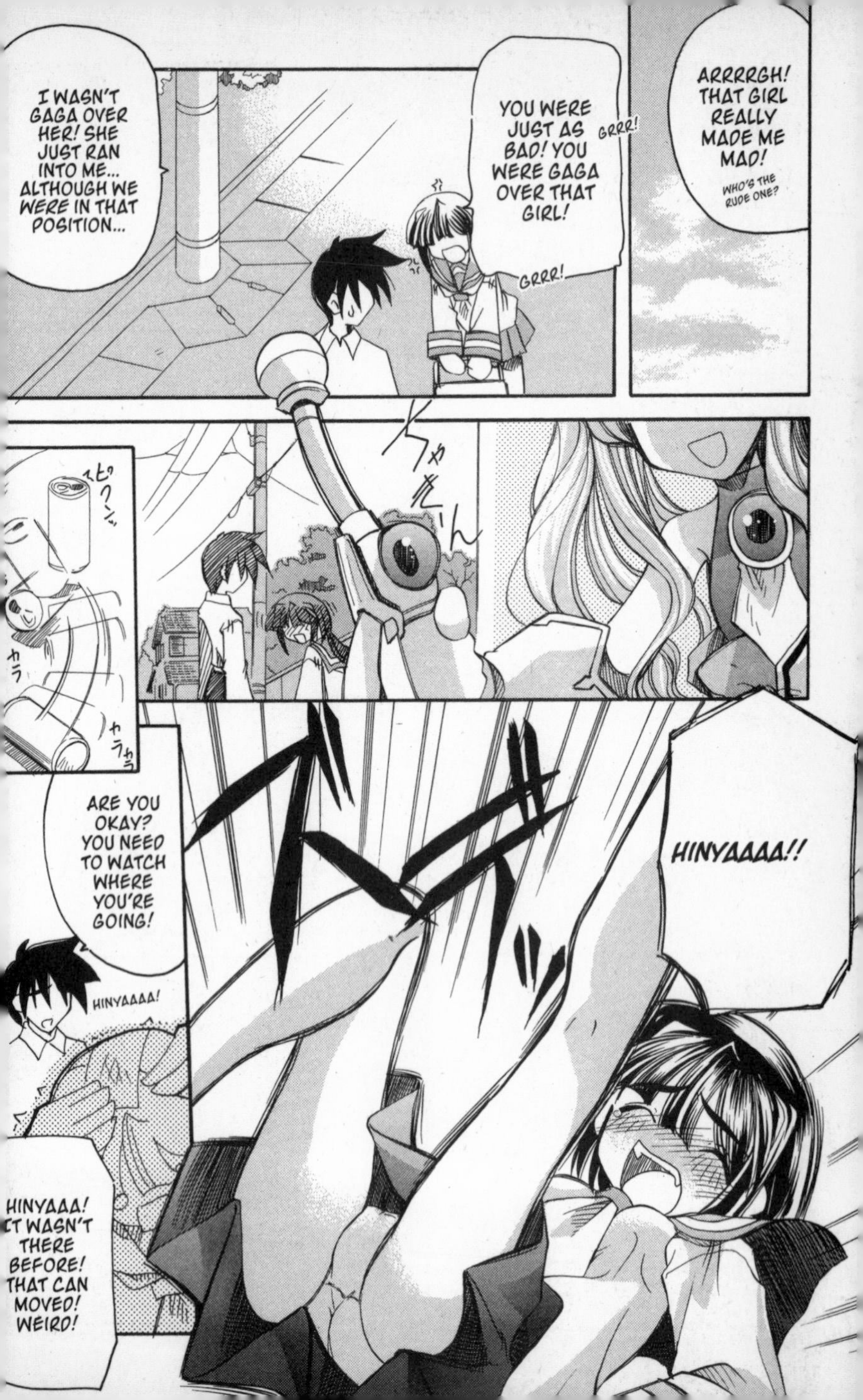
ARRRRGH! THAT GIRL REALLY MADE ME MAD!
WHO'S THE RUDE ONE?
YOU WERE JUST AS BAD! YOU WERE GAGA OVER THAT GIRL!
GRRR!
GRRR!
I WASN'T GAGA OVER HER! SHE JUST RAN INTO ME... ALTHOUGH WE WERE IN THAT POSITION...
HINYAAAA!!
ARE YOU OKAY? YOU NEED TO WATCH WHERE YOU'RE GOING!
HINYAAAA!
HINYAAA! IT WASN'T THERE BEFORE! THAT CAN MOVED! WEIRD!

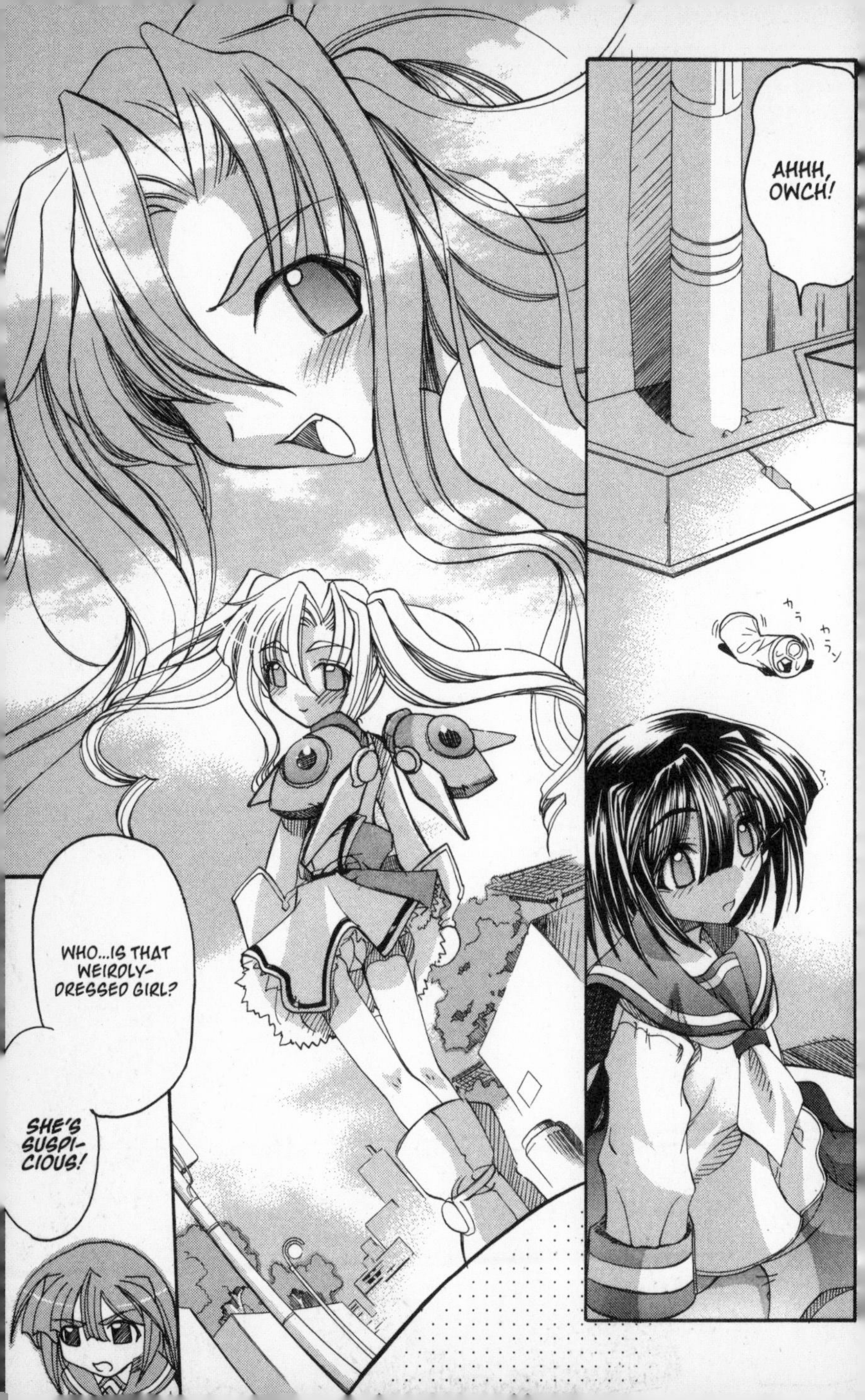
AHHH, OWCH!
カラ
カラン
WHO...IS THAT WEIRDLY-DRESSED GIRL?
SHE'S SUSPICIOUS!

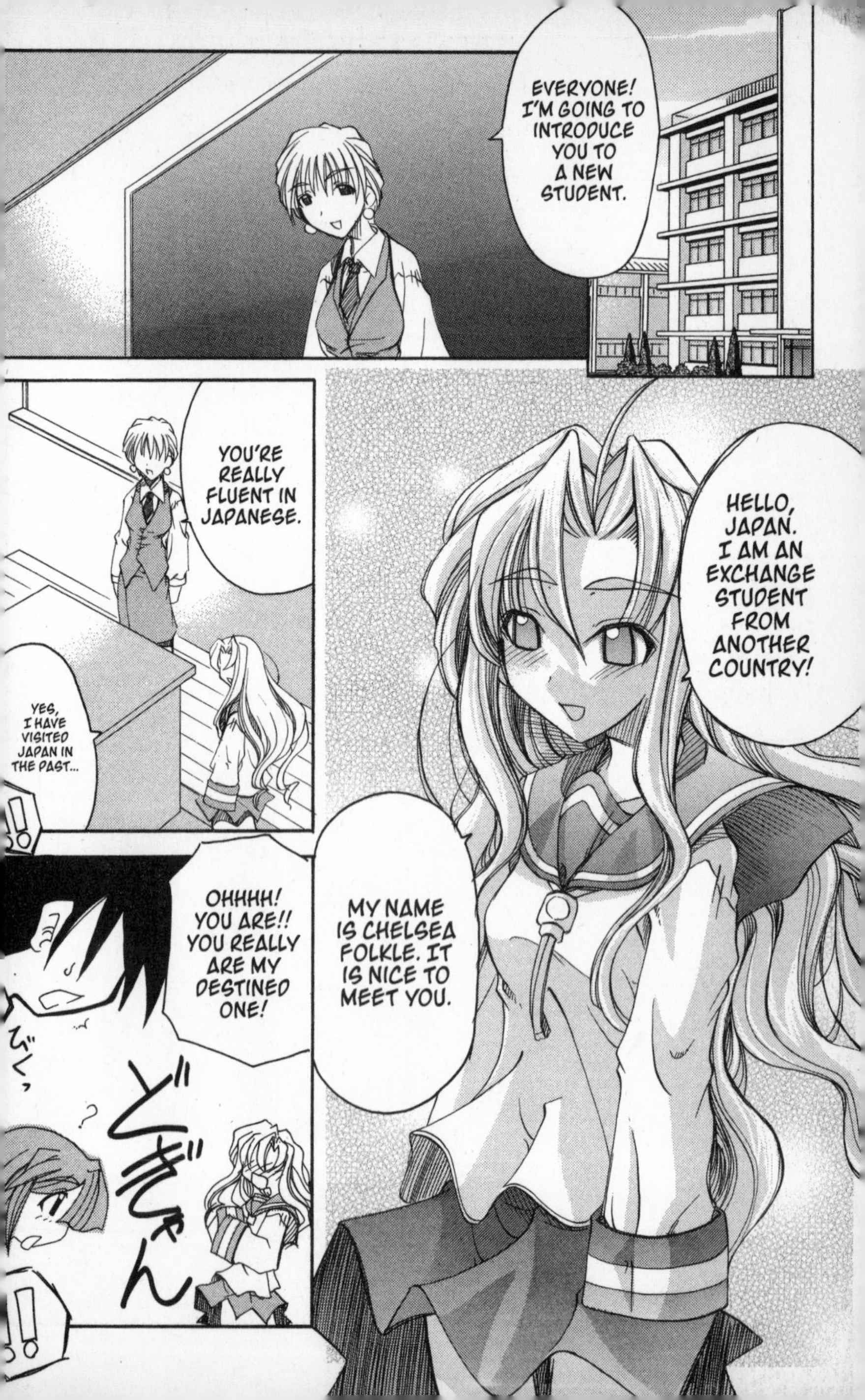
EVERYONE! I'M GOING TO INTRODUCE YOU TO A NEW STUDENT.
HELLO, JAPAN. I AM AN EXCHANGE STUDENT FROM ANOTHER COUNTRY!
MY NAME IS CHELSEA FOLKLE. IT IS NICE TO MEET YOU.
YOU'RE REALLY FLUENT IN JAPANESE.
YES, I HAVE VISITED JAPAN IN THE PAST...
!!
OHHHH! YOU ARE!! YOU REALLY ARE MY DESTINED ONE!
どぎゃん
びく、
?
!!

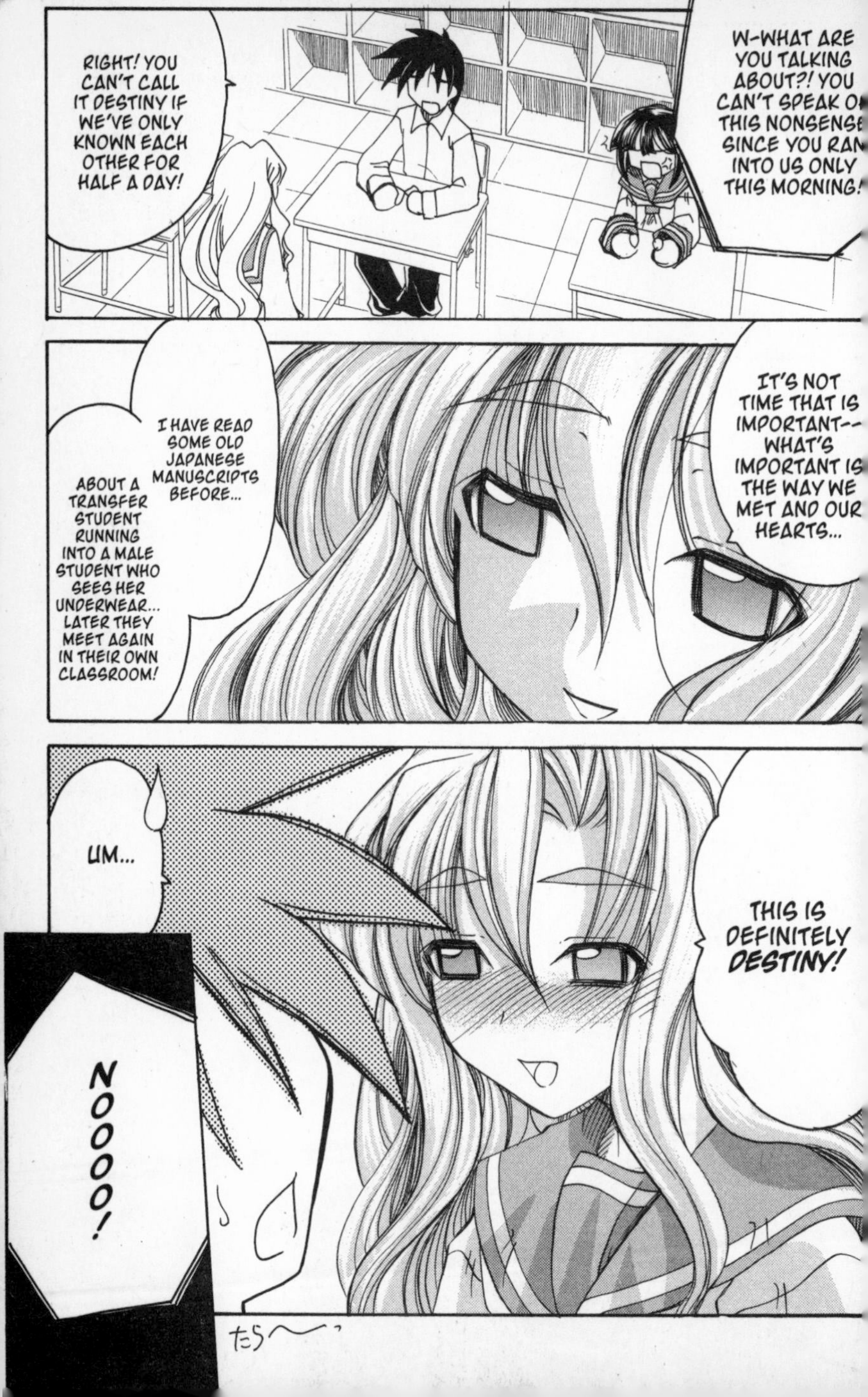
W-WHAT ARE YOU TALKING ABOUT?! YOU CAN'T SPEAK OF THIS NONSENSE SINCE YOU RAN INTO US ONLY THIS MORNING!
RIGHT! YOU CAN'T CALL IT DESTINY IF WE'VE ONLY KNOWN EACH OTHER FOR HALF A DAY!
IT'S NOT TIME THAT IS IMPORTANT--WHAT'S IMPORTANT IS THE WAY WE MET AND OUR HEARTS...
I HAVE READ SOME OLD JAPANESE MANUSCRIPTS BEFORE...
ABOUT A TRANSFER STUDENT RUNNING INTO A MALE STUDENT WHO SEES HER UNDERWEAR... LATER THEY MEET AGAIN IN THEIR OWN CLASSROOM!
THIS IS DEFINITELY ***DESTINY!***
UM...
NOOOOO!
たら〜

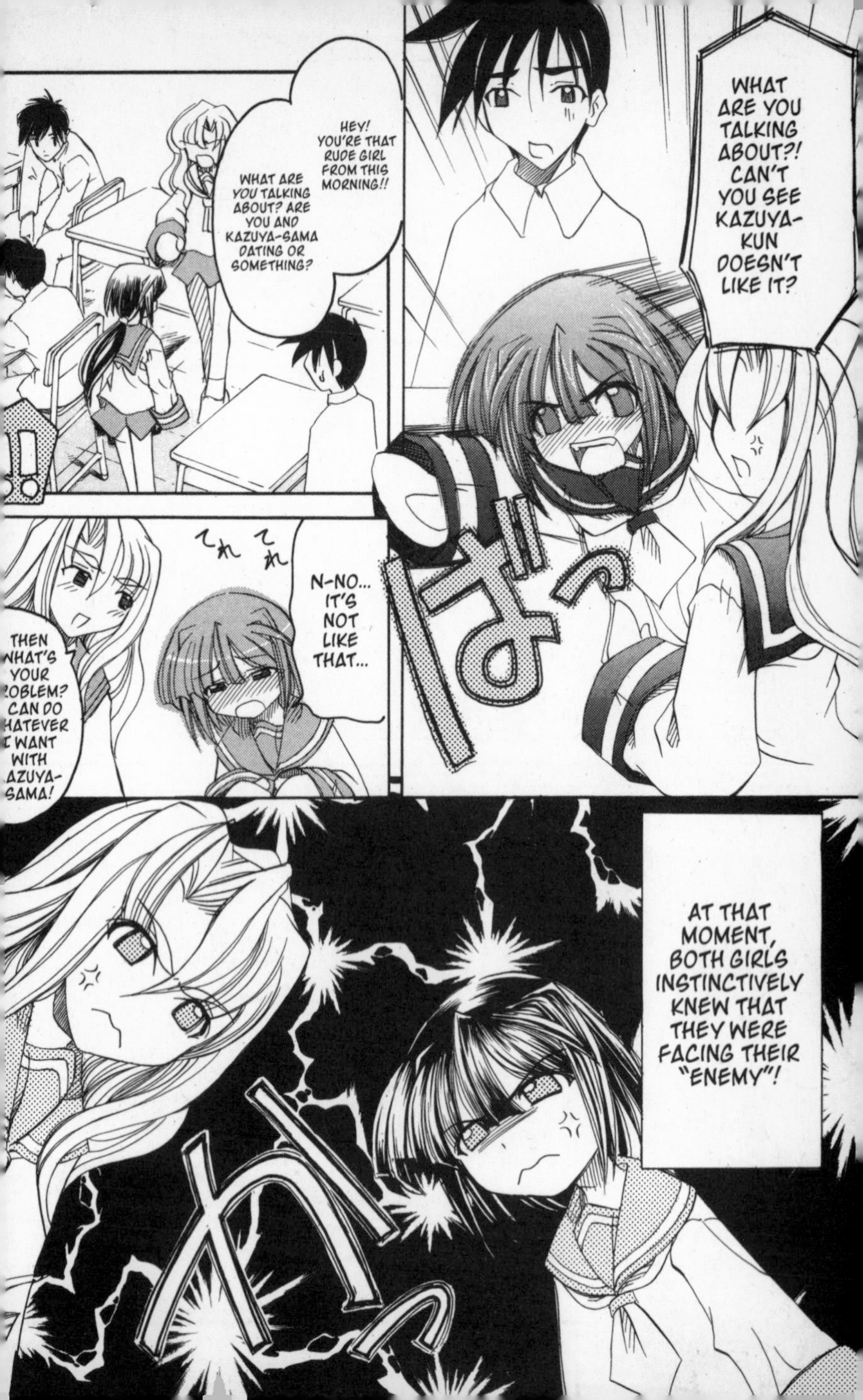
WHAT ARE YOU TALKING ABOUT?! CAN'T YOU SEE KAZUYA-KUN DOESN'T LIKE IT?
ばっ
HEY! YOU'RE THAT RUDE GIRL FROM THIS MORNING!!
WHAT ARE YOU TALKING ABOUT? ARE YOU AND KAZUYA-SAMA DATING OR SOMETHING?
!!
てれ てれ
N-NO... IT'S NOT LIKE THAT...
THEN WHAT'S YOUR ROBLEM? CAN DO HATEVER WANT WITH AZUYA-SAMA!
AT THAT MOMENT, BOTH GIRLS INSTINCTIVELY KNEW THAT THEY WERE FACING THEIR "ENEMY"!

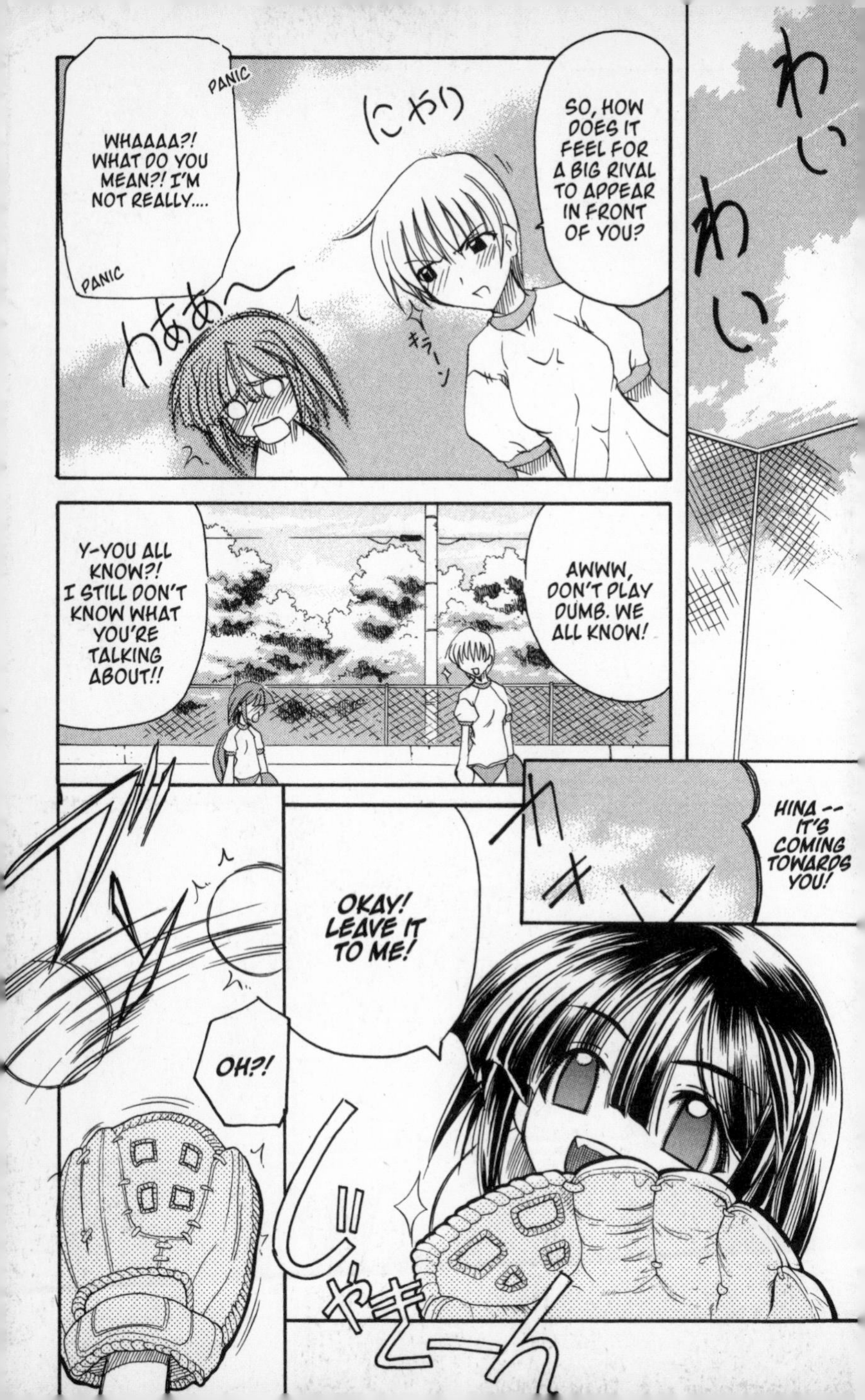

わいわい
SO, HOW DOES IT FEEL FOR A BIG RIVAL TO APPEAR IN FRONT OF YOU?
にやり
キラーン
PANIC
WHAAAA?! WHAT DO YOU MEAN?! I'M NOT REALLY....
PANIC
わああ〜
AWWW, DON'T PLAY DUMB. WE ALL KNOW!
Y-YOU ALL KNOW?! I STILL DON'T KNOW WHAT YOU'RE TALKING ABOUT!!
HINA -- IT'S COMING TOWARDS YOU!
OKAY! LEAVE IT TO ME!
じゃきーん
OH?!

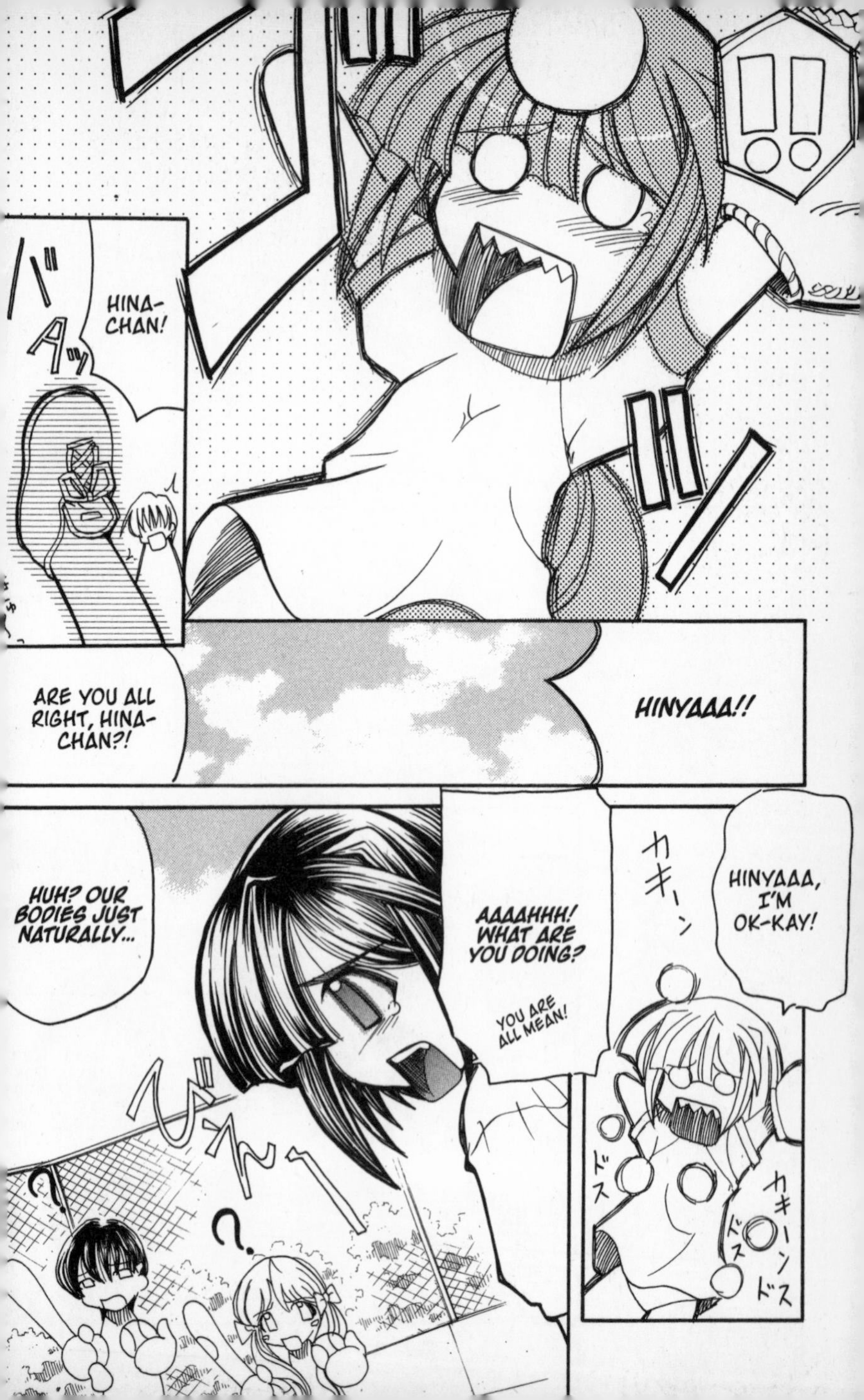
!!
HINA-CHAN!
バAッ
HINYAAA!!
ARE YOU ALL RIGHT, HINA-CHAN?!
HINYAAA, I'M OK-KAY!
カキーン
ドス
カキーンドスドス
AAAAHHH! WHAT ARE YOU DOING?
YOU ARE ALL MEAN!
HUH? OUR BODIES JUST NATURALLY...
びえ〜ん

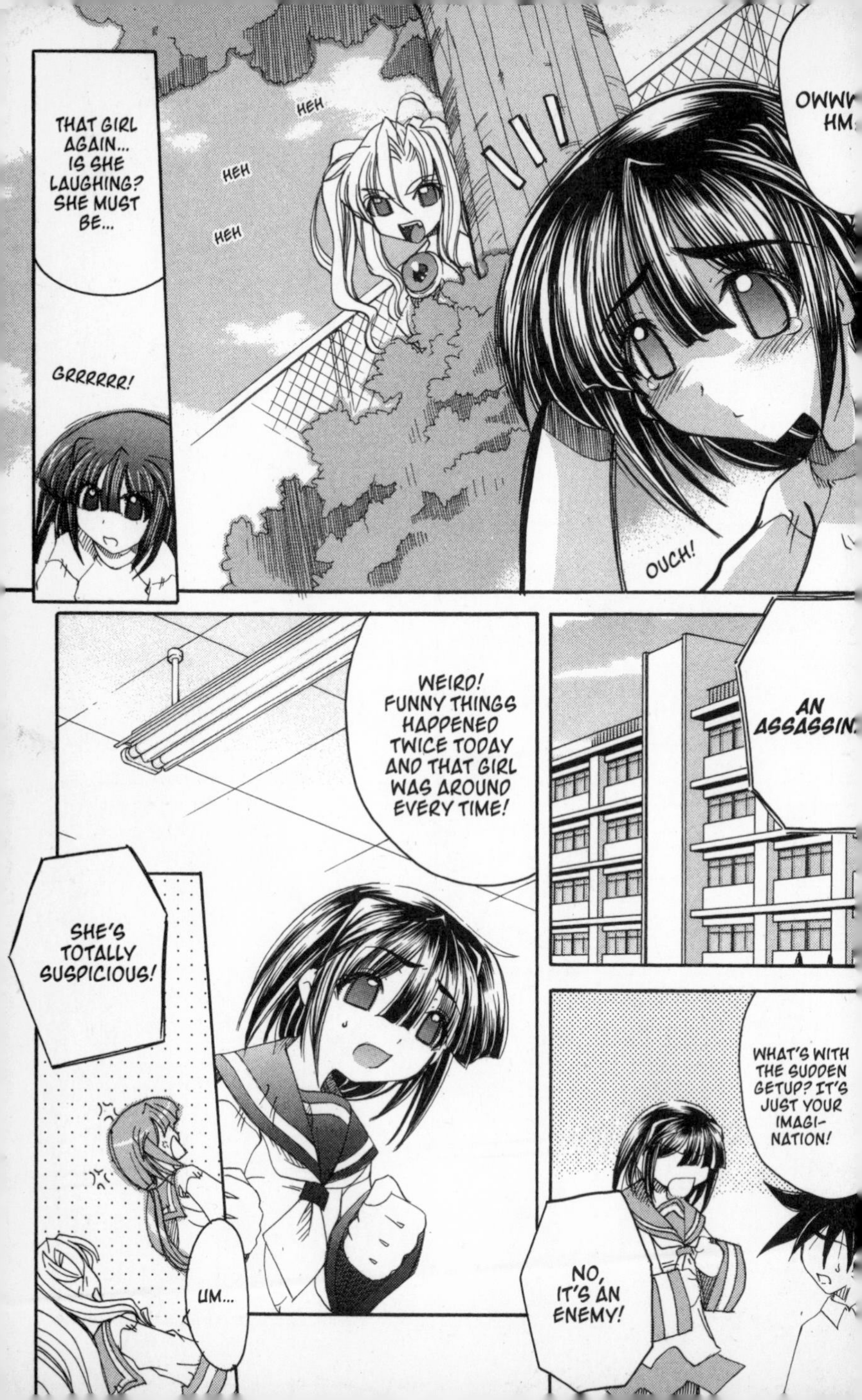
OWWW
HM
HEH
HEH
HEH
OUCH!
THAT GIRL AGAIN... IS SHE LAUGHING? SHE MUST BE...
GRRRRRR!
AN ASSASSIN.
WHAT'S WITH THE SUDDEN GETUP? IT'S JUST YOUR IMAGI-NATION!
NO, IT'S AN ENEMY!
WEIRD! FUNNY THINGS HAPPENED TWICE TODAY AND THAT GIRL WAS AROUND EVERY TIME!
SHE'S TOTALLY SUSPICIOUS!
UM...

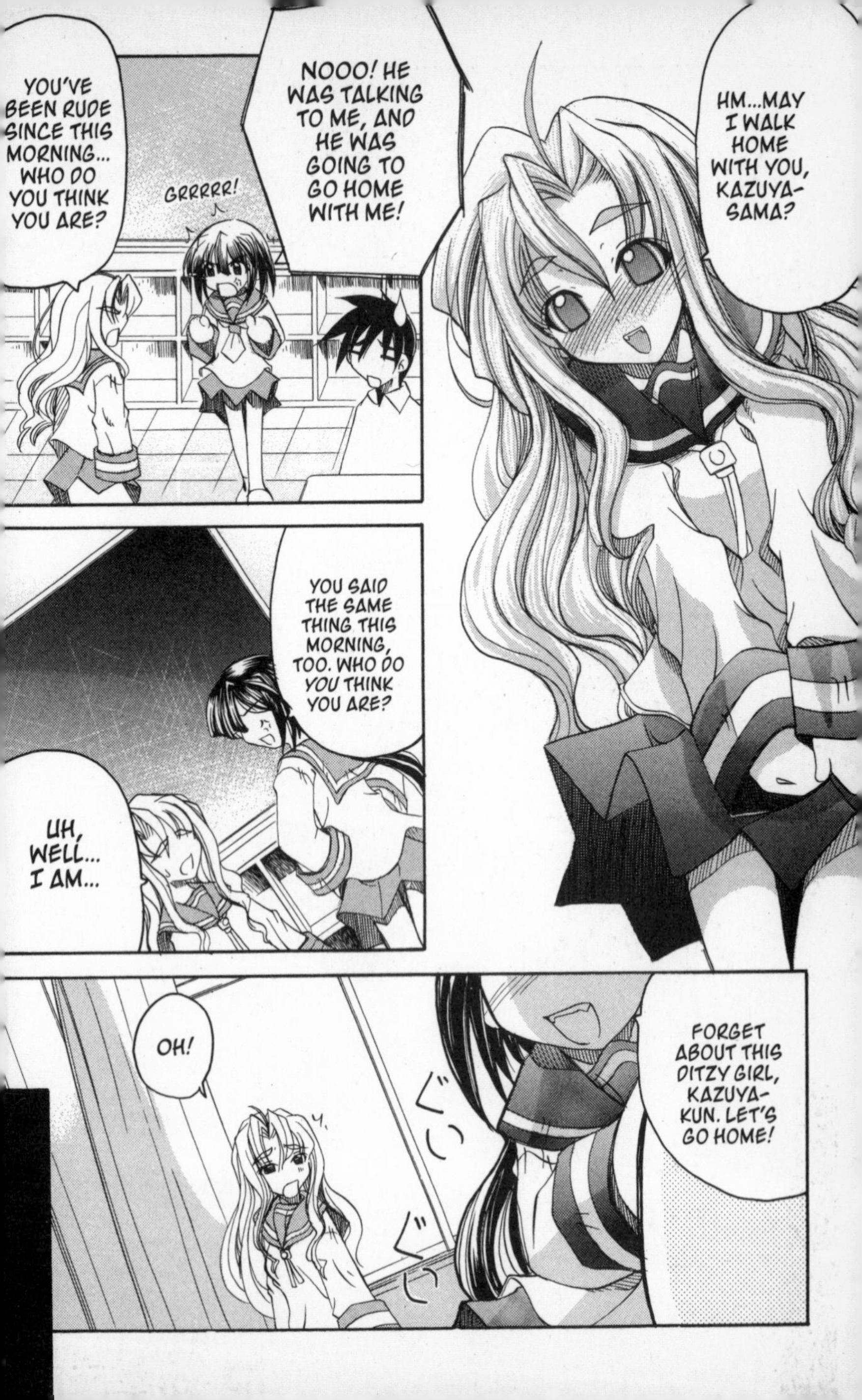
HM...MAY I WALK HOME WITH YOU, KAZUYA-SAMA?
NOOO! HE WAS TALKING TO ME, AND HE WAS GOING TO GO HOME WITH ME!
GRRRRR!
YOU'VE BEEN RUDE SINCE THIS MORNING... WHO DO YOU THINK YOU ARE?
YOU SAID THE SAME THING THIS MORNING, TOO. WHO DO *YOU* THINK YOU ARE?
UH, WELL... I AM...
FORGET ABOUT THIS DITZY GIRL, KAZUYA-KUN. LET'S GO HOME!
OH!

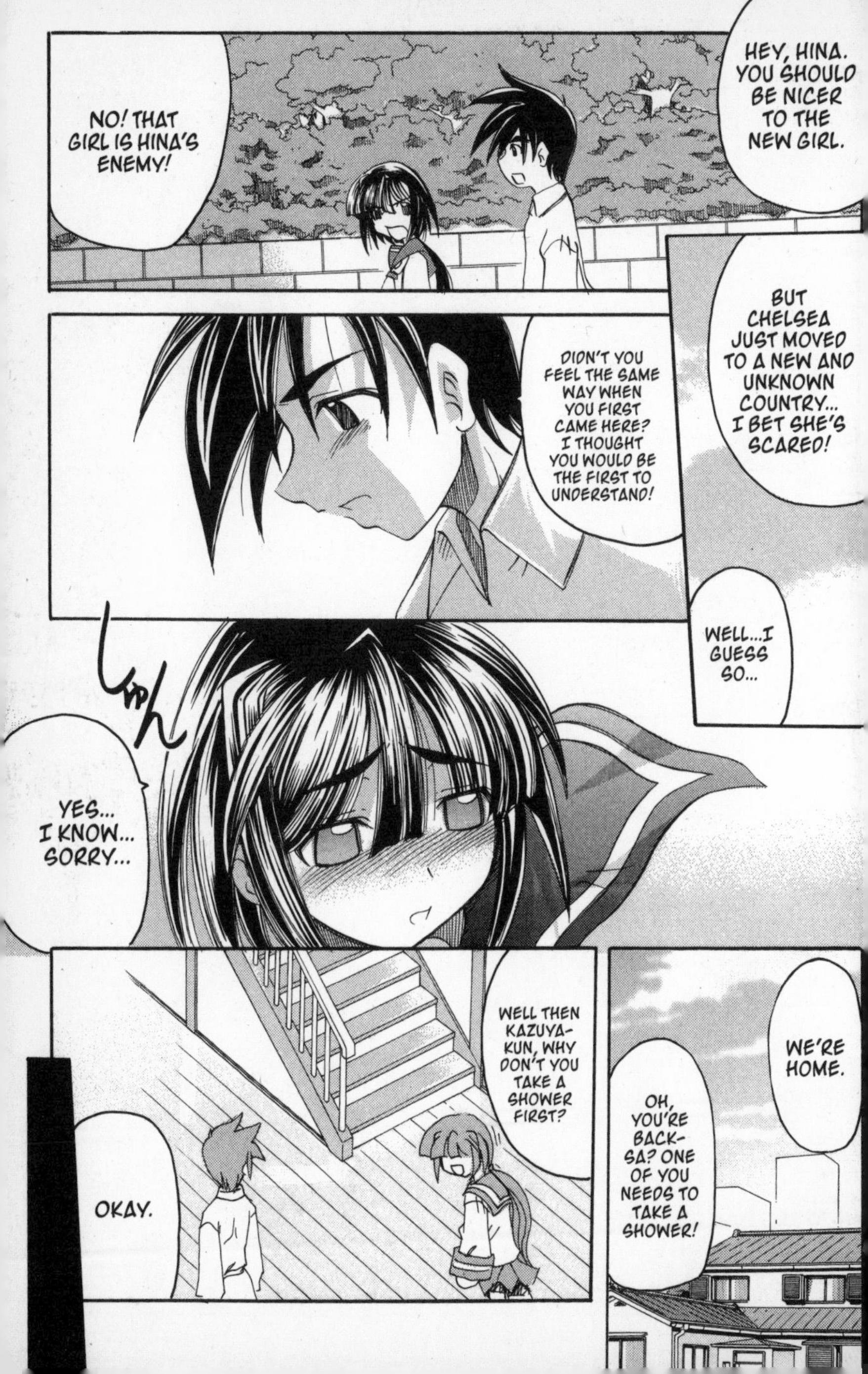
HEY, HINA. YOU SHOULD BE NICER TO THE NEW GIRL.
NO! THAT GIRL IS HINA'S ENEMY!
BUT CHELSEA JUST MOVED TO A NEW AND UNKNOWN COUNTRY... I BET SHE'S SCARED!
DIDN'T YOU FEEL THE SAME WAY WHEN YOU FIRST CAME HERE? I THOUGHT YOU WOULD BE THE FIRST TO UNDERSTAND!
WELL...I GUESS SO...
YES... I KNOW... SORRY...
WE'RE HOME.
OH, YOU'RE BACK-SA? ONE OF YOU NEEDS TO TAKE A SHOWER!
WELL THEN KAZUYA-KUN, WHY DON'T YOU TAKE A SHOWER FIRST?
OKAY.

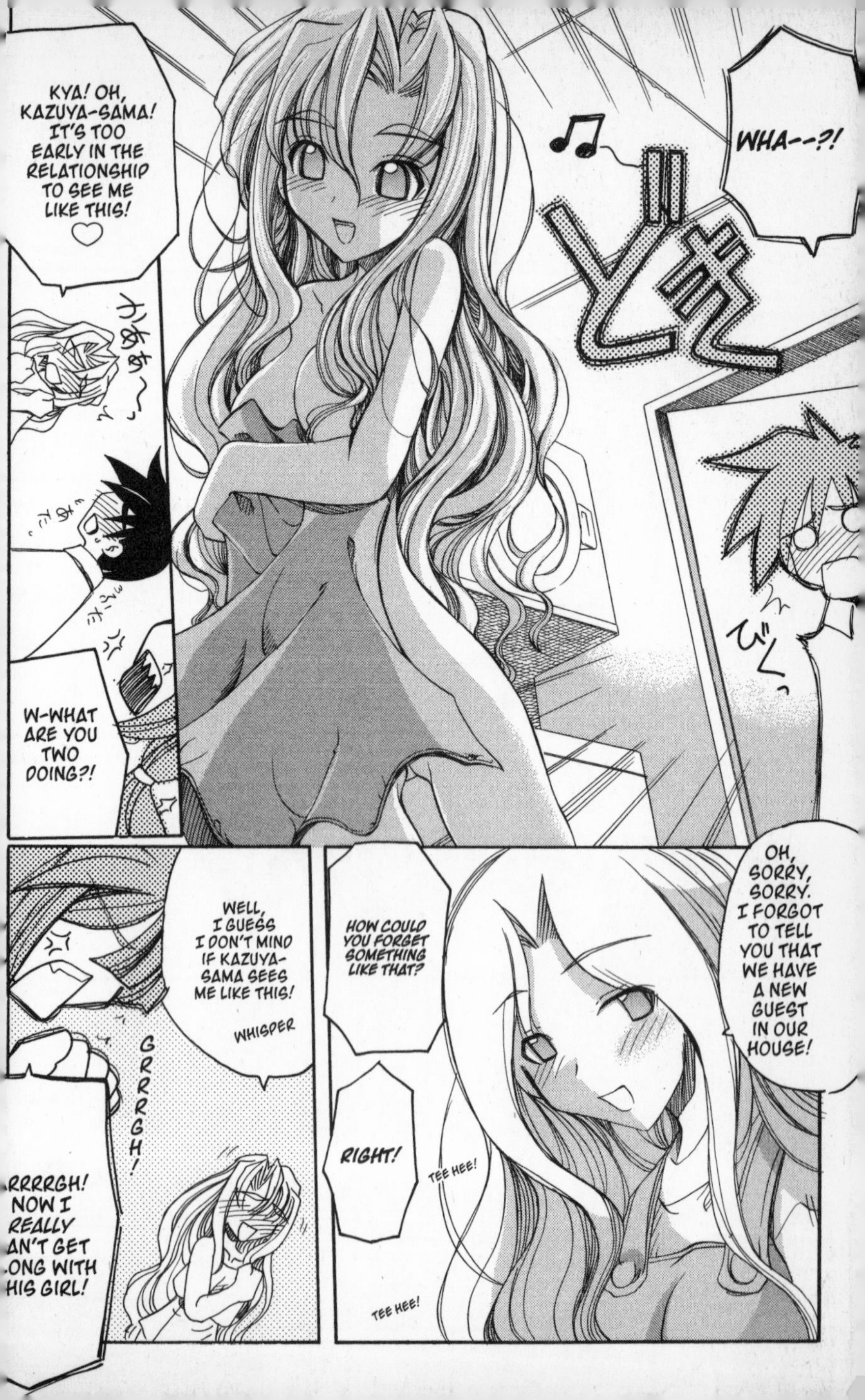
WHA--?!
どき
びくっ
KYA! OH, KAZUYA-SAMA! IT'S TOO EARLY IN THE RELATIONSHIP TO SEE ME LIKE THIS! ♡
W-WHAT ARE YOU TWO DOING?!
OH, SORRY, SORRY. I FORGOT TO TELL YOU THAT WE HAVE A NEW GUEST IN OUR HOUSE!
HOW COULD YOU FORGET SOMETHING LIKE THAT?
RIGHT!
TEE HEE!
TEE HEE!
WELL, I GUESS I DON'T MIND IF KAZUYA-SAMA SEES ME LIKE THIS!
WHISPER
GRRRRGH!
RRRRGH! NOW I REALLY AN'T GET ONG WITH HIS GIRL!

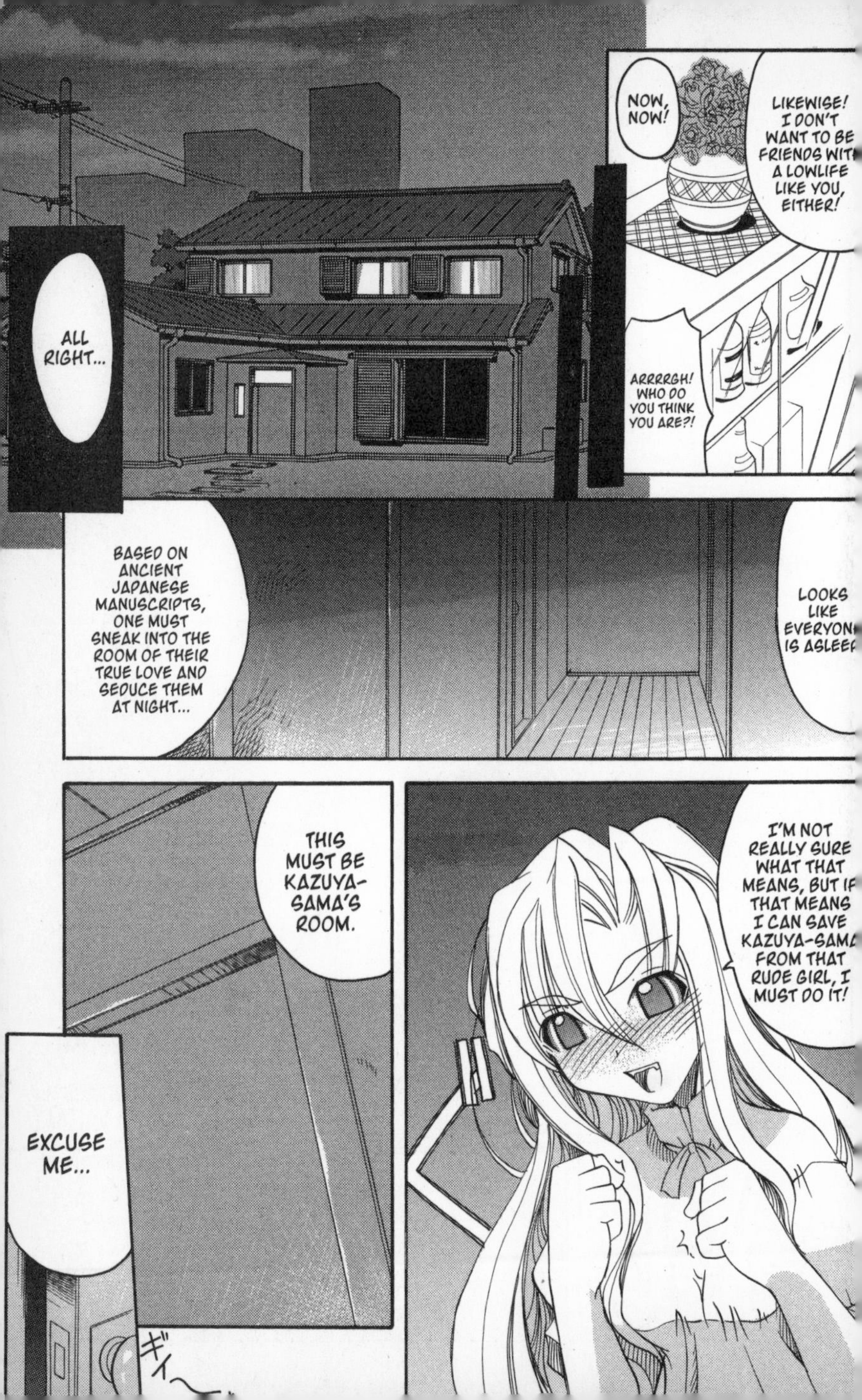
LIKEWISE! I DON'T WANT TO BE FRIENDS WITH A LOWLIFE LIKE YOU, EITHER!
NOW, NOW!
ARRRRGH! WHO DO YOU THINK YOU ARE?!
ALL RIGHT...
LOOKS LIKE EVERYON IS ASLEE
BASED ON ANCIENT JAPANESE MANUSCRIPTS, ONE MUST SNEAK INTO THE ROOM OF THEIR TRUE LOVE AND SEDUCE THEM AT NIGHT...
I'M NOT REALLY SURE WHAT THAT MEANS, BUT IF THAT MEANS I CAN SAVE KAZUYA-SAMA FROM THAT RUDE GIRL, I MUST DO IT!
THIS MUST BE KAZUYA-SAMA'S ROOM.
EXCUSE ME...
ギィ～

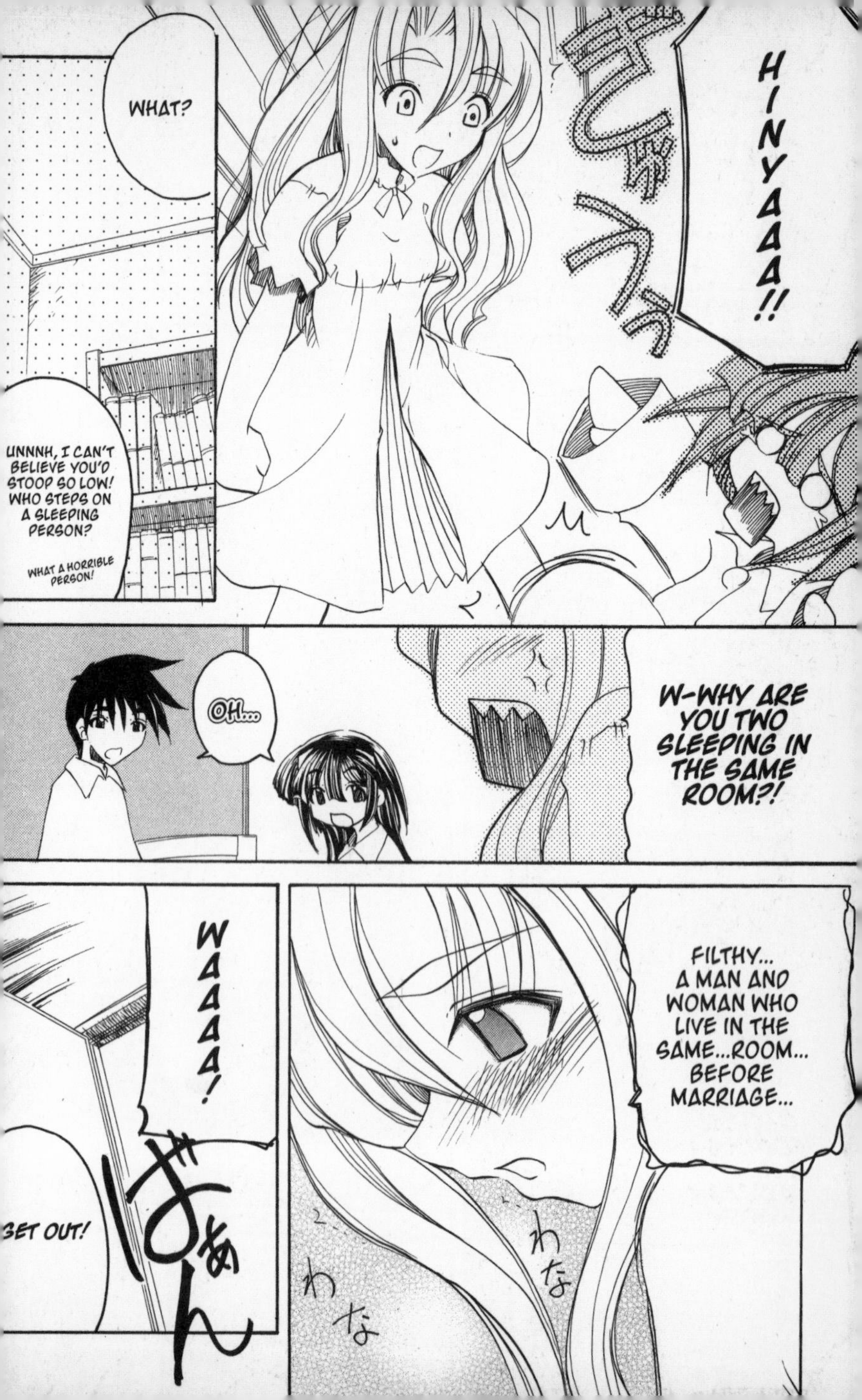

ぎゅうっ
HINYAAAA!!
WHAT?
UNNNH, I CAN'T BELIEVE YOU'D STOOP SO LOW! WHO STEPS ON A SLEEPING PERSON?
WHAT A HORRIBLE PERSON!
W-WHY ARE YOU TWO SLEEPING IN THE SAME ROOM?!
OH...
FILTHY... A MAN AND WOMAN WHO LIVE IN THE SAME...ROOM... BEFORE MARRIAGE...
わなわな
わなわな
WAAAAA!
GET OUT!
ばぁん

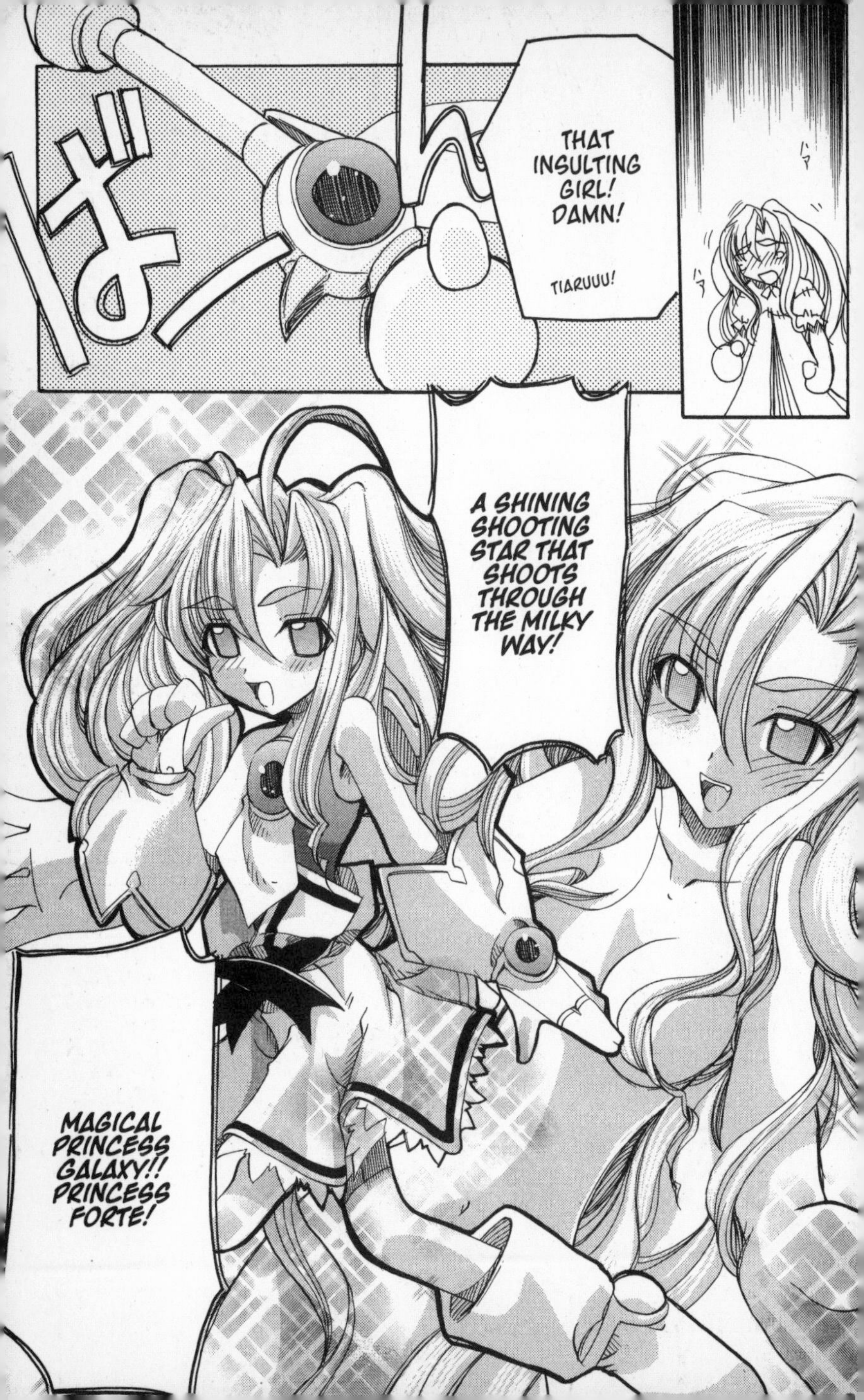
THAT INSULTING GIRL! DAMN!
TIARUUU!
A SHINING SHOOTING STAR THAT SHOOTS THROUGH THE MILKY WAY!
MAGICAL PRINCESS GALAXY!! PRINCESS FORTE!

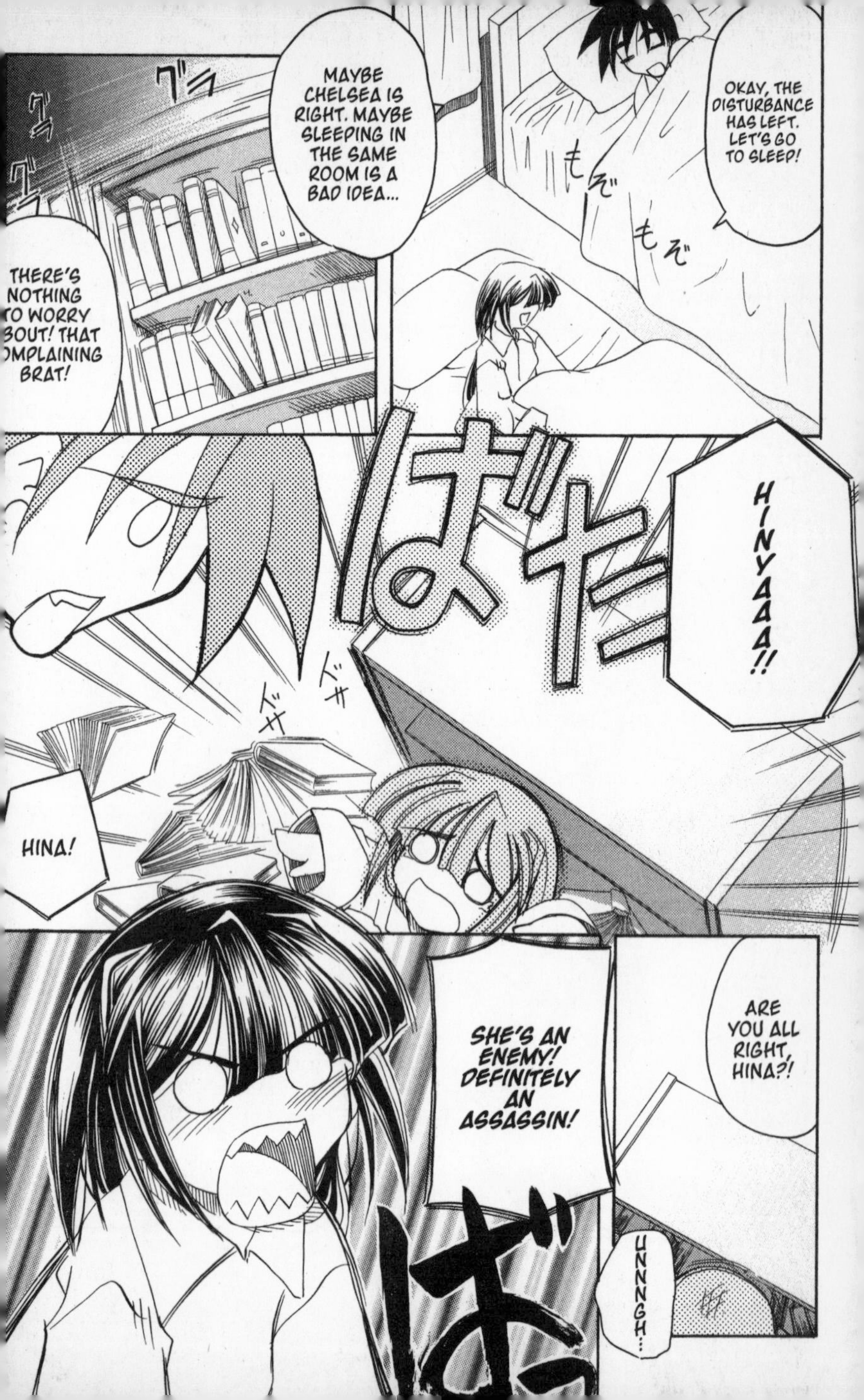
OKAY, THE DISTURBANCE HAS LEFT. LET'S GO TO SLEEP!
もぞ
もぞ
MAYBE CHELSEA IS RIGHT. MAYBE SLEEPING IN THE SAME ROOM IS A BAD IDEA...
THERE'S NOTHING TO WORRY BOUT! THAT OMPLAINING BRAT!
HINYAAAA!!
ドサ
ドサ
HINA!
ARE YOU ALL RIGHT, HINA?!
UNNNGH..
SHE'S AN ENEMY! DEFINITELY AN ASSASSIN!

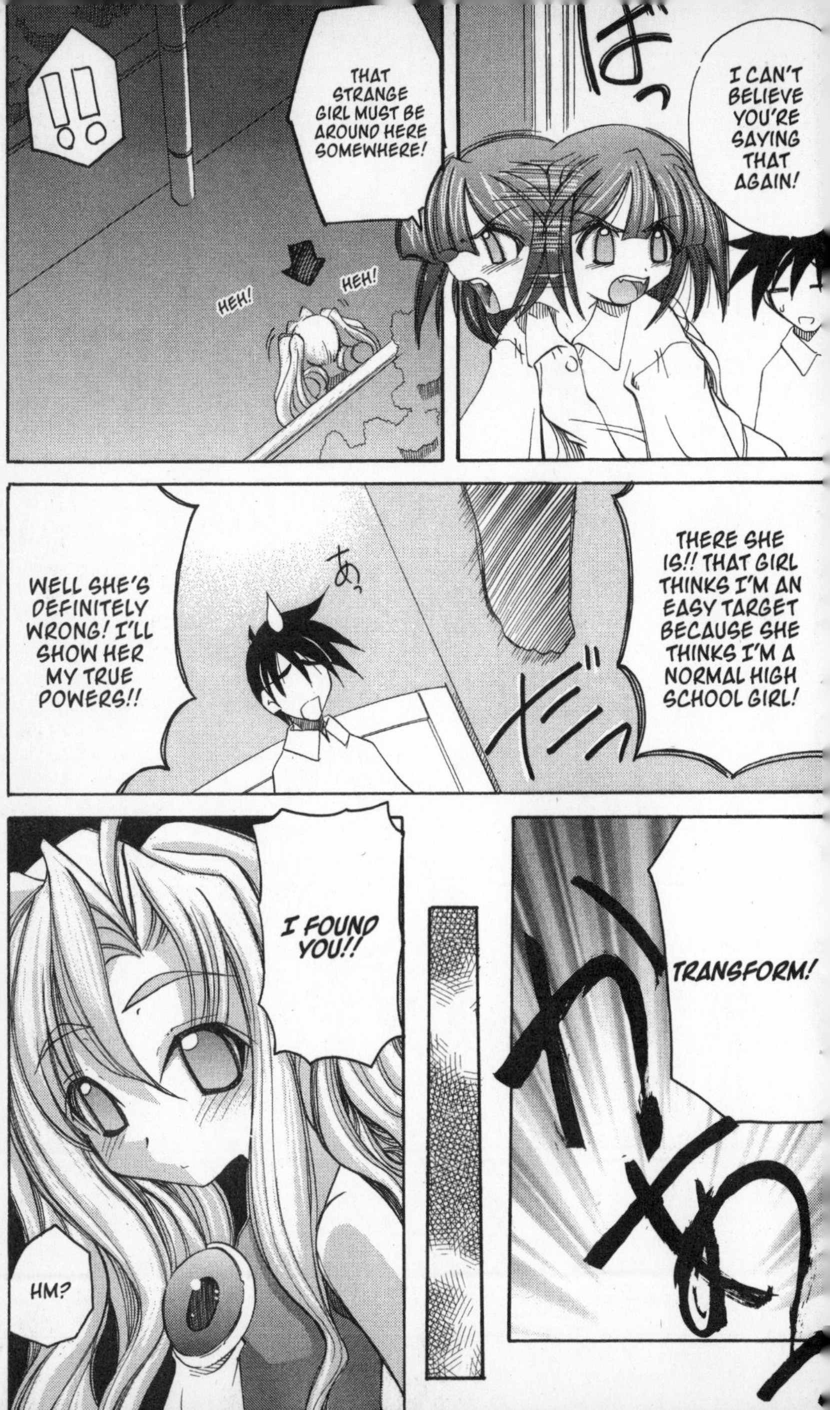
ばっ
I CAN'T BELIEVE YOU'RE SAYING THAT AGAIN!
THAT STRANGE GIRL MUST BE AROUND HERE SOMEWHERE!
!!
HEH!
HEH!
THERE SHE IS!! THAT GIRL THINKS I'M AN EASY TARGET BECAUSE SHE THINKS I'M A NORMAL HIGH SCHOOL GIRL!
ダッ
あっ
WELL SHE'S DEFINITELY WRONG! I'LL SHOW HER MY TRUE POWERS!!
TRANSFORM!
I FOUND YOU!!
HM?

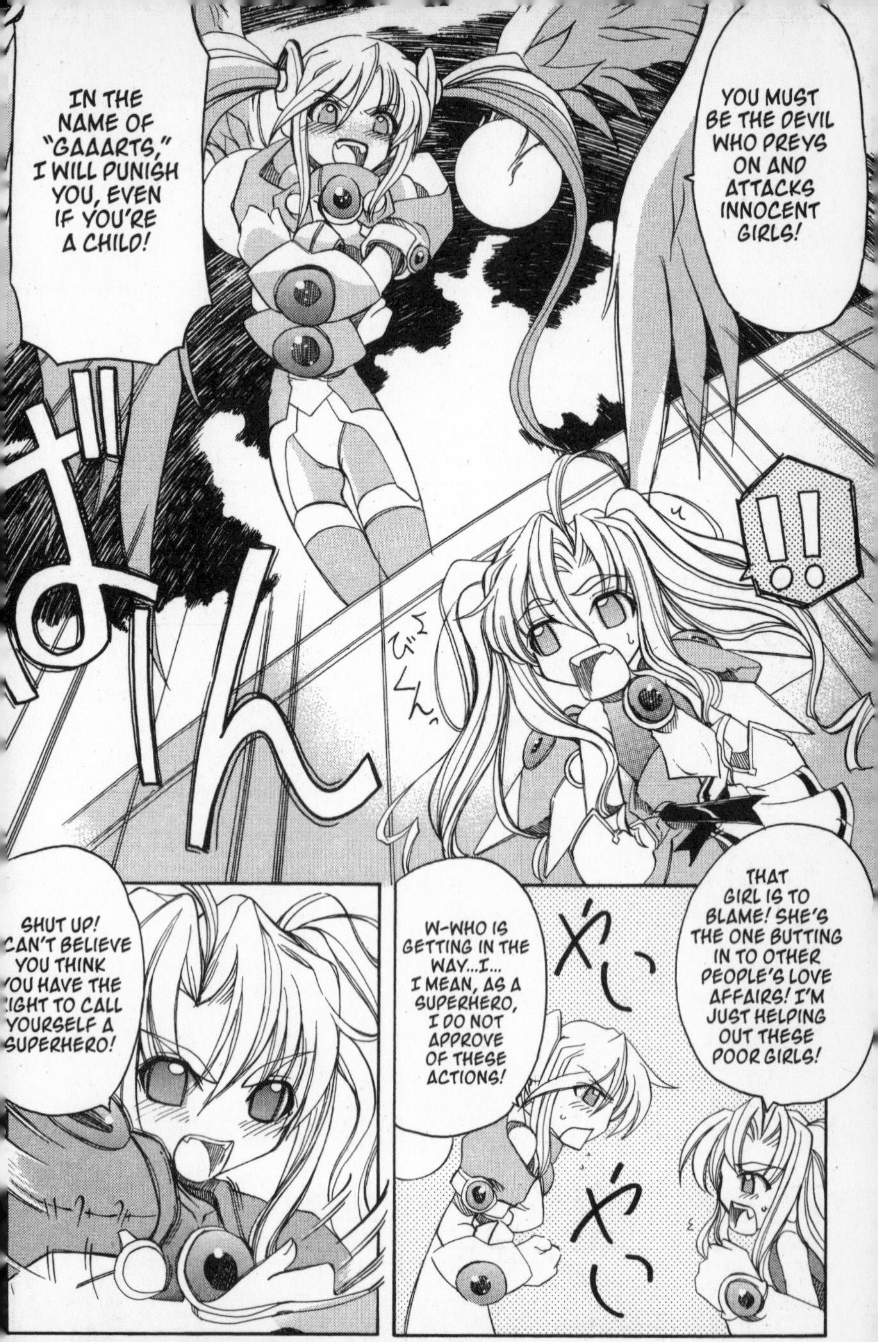
YOU MUST BE THE DEVIL WHO PREYS ON AND ATTACKS INNOCENT GIRLS!
IN THE NAME OF "GAAARTS," I WILL PUNISH YOU, EVEN IF YOU'RE A CHILD!
!!
THAT GIRL IS TO BLAME! SHE'S THE ONE BUTTING IN TO OTHER PEOPLE'S LOVE AFFAIRS! I'M JUST HELPING OUT THESE POOR GIRLS!
やい
やい
W-WHO IS GETTING IN THE WAY...I... I MEAN, AS A SUPERHERO, I DO NOT APPROVE OF THESE ACTIONS!
SHUT UP! I CAN'T BELIEVE YOU THINK YOU HAVE THE RIGHT TO CALL YOURSELF A SUPERHERO!

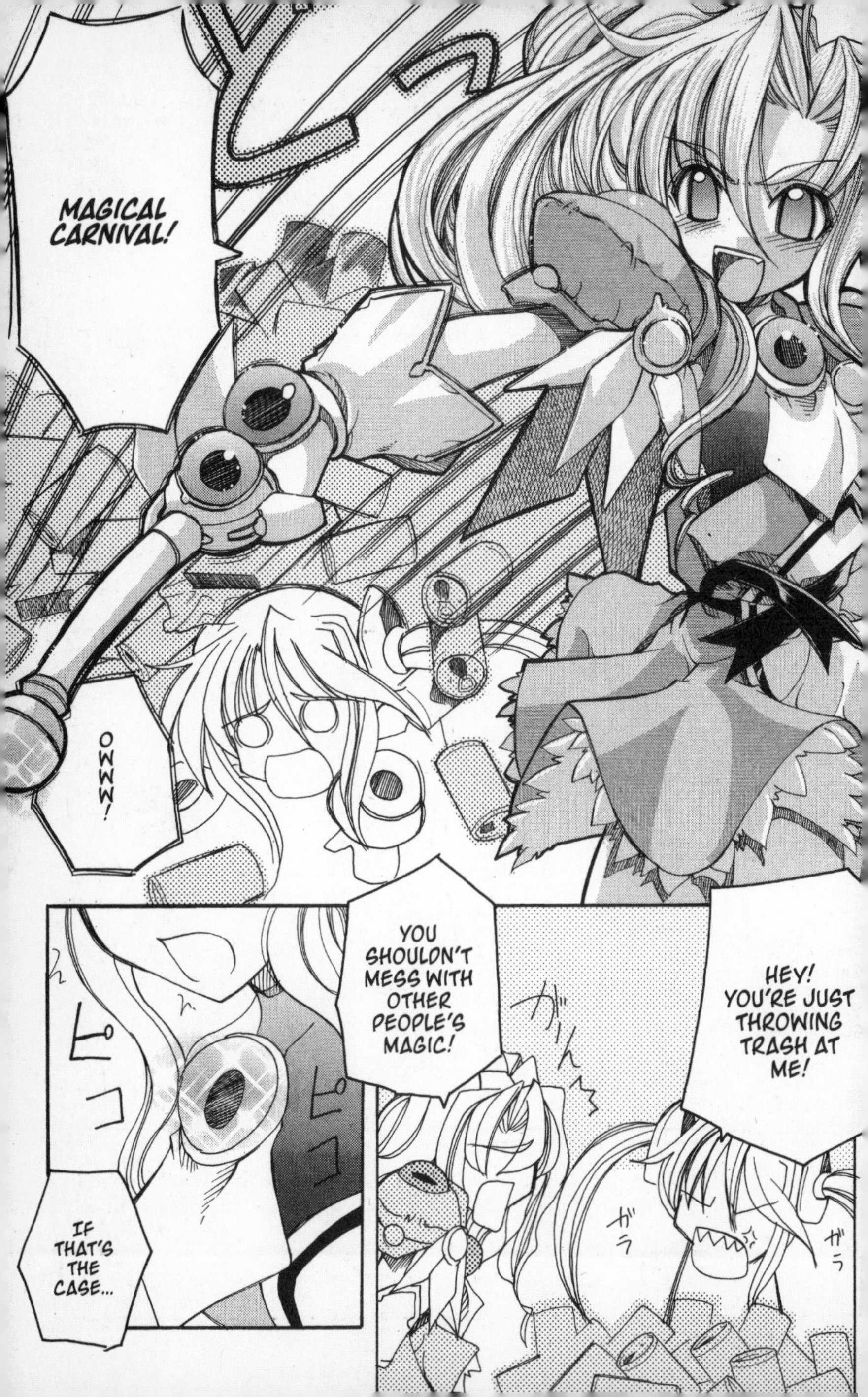
MAGICAL CARNIVAL!
OWWW!
HEY! YOU'RE JUST THROWING TRASH AT ME!
YOU SHOULDN'T MESS WITH OTHER PEOPLE'S MAGIC!
IF THAT'S THE CASE...

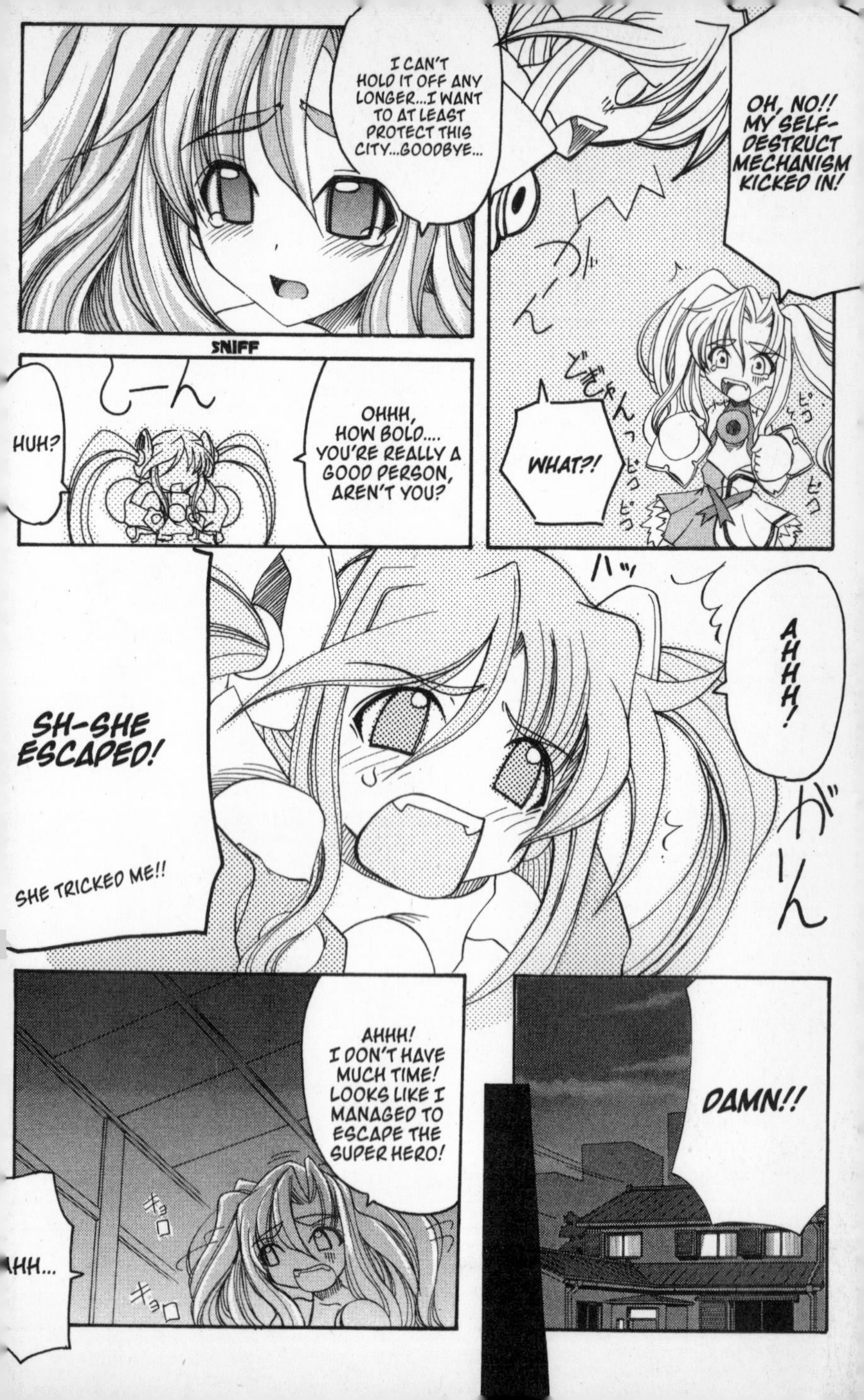

OH, NO!! MY SELF-DESTRUCT MECHANISM KICKED IN!
WHAT?!
I CAN'T HOLD IT OFF ANY LONGER...I WANT TO AT LEAST PROTECT THIS CITY...GOODBYE...
SNIFF
OHHH, HOW BOLD.... YOU'RE REALLY A GOOD PERSON, AREN'T YOU?
HUH?
AHHH!
SH-SHE ESCAPED!
SHE TRICKED ME!!
DAMN!!
AHHH! I DON'T HAVE MUCH TIME! LOOKS LIKE I MANAGED TO ESCAPE THE SUPER HERO!
HH...

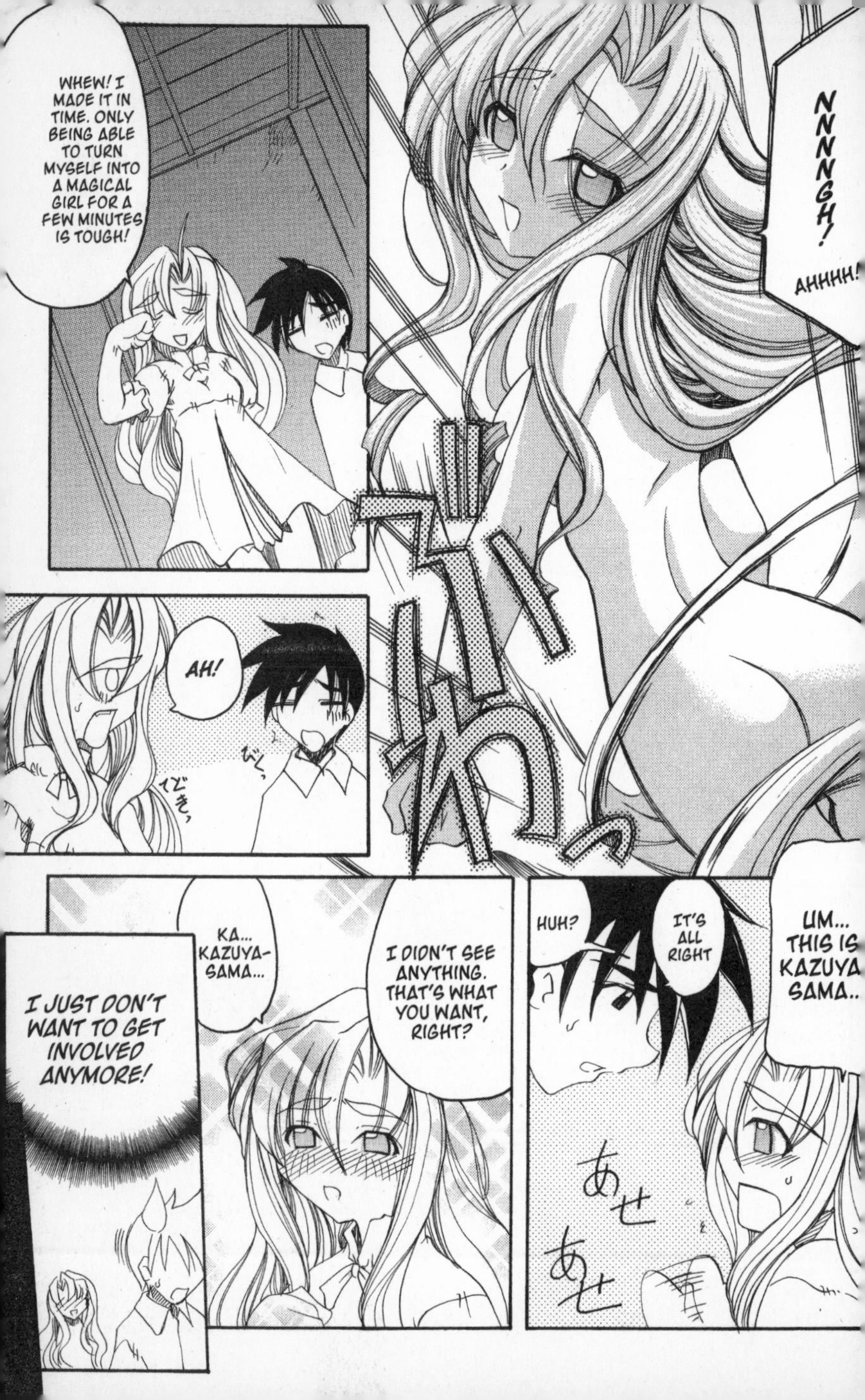
NNNNGH!
AHHHH!
WHEW! I MADE IT IN TIME. ONLY BEING ABLE TO TURN MYSELF INTO A MAGICAL GIRL FOR A FEW MINUTES IS TOUGH!
AH!
UM... THIS IS KAZUYA SAMA..
IT'S ALL RIGHT
HUH?
I DIDN'T SEE ANYTHING. THAT'S WHAT YOU WANT, RIGHT?
KA... KAZUYA-SAMA...
I JUST DON'T WANT TO GET INVOLVED ANYMORE!
あせあせ

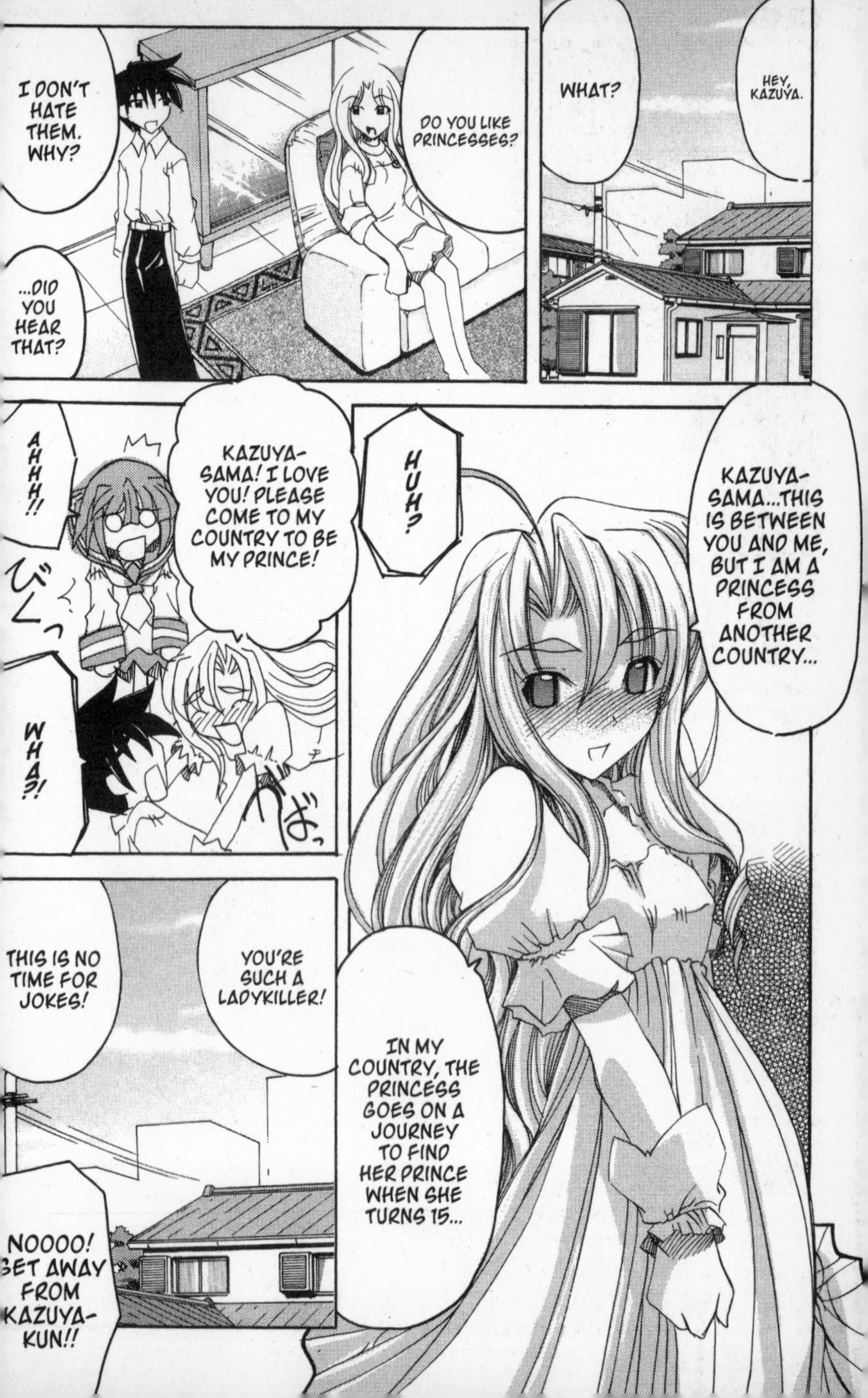
HEY, KAZUYA.
WHAT?
DO YOU LIKE PRINCESSES?
I DON'T HATE THEM. WHY?
...DID YOU HEAR THAT?
KAZUYA-SAMA...THIS IS BETWEEN YOU AND ME, BUT I AM A PRINCESS FROM ANOTHER COUNTRY...
HUH?
IN MY COUNTRY, THE PRINCESS GOES ON A JOURNEY TO FIND HER PRINCE WHEN SHE TURNS 15...
KAZUYA-SAMA! I LOVE YOU! PLEASE COME TO MY COUNTRY TO BE MY PRINCE!
AHHH!!
びくっ
WHA?!
がばっ
YOU'RE SUCH A LADYKILLER!
THIS IS NO TIME FOR JOKES!
NOOOO! GET AWAY FROM KAZUYA-KUN!!

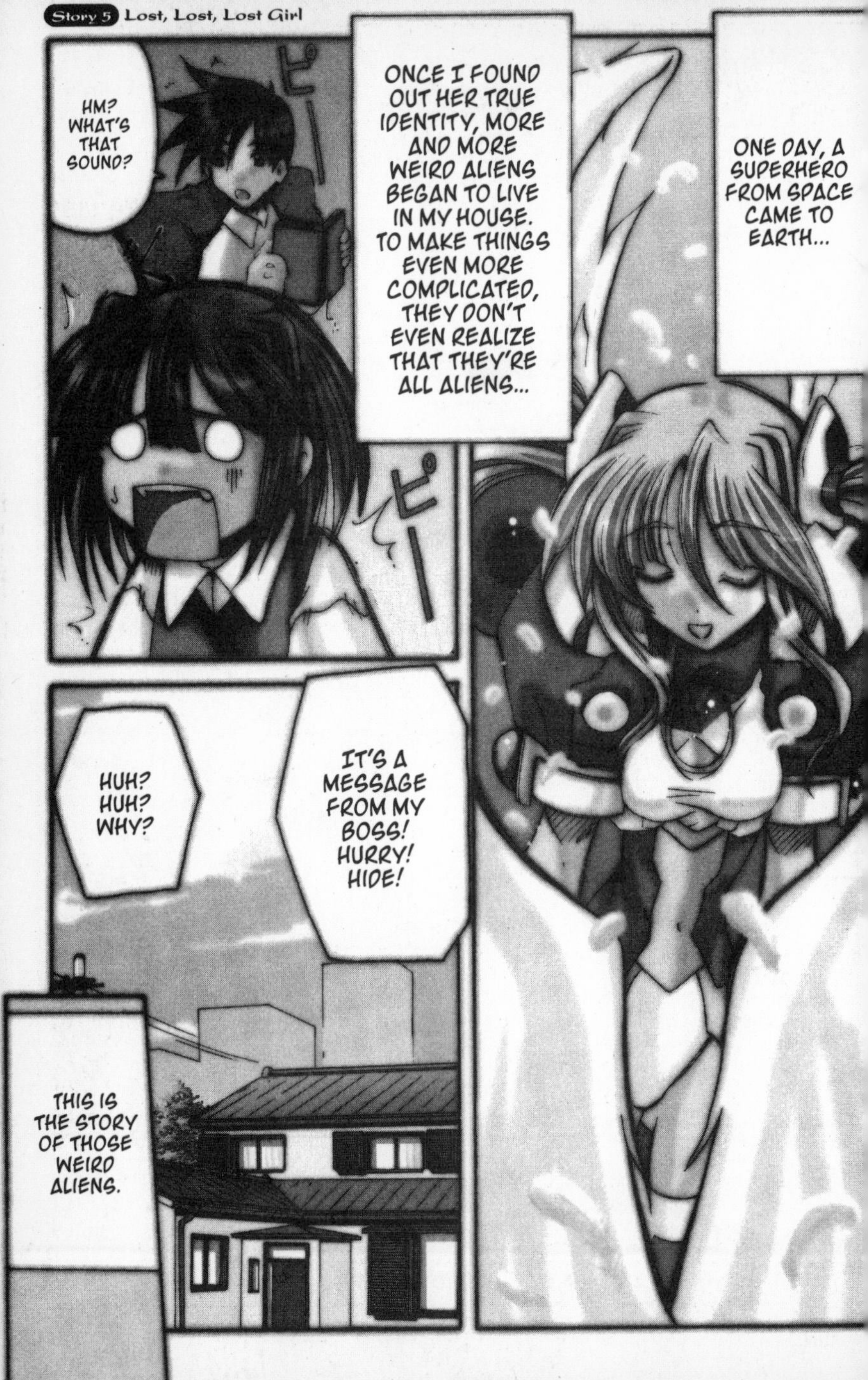
ONE DAY, A SUPERHERO FROM SPACE CAME TO EARTH...
ONCE I FOUND OUT HER TRUE IDENTITY, MORE AND MORE WEIRD ALIENS BEGAN TO LIVE IN MY HOUSE. TO MAKE THINGS EVEN MORE COMPLICATED, THEY DON'T EVEN REALIZE THAT THEY'RE ALL ALIENS...
ピー
HM? WHAT'S THAT SOUND?
ピー
IT'S A MESSAGE FROM MY BOSS! HURRY! HIDE!
HUH? HUH? WHY?
THIS IS THE STORY OF THOSE WEIRD ALIENS.

Story 5

Lost, Lost, Lost Girl

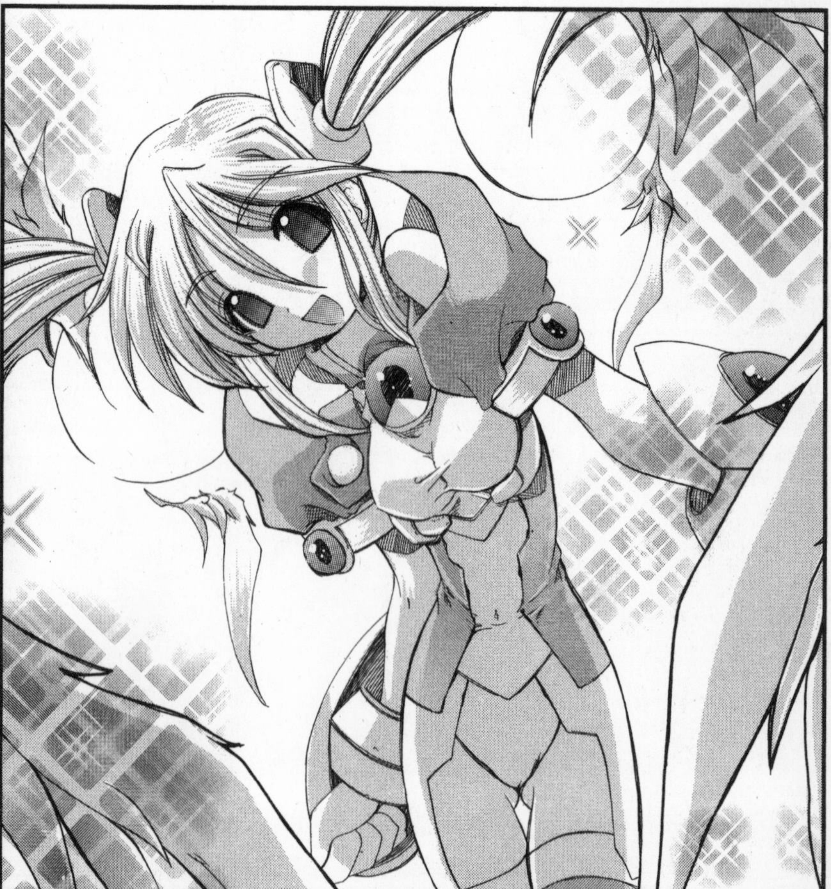

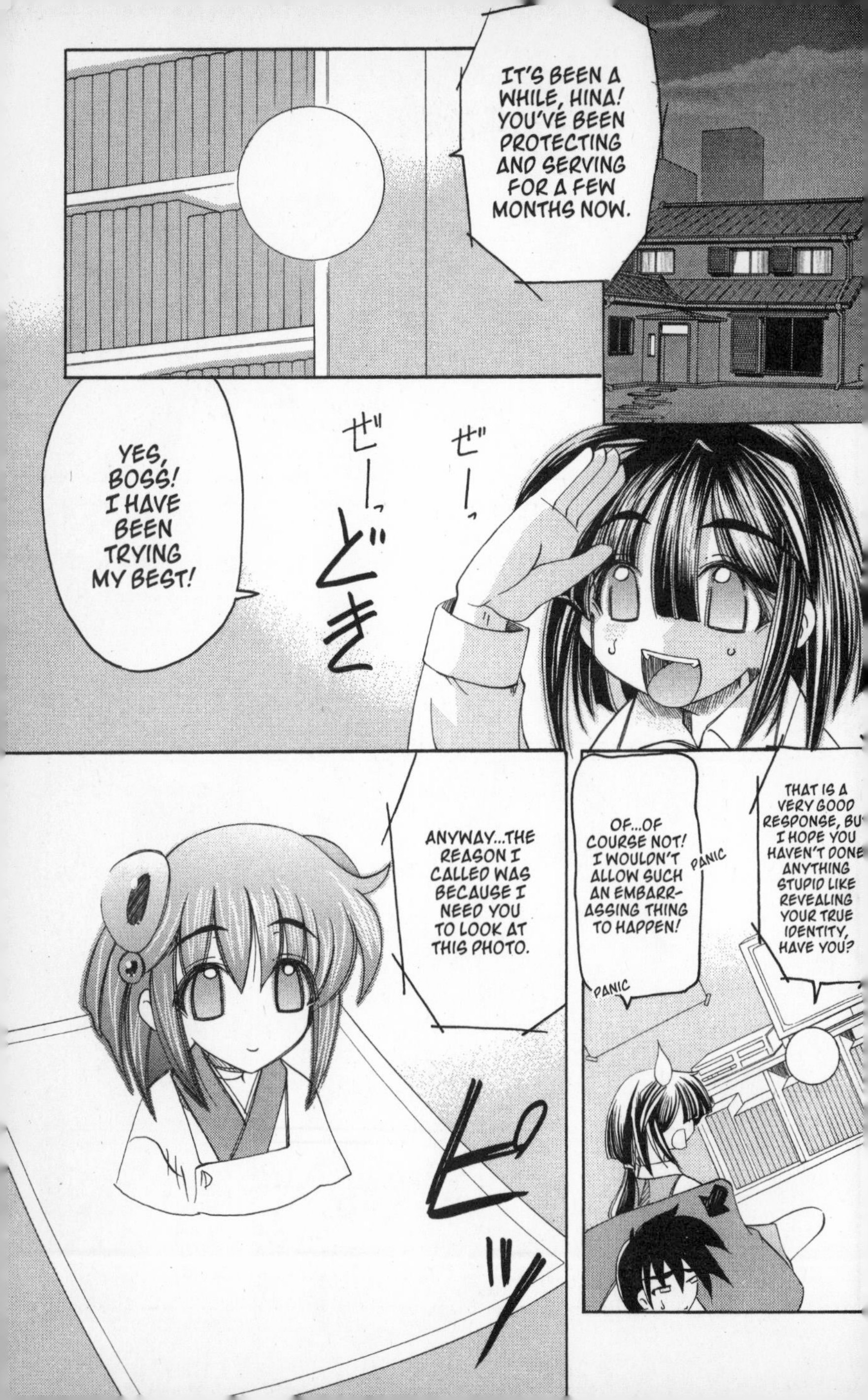
IT'S BEEN A WHILE, HINA! YOU'VE BEEN PROTECTING AND SERVING FOR A FEW MONTHS NOW.
YES, BOSS! I HAVE BEEN TRYING MY BEST!
ぜーっ
ぜーっ
どき
THAT IS A VERY GOOD RESPONSE, BU I HOPE YOU HAVEN'T DONE ANYTHING STUPID LIKE REVEALING YOUR TRUE IDENTITY, HAVE YOU?
OF...OF COURSE NOT! I WOULDN'T ALLOW SUCH AN EMBARR-ASSING THING TO HAPPEN!
PANIC
PANIC
ANYWAY...THE REASON I CALLED WAS BECAUSE I NEED YOU TO LOOK AT THIS PHOTO.
ピッ

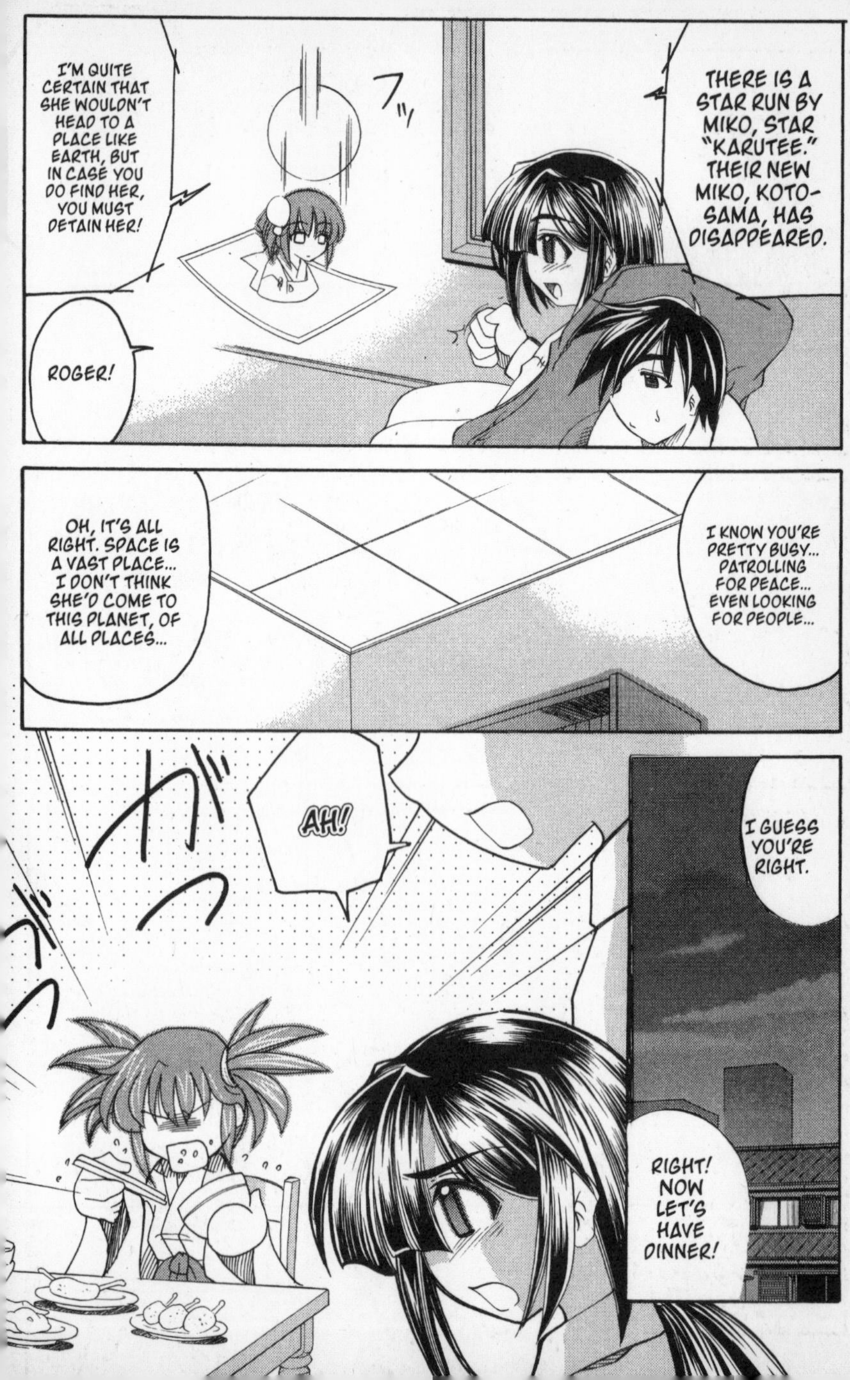
THERE IS A STAR RUN BY MIKO, STAR "KARUTEE." THEIR NEW MIKO, KOTO-SAMA, HAS DISAPPEARED.
I'M QUITE CERTAIN THAT SHE WOULDN'T HEAD TO A PLACE LIKE EARTH, BUT IN CASE YOU DO FIND HER, YOU MUST DETAIN HER!
ROGER!
I KNOW YOU'RE PRETTY BUSY... PATROLLING FOR PEACE... EVEN LOOKING FOR PEOPLE...
OH, IT'S ALL RIGHT. SPACE IS A VAST PLACE... I DON'T THINK SHE'D COME TO THIS PLANET, OF ALL PLACES...
I GUESS YOU'RE RIGHT.
RIGHT! NOW LET'S HAVE DINNER!
AH!

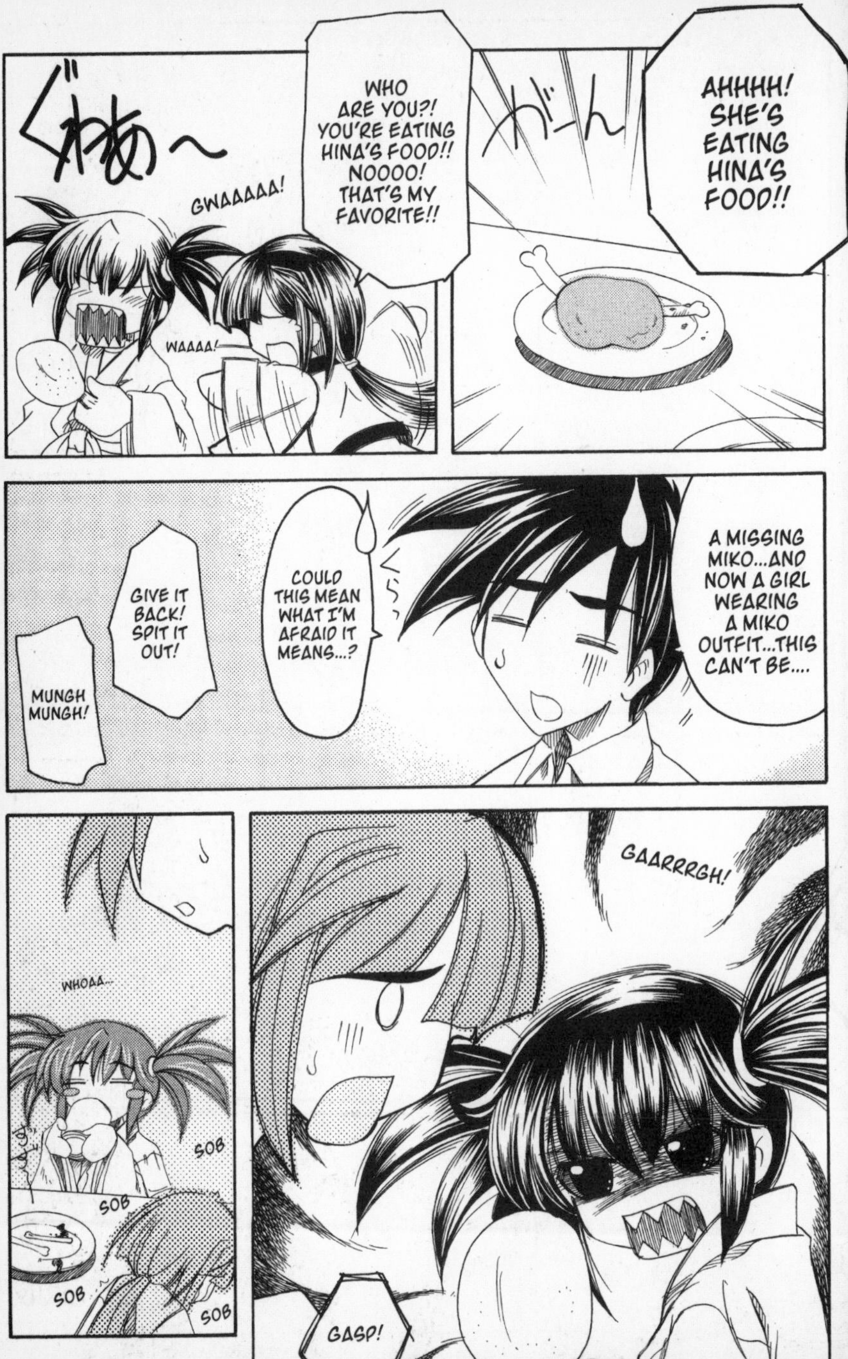
AHHHH! SHE'S EATING HINA'S FOOD!!
がーん
WHO ARE YOU?! YOU'RE EATING HINA'S FOOD!! NOOOO! THAT'S MY FAVORITE!!
ぐわあ～
GWAAAAAA!
WAAAA!
A MISSING MIKO...AND NOW A GIRL WEARING A MIKO OUTFIT...THIS CAN'T BE....
くらっ
COULD THIS MEAN WHAT I'M AFRAID IT MEANS...?
GIVE IT BACK! SPIT IT OUT!
MUNGH MUNGH!
GAARRRGH!
GASP!
WHOAA...
SOB
SOB
SOB
SOB

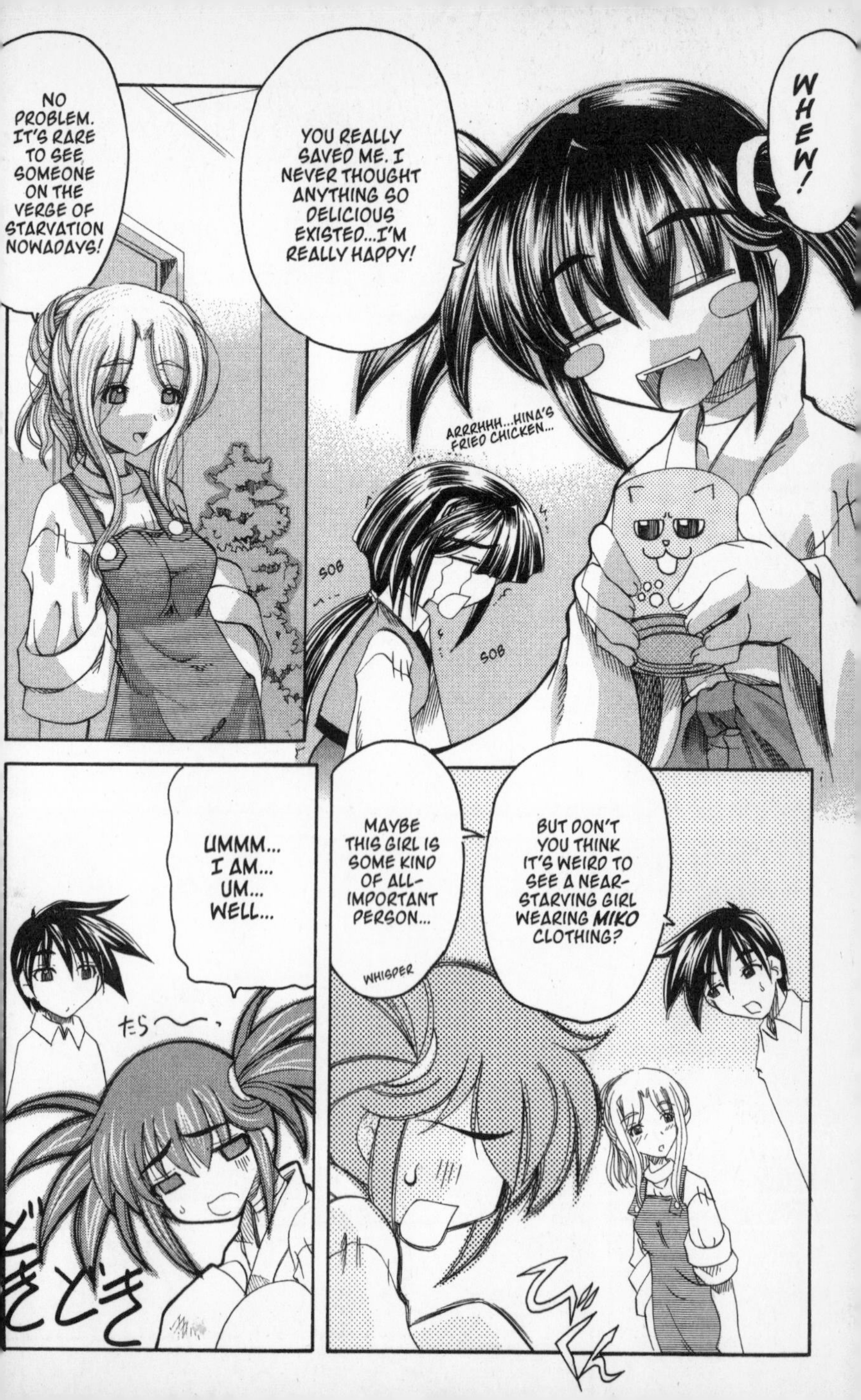
WHEW!
YOU REALLY SAVED ME. I NEVER THOUGHT ANYTHING SO DELICIOUS EXISTED...I'M REALLY HAPPY!
ARRRHHH...HINA'S FRIED CHICKEN...
SOB
SOB
NO PROBLEM. IT'S RARE TO SEE SOMEONE ON THE VERGE OF STARVATION NOWADAYS!
BUT DON'T YOU THINK IT'S WEIRD TO SEE A NEAR-STARVING GIRL WEARING MIKO CLOTHING?
MAYBE THIS GIRL IS SOME KIND OF ALL-IMPORTANT PERSON...
WHISPER
UMMM... I AM... UM... WELL...
たら〜
どきどき

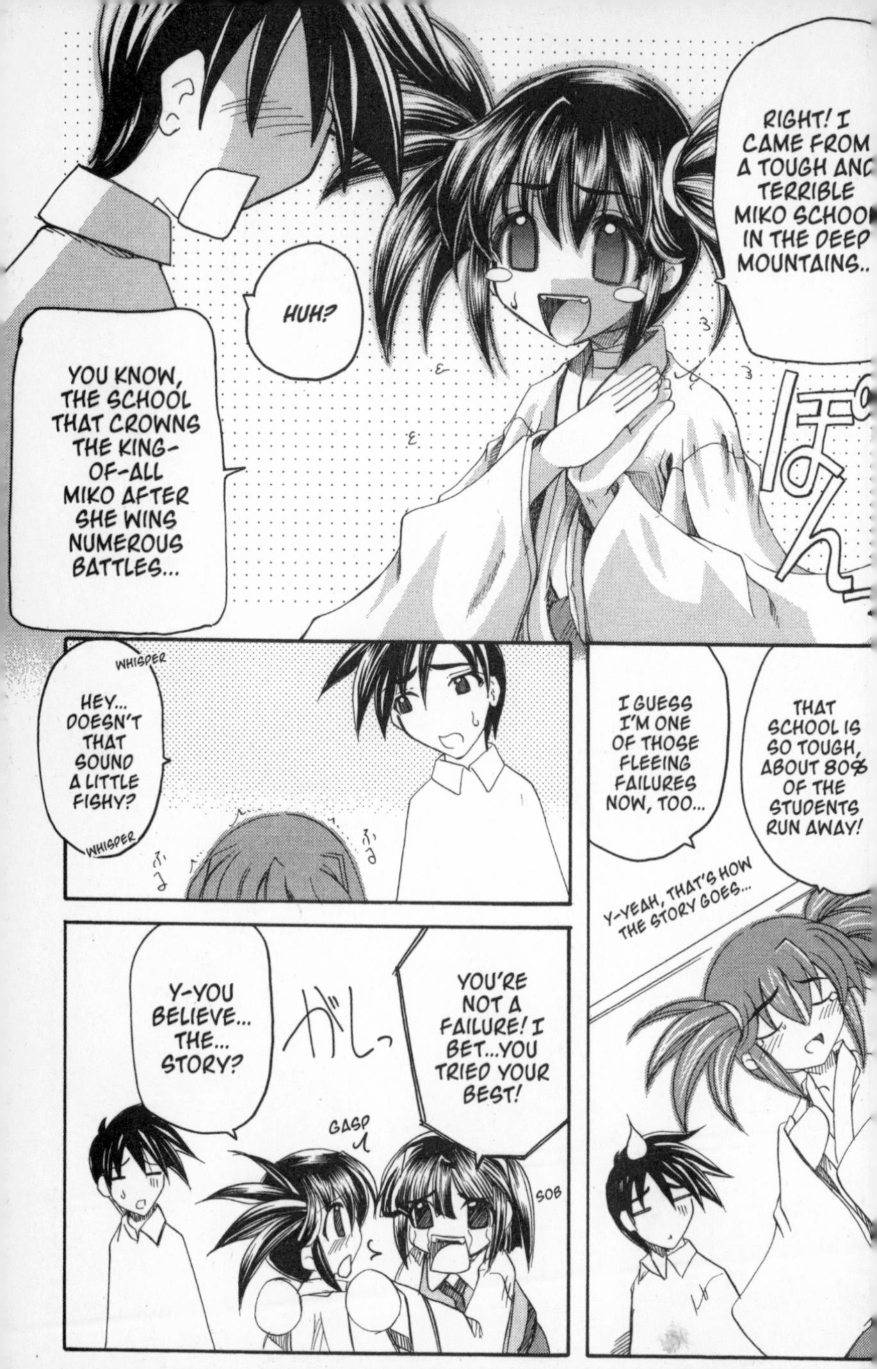
RIGHT! I CAME FROM A TOUGH AND TERRIBLE MIKO SCHOOL IN THE DEEP MOUNTAINS..
ぽん
HUH?
YOU KNOW, THE SCHOOL THAT CROWNS THE KING-OF-ALL MIKO AFTER SHE WINS NUMEROUS BATTLES...
THAT SCHOOL IS SO TOUGH, ABOUT 80% OF THE STUDENTS RUN AWAY!
I GUESS I'M ONE OF THOSE FLEEING FAILURES NOW, TOO...
Y-YEAH, THAT'S HOW THE STORY GOES...
WHISPER
HEY... DOESN'T THAT SOUND A LITTLE FISHY?
WHISPER
YOU'RE NOT A FAILURE! I BET...YOU TRIED YOUR BEST!
がしっ
Y-YOU BELIEVE... THE... STORY?
GASP
SOB

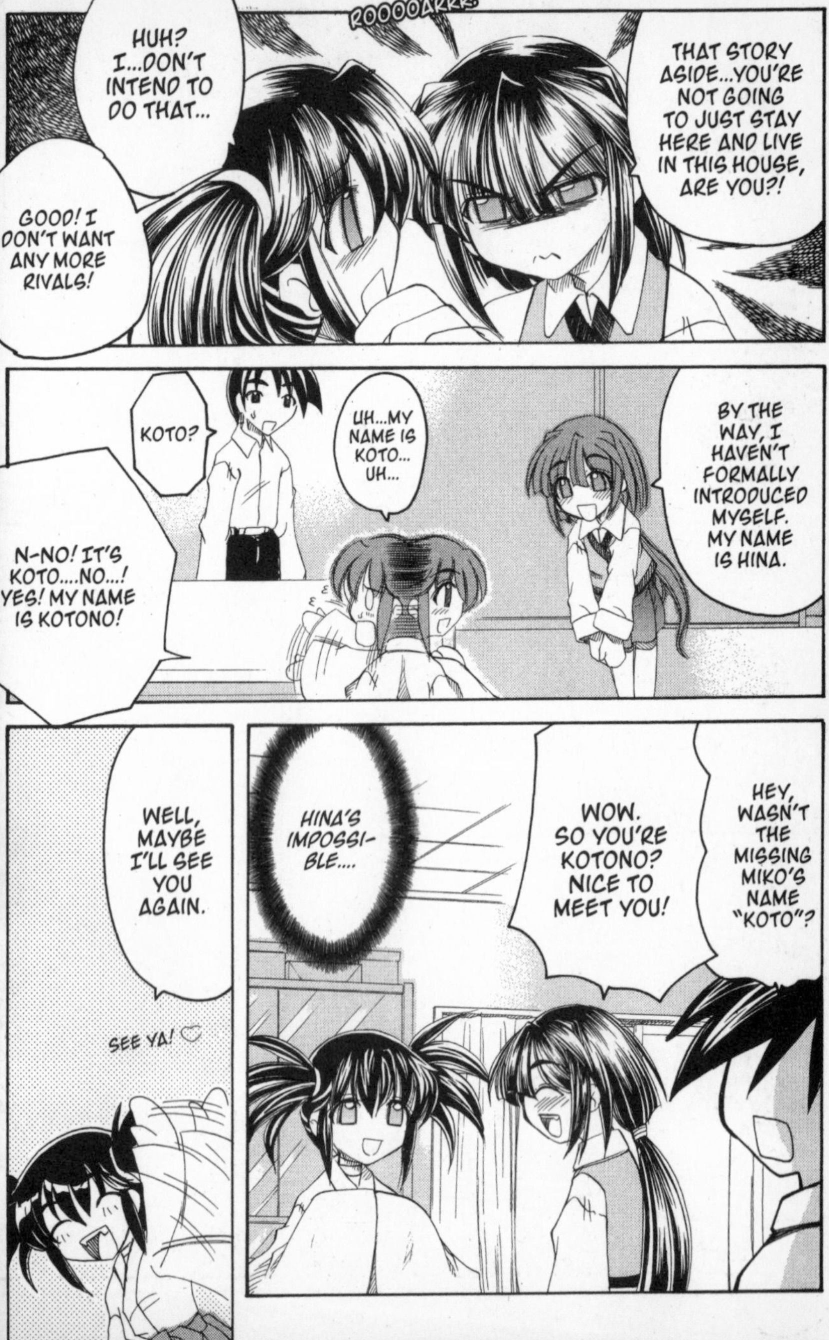
ROOOOARRR!
THAT STORY ASIDE...YOU'RE NOT GOING TO JUST STAY HERE AND LIVE IN THIS HOUSE, ARE YOU?!
HUH? I...DON'T INTEND TO DO THAT...
GOOD! I DON'T WANT ANY MORE RIVALS!
BY THE WAY, I HAVEN'T FORMALLY INTRODUCED MYSELF. MY NAME IS HINA.
UH...MY NAME IS KOTO... UH...
KOTO?
N-NO! IT'S KOTO....NO...! YES! MY NAME IS KOTONO!
HEY, WASN'T THE MISSING MIKO'S NAME "KOTO"?
WOW. SO YOU'RE KOTONO? NICE TO MEET YOU!
HINA'S IMPOSSIBLE....
WELL, MAYBE I'LL SEE YOU AGAIN.
SEE YA! ♡

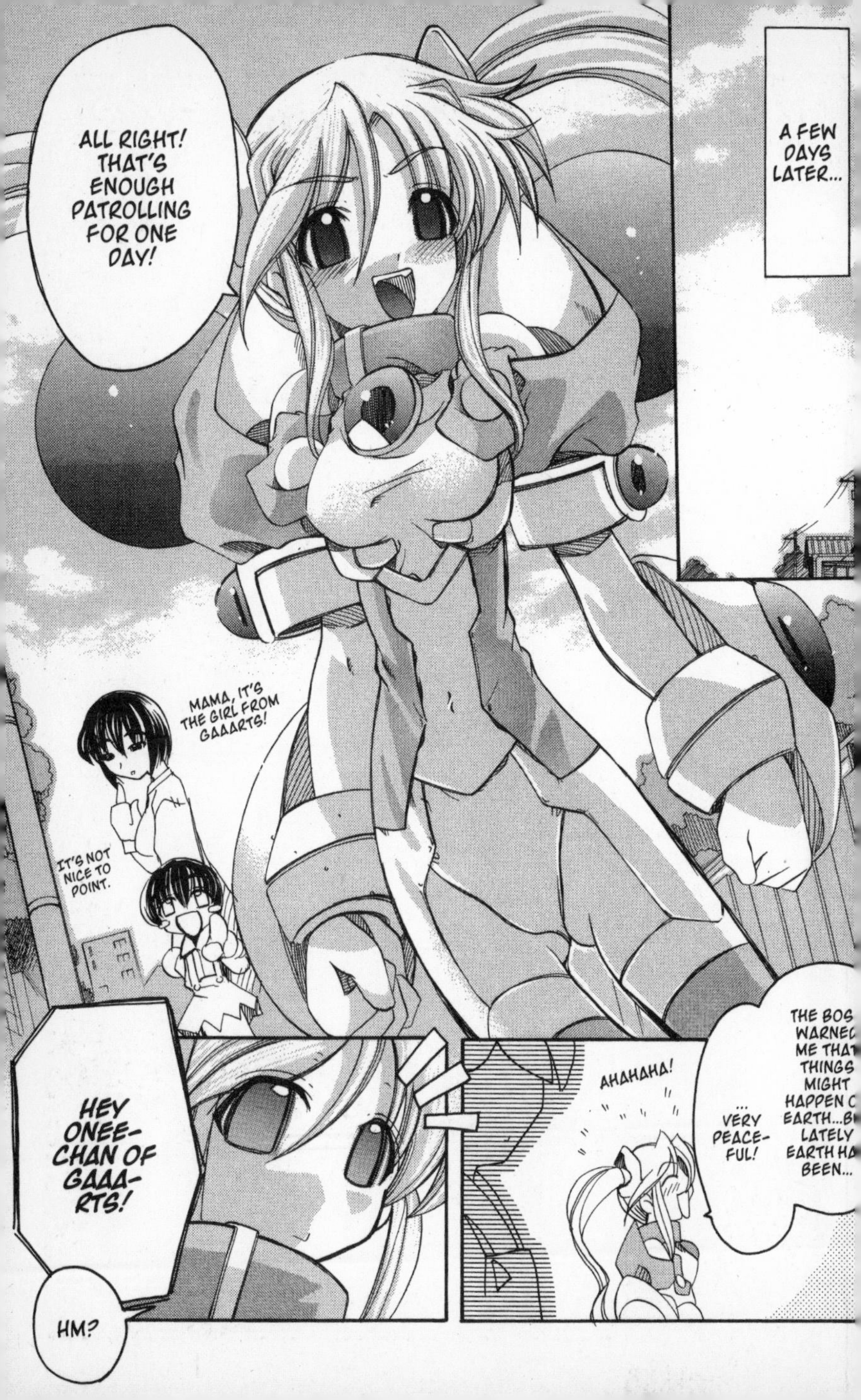
A FEW DAYS LATER...
ALL RIGHT! THAT'S ENOUGH PATROLLING FOR ONE DAY!
MAMA, IT'S THE GIRL FROM GAAARTS!
IT'S NOT NICE TO POINT.
THE BOS WARNED ME THAT THINGS MIGHT HAPPEN O EARTH...B LATELY EARTH HA BEEN...
... VERY PEACE-FUL!
AHAHAHA!
HEY ONEE-CHAN OF GAAA-RTS!
HM?

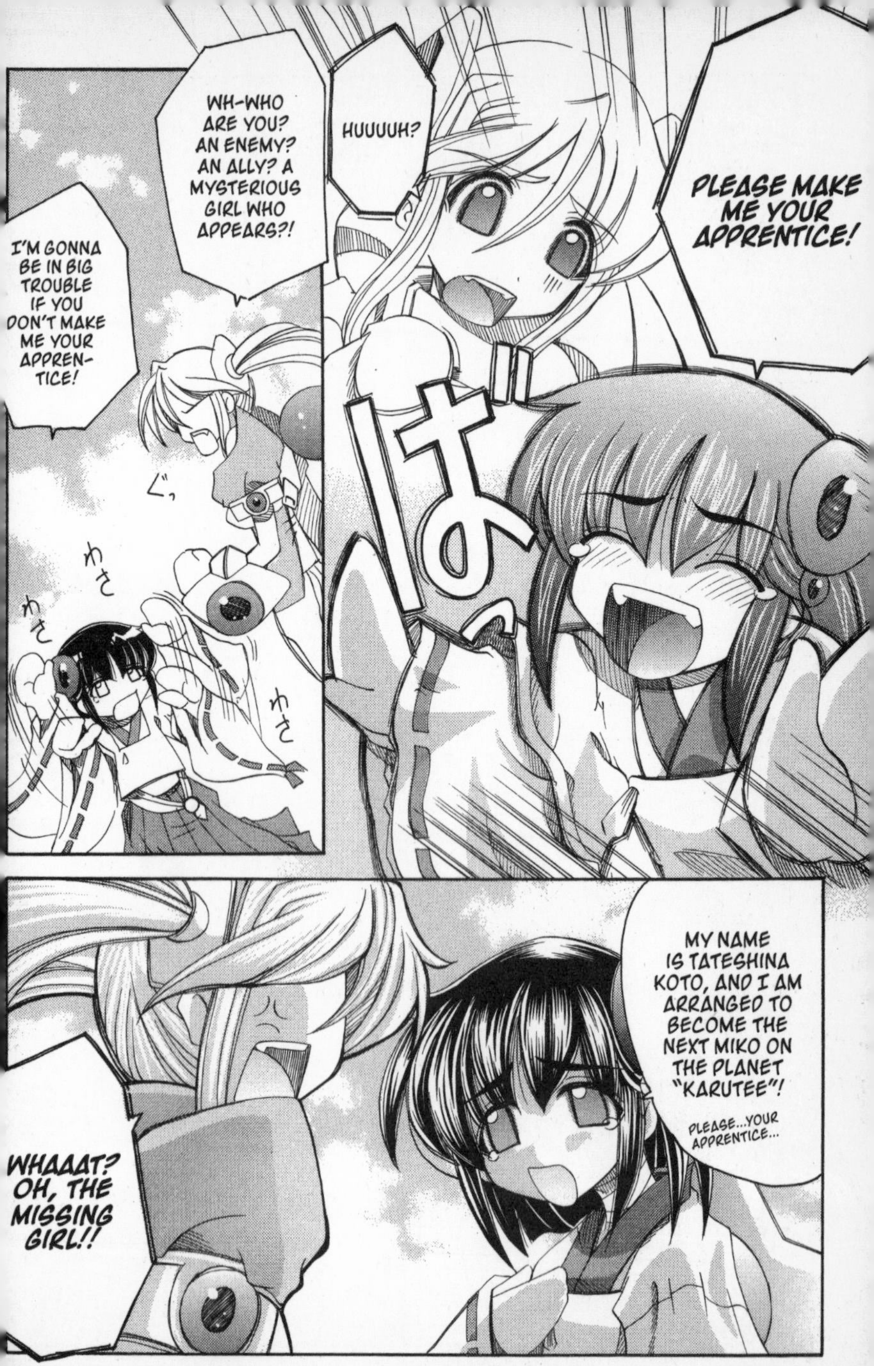

PLEASE MAKE ME YOUR APPRENTICE!
HUUUUH?
ぱっ
WH-WHO ARE YOU? AN ENEMY? AN ALLY? A MYSTERIOUS GIRL WHO APPEARS?!
I'M GONNA BE IN BIG TROUBLE IF YOU DON'T MAKE ME YOUR APPREN-TICE!
ぐっ
わさ
わさ
わさ
MY NAME IS TATESHINA KOTO, AND I AM ARRANGED TO BECOME THE NEXT MIKO ON THE PLANET "KARUTEE"!
PLEASE...YOUR APPRENTICE...
WHAAAT? OH, THE MISSING GIRL!!

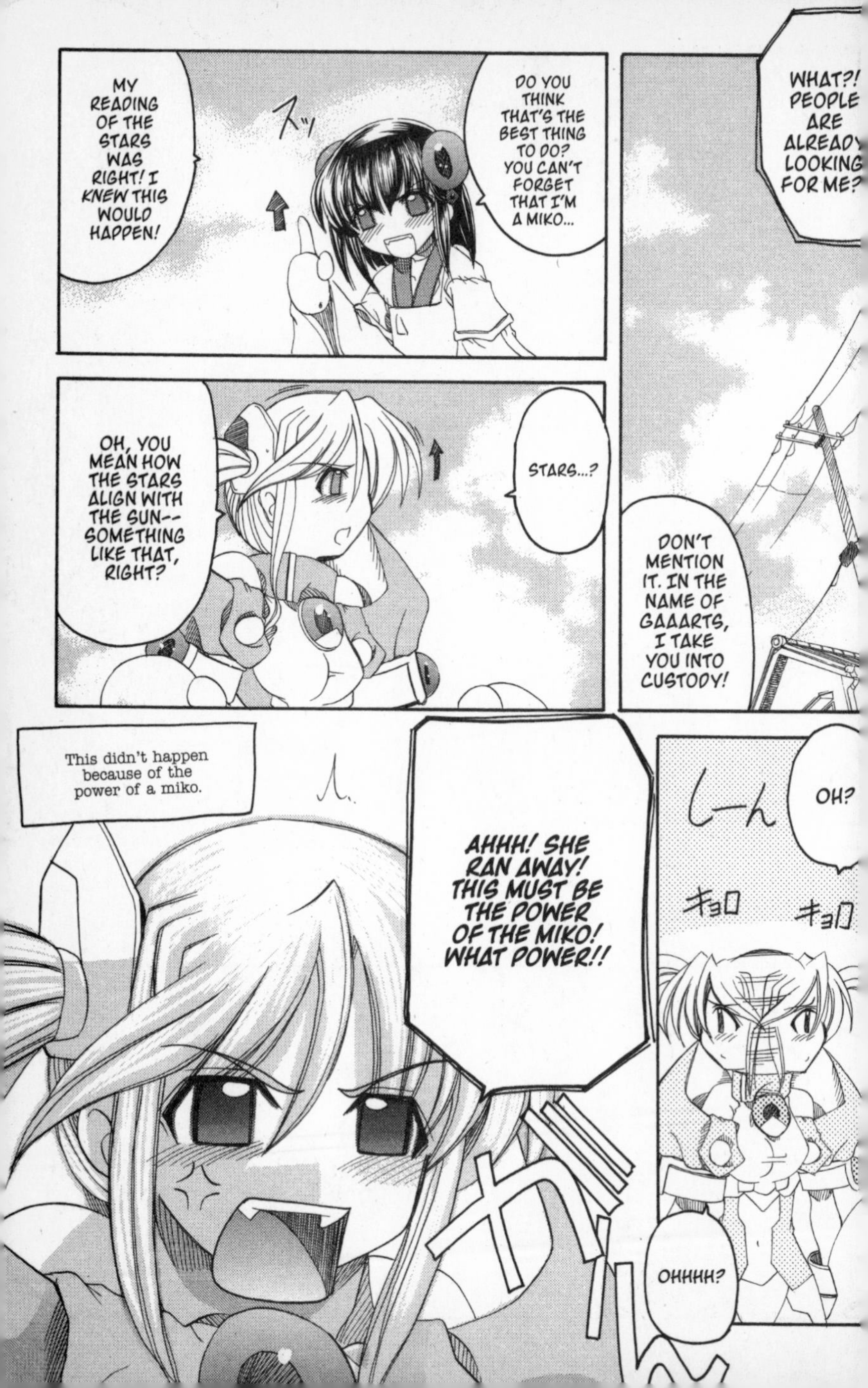
WHAT?! PEOPLE ARE ALREADY LOOKING FOR ME?
DON'T MENTION IT. IN THE NAME OF GAAARTS, I TAKE YOU INTO CUSTODY!
DO YOU THINK THAT'S THE BEST THING TO DO? YOU CAN'T FORGET THAT I'M A MIKO...
ズッ
MY READING OF THE STARS WAS RIGHT! I KNEW THIS WOULD HAPPEN!
STARS...?
OH, YOU MEAN HOW THE STARS ALIGN WITH THE SUN--SOMETHING LIKE THAT, RIGHT?
OH?
しーん
キョロ
キョロ
OHHHH?
AHHH! SHE RAN AWAY! THIS MUST BE THE POWER OF THE MIKO! WHAT POWER!!
This didn't happen because of the power of a miko.

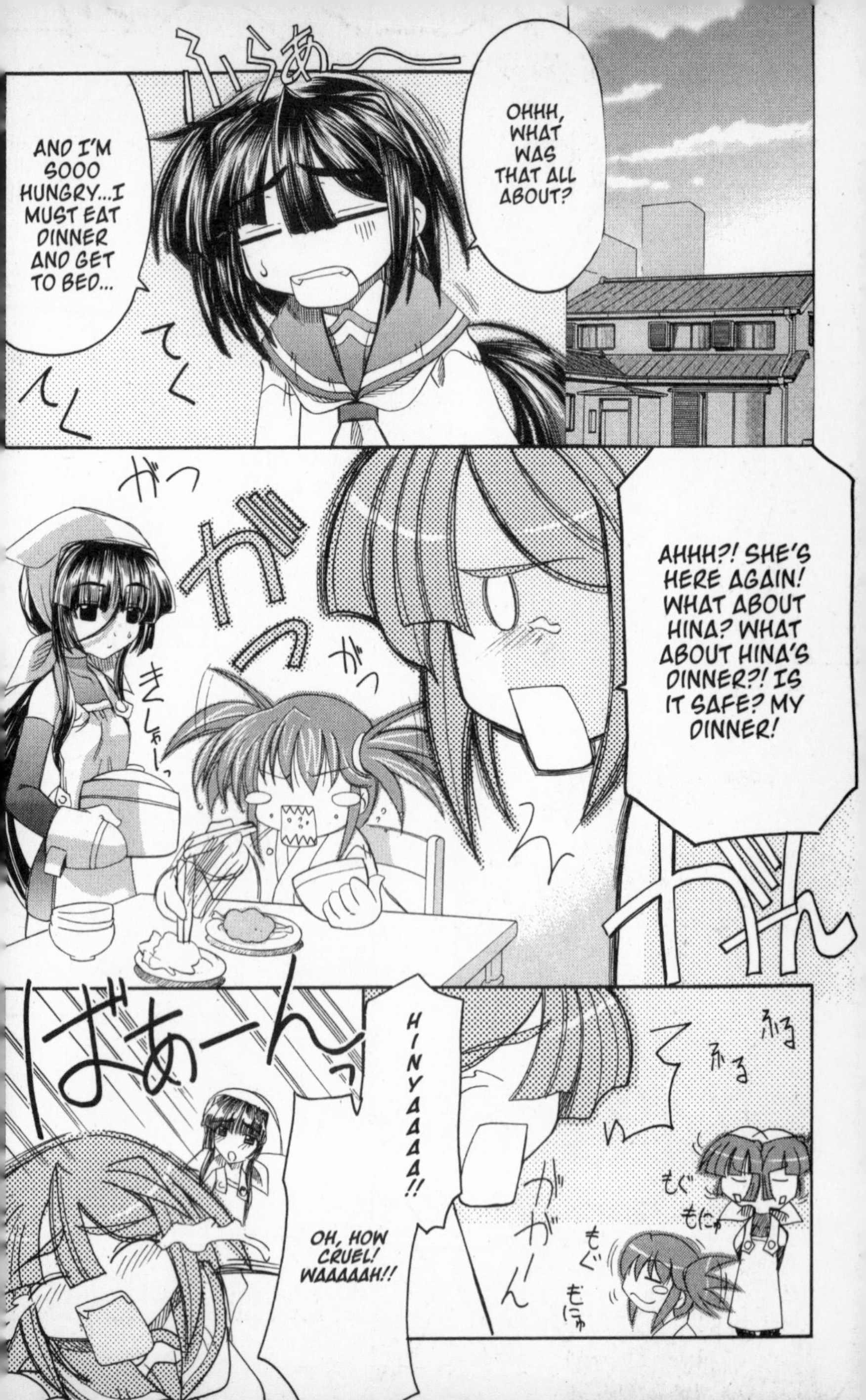
ふらあ〜
OHHH, WHAT WAS THAT ALL ABOUT?
AND I'M SOOO HUNGRY...I MUST EAT DINNER AND GET TO BED...
てくてく
AHHH?! SHE'S HERE AGAIN! WHAT ABOUT HINA? WHAT ABOUT HINA'S DINNER?! IS IT SAFE? MY DINNER!
わぁん
がつがつ
がつ
ぷるぷる
もぐもにゅ
もぐもにゅ
がーん
HINYAAAAA!!
OH, HOW CRUEL! WAAAAAH!!
ばあーんっ

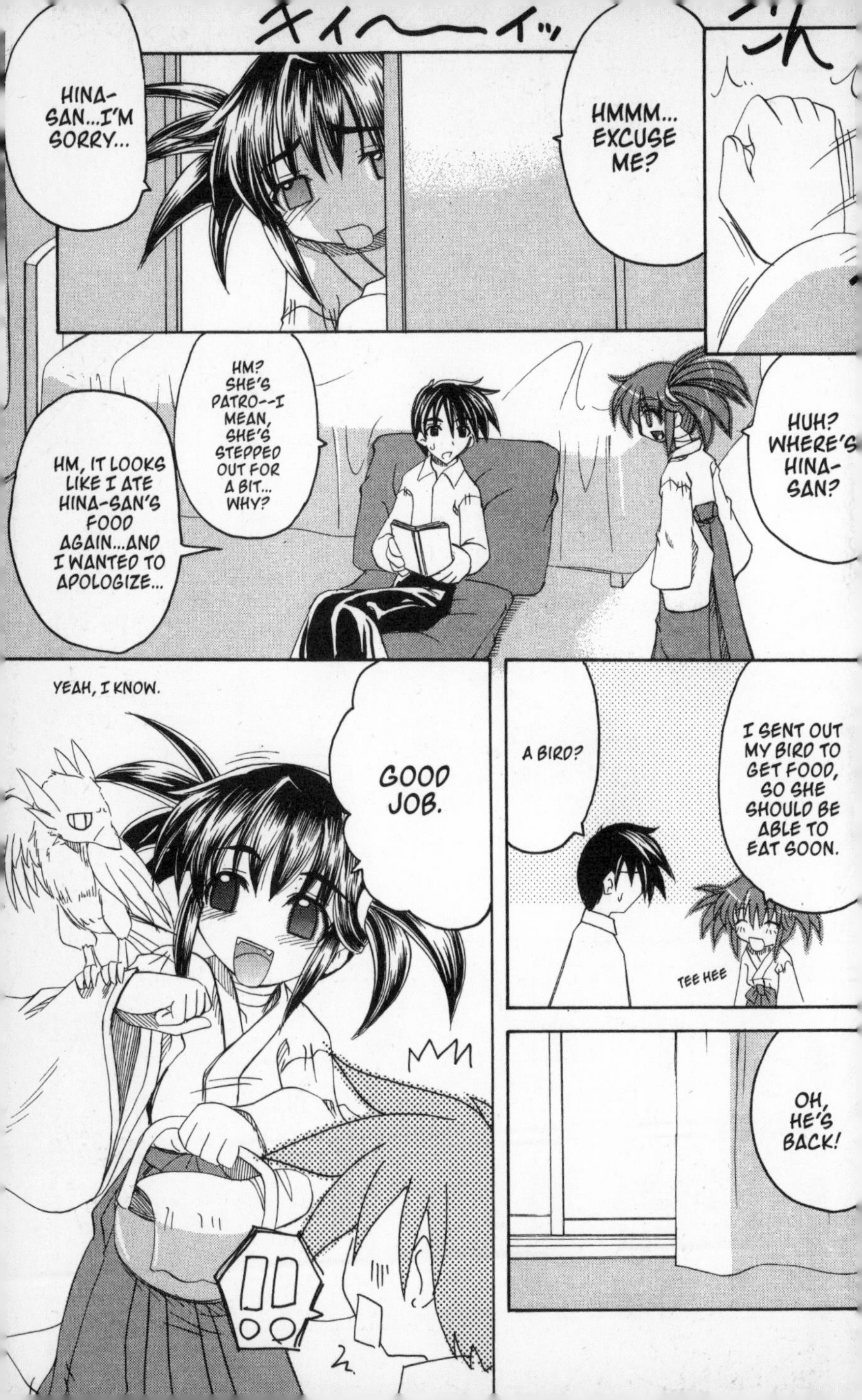
こん
HMMM... EXCUSE ME?
キィ〜〜イッ
HINA-SAN...I'M SORRY...
HUH? WHERE'S HINA-SAN?
HM? SHE'S PATRO--I MEAN, SHE'S STEPPED OUT FOR A BIT... WHY?
HM, IT LOOKS LIKE I ATE HINA-SAN'S FOOD AGAIN...AND I WANTED TO APOLOGIZE...
I SENT OUT MY BIRD TO GET FOOD, SO SHE SHOULD BE ABLE TO EAT SOON.
A BIRD?
TEE HEE
OH, HE'S BACK!
GOOD JOB.
YEAH, I KNOW.
!!

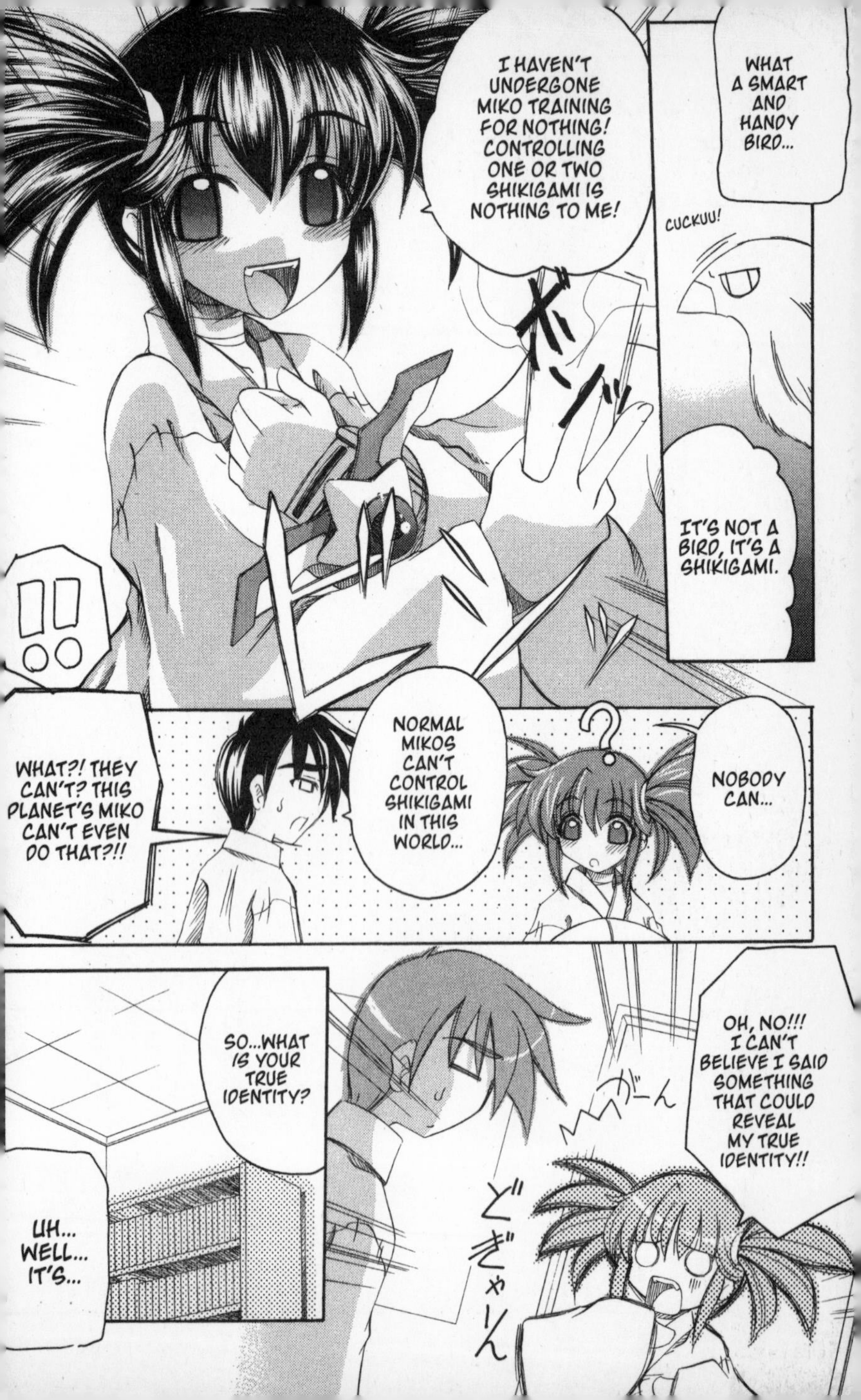

WHAT A SMART AND HANDY BIRD...
CUCKUU!
IT'S NOT A BIRD, IT'S A SHIKIGAMI.
I HAVEN'T UNDERGONE MIKO TRAINING FOR NOTHING! CONTROLLING ONE OR TWO SHIKIGAMI IS NOTHING TO ME!
ボンッ
!!
NOBODY CAN...
NORMAL MIKOS CAN'T CONTROL SHIKIGAMI IN THIS WORLD...
WHAT?! THEY CAN'T? THIS PLANET'S MIKO CAN'T EVEN DO THAT?!!
OH, NO!!! I CAN'T BELIEVE I SAID SOMETHING THAT COULD REVEAL MY TRUE IDENTITY!!
がーん
どぎゃーん
SO...WHAT IS YOUR TRUE IDENTITY?
UH... WELL... IT'S...

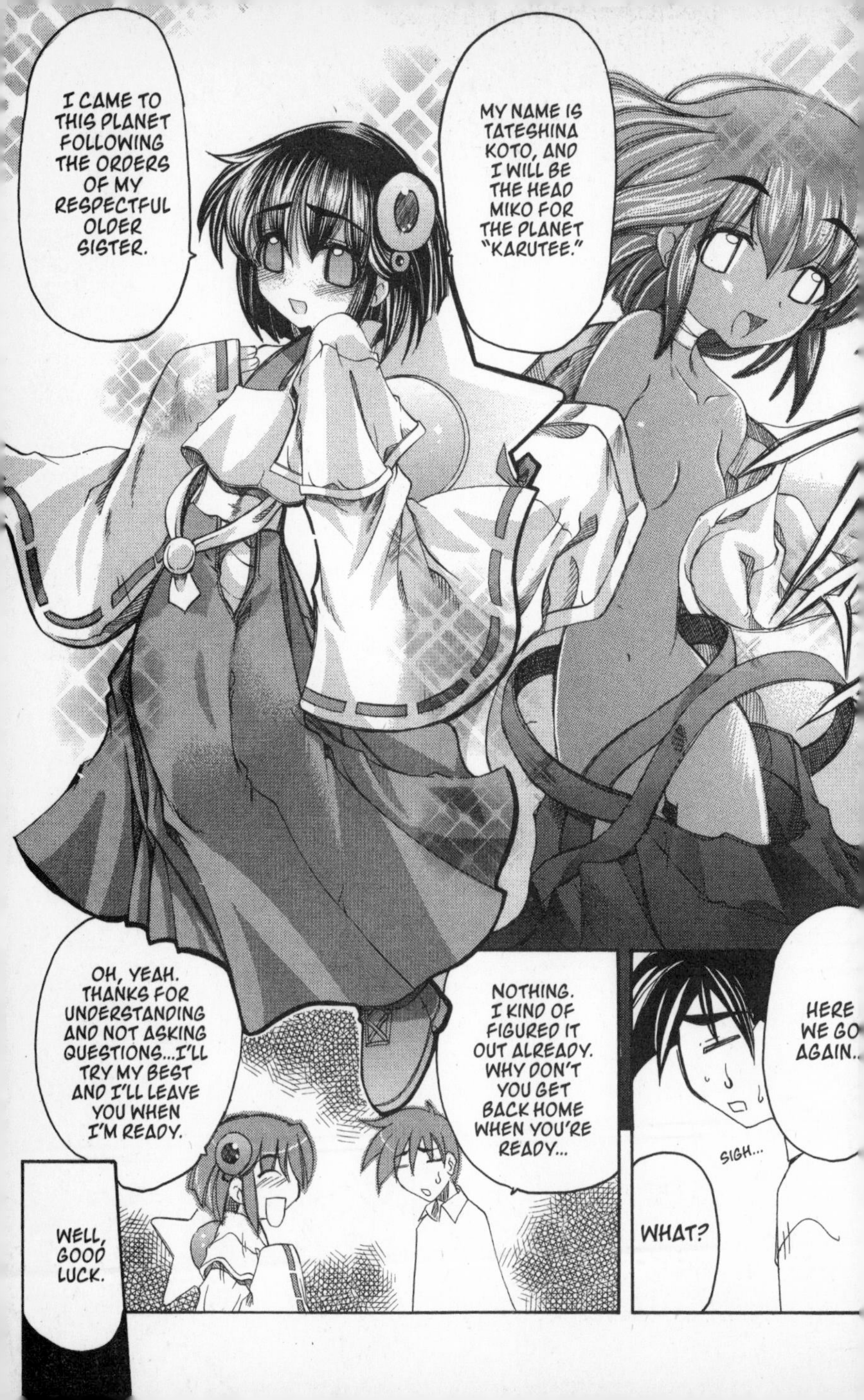
MY NAME IS TATESHINA KOTO, AND I WILL BE THE HEAD MIKO FOR THE PLANET "KARUTEE."
I CAME TO THIS PLANET FOLLOWING THE ORDERS OF MY RESPECTFUL OLDER SISTER.
HERE WE GO AGAIN...
SIGH...
WHAT?
NOTHING. I KIND OF FIGURED IT OUT ALREADY. WHY DON'T YOU GET BACK HOME WHEN YOU'RE READY...
OH, YEAH. THANKS FOR UNDERSTANDING AND NOT ASKING QUESTIONS...I'LL TRY MY BEST AND I'LL LEAVE YOU WHEN I'M READY.
WELL, GOOD LUCK.

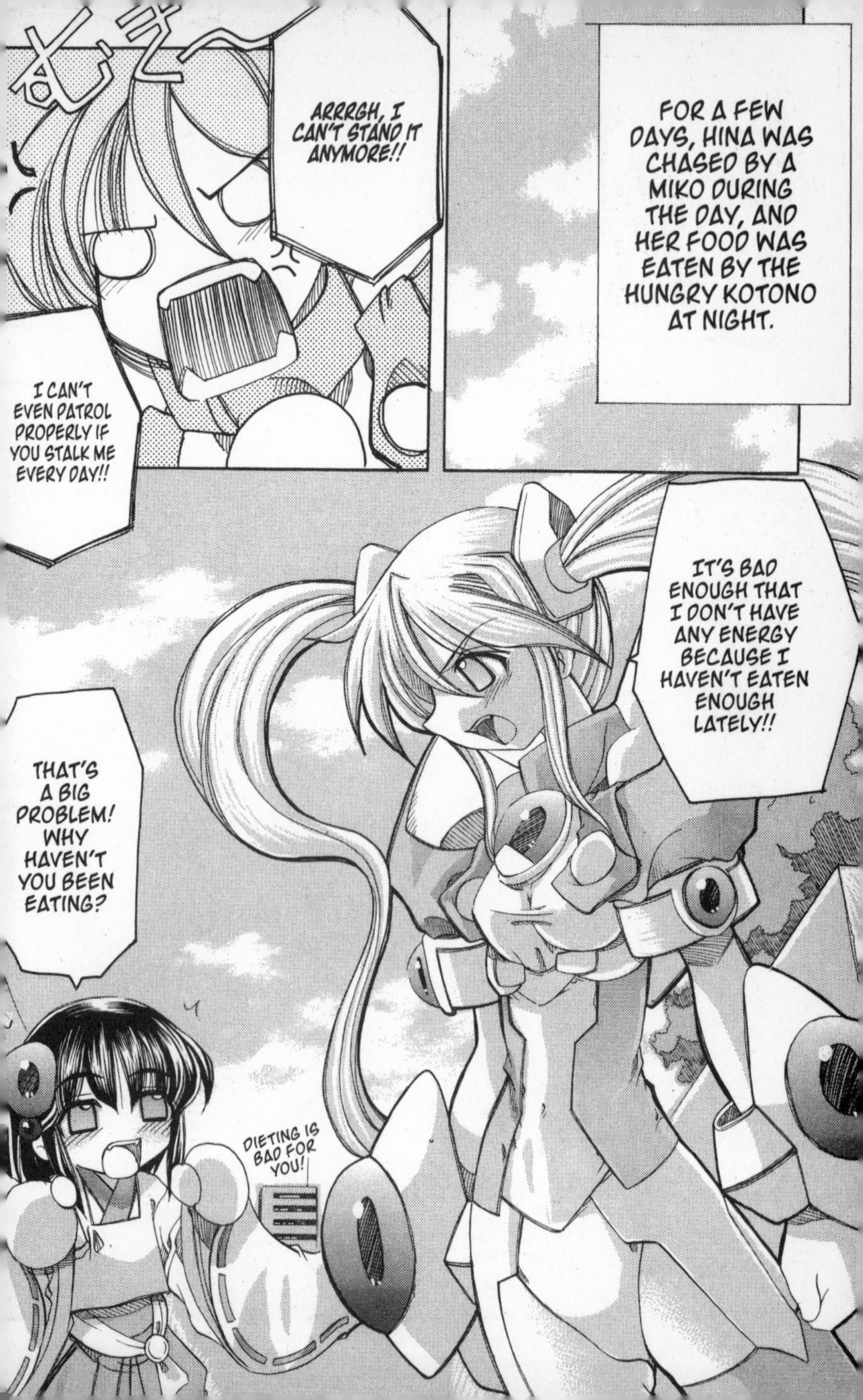
FOR A FEW DAYS, HINA WAS CHASED BY A MIKO DURING THE DAY, AND HER FOOD WAS EATEN BY THE HUNGRY KOTONO AT NIGHT.
ARRRGH, I CAN'T STAND IT ANYMORE!!
I CAN'T EVEN PATROL PROPERLY IF YOU STALK ME EVERY DAY!!
IT'S BAD ENOUGH THAT I DON'T HAVE ANY ENERGY BECAUSE I HAVEN'T EATEN ENOUGH LATELY!!
THAT'S A BIG PROBLEM! WHY HAVEN'T YOU BEEN EATING?
DIETING IS BAD FOR YOU!

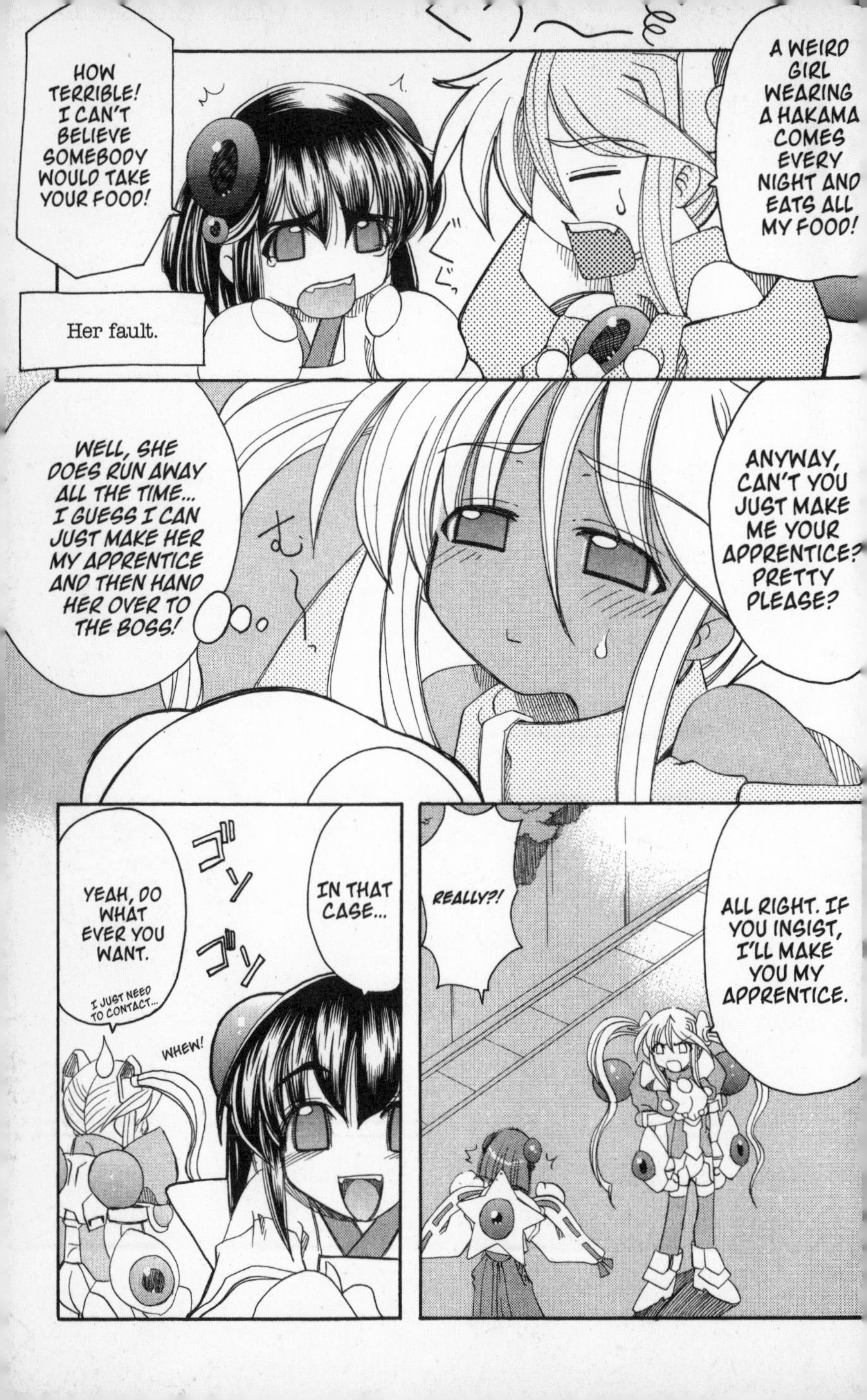
A WEIRD GIRL WEARING A HAKAMA COMES EVERY NIGHT AND EATS ALL MY FOOD!
HOW TERRIBLE! I CAN'T BELIEVE SOMEBODY WOULD TAKE YOUR FOOD!
Her fault.
ANYWAY, CAN'T YOU JUST MAKE ME YOUR APPRENTICE? PRETTY PLEASE?
WELL, SHE DOES RUN AWAY ALL THE TIME... I GUESS I CAN JUST MAKE HER MY APPRENTICE AND THEN HAND HER OVER TO THE BOSS!
ALL RIGHT. IF YOU INSIST, I'LL MAKE YOU MY APPRENTICE.
REALLY?!
IN THAT CASE...
YEAH, DO WHAT EVER YOU WANT.
I JUST NEED TO CONTACT...
WHEW!

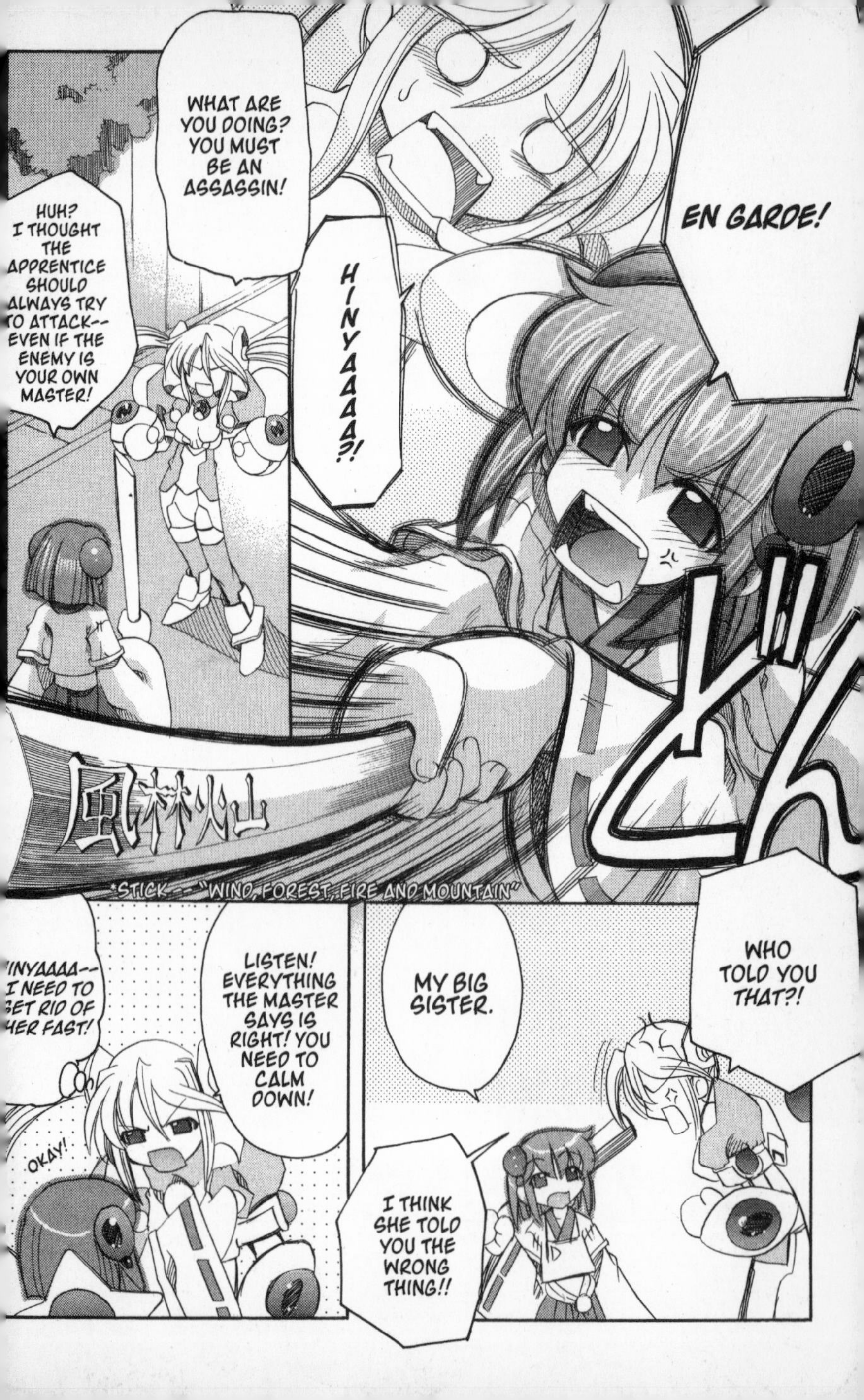
EN GARDE!
WHAT ARE YOU DOING? YOU MUST BE AN ASSASSIN!
HINYAAAAA?!
HUH? I THOUGHT THE APPRENTICE SHOULD ALWAYS TRY TO ATTACK--EVEN IF THE ENEMY IS YOUR OWN MASTER!
風林火山
*STICK -- "WIND, FOREST, FIRE AND MOUNTAIN"
WHO TOLD YOU THAT?!
MY BIG SISTER.
I THINK SHE TOLD YOU THE WRONG THING!!
LISTEN! EVERYTHING THE MASTER SAYS IS RIGHT! YOU NEED TO CALM DOWN!
INYAAAA-- I NEED TO ET RID OF HER FAST!
OKAY!

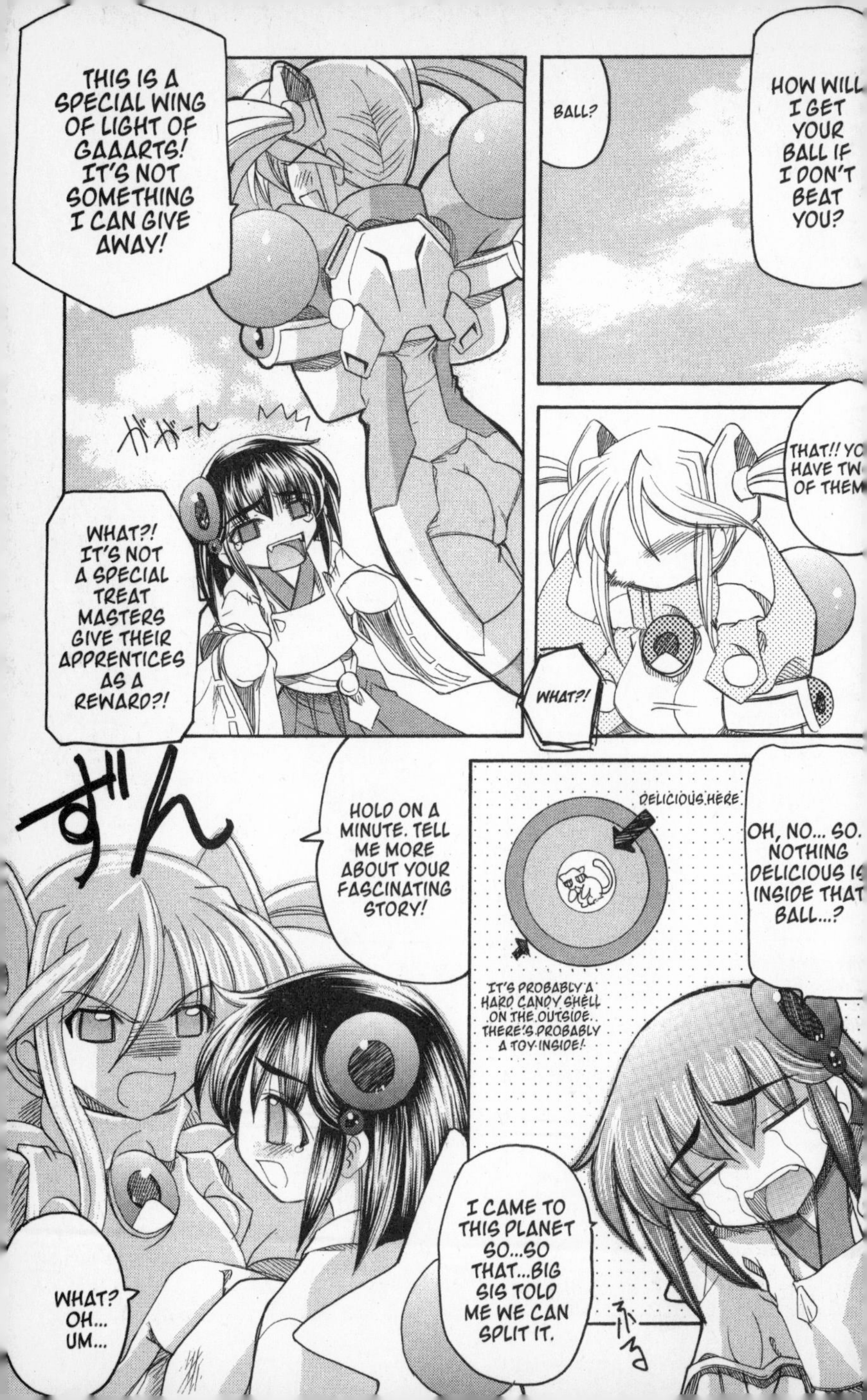
HOW WILL I GET YOUR BALL IF I DON'T BEAT YOU?
BALL?
THAT!! YO HAVE TW OF THEM
WHAT?!
THIS IS A SPECIAL WING OF LIGHT OF GAAARTS! IT'S NOT SOMETHING I CAN GIVE AWAY!
ががーん
WHAT?! IT'S NOT A SPECIAL TREAT MASTERS GIVE THEIR APPRENTICES AS A REWARD?!
OH, NO... SO. NOTHING DELICIOUS IS INSIDE THAT BALL...?
DELICIOUS HERE
IT'S PROBABLY A HARD CANDY SHELL ON THE OUTSIDE. THERE'S PROBABLY A TOY INSIDE!
I CAME TO THIS PLANET SO...SO THAT...BIG SIS TOLD ME WE CAN SPLIT IT.
ずん
HOLD ON A MINUTE. TELL ME MORE ABOUT YOUR FASCINATING STORY!
WHAT? OH... UM...

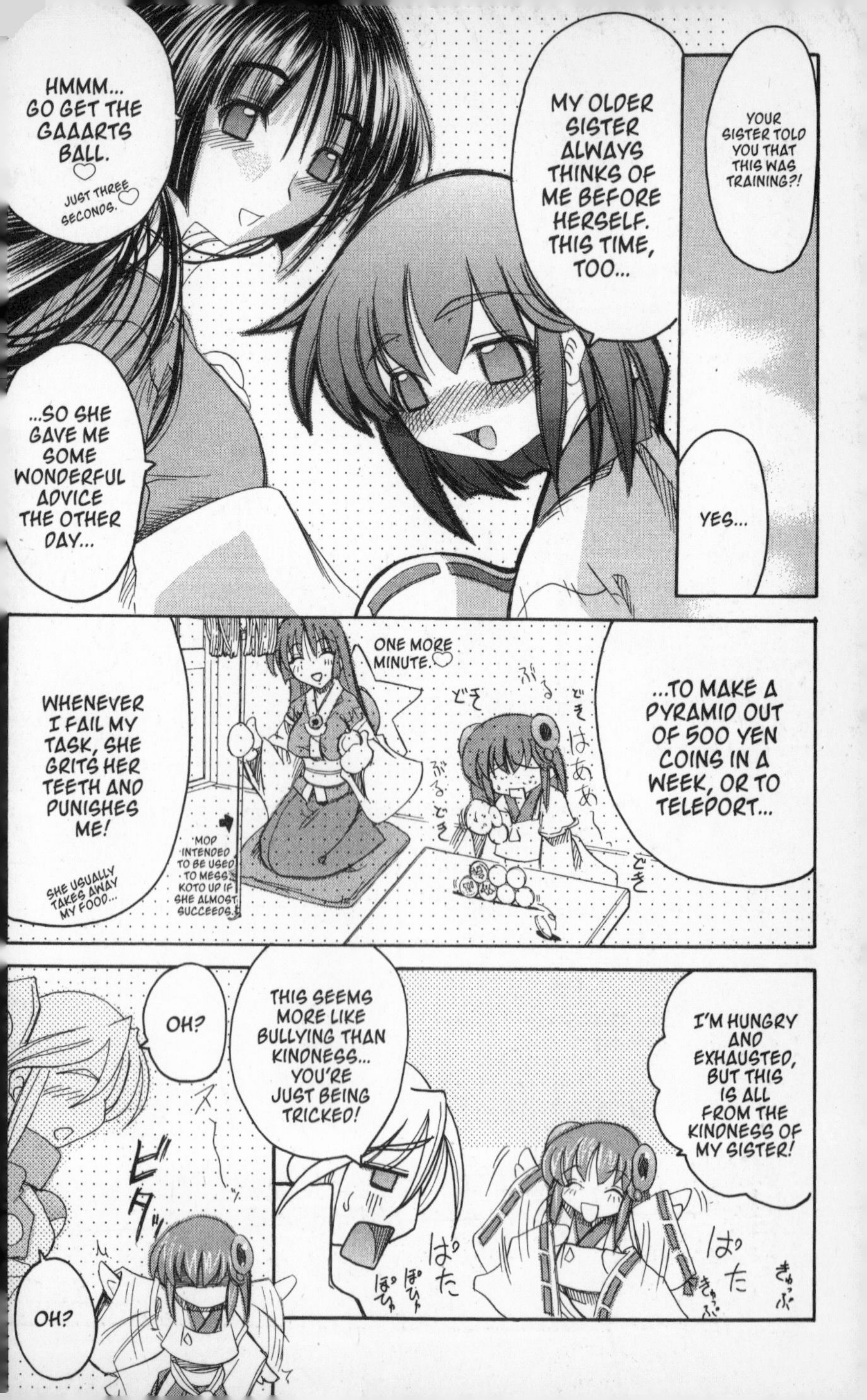
YOUR SISTER TOLD YOU THAT THIS WAS TRAINING?!
YES...
MY OLDER SISTER ALWAYS THINKS OF ME BEFORE HERSELF. THIS TIME, TOO...
HMMM... GO GET THE GAAARTS BALL. ♡
JUST THREE SECONDS. ♡
...SO SHE GAVE ME SOME WONDERFUL ADVICE THE OTHER DAY...
...TO MAKE A PYRAMID OUT OF 500 YEN COINS IN A WEEK, OR TO TELEPORT...
ONE MORE MINUTE. ♡
WHENEVER I FAIL MY TASK, SHE GRITS HER TEETH AND PUNISHES ME!
MOP INTENDED TO BE USED TO MESS KOTO UP IF SHE ALMOST SUCCEEDS.
SHE USUALLY TAKES AWAY MY FOOD...
I'M HUNGRY AND EXHAUSTED, BUT THIS IS ALL FROM THE KINDNESS OF MY SISTER!
THIS SEEMS MORE LIKE BULLYING THAN KINDNESS... YOU'RE JUST BEING TRICKED!
OH?
OH?

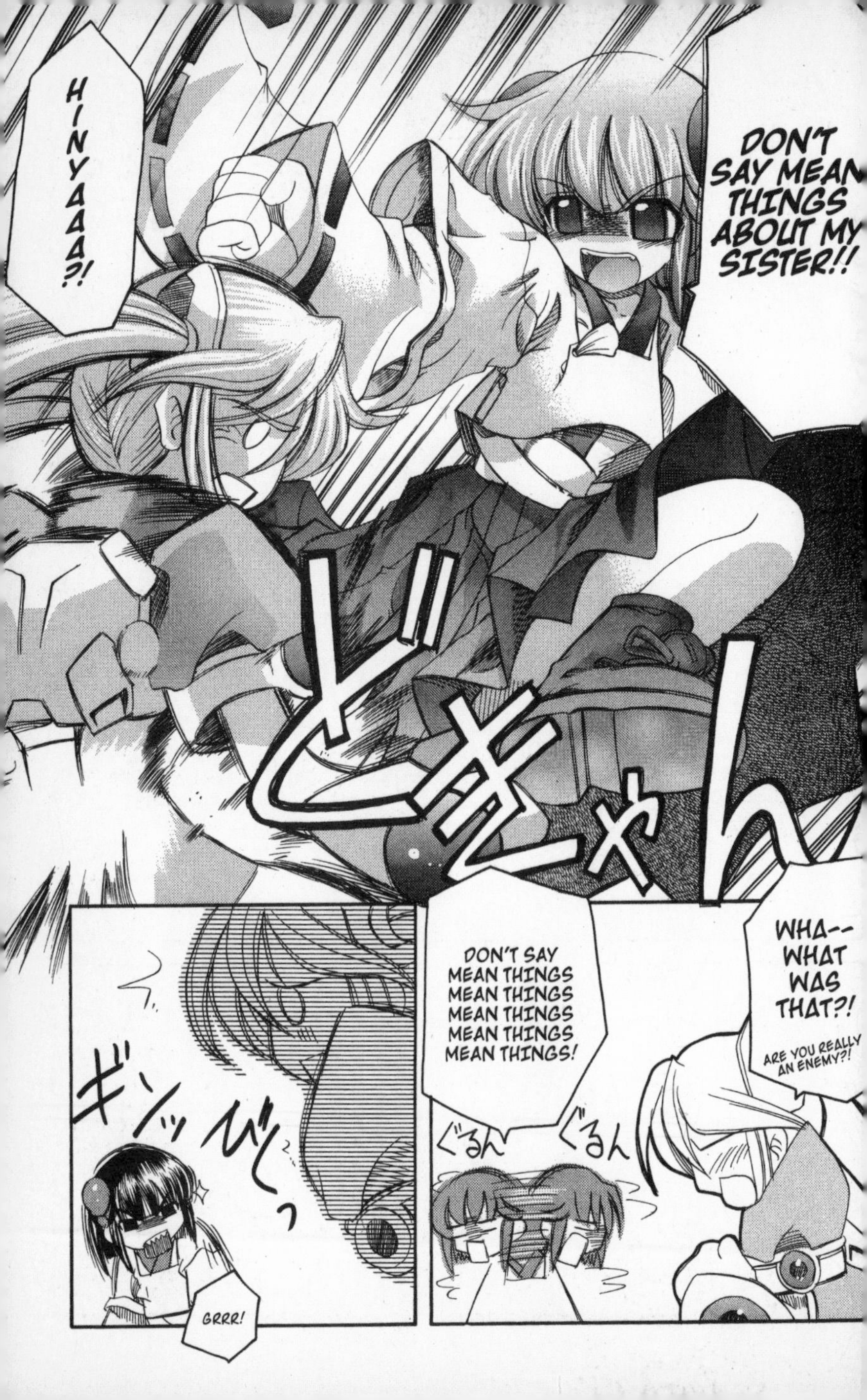
DON'T SAY MEAN THINGS ABOUT MY SISTER!!
HINYAAAA?!
どぎゃん
WHA-- WHAT WAS THAT?!
ARE YOU REALLY AN ENEMY?!
DON'T SAY MEAN THINGS MEAN THINGS MEAN THINGS MEAN THINGS MEAN THINGS!
ぐるん
ぐるん
ギンッ
びくっ
GRRR!

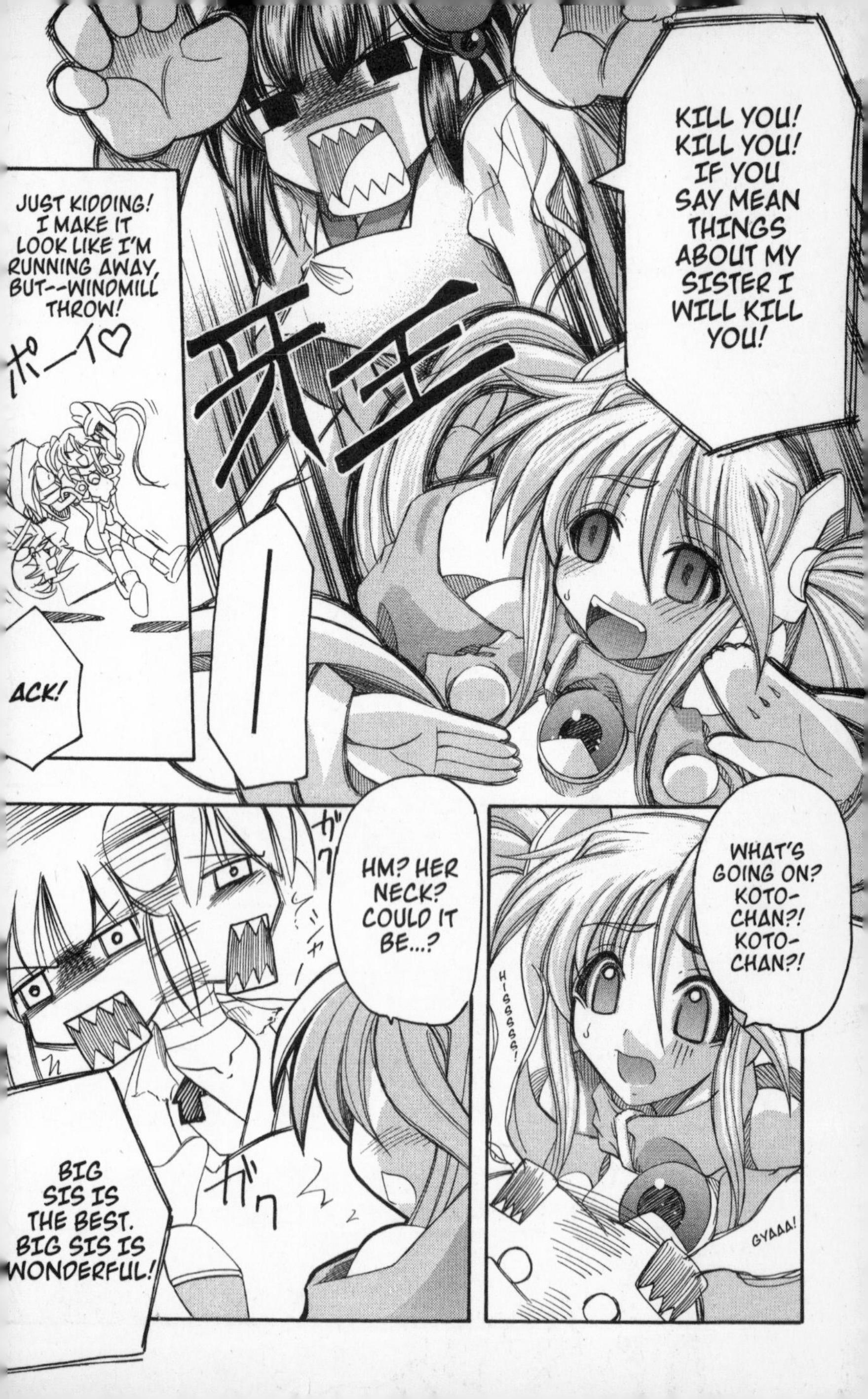
KILL YOU! KILL YOU! IF YOU SAY MEAN THINGS ABOUT MY SISTER I WILL KILL YOU!
JUST KIDDING! I MAKE IT LOOK LIKE I'M RUNNING AWAY, BUT--WINDMILL THROW!
ポーイ♡
ACK!
WHAT'S GOING ON? KOTO-CHAN?! KOTO-CHAN?!
HISSSSS!
GYAAA!
HM? HER NECK? COULD IT BE...?
ガク
BIG SIS IS THE BEST. BIG SIS IS WONDERFUL!
ガク

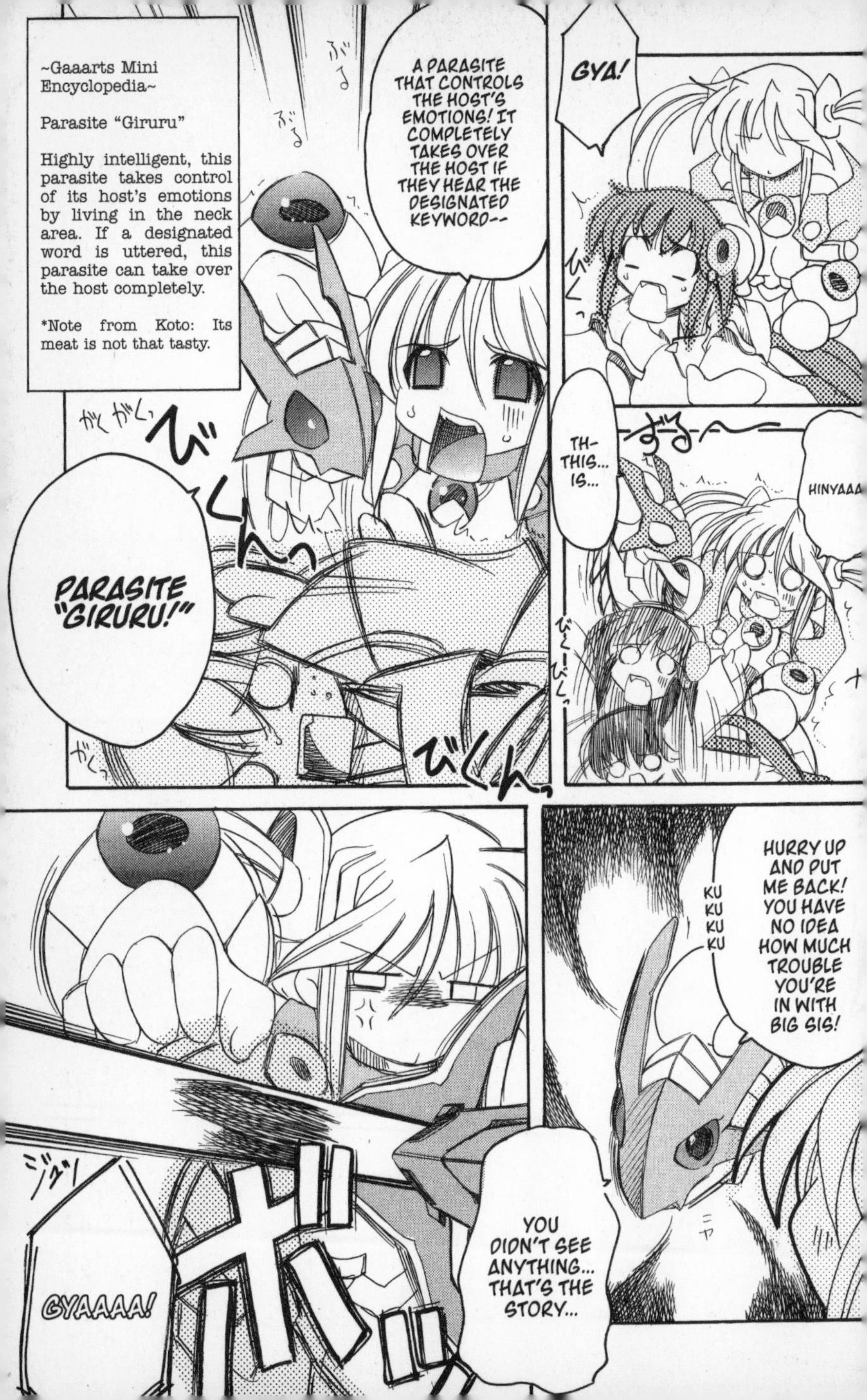
GYA!
TH- THIS... IS...
HINYAAA
A PARASITE THAT CONTROLS THE HOST'S EMOTIONS! IT COMPLETELY TAKES OVER THE HOST IF THEY HEAR THE DESIGNATED KEYWORD--
~Gaaarts Mini Encyclopedia~
Parasite "Giruru"
Highly intelligent, this parasite takes control of its host's emotions by living in the neck area. If a designated word is uttered, this parasite can take over the host completely.
*Note from Koto: Its meat is not that tasty.
PARASITE "GIRURU!"
HURRY UP AND PUT ME BACK! YOU HAVE NO IDEA HOW MUCH TROUBLE YOU'RE IN WITH BIG SIS!
KU KU KU KU
YOU DIDN'T SEE ANYTHING... THAT'S THE STORY...
GYAAAA!

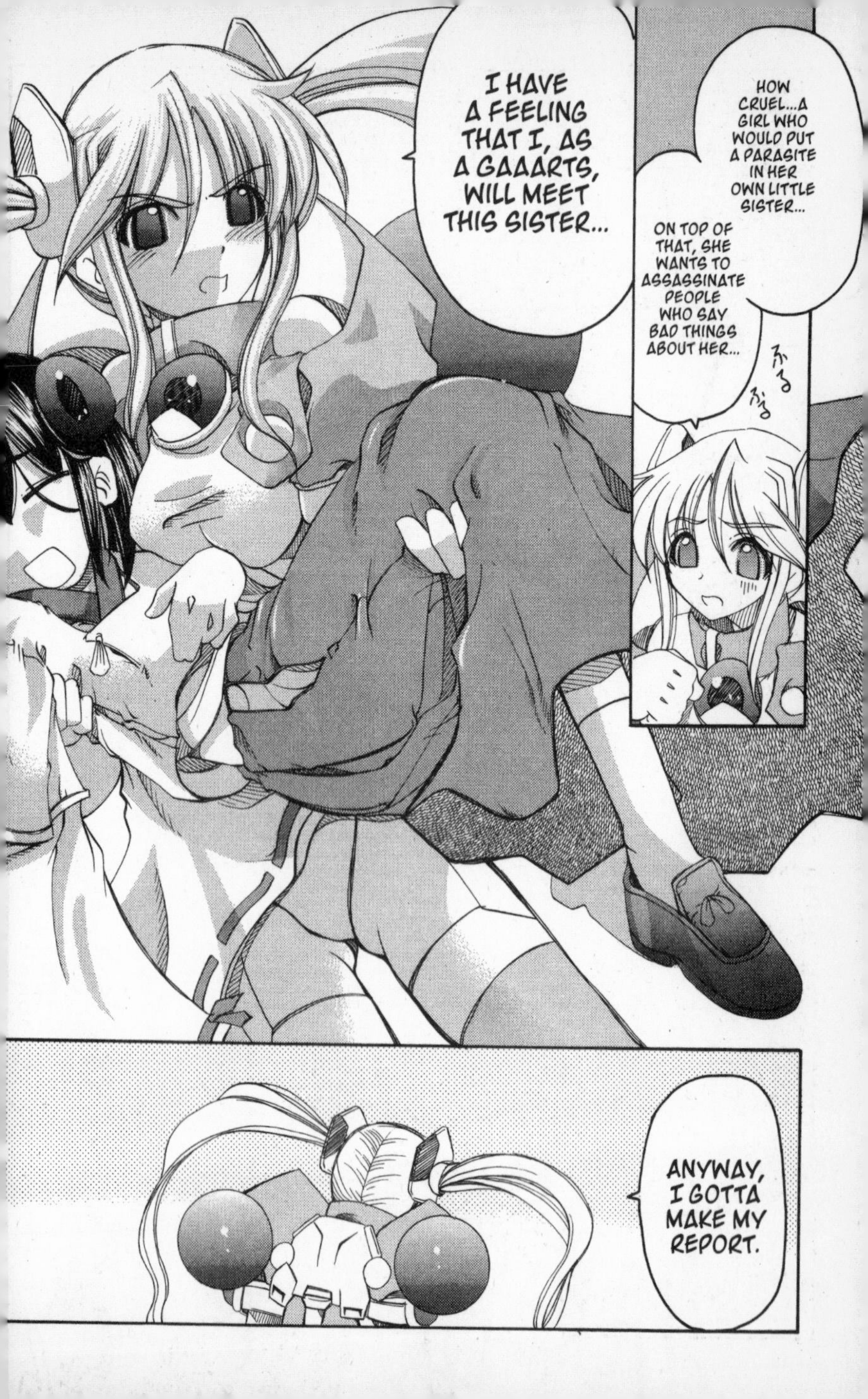
HOW CRUEL...A GIRL WHO WOULD PUT A PARASITE IN HER OWN LITTLE SISTER...
ON TOP OF THAT, SHE WANTS TO ASSASSINATE PEOPLE WHO SAY BAD THINGS ABOUT HER...
I HAVE A FEELING THAT I, AS A GAAARTS, WILL MEET THIS SISTER...
ANYWAY, I GOTTA MAKE MY REPORT.

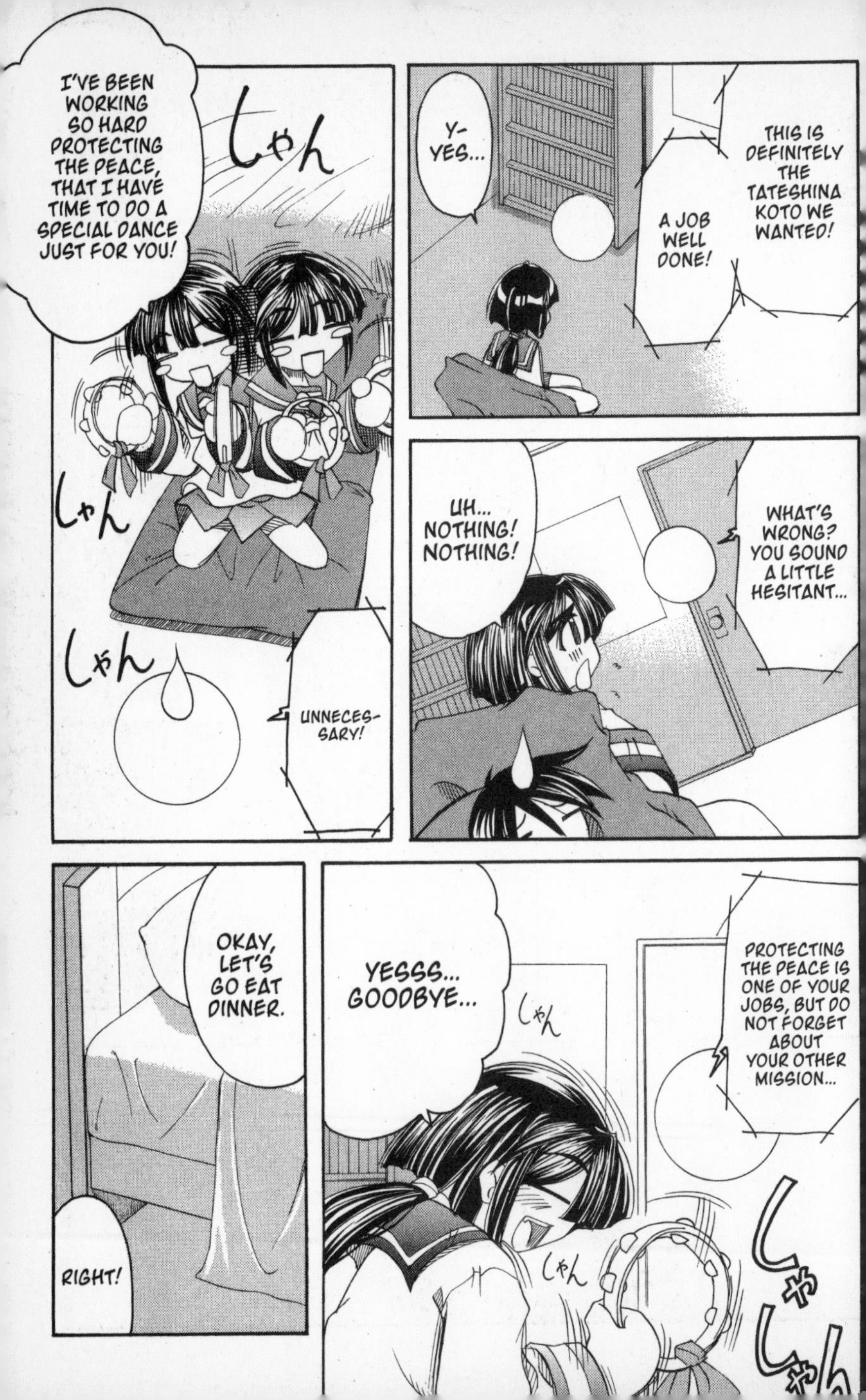
THIS IS DEFINITELY THE TATESHINA KOTO WE WANTED!
A JOB WELL DONE!
Y-YES...
WHAT'S WRONG? YOU SOUND A LITTLE HESITANT...
UH... NOTHING! NOTHING!
I'VE BEEN WORKING SO HARD PROTECTING THE PEACE, THAT I HAVE TIME TO DO A SPECIAL DANCE JUST FOR YOU!
しゃん
しゃん
しゃん
UNNECES-SARY!
PROTECTING THE PEACE IS ONE OF YOUR JOBS, BUT DO NOT FORGET ABOUT YOUR OTHER MISSION...
しゃん
YESSS... GOODBYE...
しゃしゃん
しゃん
OKAY, LET'S GO EAT DINNER.
RIGHT!

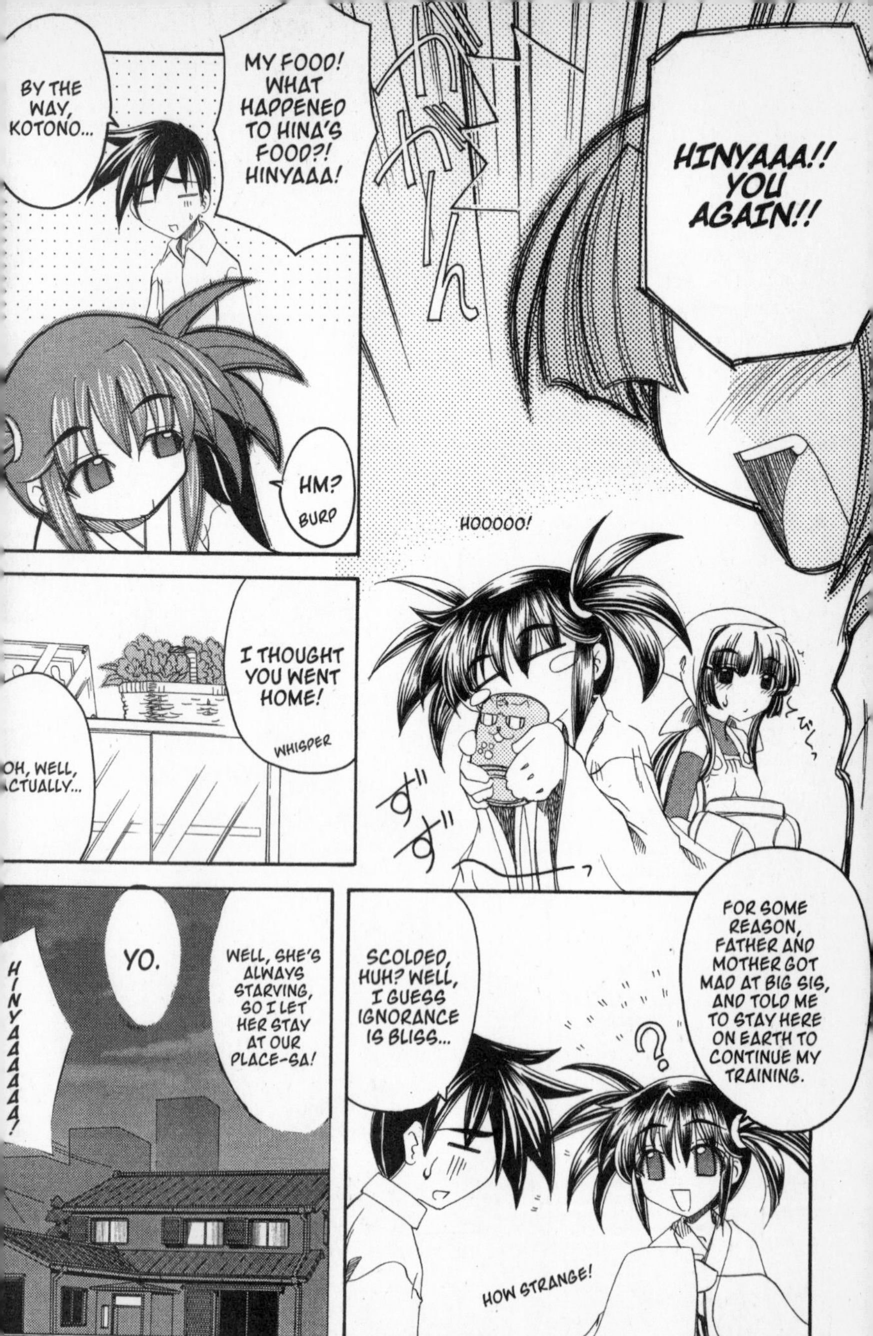
HINYAAA!! YOU AGAIN!!
HOOOOO!
MY FOOD! WHAT HAPPENED TO HINA'S FOOD?! HINYAAA!
BY THE WAY, KOTONO...
HM?
BURP
I THOUGHT YOU WENT HOME!
WHISPER
OH, WELL, ACTUALLY...
FOR SOME REASON, FATHER AND MOTHER GOT MAD AT BIG SIS, AND TOLD ME TO STAY HERE ON EARTH TO CONTINUE MY TRAINING.
SCOLDED, HUH? WELL, I GUESS IGNORANCE IS BLISS...
HOW STRANGE!
WELL, SHE'S ALWAYS STARVING, SO I LET HER STAY AT OUR PLACE-SA!
YO.
HINYAAAAAAAA!

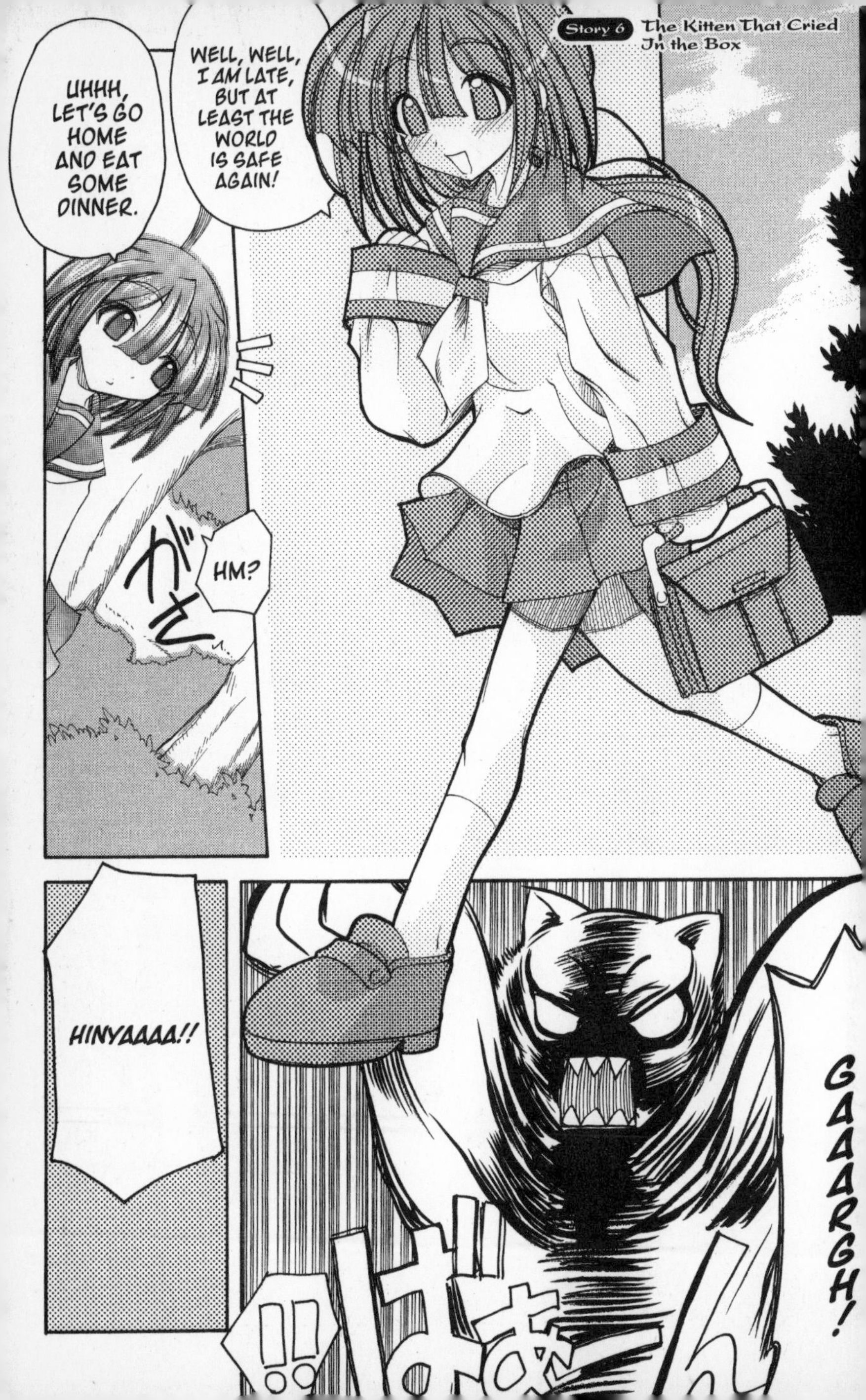

Story 6 The Kitten That Cried In the Box
WELL, WELL, I AM LATE, BUT AT LEAST THE WORLD IS SAFE AGAIN!
UHHH, LET'S GO HOME AND EAT SOME DINNER.
がさ
HM?
GAAARGH!
ばぁーん!!
HINYAAAA!!

Story 6

The Kitten That Cried In the Box

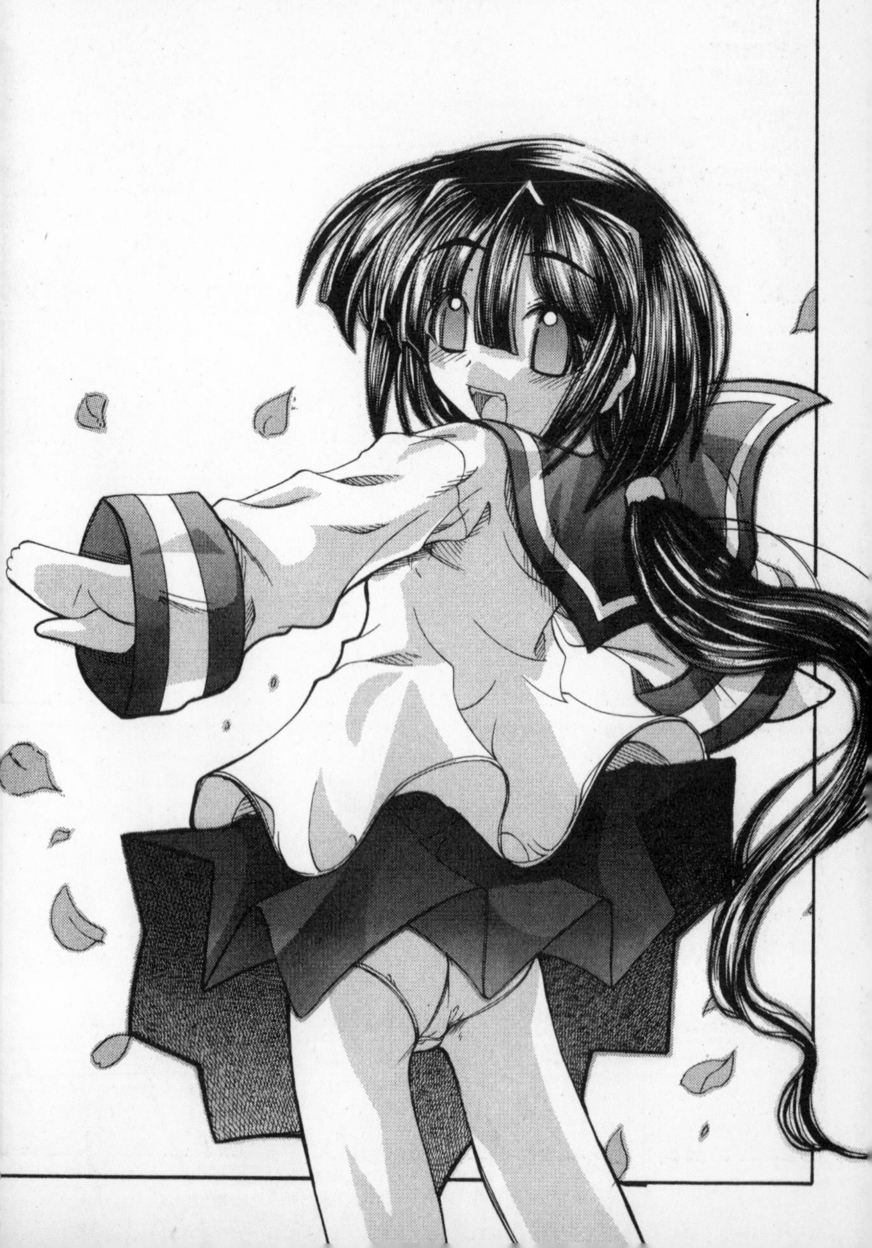

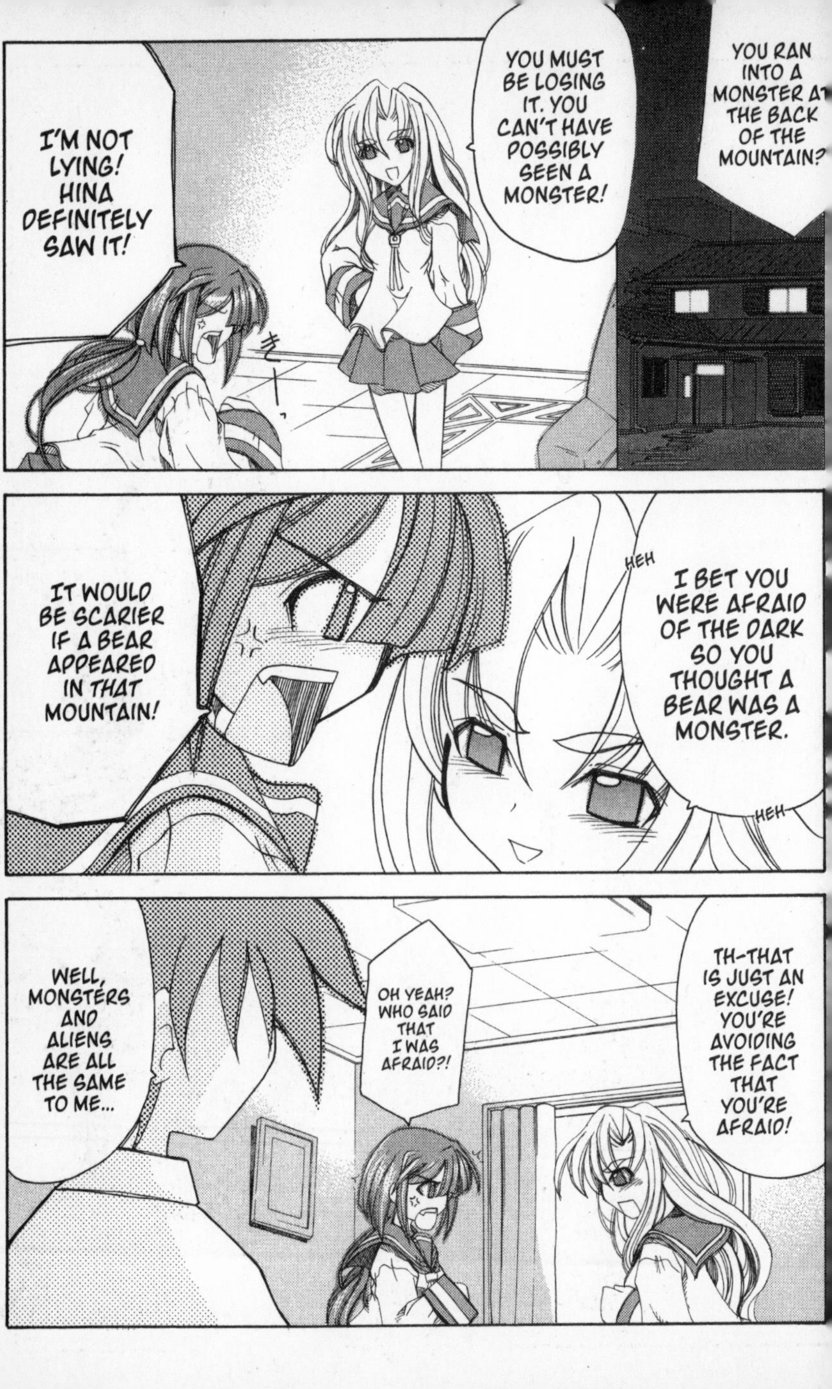
YOU RAN INTO A MONSTER AT THE BACK OF THE MOUNTAIN?
YOU MUST BE LOSING IT. YOU CAN'T HAVE POSSIBLY SEEN A MONSTER!
I'M NOT LYING! HINA DEFINITELY SAW IT!
HEH
I BET YOU WERE AFRAID OF THE DARK SO YOU THOUGHT A BEAR WAS A MONSTER.
HEH
IT WOULD BE SCARIER IF A BEAR APPEARED IN THAT MOUNTAIN!
TH-THAT IS JUST AN EXCUSE! YOU'RE AVOIDING THE FACT THAT YOU'RE AFRAID!
OH YEAH? WHO SAID THAT I WAS AFRAID?!
WELL, MONSTERS AND ALIENS ARE ALL THE SAME TO ME...

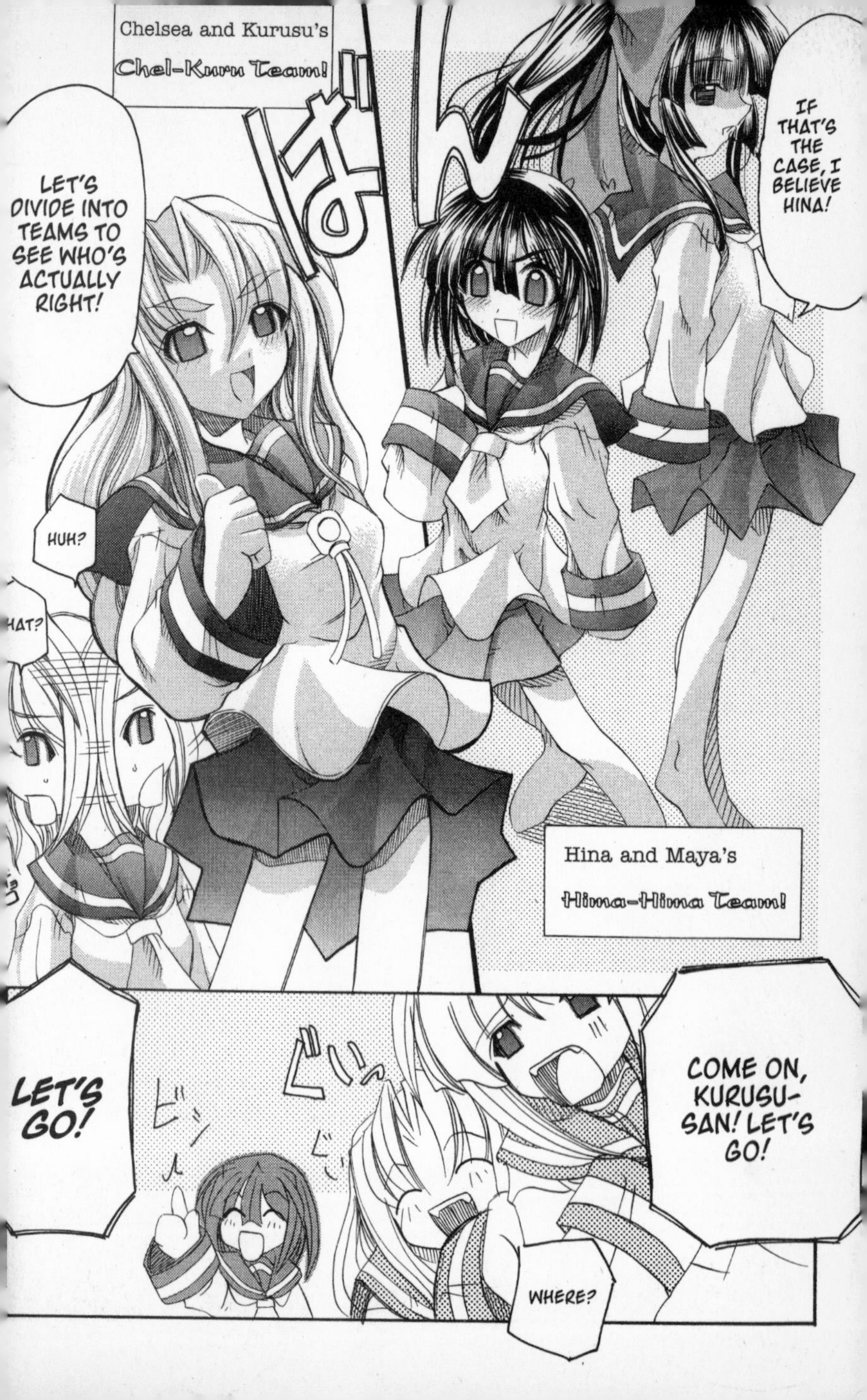
IF THAT'S THE CASE, I BELIEVE HINA!
Chelsea and Kurusu's
Chel-Kuru Team!
LET'S DIVIDE INTO TEAMS TO SEE WHO'S ACTUALLY RIGHT!
HUH?
HAT?
Hina and Maya's
Hima-Hima Team!
COME ON, KURUSU-SAN! LET'S GO!
LET'S GO!
WHERE?

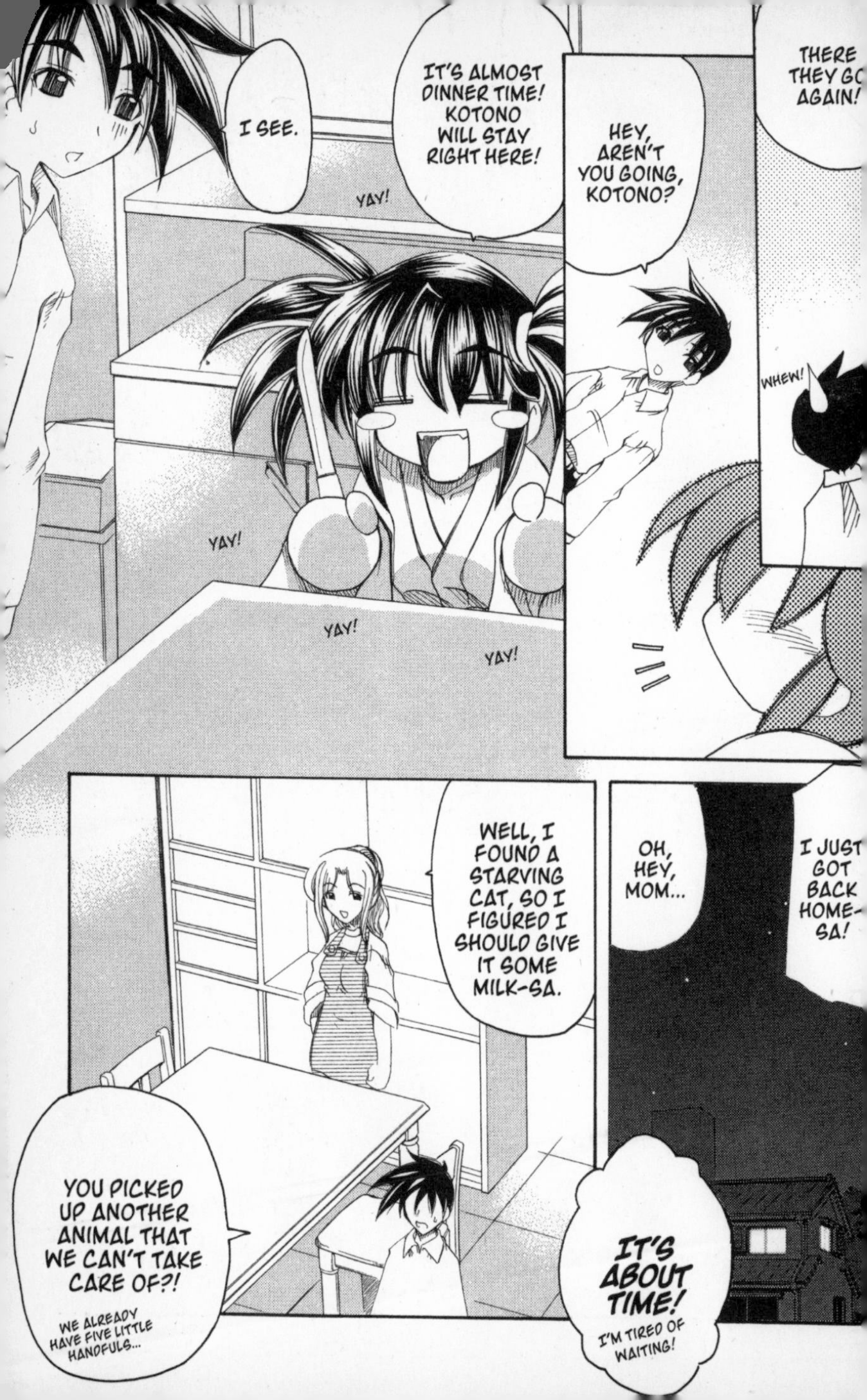
THERE THEY GO AGAIN!
WHEW!
HEY, AREN'T YOU GOING, KOTONO?
IT'S ALMOST DINNER TIME! KOTONO WILL STAY RIGHT HERE!
I SEE.
YAY!
YAY!
YAY!
YAY!
I JUST GOT BACK HOME-SA!
OH, HEY, MOM...
IT'S ABOUT TIME!
I'M TIRED OF WAITING!
WELL, I FOUND A STARVING CAT, SO I FIGURED I SHOULD GIVE IT SOME MILK-SA.
YOU PICKED UP ANOTHER ANIMAL THAT WE CAN'T TAKE CARE OF?!
WE ALREADY HAVE FIVE LITTLE HANDFULS...

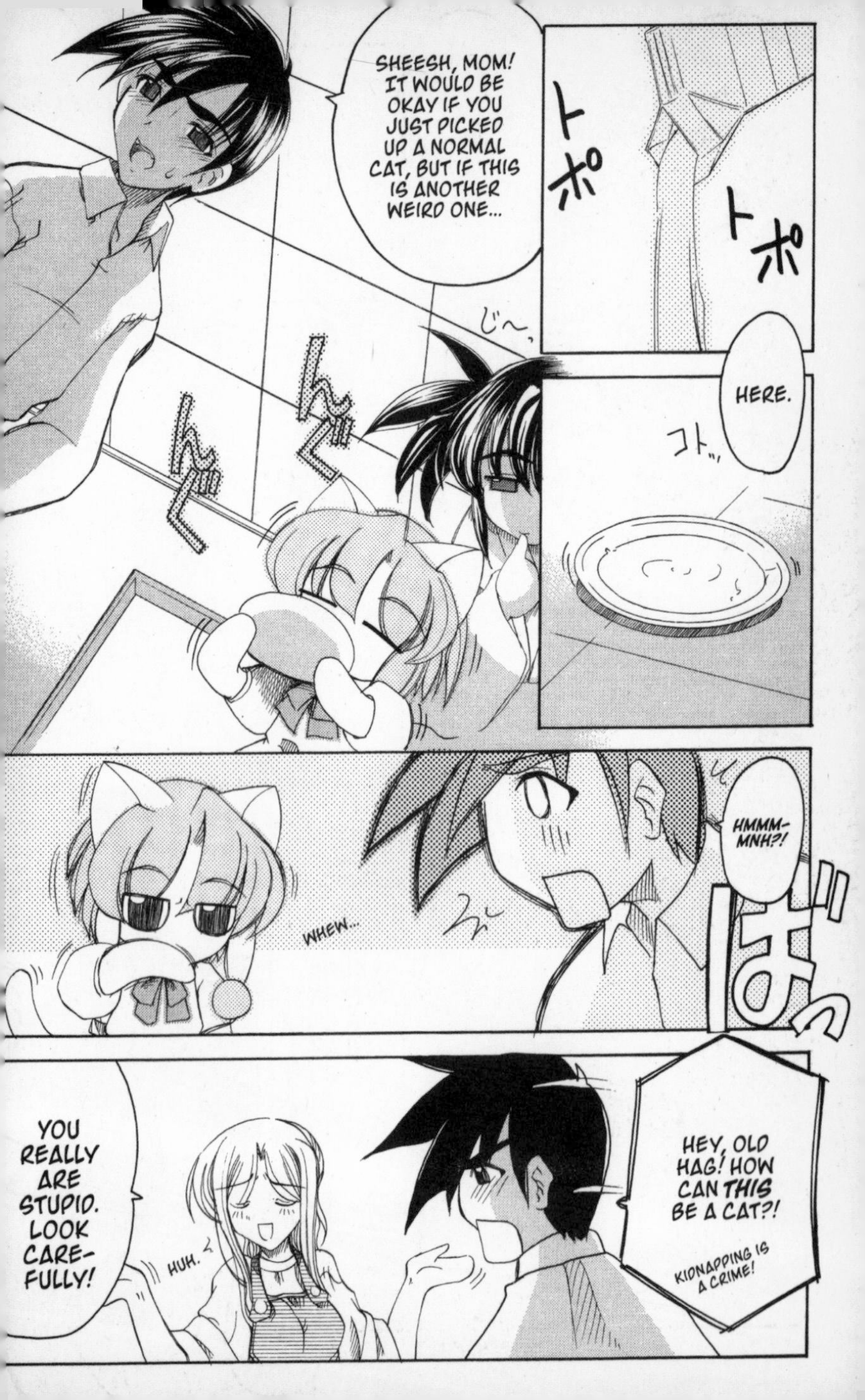
トポ
トポ
HERE.
コト,,
SHEESH, MOM! IT WOULD BE OKAY IF YOU JUST PICKED UP A NORMAL CAT, BUT IF THIS IS ANOTHER WEIRD ONE...
じ〜,
んぐ
んぐ
HMMMM-MNH?!
ばっ
WHEW...
HEY, OLD HAG! HOW CAN THIS BE A CAT?!
KIDNAPPING IS A CRIME!
YOU REALLY ARE STUPID. LOOK CARE-FULLY!
HUH.

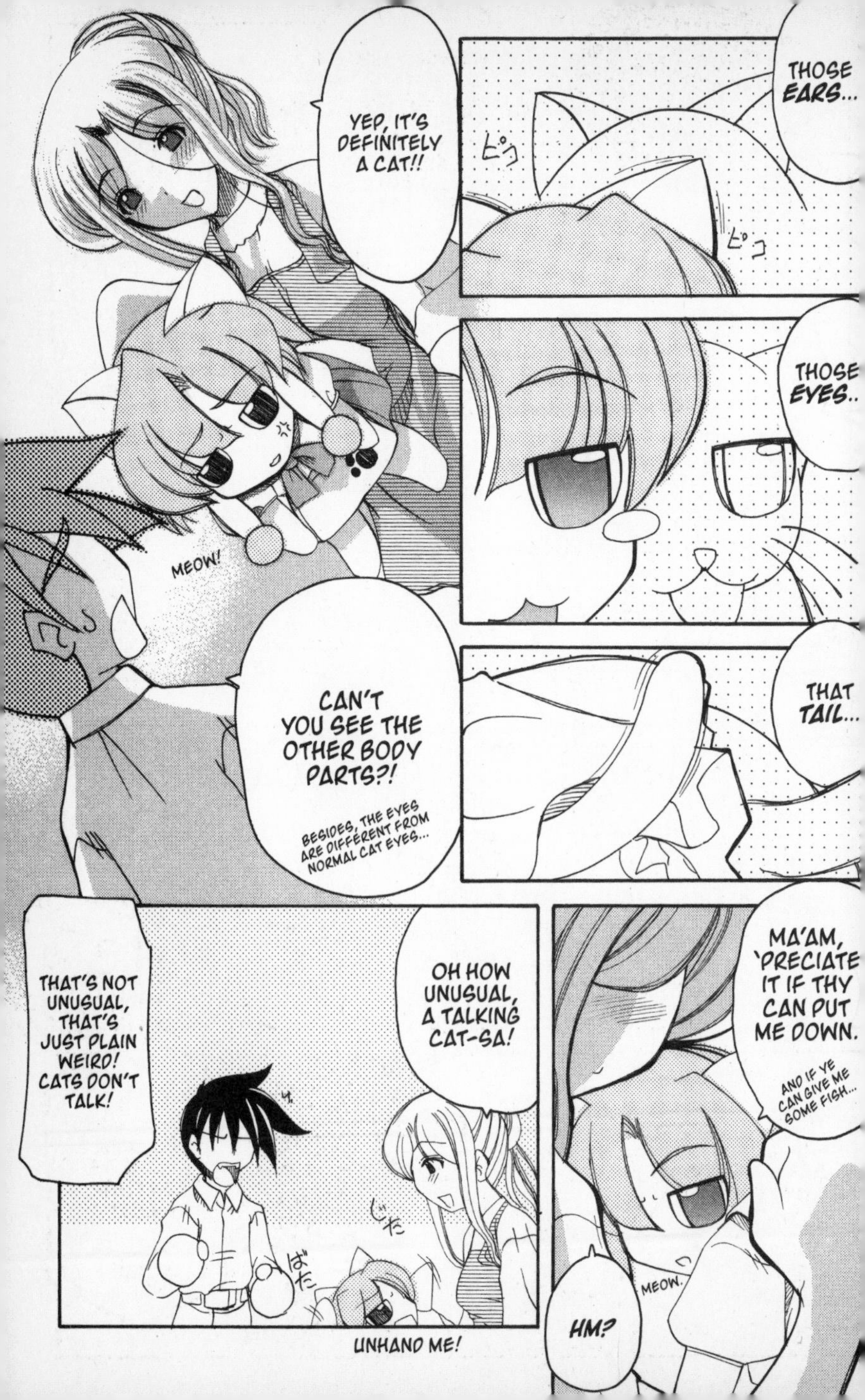

THOSE EARS...
THOSE EYES...
THAT TAIL...
YEP, IT'S DEFINITELY A CAT!!
MEOW!
CAN'T YOU SEE THE OTHER BODY PARTS?!
BESIDES, THE EYES ARE DIFFERENT FROM NORMAL CAT EYES...
MA'AM, 'PRECIATE IT IF THY CAN PUT ME DOWN.
AND IF YE CAN GIVE ME SOME FISH...
MEOW.
HM?
OH HOW UNUSUAL, A TALKING CAT-SA!
THAT'S NOT UNUSUAL, THAT'S JUST PLAIN WEIRD! CATS DON'T TALK!
UNHAND ME!

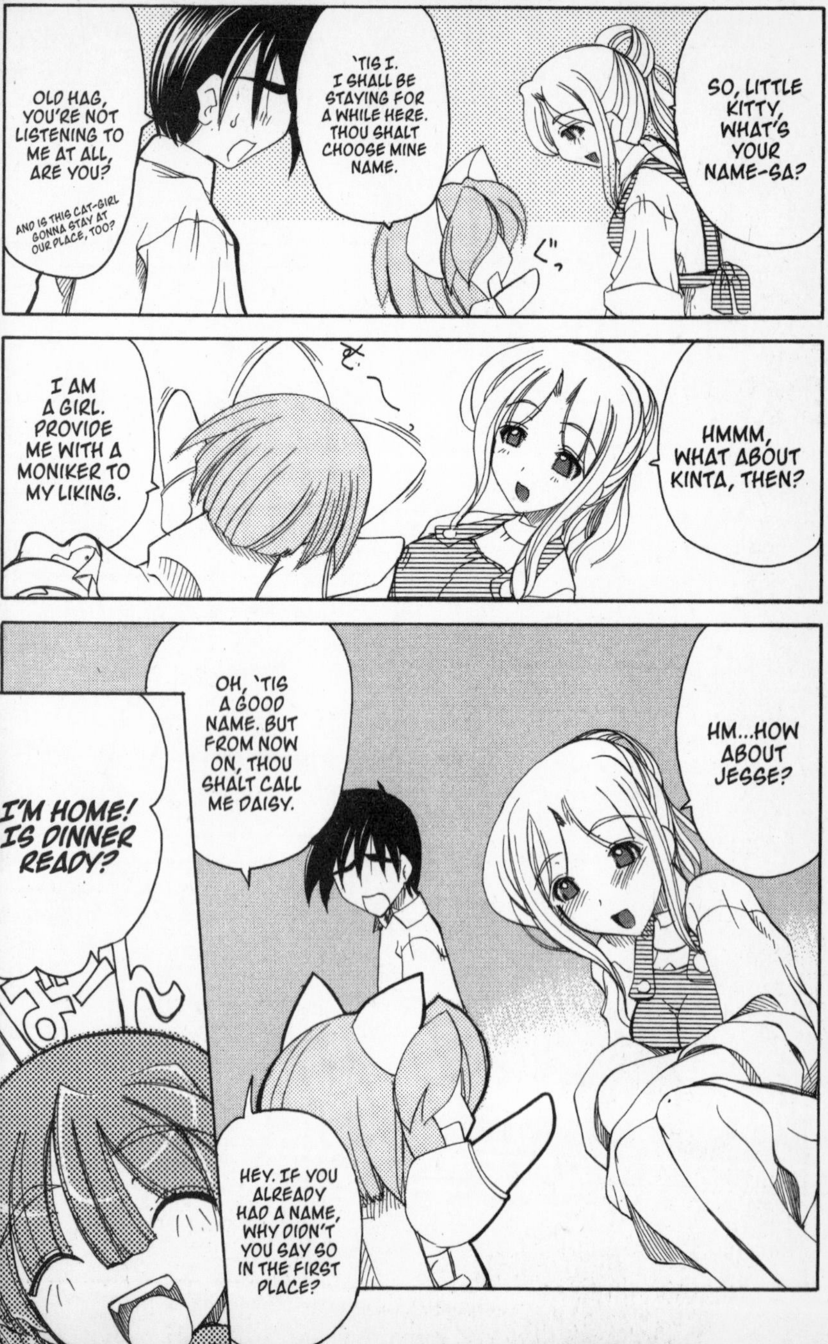
SO, LITTLE KITTY, WHAT'S YOUR NAME-SA?
ぐっ
`TIS I. I SHALL BE STAYING FOR A WHILE HERE. THOU SHALT CHOOSE MINE NAME.
OLD HAG, YOU'RE NOT LISTENING TO ME AT ALL, ARE YOU?
AND IS THIS CAT-GIRL GONNA STAY AT OUR PLACE, TOO?
HMMM, WHAT ABOUT KINTA, THEN?
I AM A GIRL. PROVIDE ME WITH A MONIKER TO MY LIKING.
HM...HOW ABOUT JESSE?
OH, `TIS A GOOD NAME. BUT FROM NOW ON, THOU SHALT CALL ME DAISY.
HEY. IF YOU ALREADY HAD A NAME, WHY DIDN'T YOU SAY SO IN THE FIRST PLACE?
I'M HOME! IS DINNER READY?

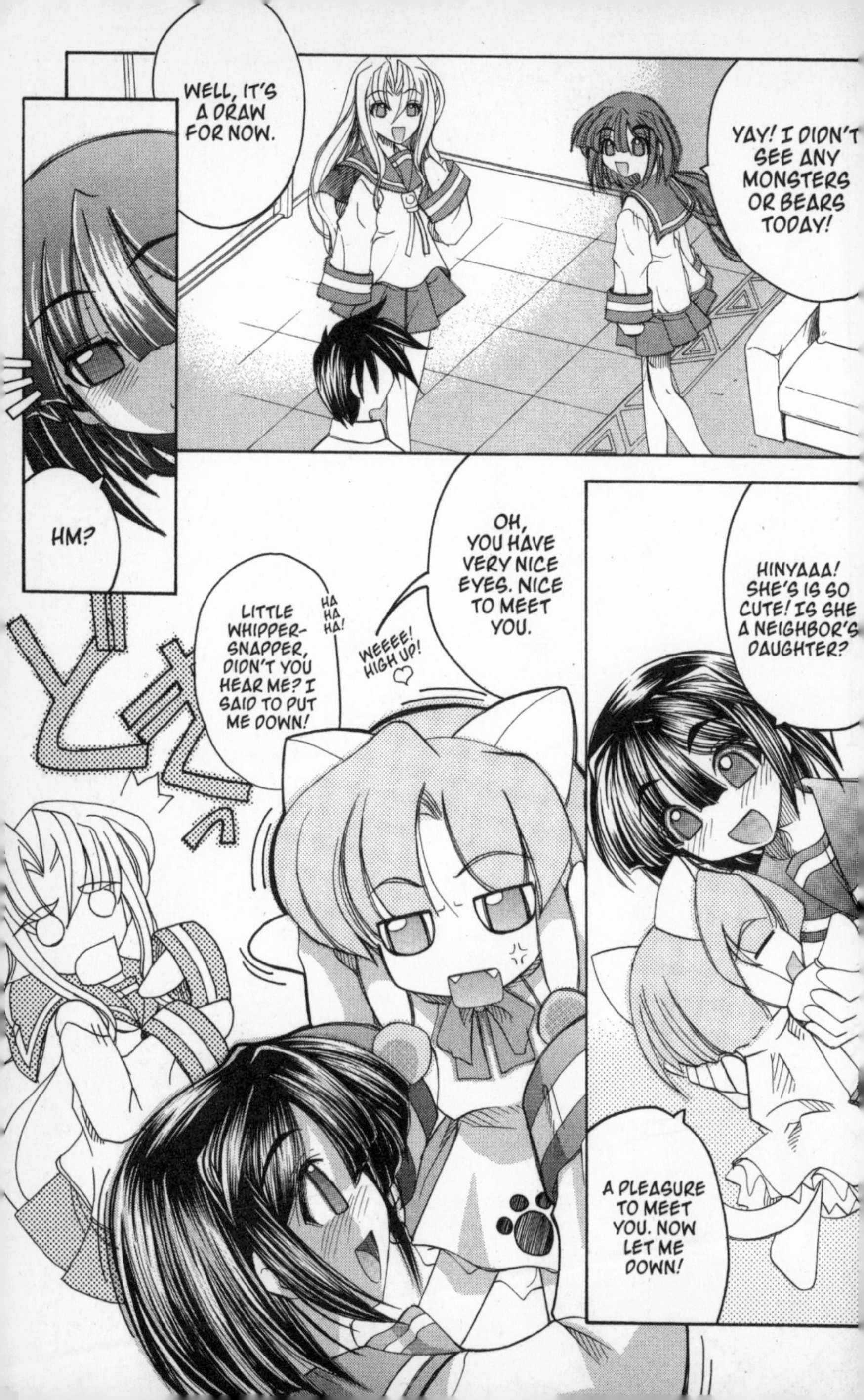
YAY! I DIDN'T SEE ANY MONSTERS OR BEARS TODAY!
WELL, IT'S A DRAW FOR NOW.
HM?
HINYAAA! SHE'S IS SO CUTE! IS SHE A NEIGHBOR'S DAUGHTER?
A PLEASURE TO MEET YOU. NOW LET ME DOWN!
OH, YOU HAVE VERY NICE EYES. NICE TO MEET YOU.
WEEEE! HIGH UP!
HA HA HA!
LITTLE WHIPPER-SNAPPER, DIDN'T YOU HEAR ME? I SAID TO PUT ME DOWN!

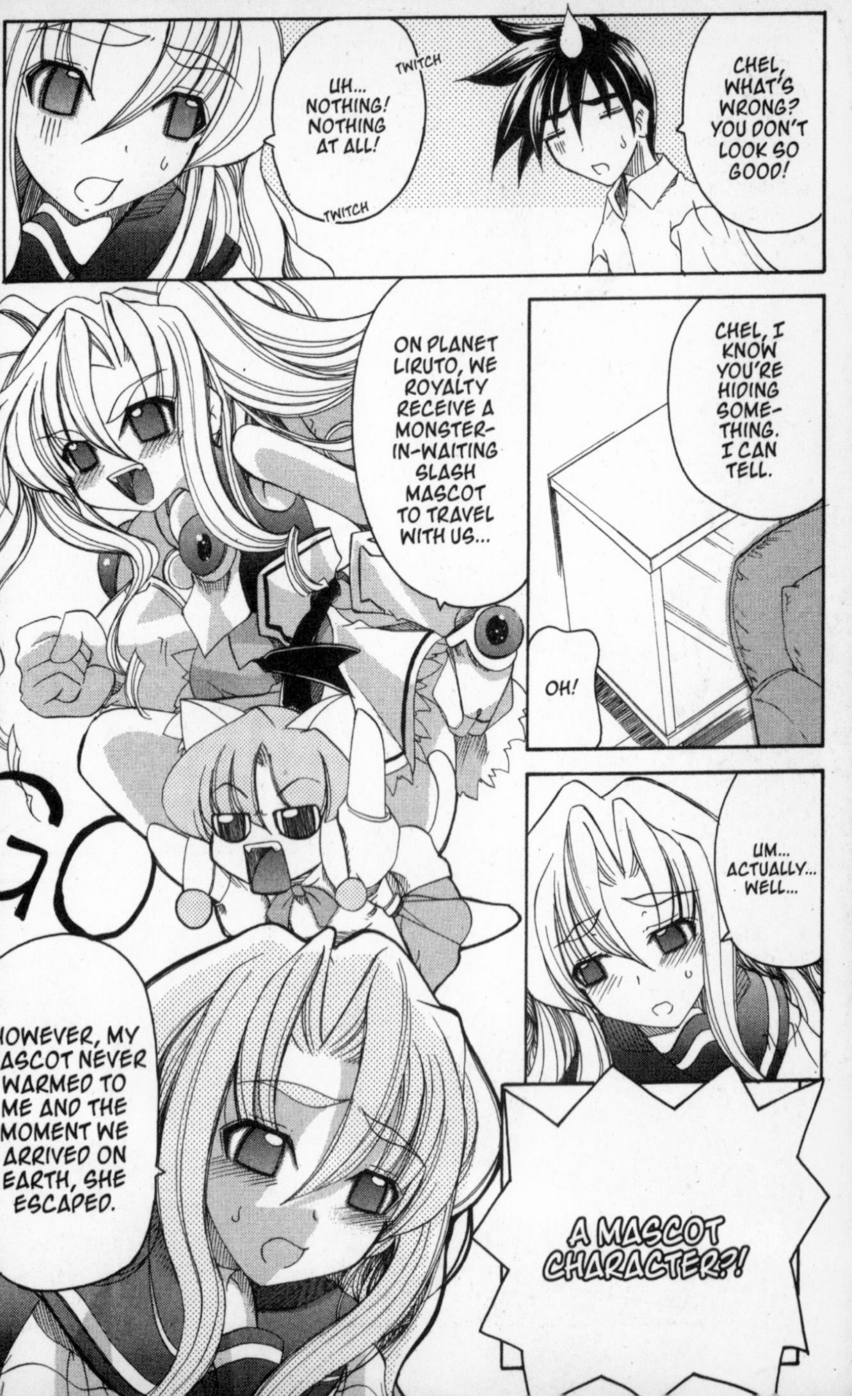
CHEL, WHAT'S WRONG? YOU DON'T LOOK SO GOOD!
TWITCH
UH... NOTHING! NOTHING AT ALL!
TWITCH
CHEL, I KNOW YOU'RE HIDING SOME-THING. I CAN TELL.
OH!
UM... ACTUALLY... WELL...
ON PLANET LIRUTO, WE ROYALTY RECEIVE A MONSTER-IN-WAITING SLASH MASCOT TO TRAVEL WITH US...
HOWEVER, MY MASCOT NEVER WARMED TO ME AND THE MOMENT WE ARRIVED ON EARTH, SHE ESCAPED.
A MASCOT CHARACTER?!

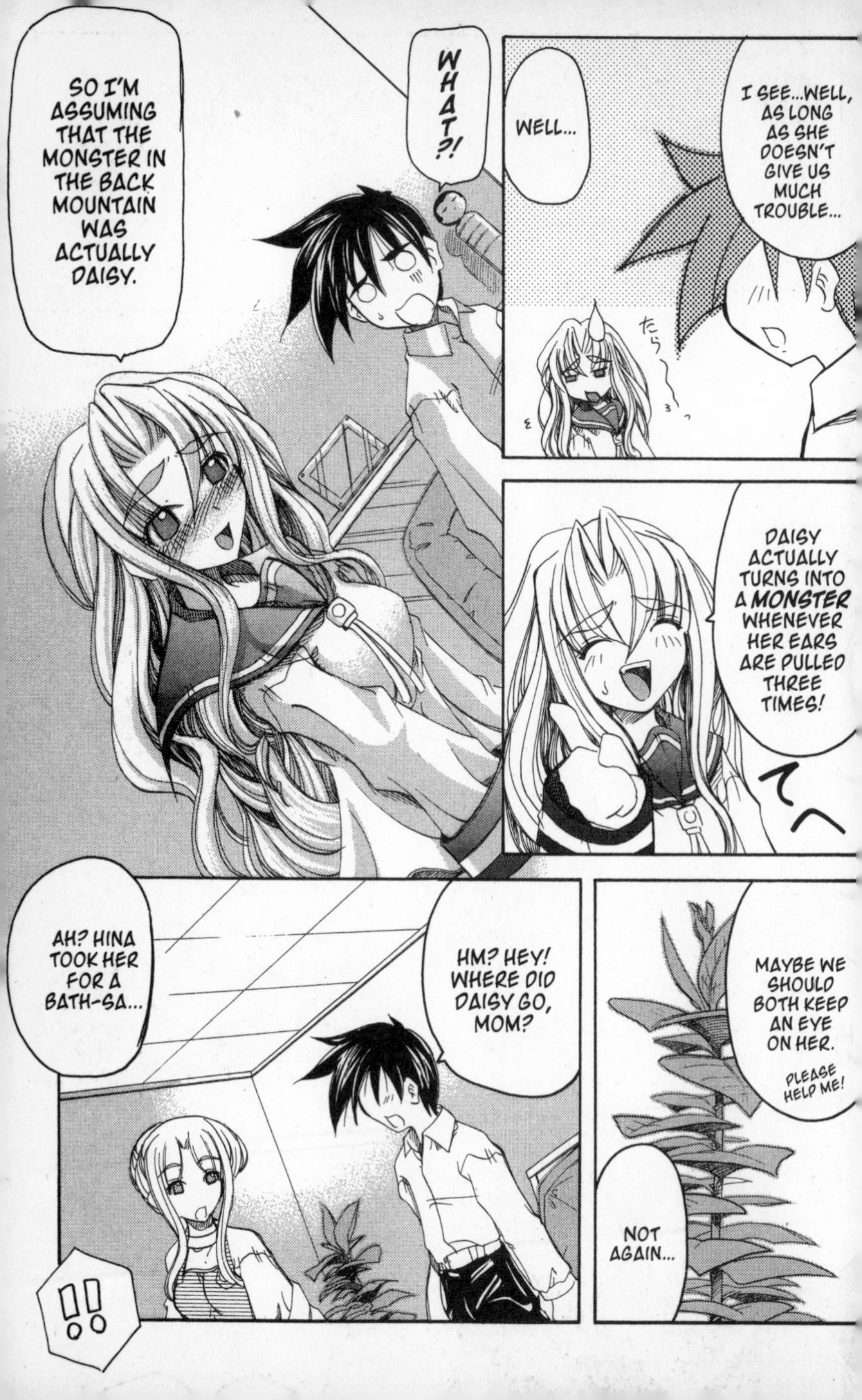
I SEE...WELL, AS LONG AS SHE DOESN'T GIVE US MUCH TROUBLE...
WELL...
たら
DAISY ACTUALLY TURNS INTO A **MONSTER** WHENEVER HER EARS ARE PULLED THREE TIMES!
てへ
WHAT?!
SO I'M ASSUMING THAT THE MONSTER IN THE BACK MOUNTAIN WAS ACTUALLY DAISY.
MAYBE WE SHOULD BOTH KEEP AN EYE ON HER.
PLEASE HELP ME!
NOT AGAIN...
HM? HEY! WHERE DID DAISY GO, MOM?
AH? HINA TOOK HER FOR A BATH-SA...
!!

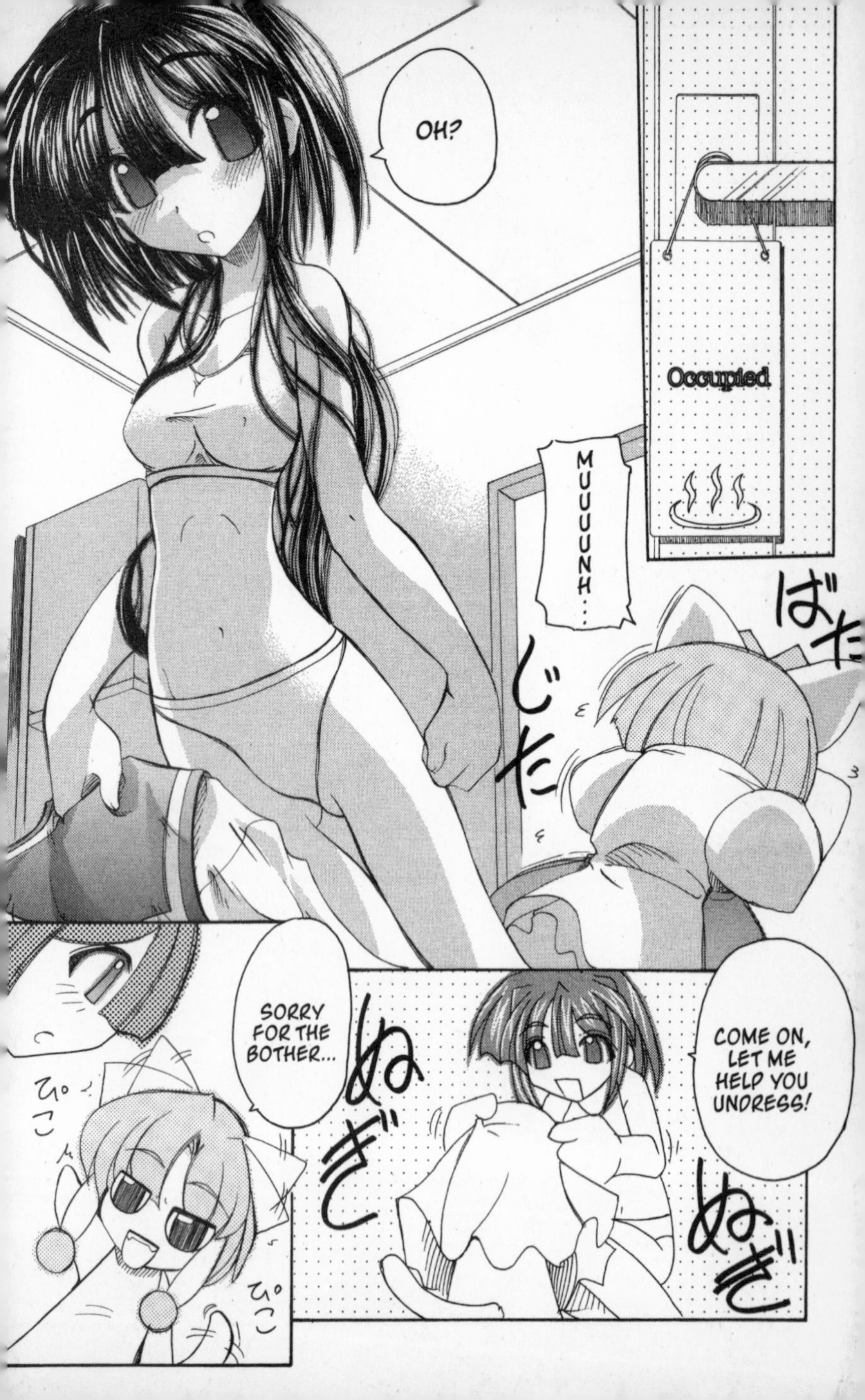
OH?
Occupied
MUUUUNH...
ばた
じた
COME ON, LET ME HELP YOU UNDRESS!
ぬぎ
ぬぎ
SORRY FOR THE BOTHER...
ぴこ
ぴこ

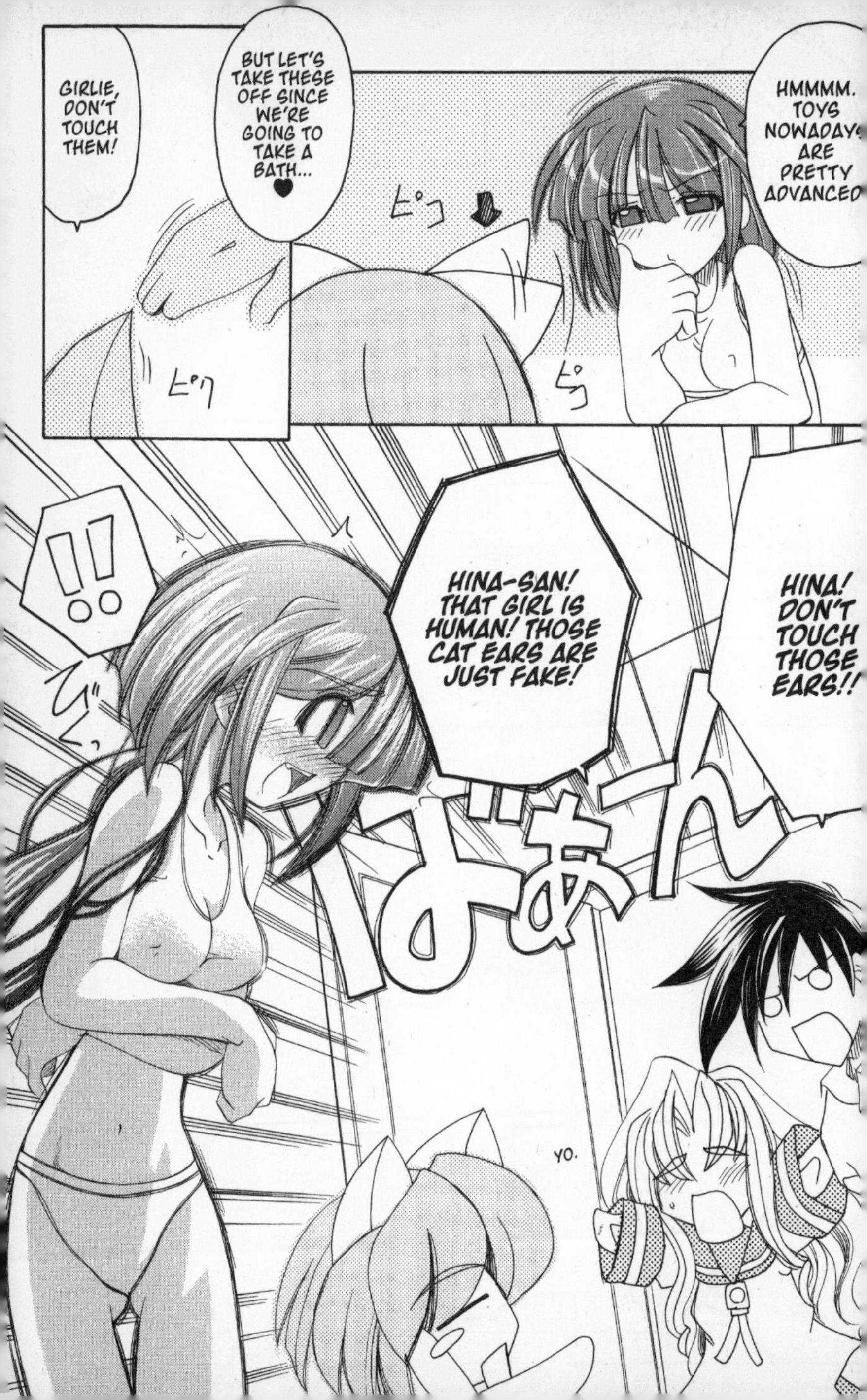
HMMMM. TOYS NOWADAYS ARE PRETTY ADVANCED
BUT LET'S TAKE THESE OFF SINCE WE'RE GOING TO TAKE A BATH...♥
GIRLIE, DON'T TOUCH THEM!
HINA! DON'T TOUCH THOSE EARS!!
HINA-SAN! THAT GIRL IS HUMAN! THOSE CAT EARS ARE JUST FAKE!
ぼあーん
!!
びくっ
YO.

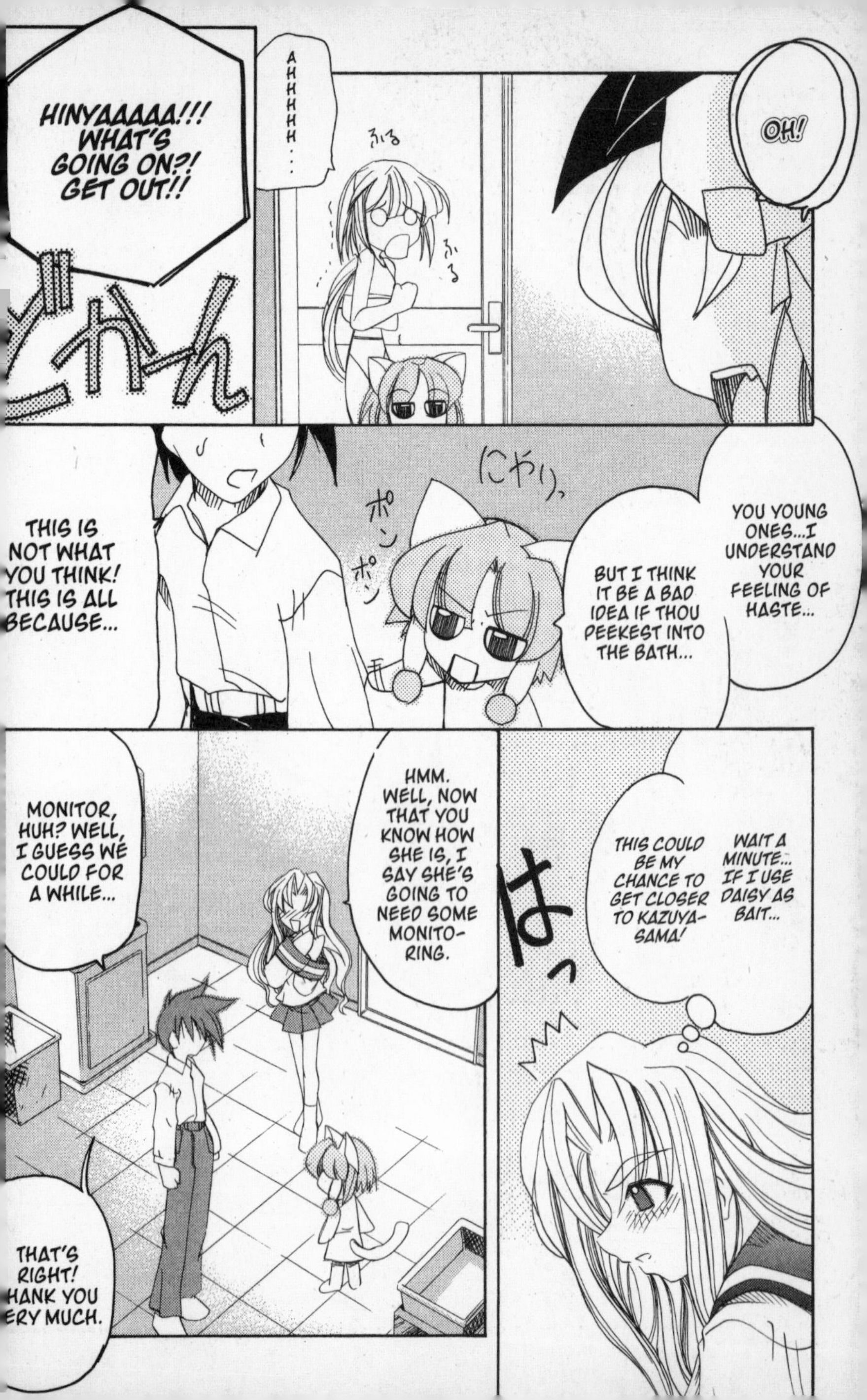
OH!
AHHHHHH...
ふる
ふる
HINYAAAAA!!! WHAT'S GOING ON?! GET OUT!!
どかん
YOU YOUNG ONES...I UNDERSTAND YOUR FEELING OF HASTE...
BUT I THINK IT BE A BAD IDEA IF THOU PEEKEST INTO THE BATH...
にやりっ
ポン
ポン
THIS IS NOT WHAT YOU THINK! THIS IS ALL BECAUSE...
WAIT A MINUTE... IF I USE DAISY AS BAIT...
THIS COULD BE MY CHANCE TO GET CLOSER TO KAZUYA-SAMA!
はっ
HMM. WELL, NOW THAT YOU KNOW HOW SHE IS, I SAY SHE'S GOING TO NEED SOME MONITO-RING.
MONITOR, HUH? WELL, I GUESS WE COULD FOR A WHILE...
THAT'S RIGHT! HANK YOU ERY MUCH.

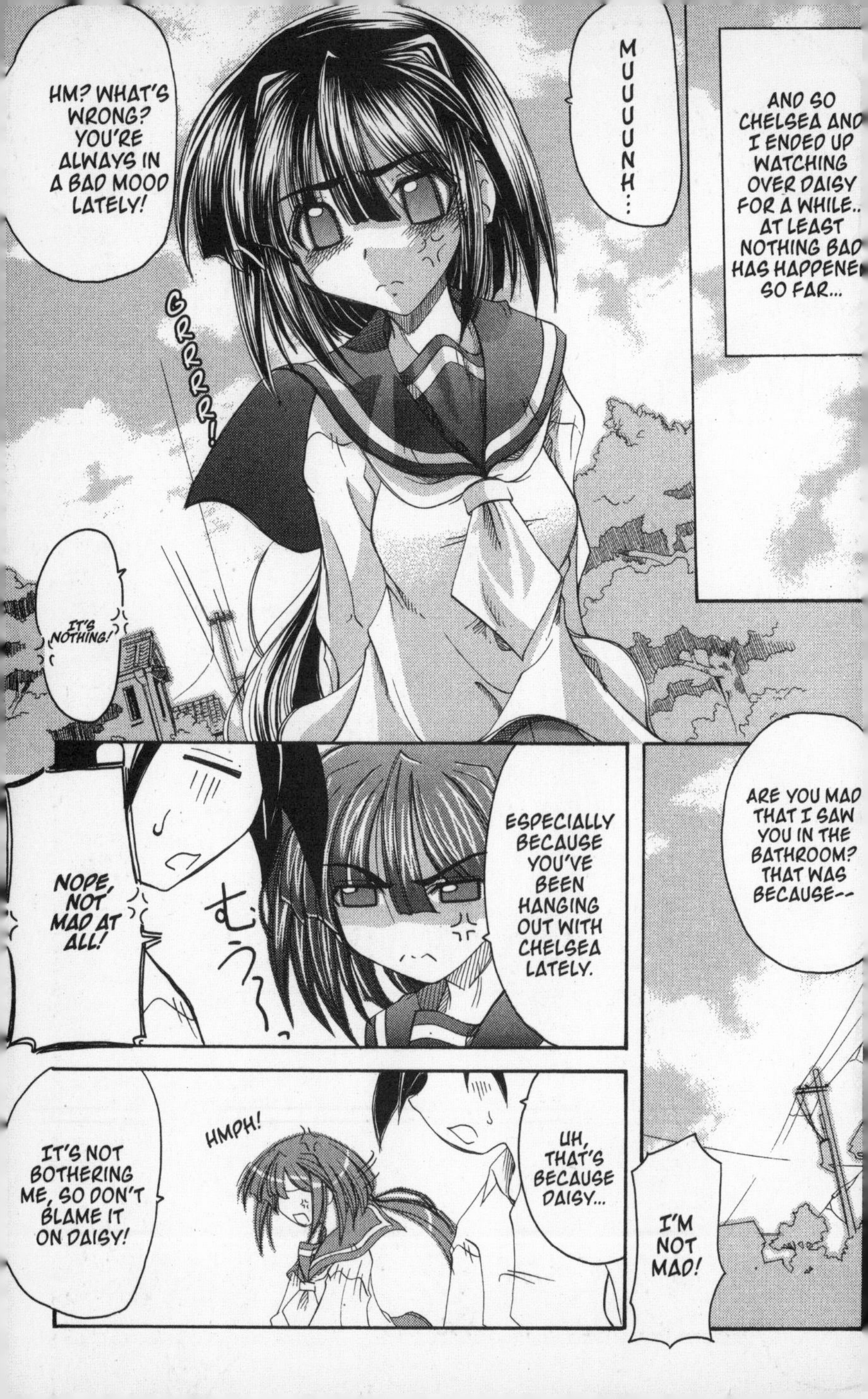
AND SO CHELSEA AND I ENDED UP WATCHING OVER DAISY FOR A WHILE.. AT LEAST NOTHING BAD HAS HAPPENE SO FAR...
MUUUUUNH...
HM? WHAT'S WRONG? YOU'RE ALWAYS IN A BAD MOOD LATELY!
GRRRRR!
IT'S NOTHING!
ARE YOU MAD THAT I SAW YOU IN THE BATHROOM? THAT WAS BECAUSE--
ESPECIALLY BECAUSE YOU'VE BEEN HANGING OUT WITH CHELSEA LATELY.
むう~
NOPE, NOT MAD AT ALL!
UH, THAT'S BECAUSE DAISY...
I'M NOT MAD!
HMPH!
IT'S NOT BOTHERING ME, SO DON'T BLAME IT ON DAISY!

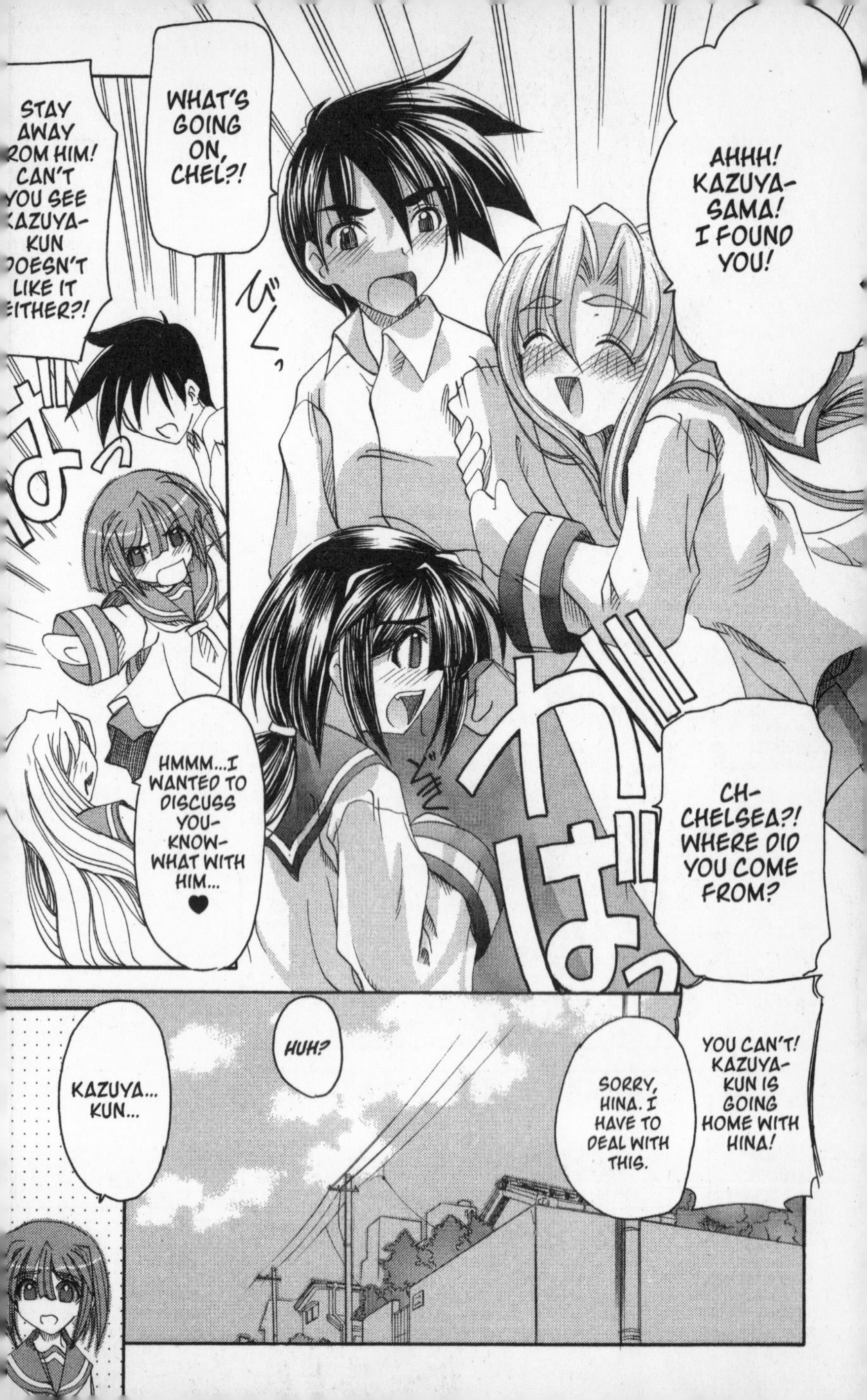

AHHH! KAZUYA-SAMA! I FOUND YOU!
WHAT'S GOING ON, CHEL?!
びくっ
わっ
ばっ
CH-CHELSEA?! WHERE DID YOU COME FROM?
STAY AWAY ROM HIM! CAN'T YOU SEE KAZUYA-KUN OESN'T LIKE IT EITHER?!
はっ
HMMM...I WANTED TO DISCUSS YOU-KNOW-WHAT WITH HIM... ♥
YOU CAN'T! KAZUYA-KUN IS GOING HOME WITH HINA!
SORRY, HINA. I HAVE TO DEAL WITH THIS.
HUH?
KAZUYA... KUN...

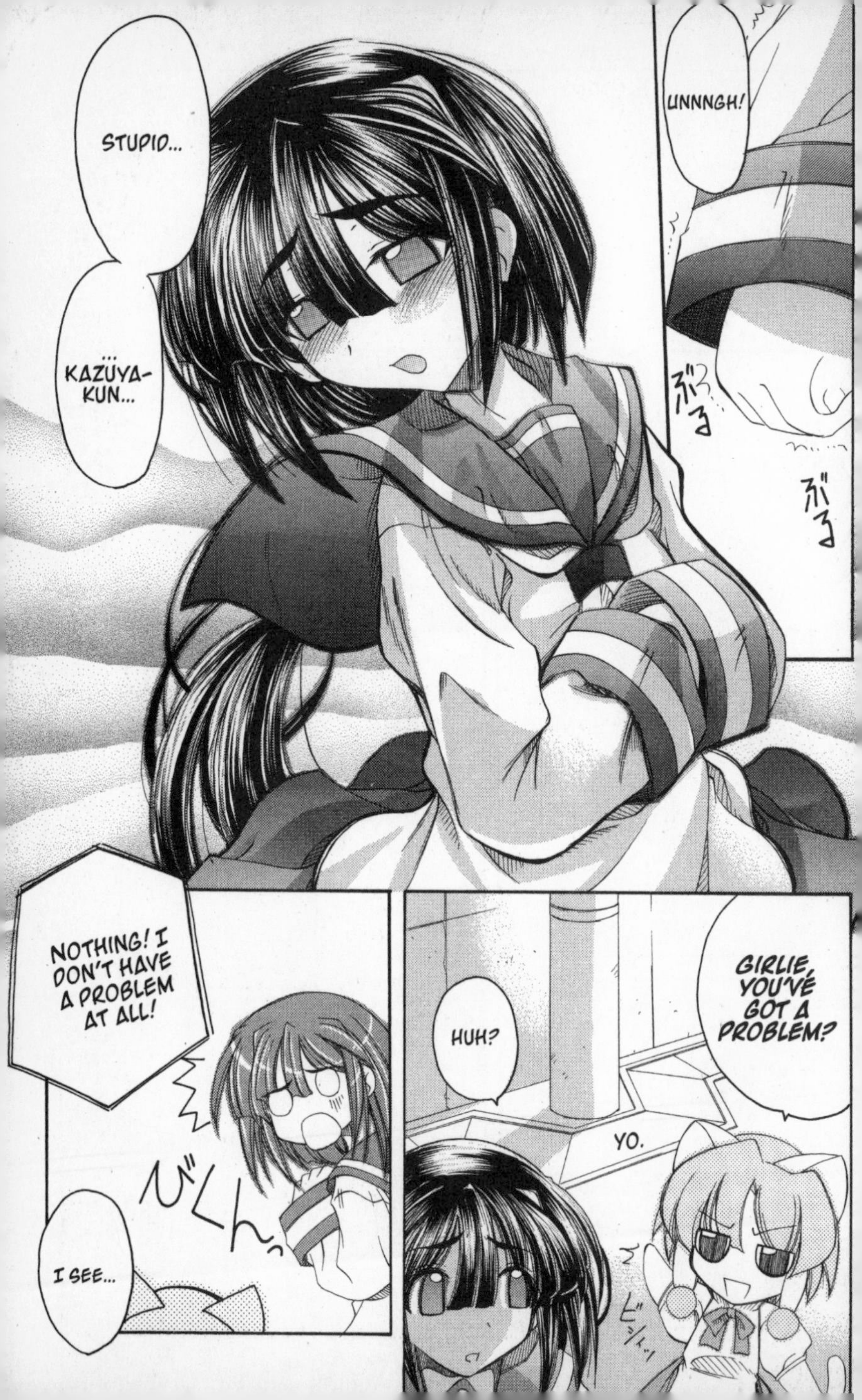
UNNNGH!
ぶる
ぶる
STUPID...
...KAZUYA-KUN...
GIRLIE, YOU'VE GOT A PROBLEM?
HUH?
YO.
NOTHING! I DON'T HAVE A PROBLEM AT ALL!
びくんっ
I SEE...

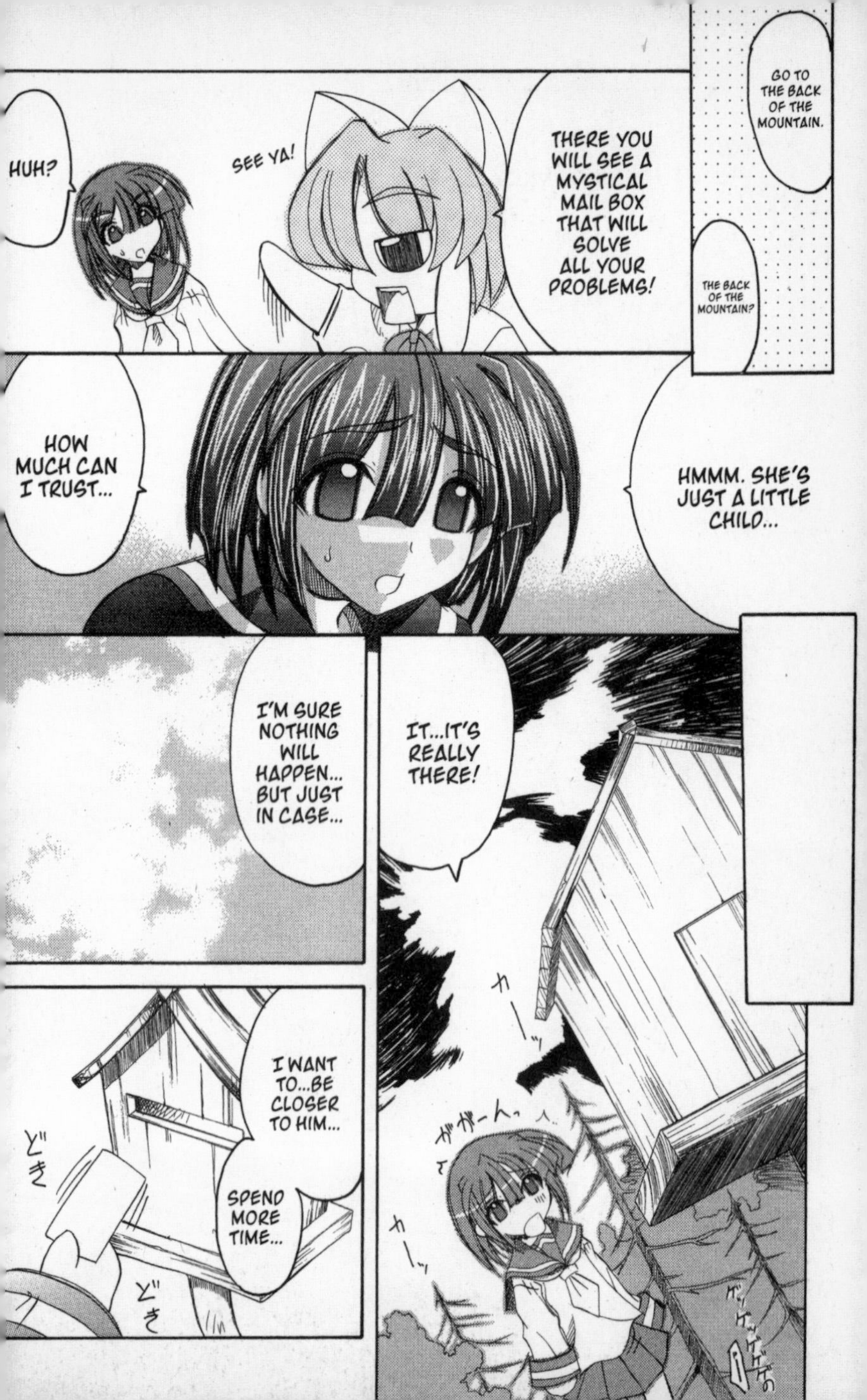
GO TO THE BACK OF THE MOUNTAIN.
THE BACK OF THE MOUNTAIN?
THERE YOU WILL SEE A MYSTICAL MAIL BOX THAT WILL SOLVE ALL YOUR PROBLEMS!
SEE YA!
HUH?
HMMM. SHE'S JUST A LITTLE CHILD...
HOW MUCH CAN I TRUST...
IT...IT'S REALLY THERE!
I'M SURE NOTHING WILL HAPPEN... BUT JUST IN CASE...
I WANT TO...BE CLOSER TO HIM...
SPEND MORE TIME...
どき
どき

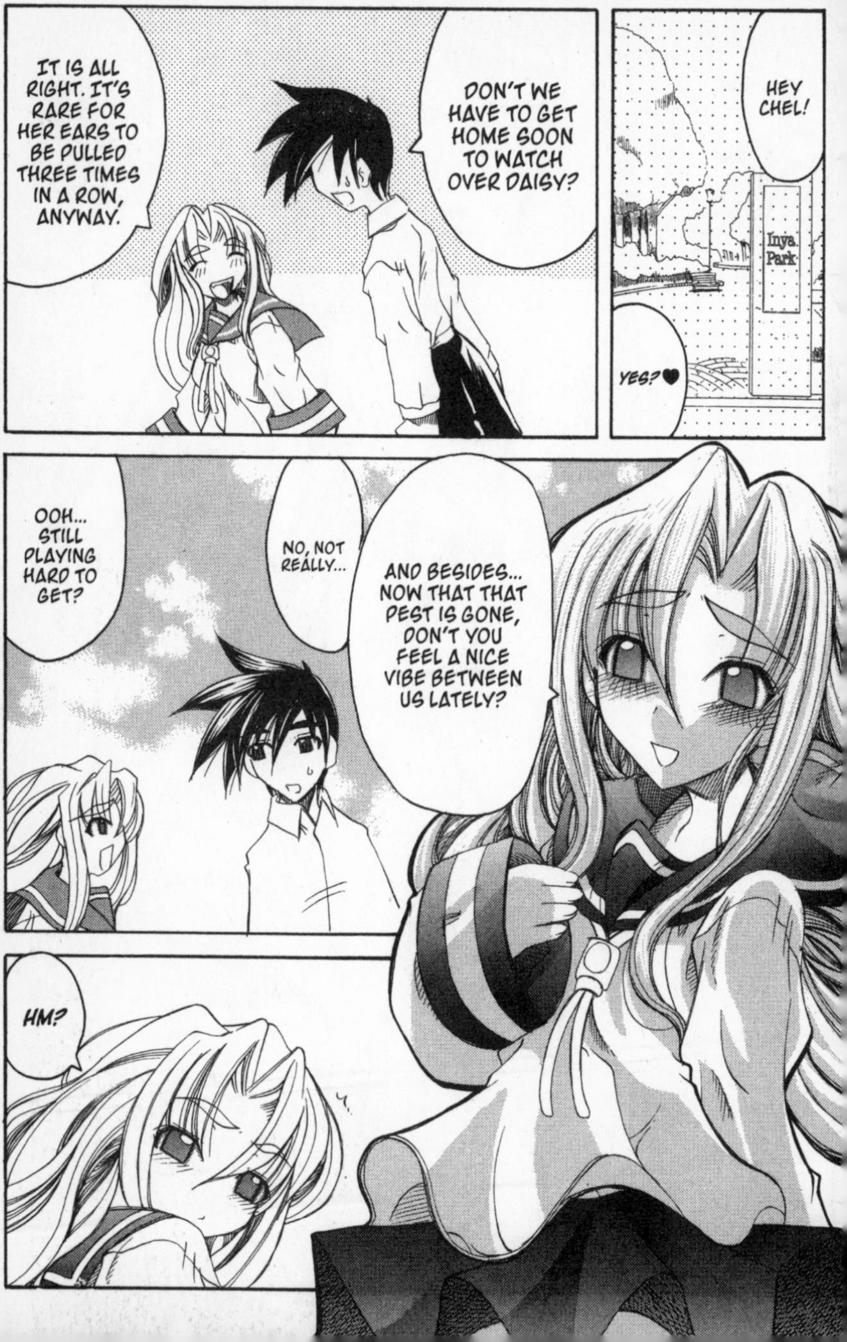
HEY CHEL!
YES? ♥
DON'T WE HAVE TO GET HOME SOON TO WATCH OVER DAISY?
IT IS ALL RIGHT. IT'S RARE FOR HER EARS TO BE PULLED THREE TIMES IN A ROW, ANYWAY.
Inya Park
AND BESIDES... NOW THAT THAT PEST IS GONE, DON'T YOU FEEL A NICE VIBE BETWEEN US LATELY?
NO, NOT REALLY...
OOH... STILL PLAYING HARD TO GET?
HM?

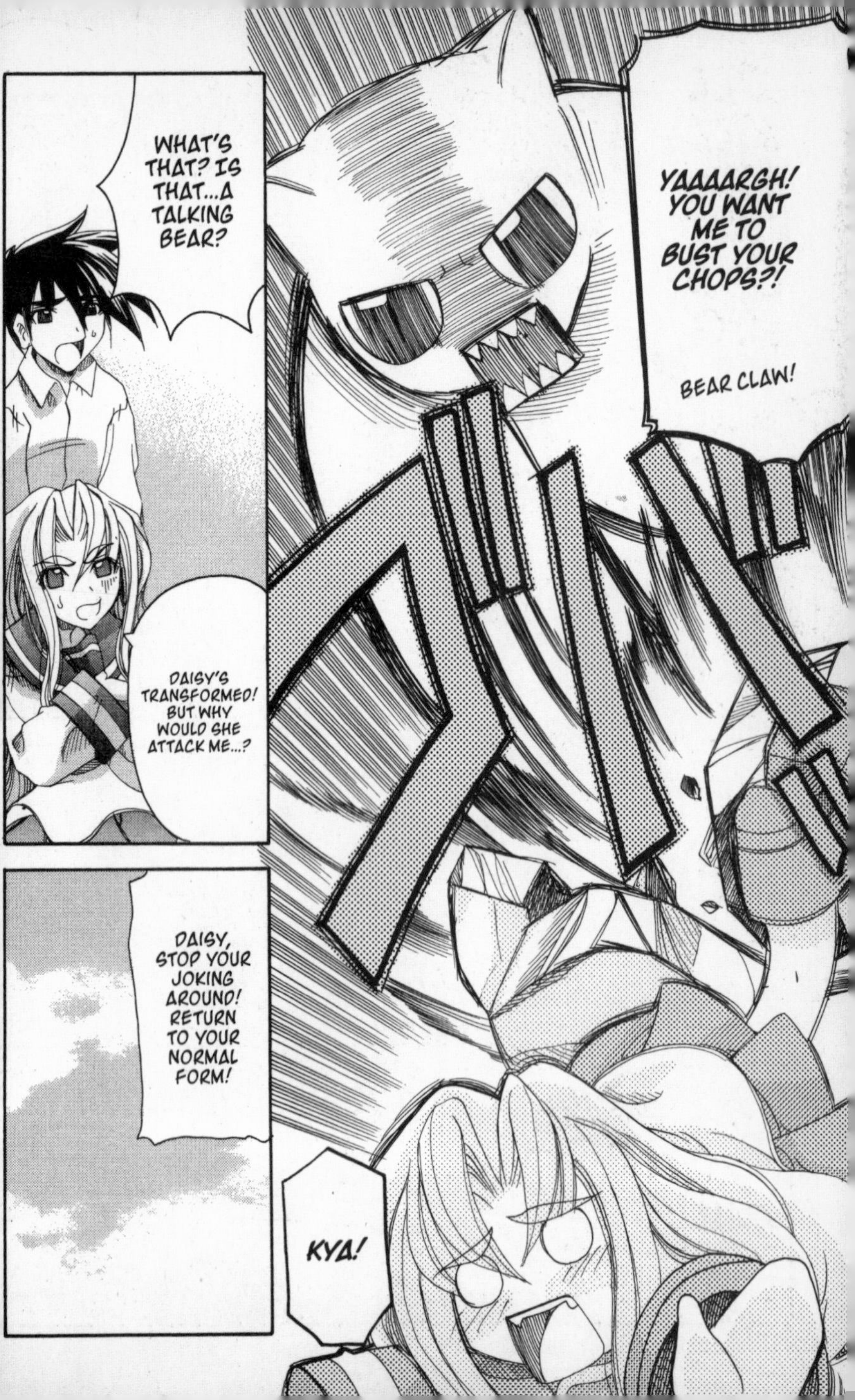
YAAAARGH! YOU WANT ME TO BUST YOUR CHOPS?!
BEAR CLAW!
KYA!
WHAT'S THAT? IS THAT...A TALKING BEAR?
DAISY'S TRANSFORMED! BUT WHY WOULD SHE ATTACK ME...?
DAISY, STOP YOUR JOKING AROUND! RETURN TO YOUR NORMAL FORM!

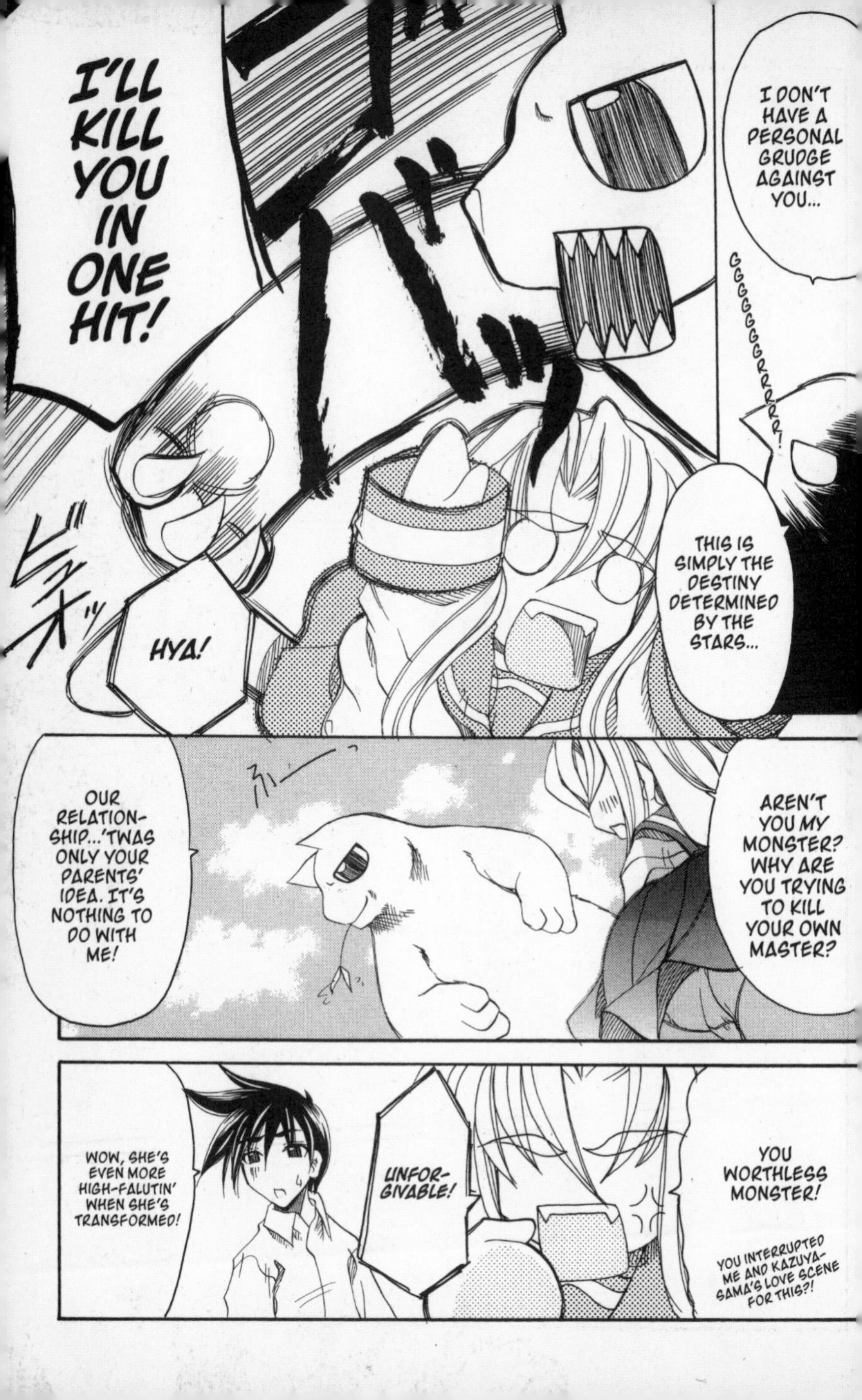
I DON'T HAVE A PERSONAL GRUDGE AGAINST YOU...
GGGGGGGRRRRR!
THIS IS SIMPLY THE DESTINY DETERMINED BY THE STARS...
I'LL KILL YOU IN ONE HIT!
HYA!
AREN'T YOU MY MONSTER? WHY ARE YOU TRYING TO KILL YOUR OWN MASTER?
OUR RELATION-SHIP...'TWAS ONLY YOUR PARENTS' IDEA. IT'S NOTHING TO DO WITH ME!
YOU WORTHLESS MONSTER!
YOU INTERRUPTED ME AND KAZUYA-SAMA'S LOVE SCENE FOR THIS?!
UNFOR-GIVABLE!
WOW, SHE'S EVEN MORE HIGH-FALUTIN' WHEN SHE'S TRANSFORMED!

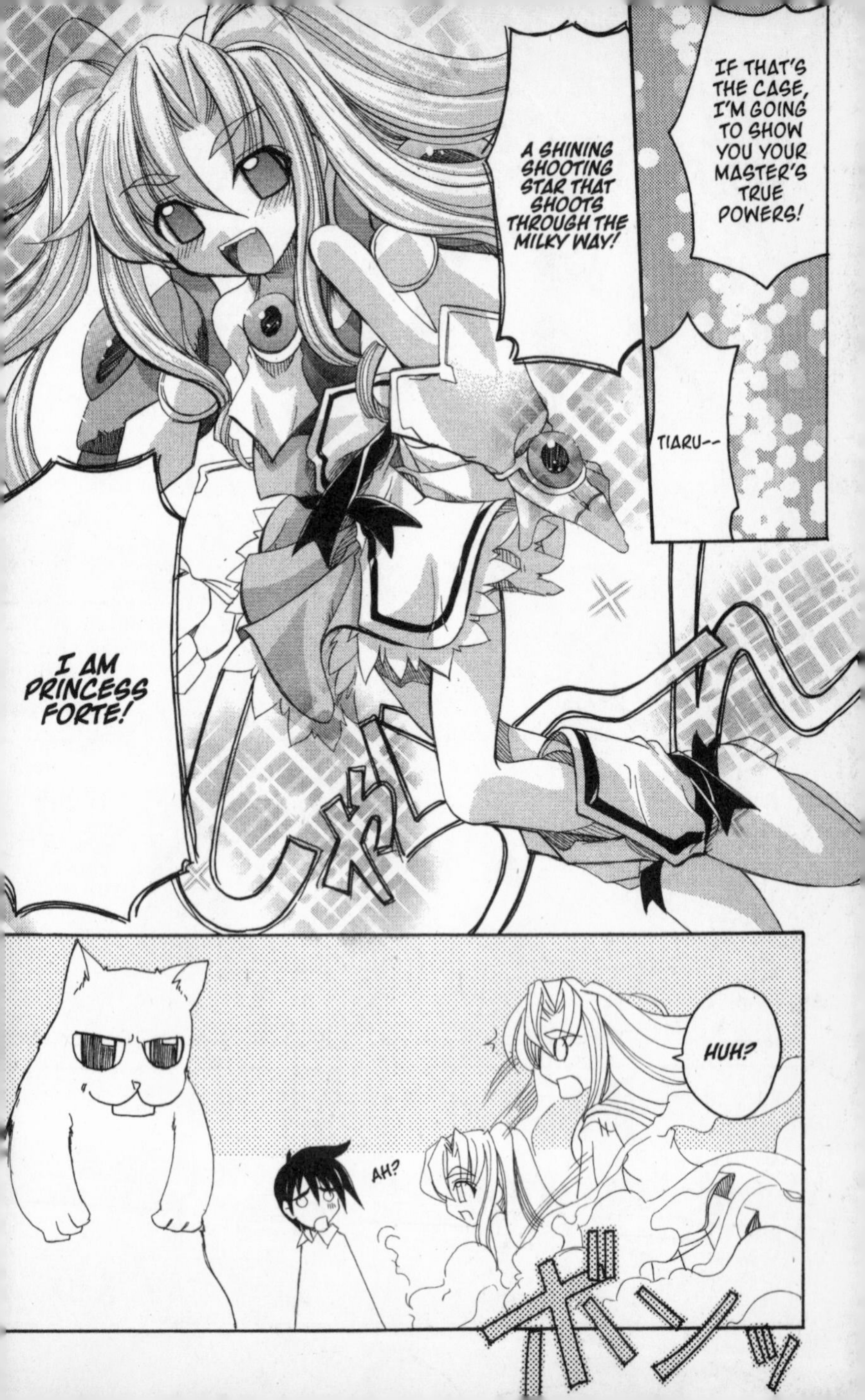
IF THAT'S THE CASE, I'M GOING TO SHOW YOU YOUR MASTER'S TRUE POWERS!
A SHINING SHOOTING STAR THAT SHOOTS THROUGH THE MILKY WAY!
TIARU--
I AM PRINCESS FORTE!
HUH?
AH?

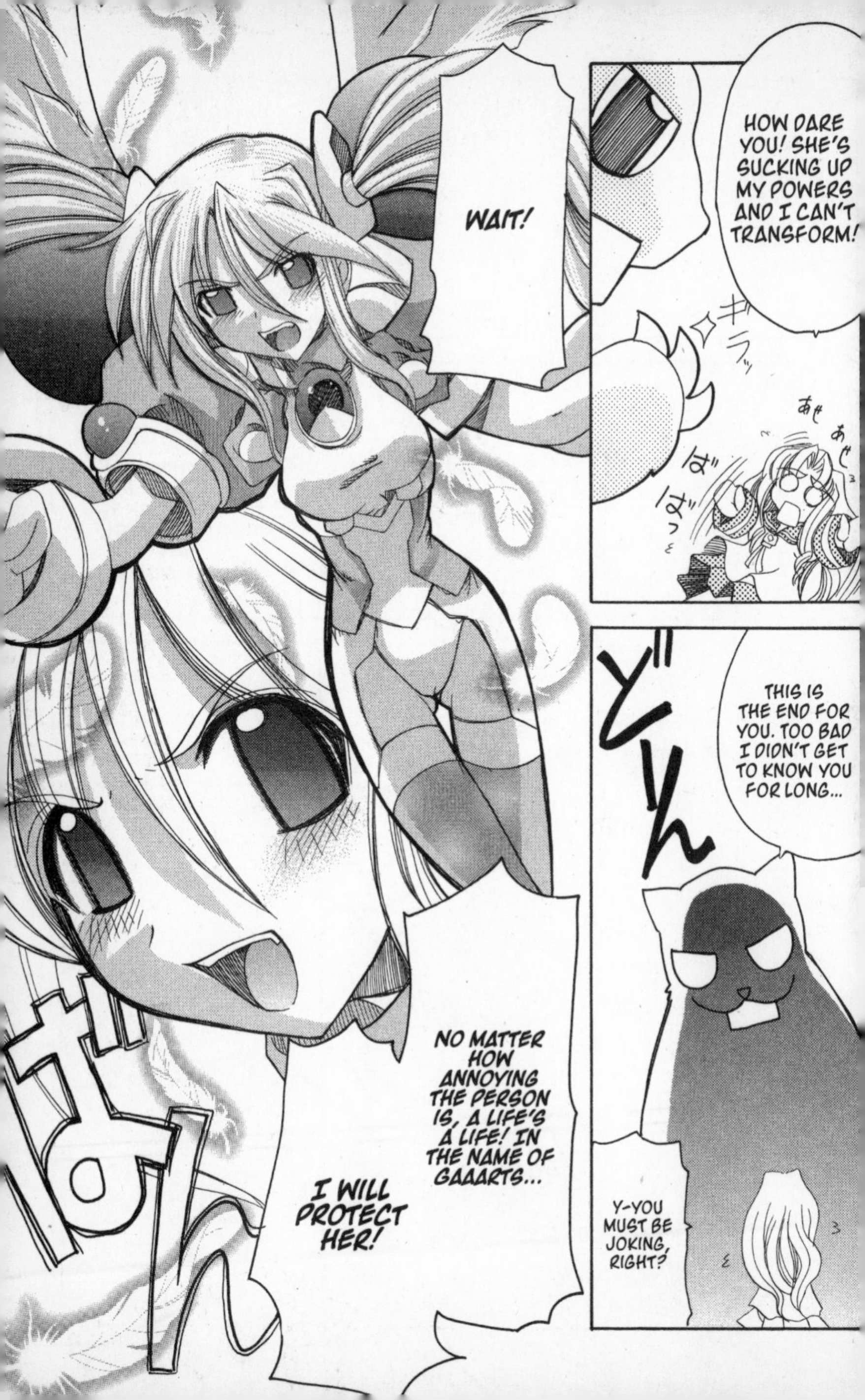
HOW DARE YOU! SHE'S SUCKING UP MY POWERS AND I CAN'T TRANSFORM!
ギラッ
THIS IS THE END FOR YOU. TOO BAD I DIDN'T GET TO KNOW YOU FOR LONG...
Y-YOU MUST BE JOKING, RIGHT?
WAIT!
NO MATTER HOW ANNOYING THE PERSON IS, A LIFE'S A LIFE! IN THE NAME OF GAAARTS...
I WILL PROTECT HER!

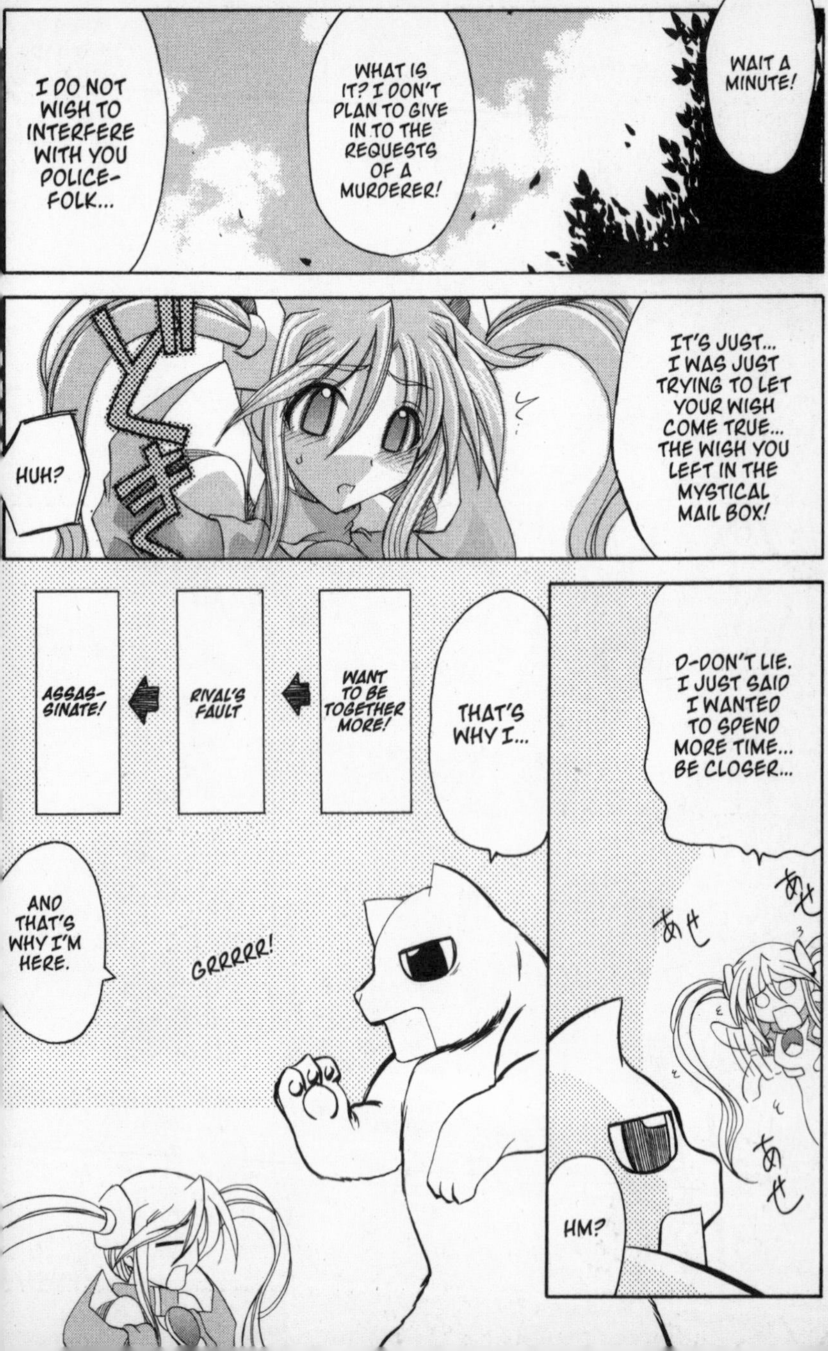
WAIT A MINUTE!
WHAT IS IT? I DON'T PLAN TO GIVE IN TO THE REQUESTS OF A MURDERER!
I DO NOT WISH TO INTERFERE WITH YOU POLICE-FOLK...
IT'S JUST... I WAS JUST TRYING TO LET YOUR WISH COME TRUE... THE WISH YOU LEFT IN THE MYSTICAL MAIL BOX!
HUH?
D-DON'T LIE. I JUST SAID I WANTED TO SPEND MORE TIME... BE CLOSER...
あせ
あせ
あせ
HM?
THAT'S WHY I...
WANT TO BE TOGETHER MORE!
RIVAL'S FAULT
ASSAS-SINATE!
GRRRRR!
AND THAT'S WHY I'M HERE.

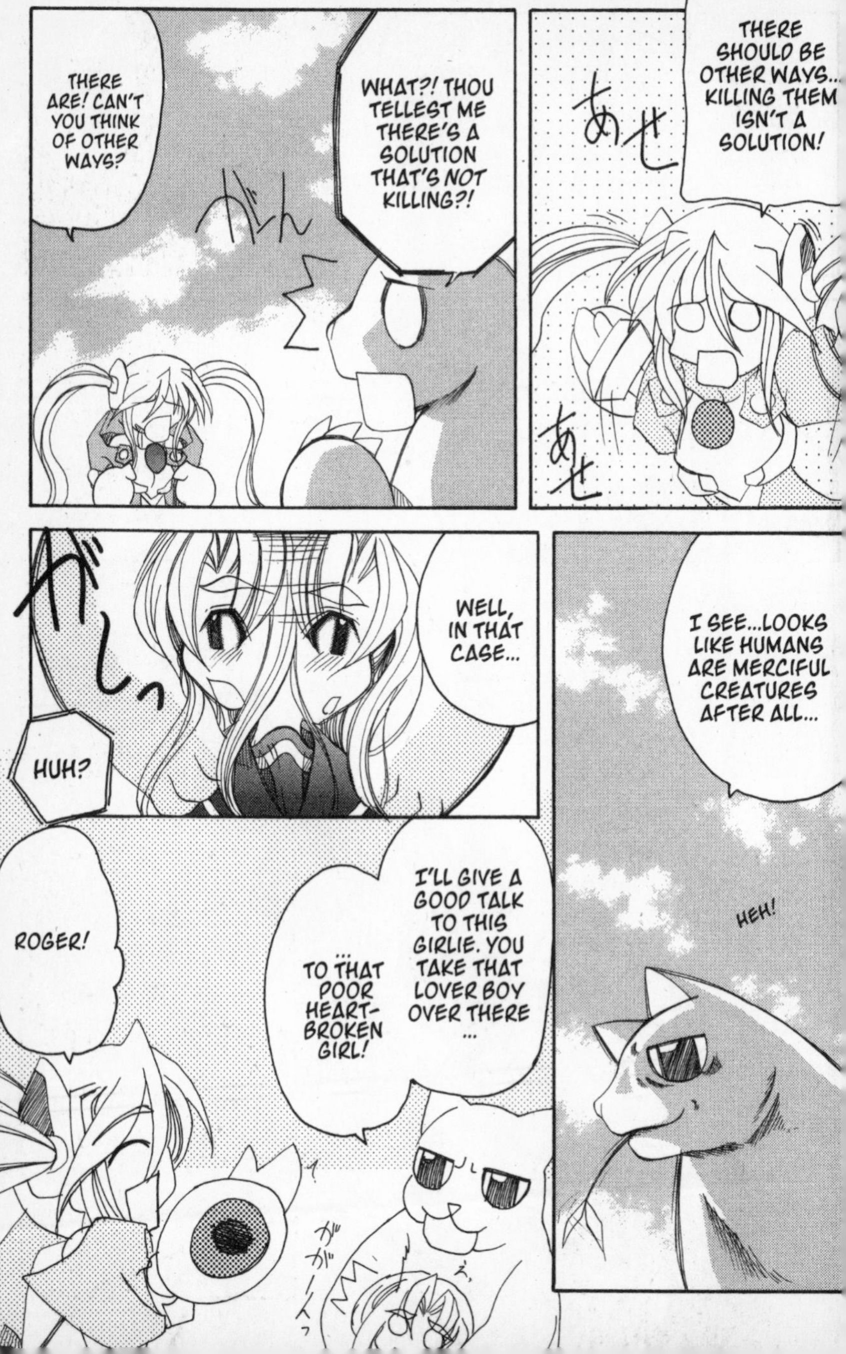
THERE SHOULD BE OTHER WAYS... KILLING THEM ISN'T A SOLUTION!
あせ
あせ
WHAT?! THOU TELLEST ME THERE'S A SOLUTION THAT'S NOT KILLING?!
THERE ARE! CAN'T YOU THINK OF OTHER WAYS?
I SEE...LOOKS LIKE HUMANS ARE MERCIFUL CREATURES AFTER ALL...
HEH!
WELL, IN THAT CASE...
HUH?
がしっ
I'LL GIVE A GOOD TALK TO THIS GIRLIE. YOU TAKE THAT LOVER BOY OVER THERE ...
... TO THAT POOR HEART-BROKEN GIRL!
ROGER!

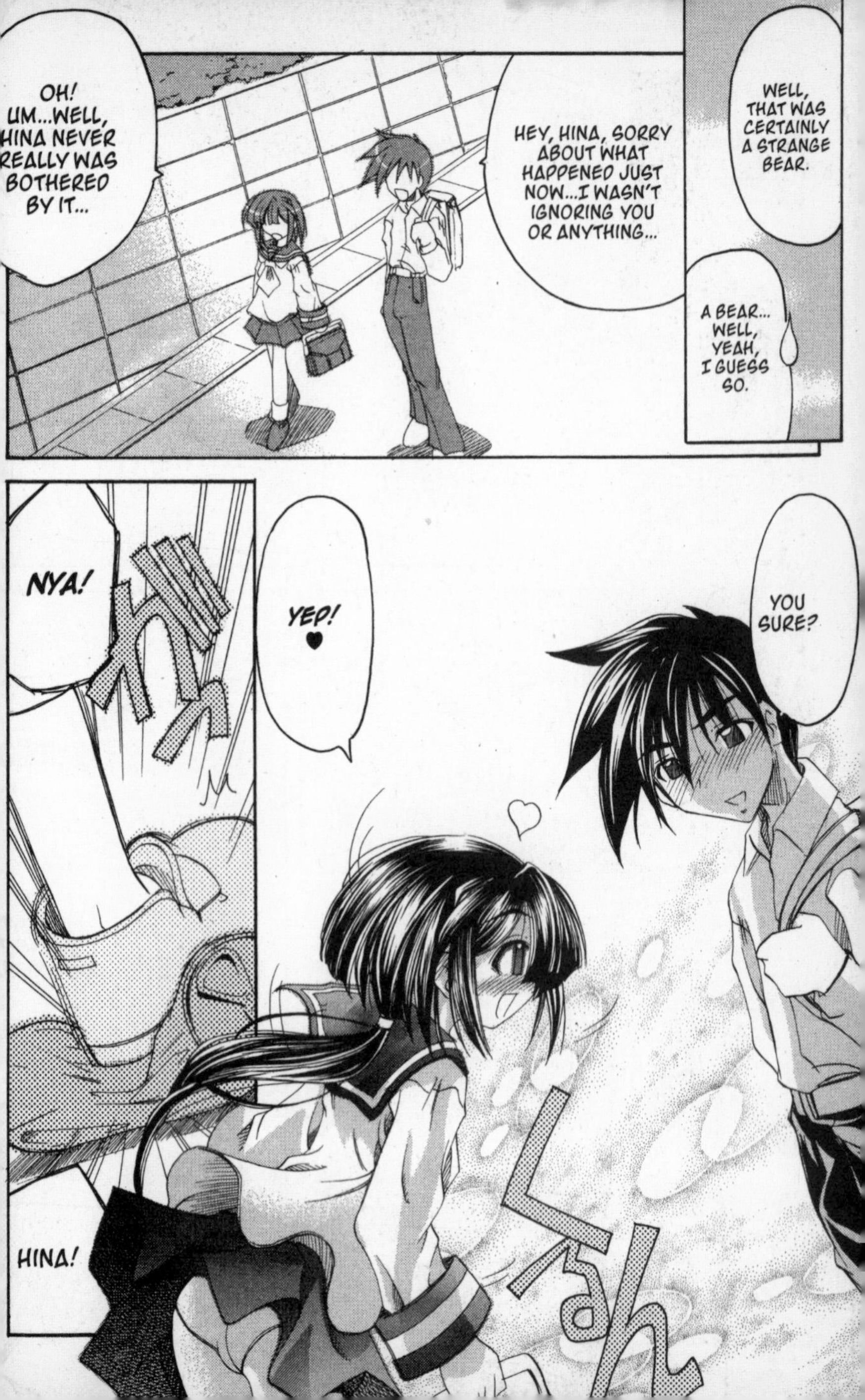
WELL, THAT WAS CERTAINLY A STRANGE BEAR.
A BEAR... WELL, YEAH, I GUESS SO.
HEY, HINA, SORRY ABOUT WHAT HAPPENED JUST NOW...I WASN'T IGNORING YOU OR ANYTHING...
OH! UM...WELL, HINA NEVER REALLY WAS BOTHERED BY IT...
YOU SURE?
YEP! ♥
NYA!
HINA!

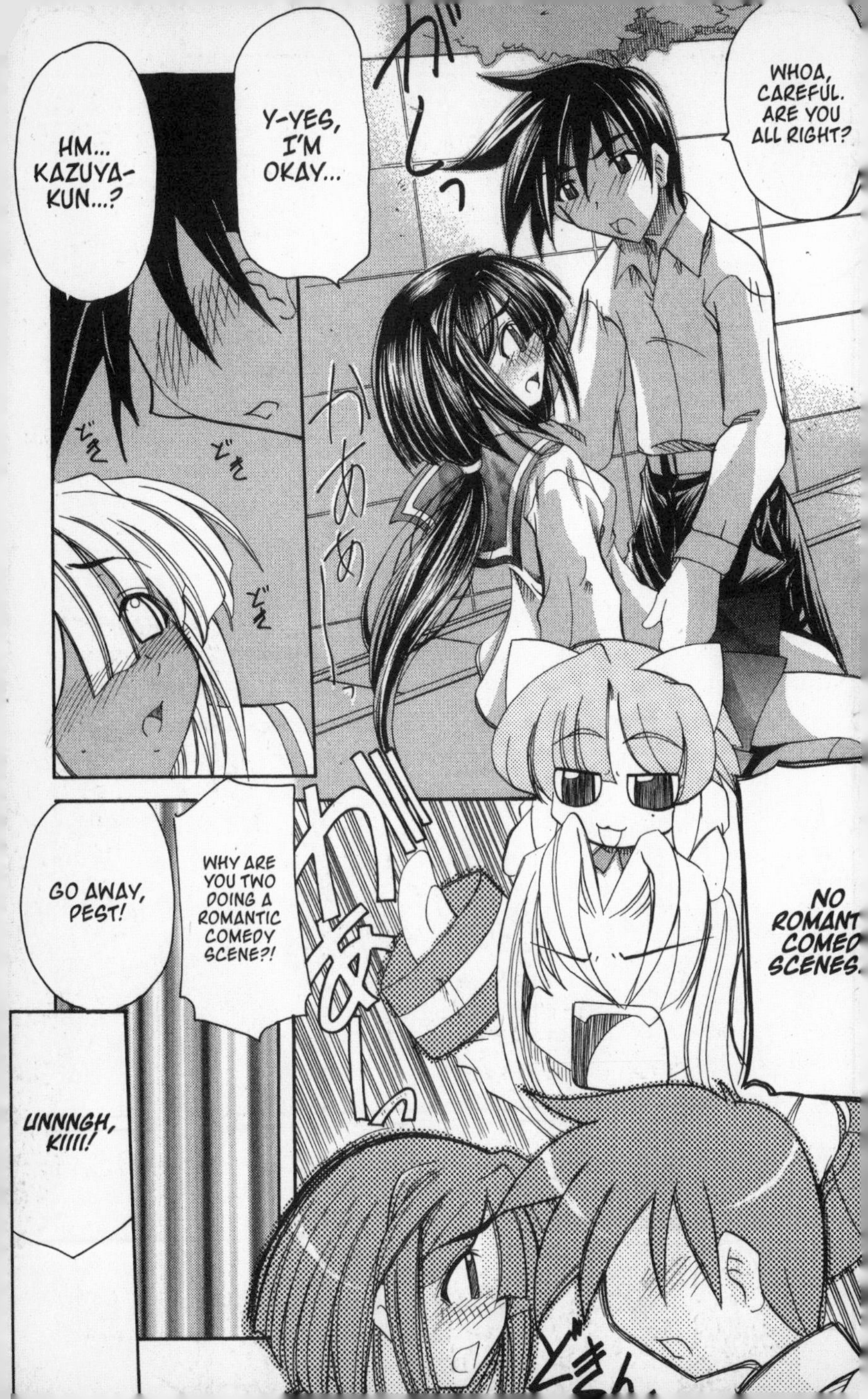

WHOA, CAREFUL. ARE YOU ALL RIGHT?
Y-YES, I'M OKAY...
HM... KAZUYA-KUN...?
NO ROMANT COMED SCENES.
WHY ARE YOU TWO DOING A ROMANTIC COMEDY SCENE?!
GO AWAY, PEST!
UNNNGH, KIIII!

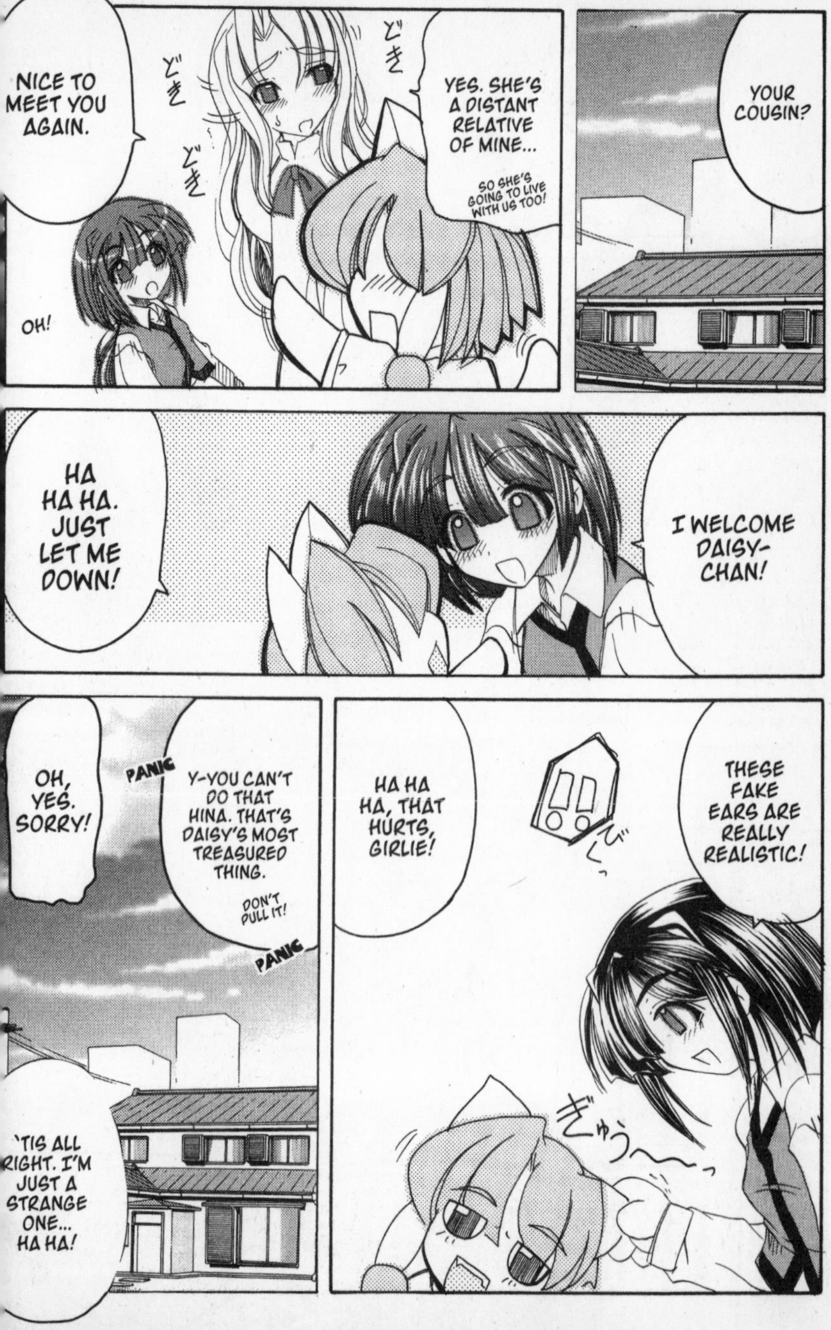

YOUR COUSIN?
どき
YES. SHE'S A DISTANT RELATIVE OF MINE...
SO SHE'S GOING TO LIVE WITH US TOO!
どき
どき
NICE TO MEET YOU AGAIN.
OH!
I WELCOME DAISY-CHAN!
HA HA HA. JUST LET ME DOWN!
THESE FAKE EARS ARE REALLY REALISTIC!
びくっ
HA HA HA, THAT HURTS, GIRLIE!
ぎゅう〜〜っ
PANIC
Y-YOU CAN'T DO THAT HINA. THAT'S DAISY'S MOST TREASURED THING.
OH, YES. SORRY!
DON'T PULL IT!
PANIC
`TIS ALL RIGHT. I'M JUST A STRANGE ONE... HA HA!

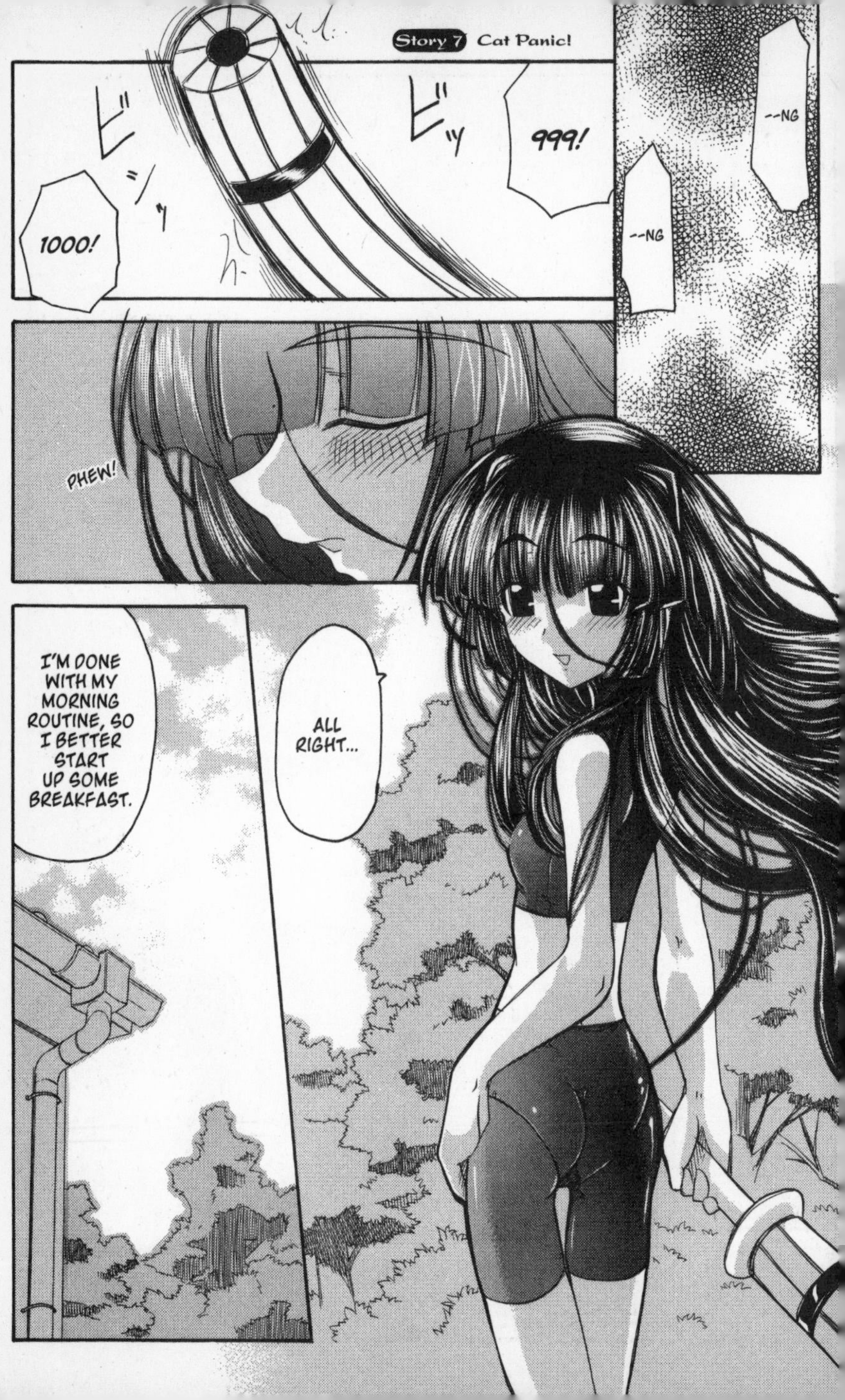
--NG
--NG
999!
1000!
PHEW!
ALL RIGHT...
I'M DONE WITH MY MORNING ROUTINE, SO I BETTER START UP SOME BREAKFAST.

Story 7

Cat Panic!

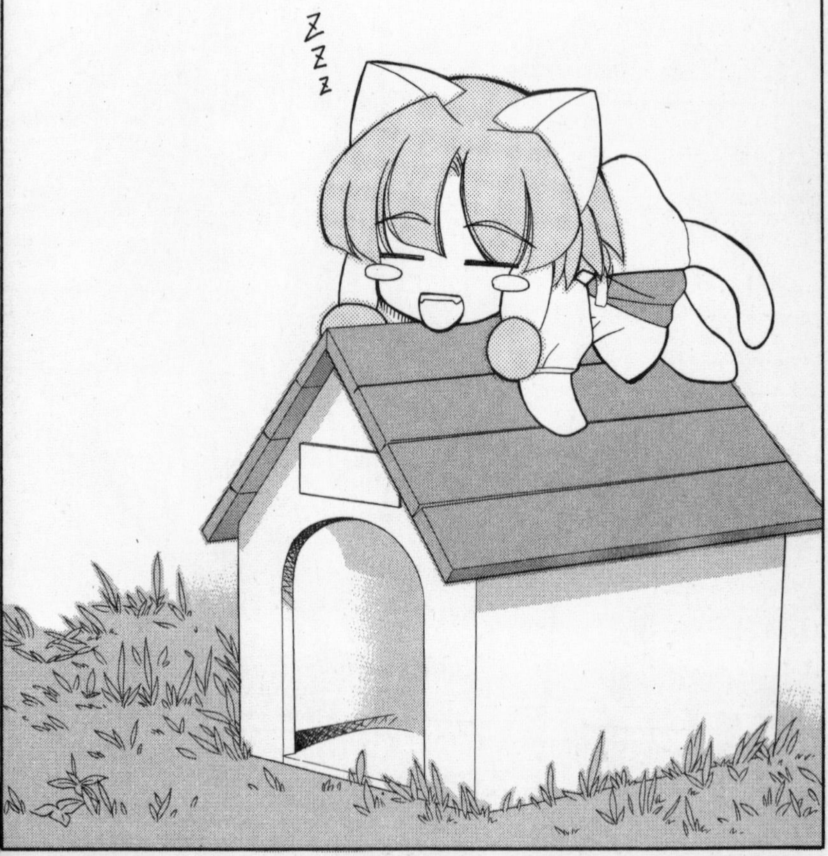
Z Z Z

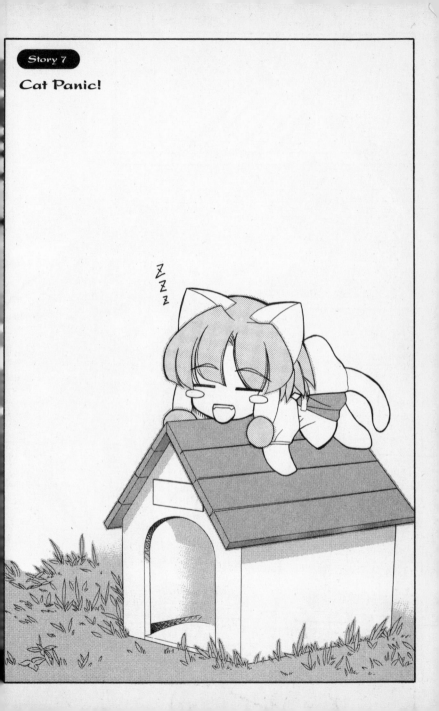

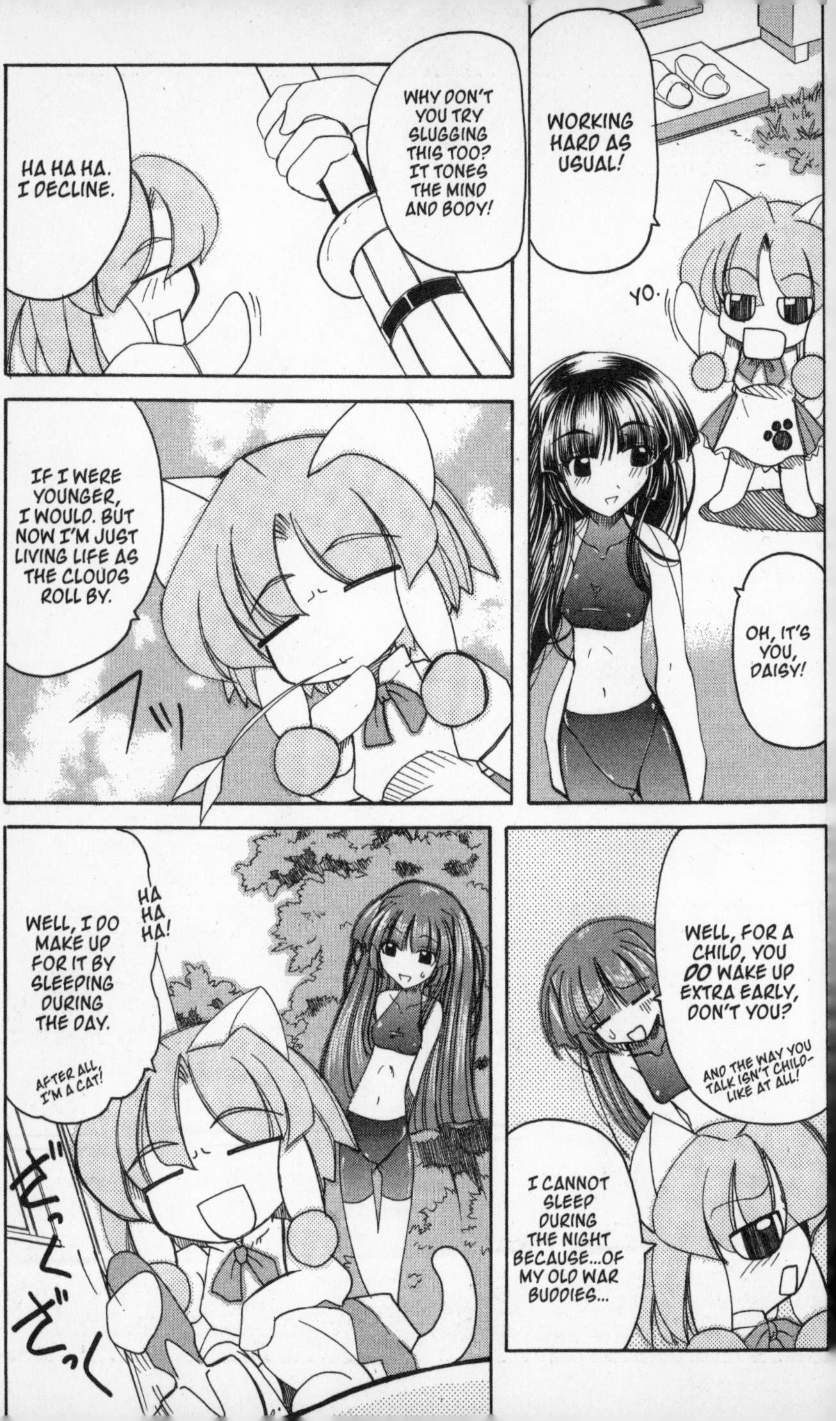
WORKING HARD AS USUAL!
YO.
OH, IT'S YOU, DAISY!
WHY DON'T YOU TRY SLUGGING THIS TOO? IT TONES THE MIND AND BODY!
HA HA HA. I DECLINE.
IF I WERE YOUNGER, I WOULD. BUT NOW I'M JUST LIVING LIFE AS THE CLOUDS ROLL BY.
WELL, FOR A CHILD, YOU DO WAKE UP EXTRA EARLY, DON'T YOU?
AND THE WAY YOU TALK ISN'T CHILD-LIKE AT ALL!
I CANNOT SLEEP DURING THE NIGHT BECAUSE...OF MY OLD WAR BUDDIES...
HA HA HA!
WELL, I DO MAKE UP FOR IT BY SLEEPING DURING THE DAY.
AFTER ALL, I'M A CAT!

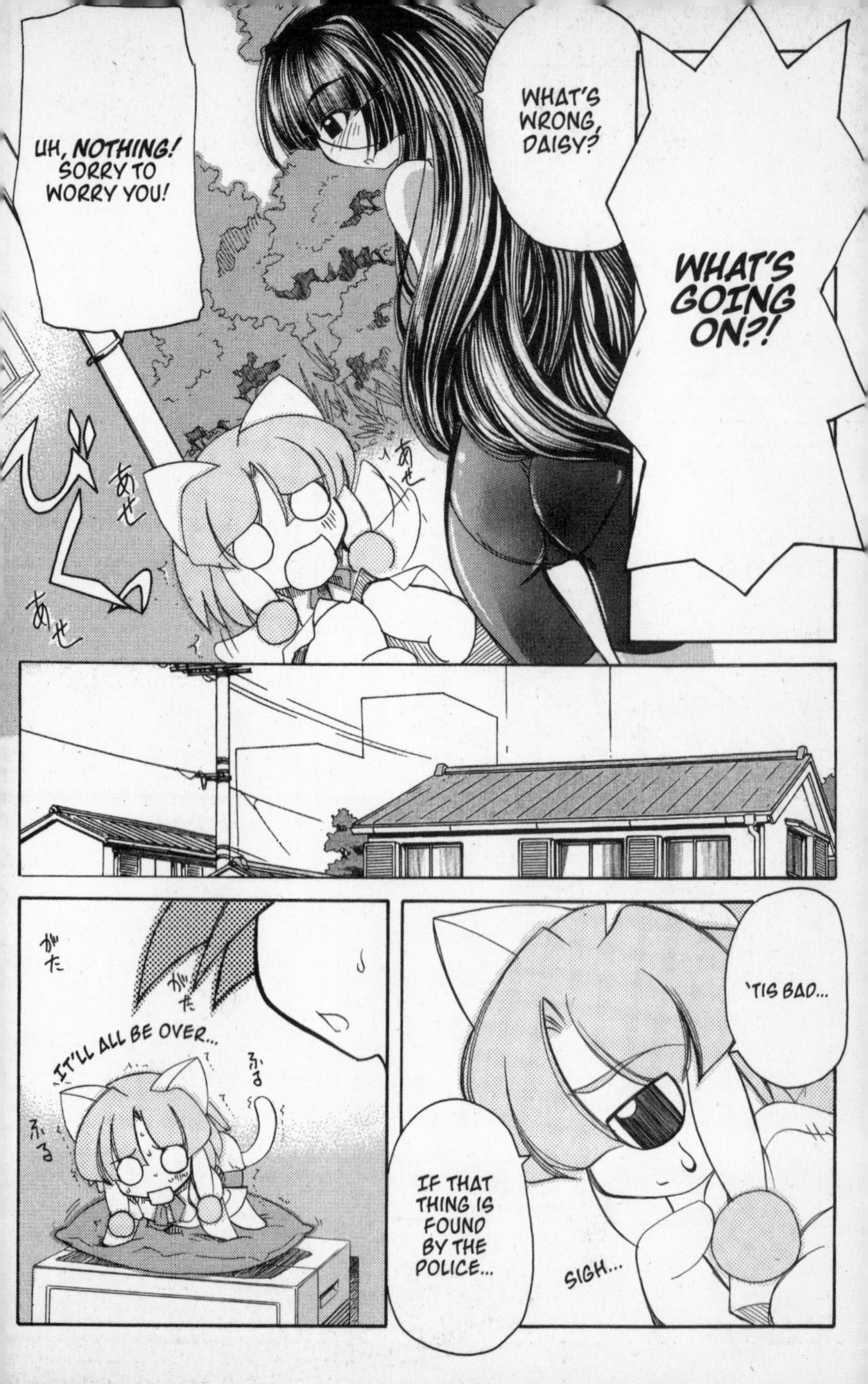
WHAT'S WRONG, DAISY?
WHAT'S GOING ON?!
UH, NOTHING! SORRY TO WORRY YOU!
あせ
あせ
あせ
'TIS BAD...
IF THAT THING IS FOUND BY THE POLICE...
SIGH...
がた
がた
IT'LL ALL BE OVER...
ふる
ふる

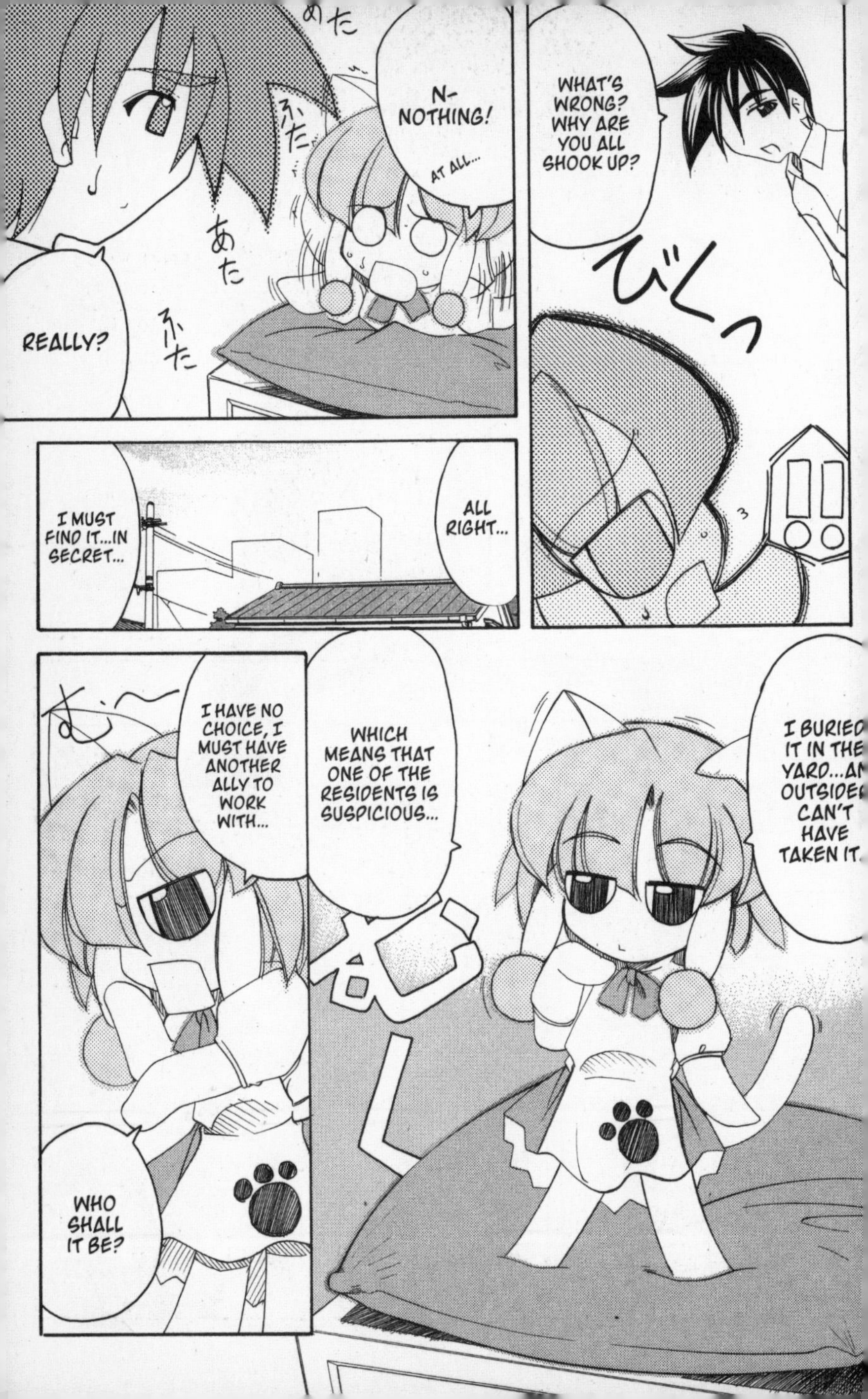
WHAT'S WRONG? WHY ARE YOU ALL SHOOK UP?
びくっ
めた
ふた
N-NOTHING!
AT ALL...
あた
ふた
REALLY?
ALL RIGHT...
I MUST FIND IT...IN SECRET...
I BURIED IT IN THE YARD...AN OUTSIDER CAN'T HAVE TAKEN IT.
WHICH MEANS THAT ONE OF THE RESIDENTS IS SUSPICIOUS...
I HAVE NO CHOICE, I MUST HAVE ANOTHER ALLY TO WORK WITH...
WHO SHALL IT BE?

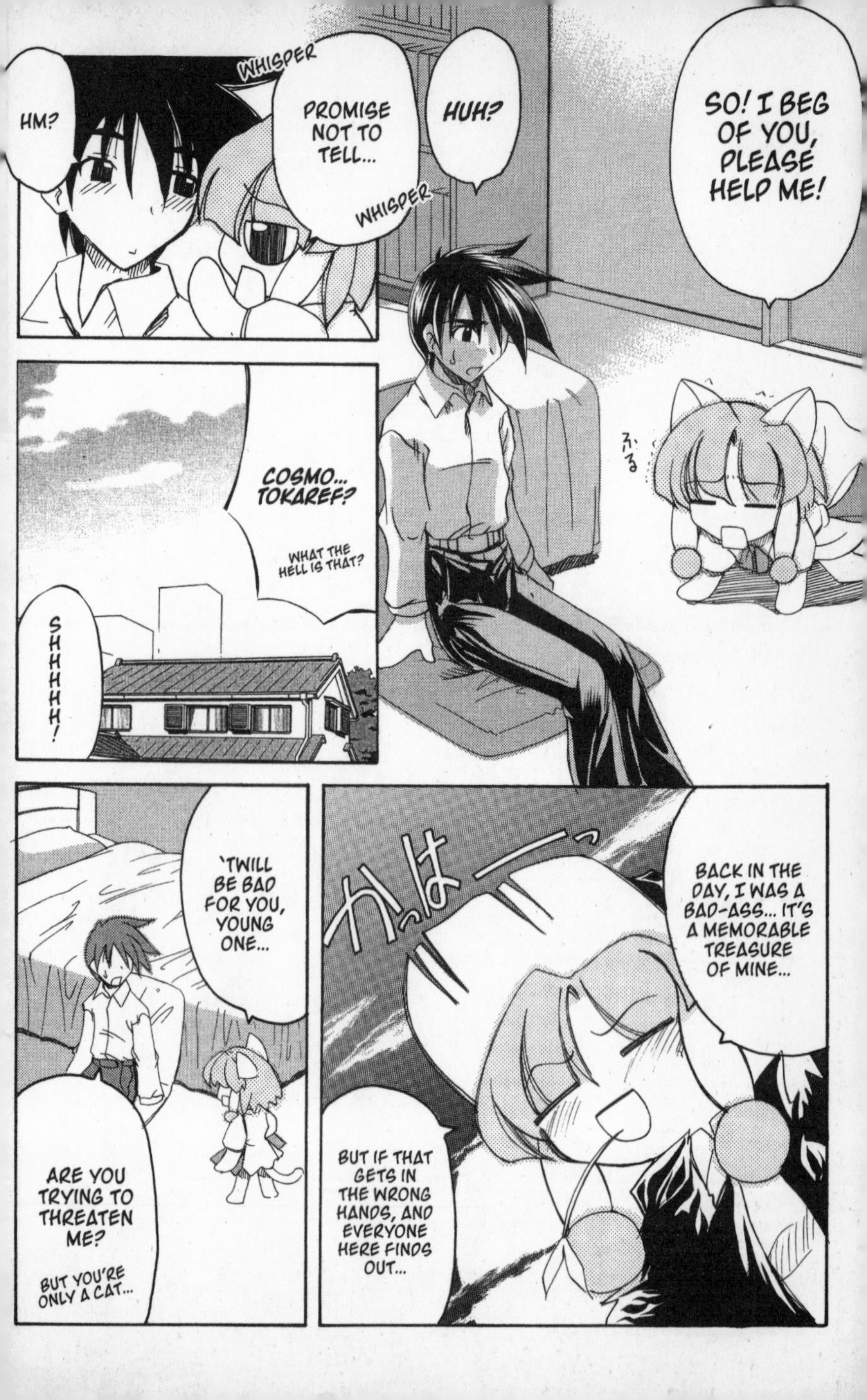
SO! I BEG OF YOU, PLEASE HELP ME!
ふる
HUH?
WHISPER
PROMISE NOT TO TELL...
WHISPER
HM?
COSMO... TOKAREF?
WHAT THE HELL IS THAT?
SHHHHHH!
BACK IN THE DAY, I WAS A BAD-ASS... IT'S A MEMORABLE TREASURE OF MINE...
わっはーー
BUT IF THAT GETS IN THE WRONG HANDS, AND EVERYONE HERE FINDS OUT...
'TWILL BE BAD FOR YOU, YOUNG ONE...
ARE YOU TRYING TO THREATEN ME?
BUT YOU'RE ONLY A CAT...

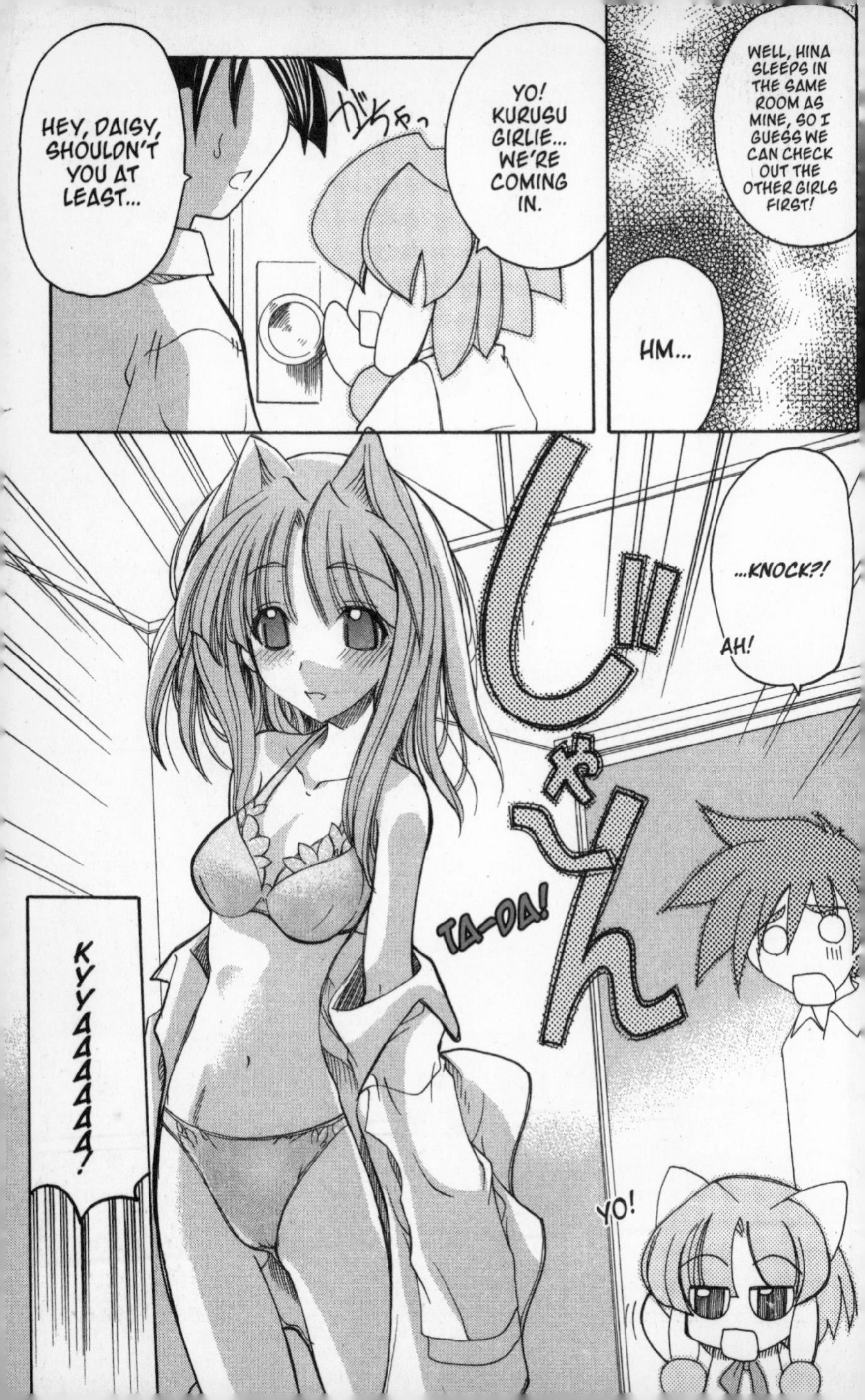
WELL, HINA SLEEPS IN THE SAME ROOM AS MINE, SO I GUESS WE CAN CHECK OUT THE OTHER GIRLS FIRST!
HM...
YO! KURUSU GIRLIE... WE'RE COMING IN.
がちゃっ
HEY, DAISY, SHOULDN'T YOU AT LEAST...
...KNOCK?!
AH!
じゃん
TA-DA!
YO!
KYYAAAAAAA!

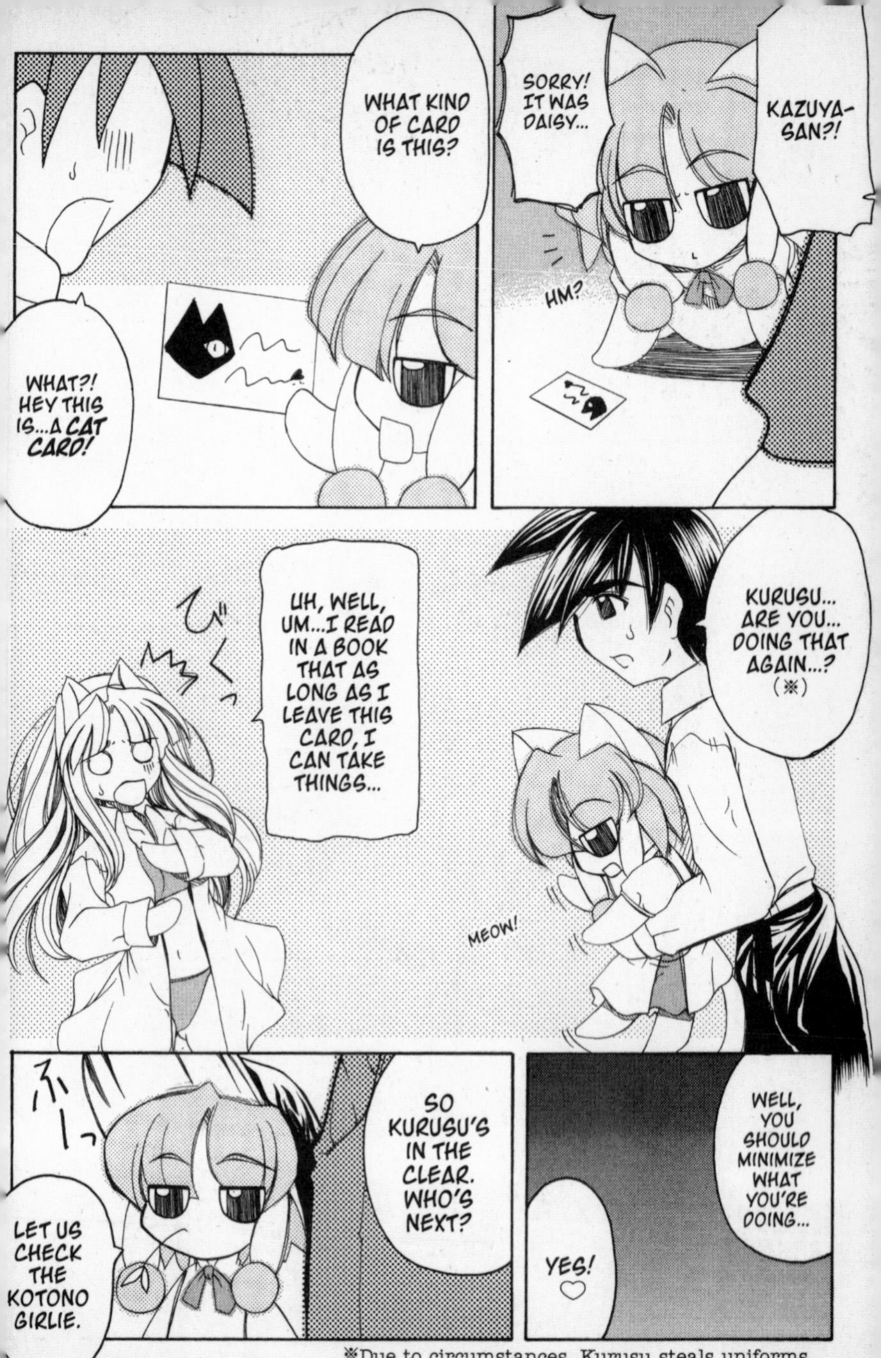
KAZUYA-SAN?!
SORRY! IT WAS DAISY...
HM?
WHAT KIND OF CARD IS THIS?
WHAT?! HEY THIS IS...A CAT CARD!
KURUSU... ARE YOU... DOING THAT AGAIN...? (※)
MEOW!
UH, WELL, UM...I READ IN A BOOK THAT AS LONG AS I LEAVE THIS CARD, I CAN TAKE THINGS...
びくっ
WELL, YOU SHOULD MINIMIZE WHAT YOU'RE DOING...
YES! ♡
SO KURUSU'S IN THE CLEAR. WHO'S NEXT?
ふーっ
LET US CHECK THE KOTONO GIRLIE.

※Due to circumstances, Kurusu steals uniforms.

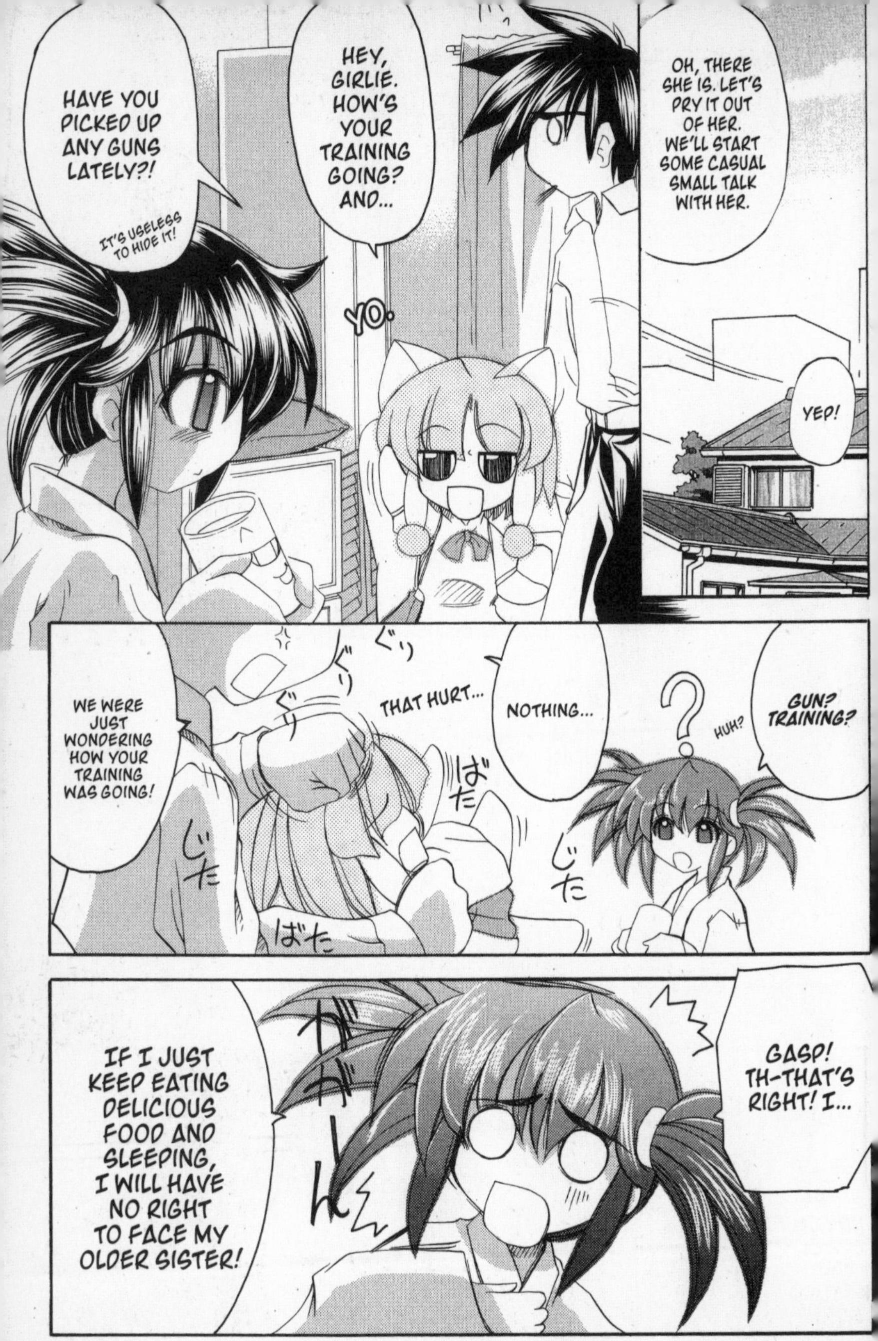
OH, THERE SHE IS. LET'S PRY IT OUT OF HER. WE'LL START SOME CASUAL SMALL TALK WITH HER.
YEP!
HEY, GIRLIE. HOW'S YOUR TRAINING GOING? AND...
YO.
HAVE YOU PICKED UP ANY GUNS LATELY?!
IT'S USELESS TO HIDE IT!
GUN? TRAINING?
HUH?
NOTHING...
THAT HURT...
ばた
ばた
じた
じた
WE WERE JUST WONDERING HOW YOUR TRAINING WAS GOING!
GASP! TH-THAT'S RIGHT! I...
IF I JUST KEEP EATING DELICIOUS FOOD AND SLEEPING, I WILL HAVE NO RIGHT TO FACE MY OLDER SISTER!

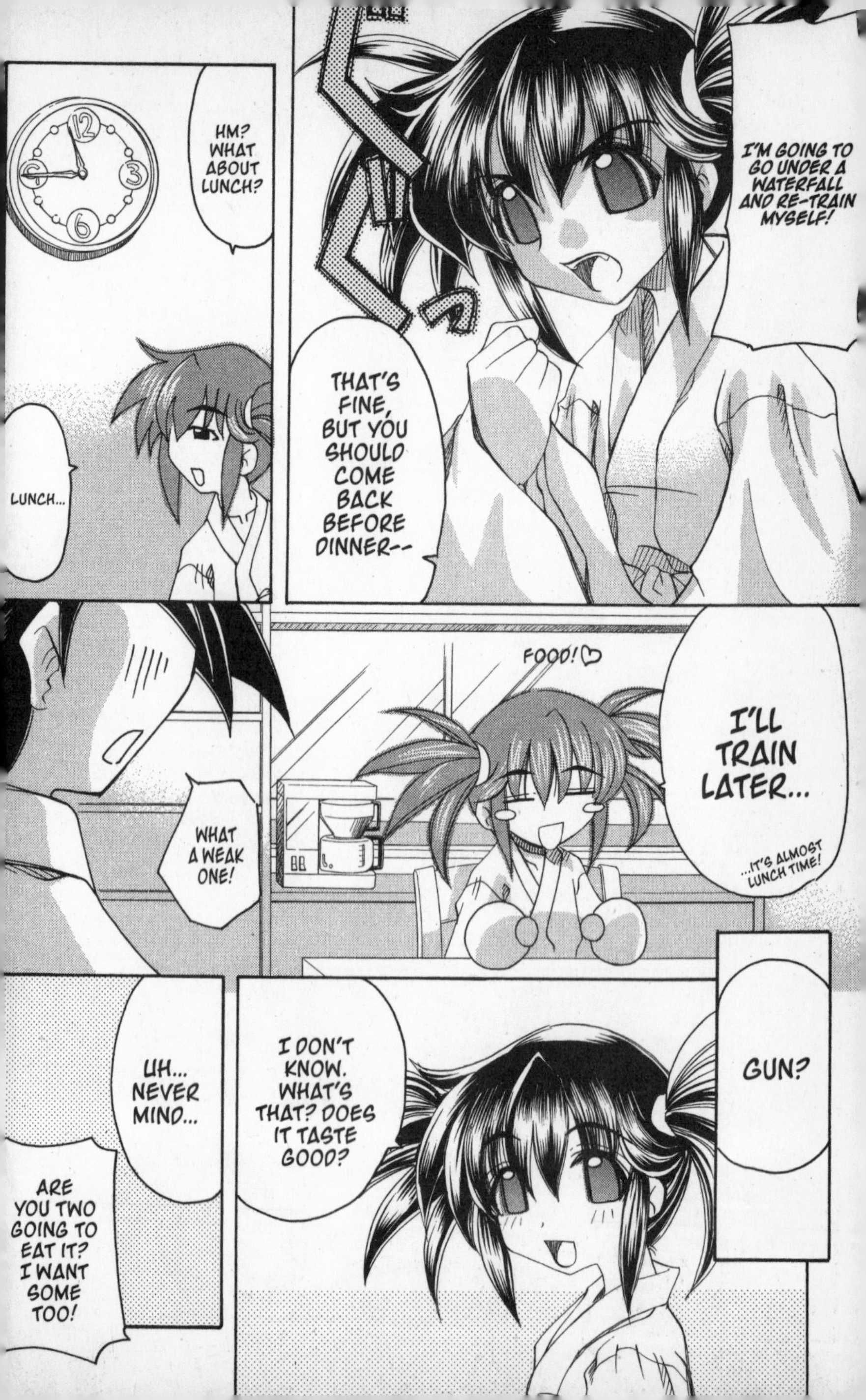

I'M GOING TO GO UNDER A WATERFALL AND RE-TRAIN MYSELF!
THAT'S FINE, BUT YOU SHOULD COME BACK BEFORE DINNER--
HM? WHAT ABOUT LUNCH?
LUNCH...
I'LL TRAIN LATER...
...IT'S ALMOST LUNCH TIME!
FOOD!♡
WHAT A WEAK ONE!
GUN?
I DON'T KNOW. WHAT'S THAT? DOES IT TASTE GOOD?
UH... NEVER MIND...
ARE YOU TWO GOING TO EAT IT? I WANT SOME TOO!

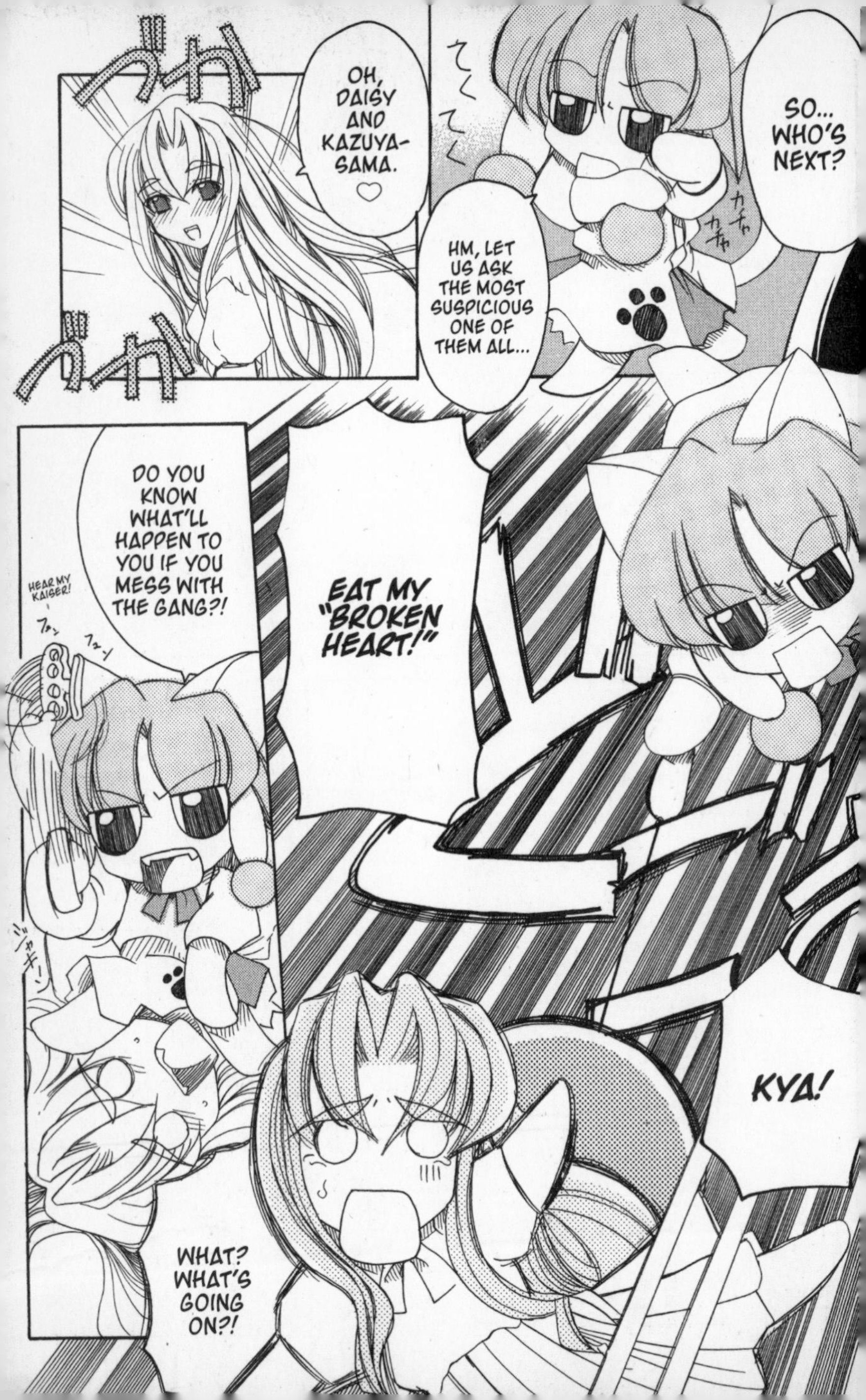
SO... WHO'S NEXT?
てくてく
カチャカチャ
HM, LET US ASK THE MOST SUSPICIOUS ONE OF THEM ALL...
ざわざわ
OH, DAISY AND KAZUYA-SAMA. ♥
EAT MY "BROKEN HEART!"
KYA!
WHAT? WHAT'S GOING ON?!
DO YOU KNOW WHAT'LL HAPPEN TO YOU IF YOU MESS WITH THE GANG?!
HEAR MY KAISER!

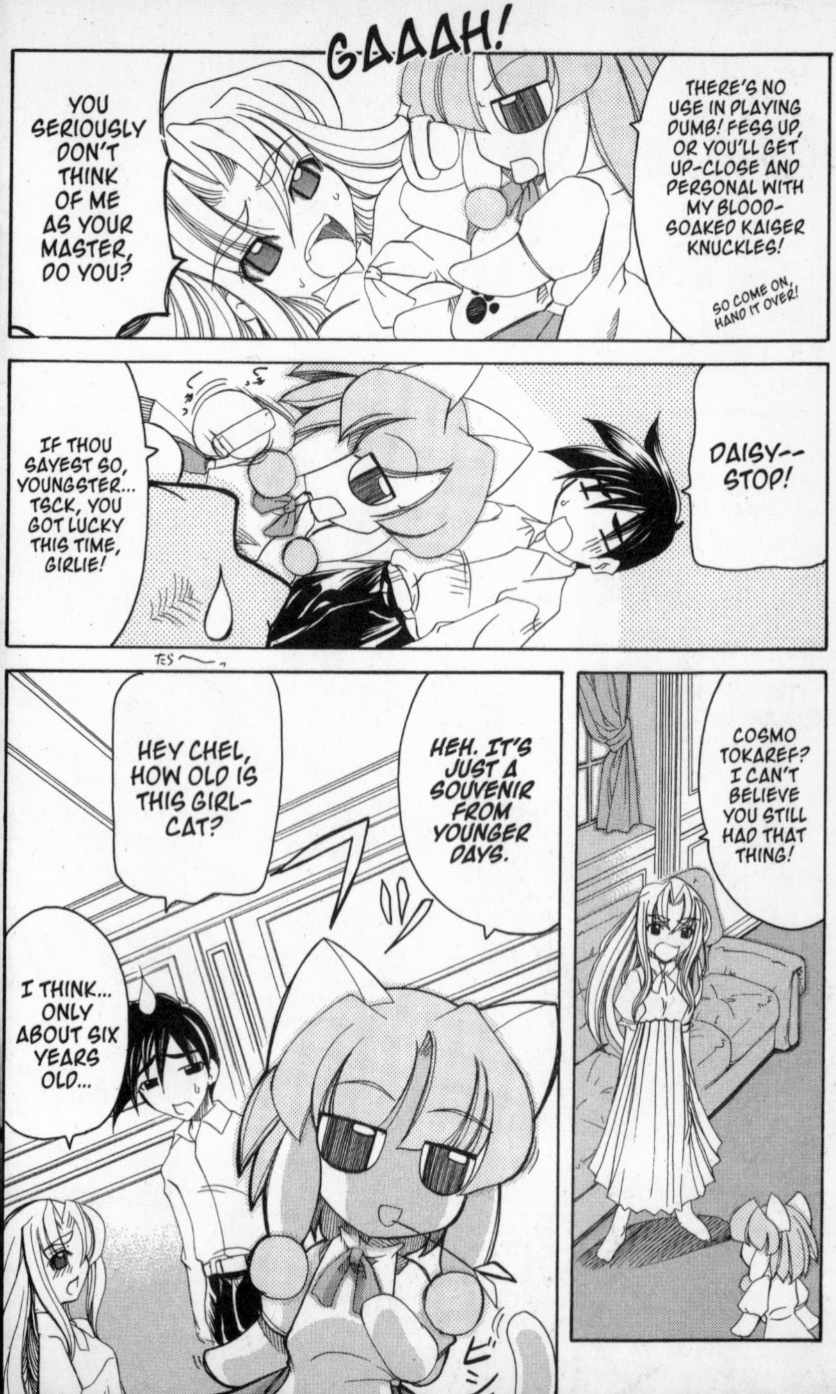
GAAAH!
THERE'S NO USE IN PLAYING DUMB! FESS UP, OR YOU'LL GET UP-CLOSE AND PERSONAL WITH MY BLOOD-SOAKED KAISER KNUCKLES!
SO COME ON, HAND IT OVER!
YOU SERIOUSLY DON'T THINK OF ME AS YOUR MASTER, DO YOU?
DAISY-- STOP!
IF THOU SAYEST SO, YOUNGSTER... TSCK, YOU GOT LUCKY THIS TIME, GIRLIE!
TES~
COSMO TOKAREF? I CAN'T BELIEVE YOU STILL HAD THAT THING!
HEH. IT'S JUST A SOUVENIR FROM YOUNGER DAYS.
HEY CHEL, HOW OLD IS THIS GIRL-CAT?
I THINK... ONLY ABOUT SIX YEARS OLD...

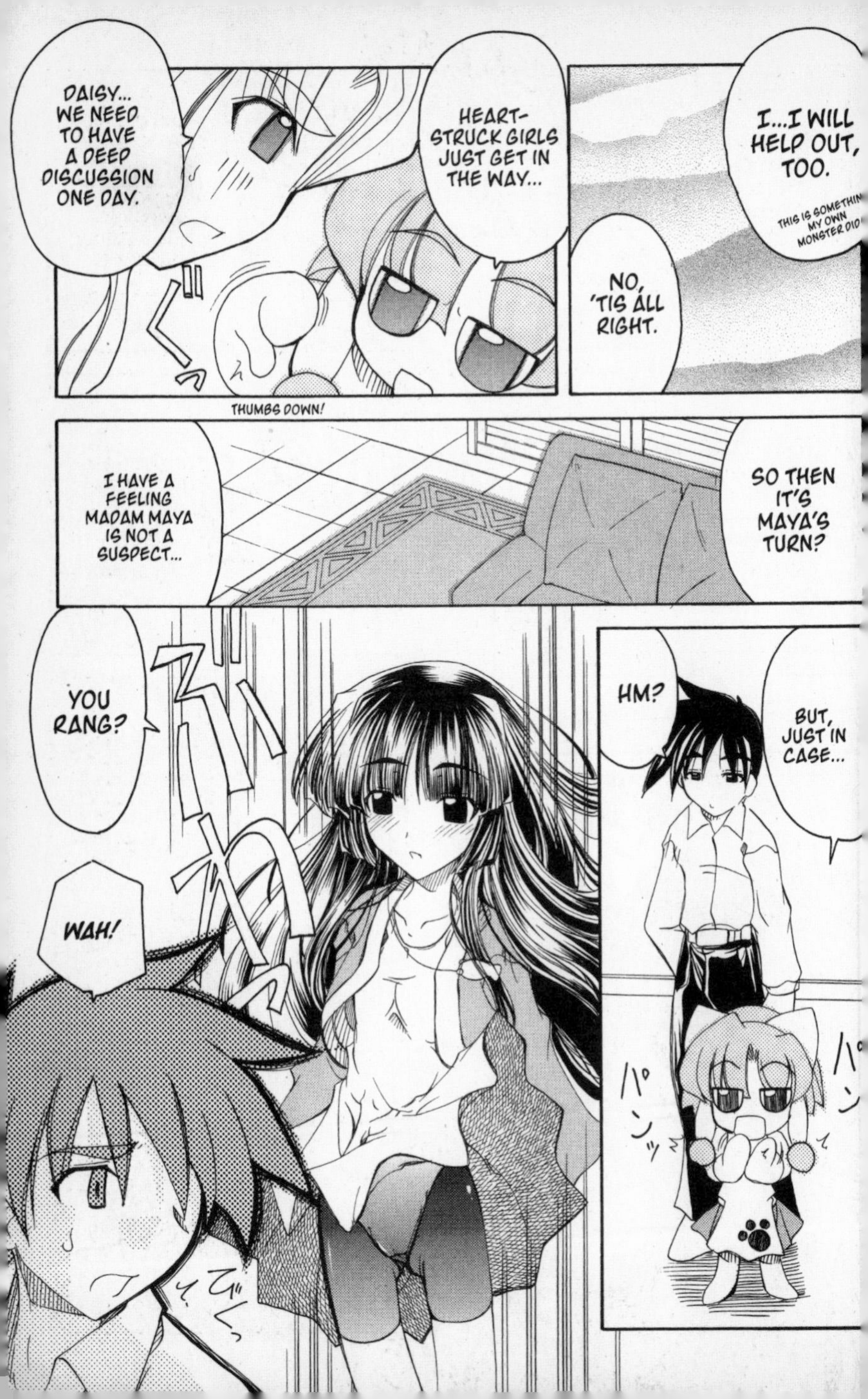
I...I WILL HELP OUT, TOO.
THIS IS SOMETHIN MY OWN MONSTER DID
NO, 'TIS ALL RIGHT.
HEART-STRUCK GIRLS JUST GET IN THE WAY...
DAISY... WE NEED TO HAVE A DEEP DISCUSSION ONE DAY.
THUMBS DOWN!
SO THEN IT'S MAYA'S TURN?
I HAVE A FEELING MADAM MAYA IS NOT A SUSPECT...
BUT, JUST IN CASE...
HM?
YOU RANG?
WAH!

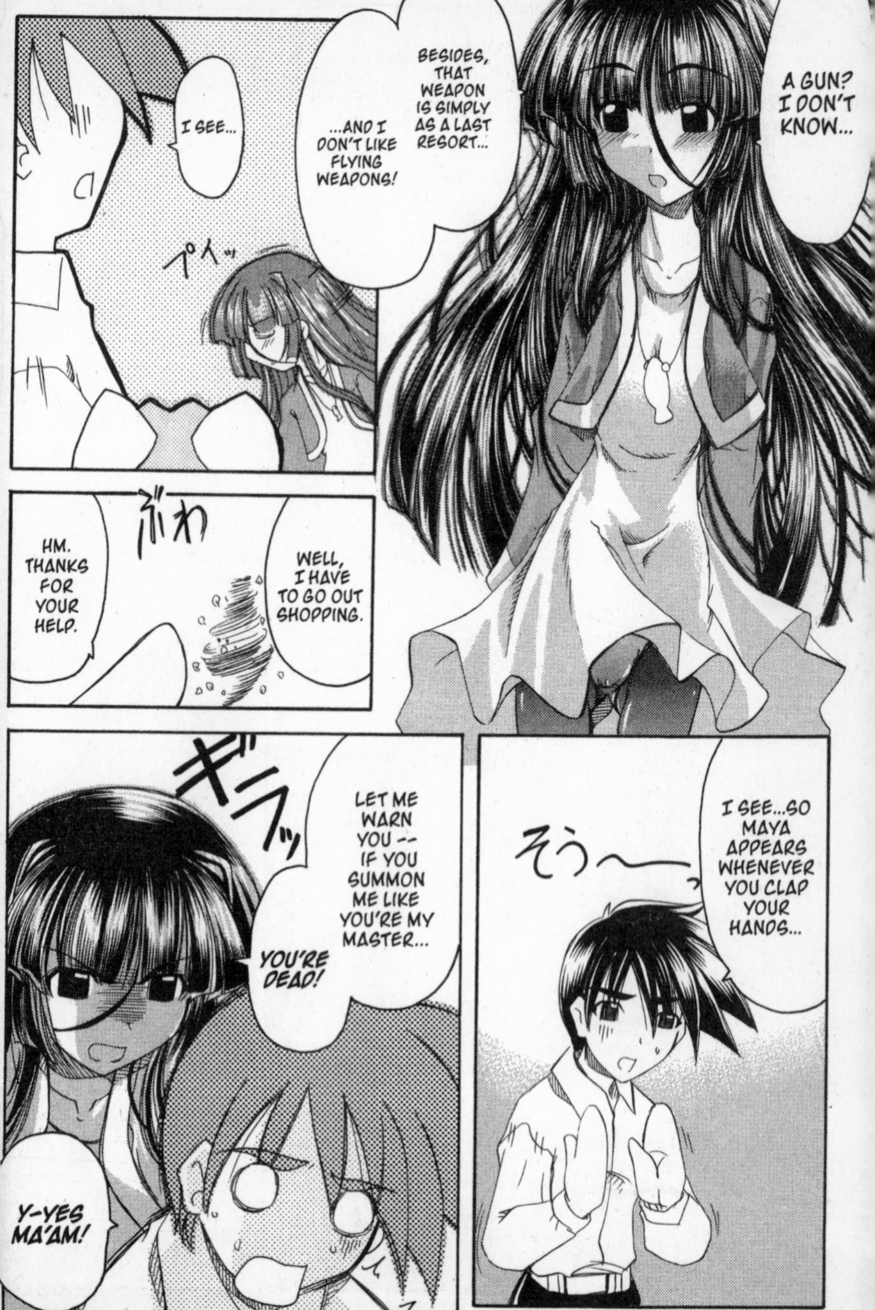
A GUN? I DON'T KNOW...
BESIDES, THAT WEAPON IS SIMPLY AS A LAST RESORT...
...AND I DON'T LIKE FLYING WEAPONS!
I SEE...
プイッ
WELL, I HAVE TO GO OUT SHOPPING.
ぶわ
HM. THANKS FOR YOUR HELP.
I SEE...SO MAYA APPEARS WHENEVER YOU CLAP YOUR HANDS...
そう〜
ギラッ
LET ME WARN YOU -- IF YOU SUMMON ME LIKE YOU'RE MY MASTER...
YOU'RE DEAD!
Y-YES MA'AM!
びくっ

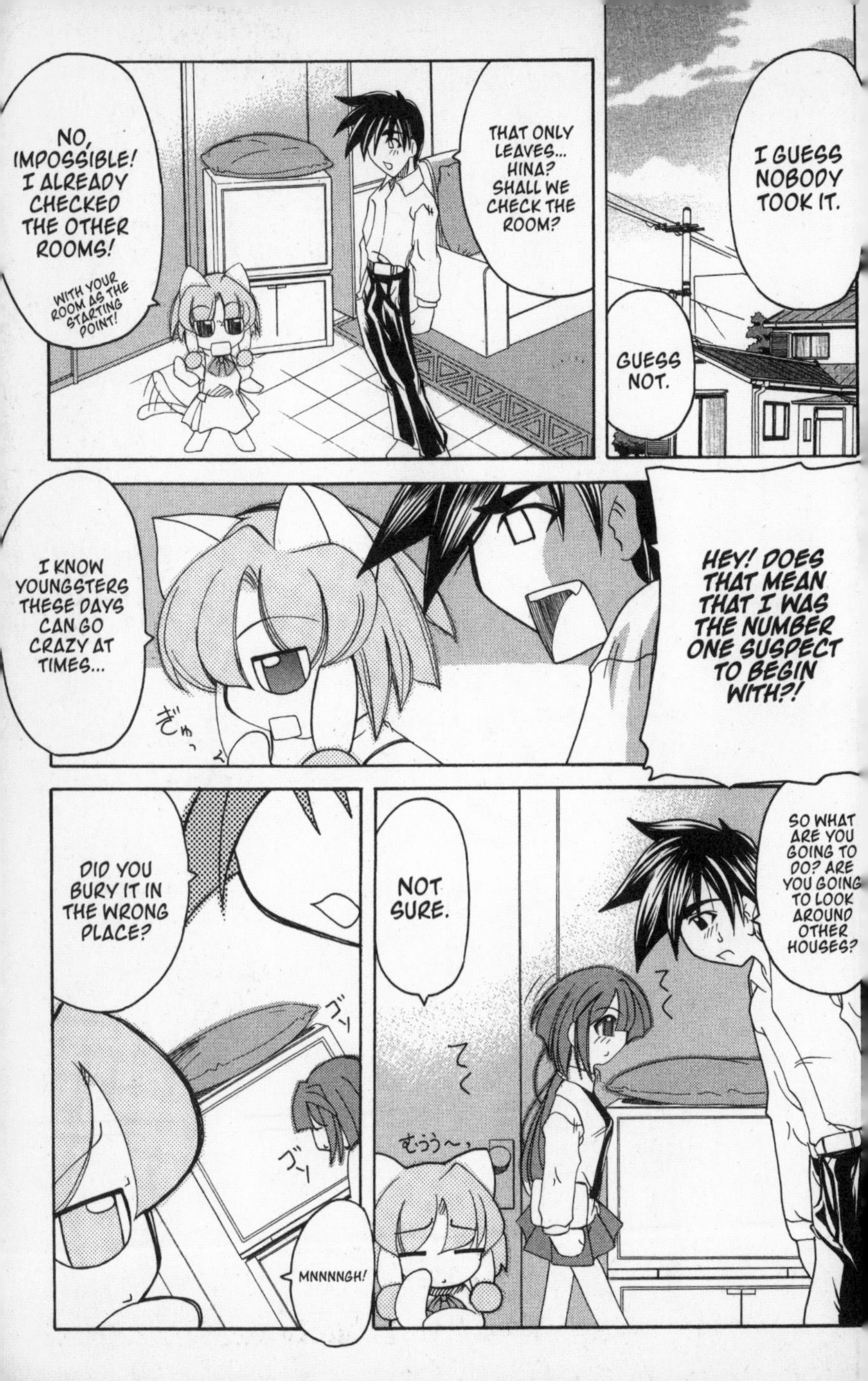
I GUESS NOBODY TOOK IT.
GUESS NOT.
THAT ONLY LEAVES... HINA? SHALL WE CHECK THE ROOM?
NO, IMPOSSIBLE! I ALREADY CHECKED THE OTHER ROOMS!
WITH YOUR ROOM AS THE STARTING POINT!
HEY! DOES THAT MEAN THAT I WAS THE NUMBER ONE SUSPECT TO BEGIN WITH?!
I KNOW YOUNGSTERS THESE DAYS CAN GO CRAZY AT TIMES...
SO WHAT ARE YOU GOING TO DO? ARE YOU GOING TO LOOK AROUND OTHER HOUSES?
NOT SURE.
DID YOU BURY IT IN THE WRONG PLACE?
MNNNNGH!

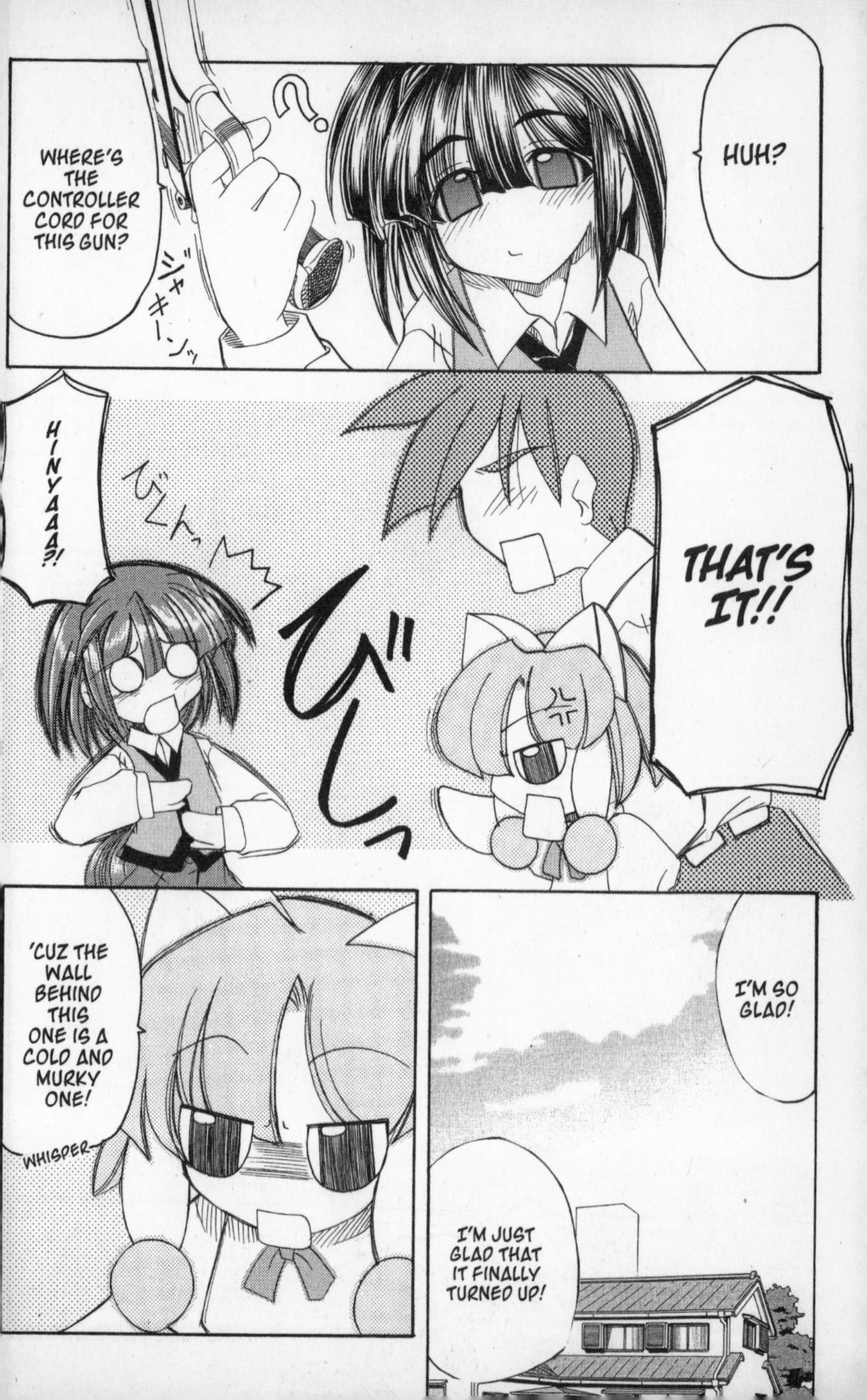
HUH?
WHERE'S THE CONTROLLER CORD FOR THIS GUN?
ジャキーンッ
THAT'S IT!!
びしっ
びくんっ
HINYAAAA?!
I'M SO GLAD!
I'M JUST GLAD THAT IT FINALLY TURNED UP!
'CUZ THE WALL BEHIND THIS ONE IS A COLD AND MURKY ONE!
WHISPER

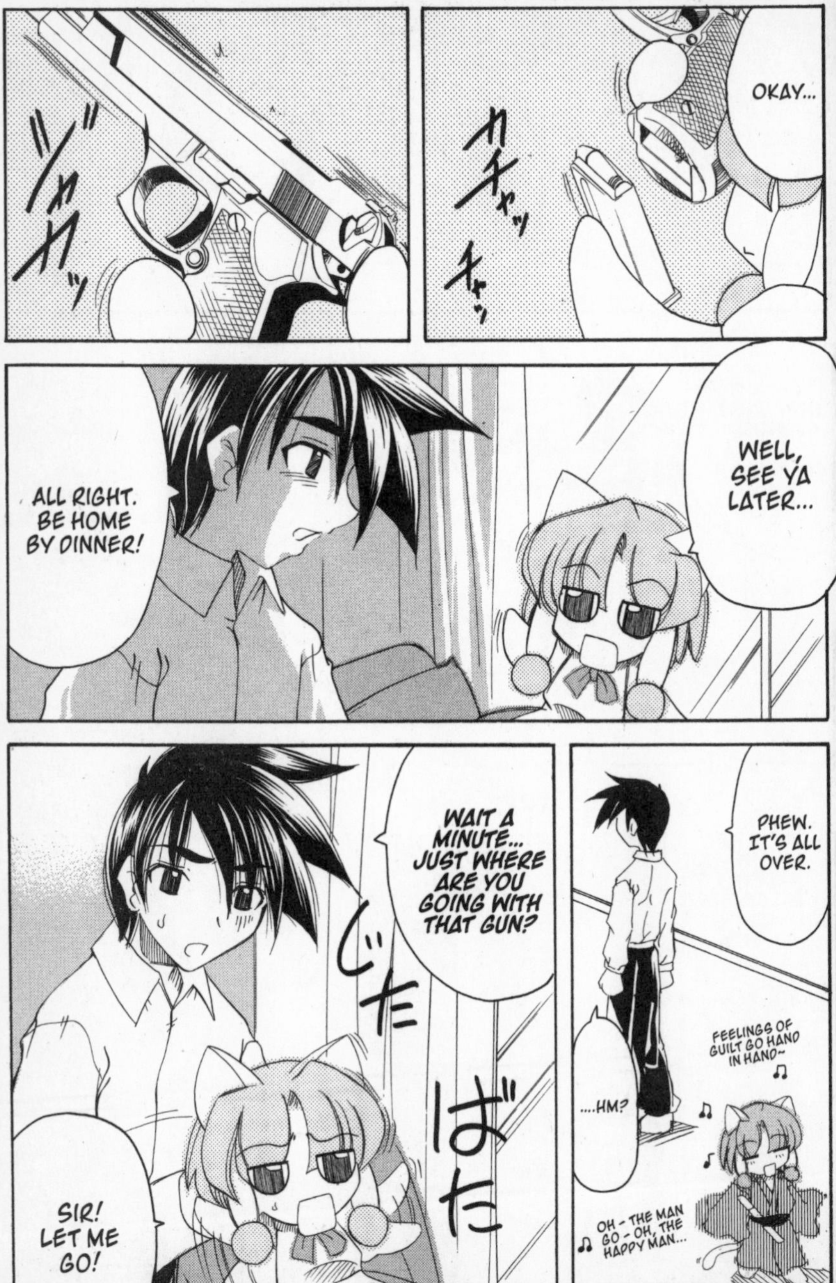
OKAY...
カチャッ
チャッ
ジャカッ
WELL, SEE YA LATER...
ALL RIGHT. BE HOME BY DINNER!
PHEW. IT'S ALL OVER.
FEELINGS OF GUILT GO HAND IN HAND~ ♪
....HM?
OH - THE MAN GO - OH, THE HAPPY MAN... ♪
WAIT A MINUTE... JUST WHERE ARE YOU GOING WITH THAT GUN?
じた
ばた
SIR! LET ME GO!

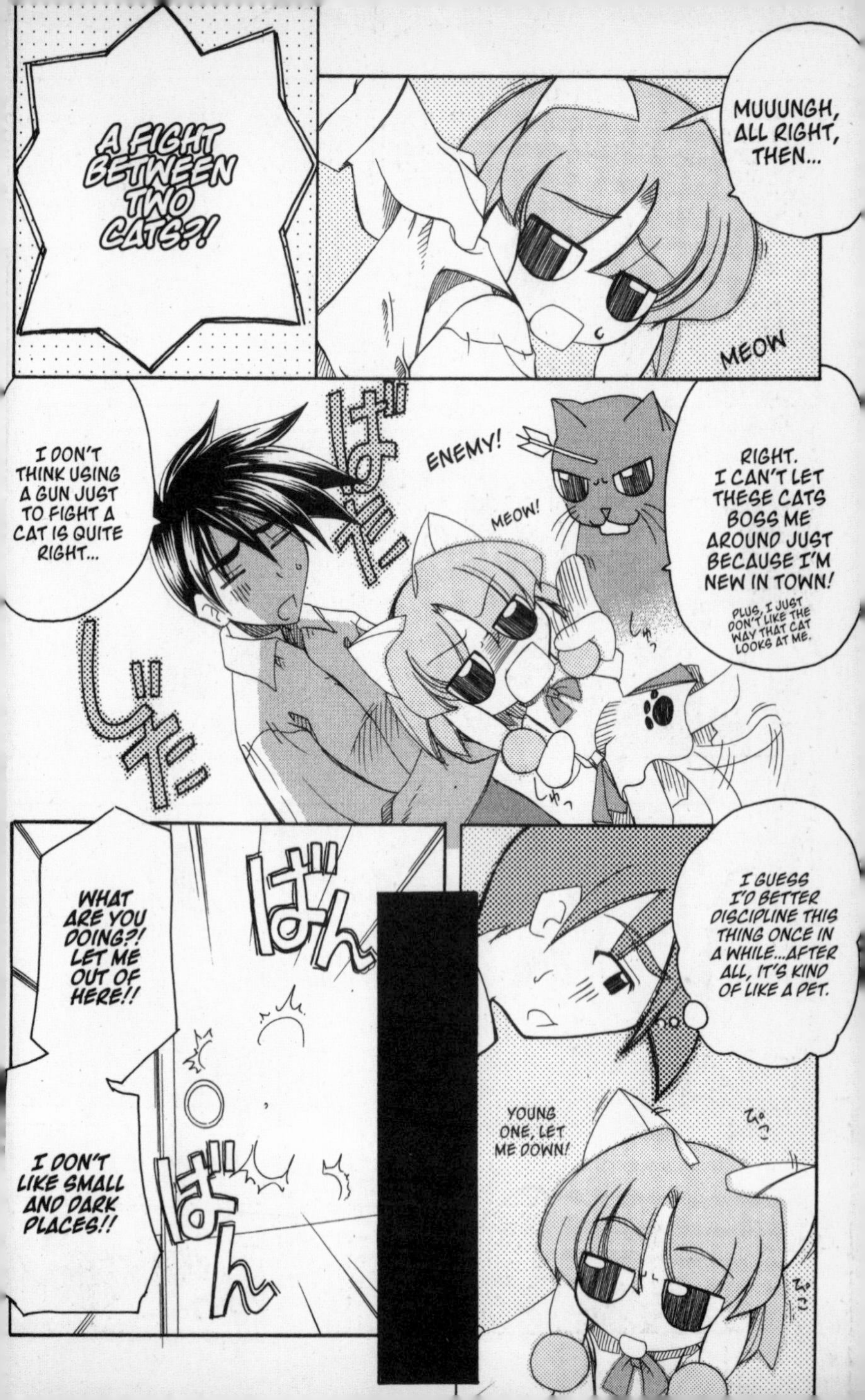
MUUUNGH, ALL RIGHT, THEN...
MEOW
A FIGHT BETWEEN TWO CATS?!
RIGHT. I CAN'T LET THESE CATS BOSS ME AROUND JUST BECAUSE I'M NEW IN TOWN!
PLUS, I JUST DON'T LIKE THE WAY THAT CAT LOOKS AT ME.
ENEMY!
MEOW!
I DON'T THINK USING A GUN JUST TO FIGHT A CAT IS QUITE RIGHT...
I GUESS I'D BETTER DISCIPLINE THIS THING ONCE IN A WHILE...AFTER ALL, IT'S KIND OF LIKE A PET.
YOUNG ONE, LET ME DOWN!
WHAT ARE YOU DOING?! LET ME OUT OF HERE!!
ばん
I DON'T LIKE SMALL AND DARK PLACES!!
ばん

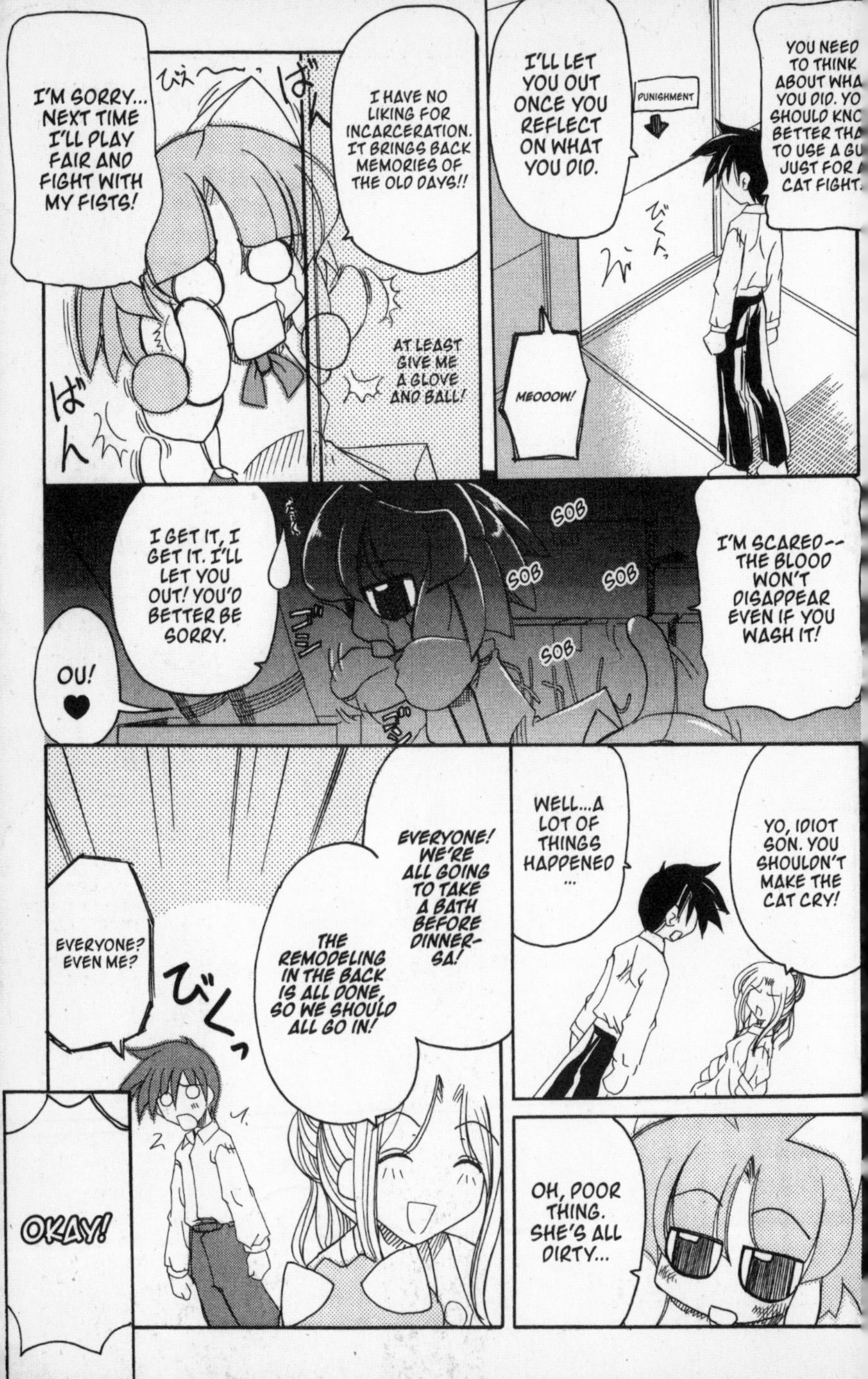
YOU NEED TO THINK ABOUT WHA YOU DID. YO SHOULD KNO BETTER THA TO USE A GU JUST FOR A CAT FIGHT.
PUNISHMENT
びくっ
I'LL LET YOU OUT ONCE YOU REFLECT ON WHAT YOU DID.
MEOOOW!
びえ〜〜
ばん
I HAVE NO LIKING FOR INCARCERATION. IT BRINGS BACK MEMORIES OF THE OLD DAYS!!
AT LEAST GIVE ME A GLOVE AND BALL!
I'M SORRY... NEXT TIME I'LL PLAY FAIR AND FIGHT WITH MY FISTS!
ばん
I'M SCARED-- THE BLOOD WON'T DISAPPEAR EVEN IF YOU WASH IT!
SOB
SOB
SOB
SOB
I GET IT, I GET IT. I'LL LET YOU OUT! YOU'D BETTER BE SORRY.
OU! ♥
YO, IDIOT SON. YOU SHOULDN'T MAKE THE CAT CRY!
WELL...A LOT OF THINGS HAPPENED...
OH, POOR THING. SHE'S ALL DIRTY...
EVERYONE! WE'RE ALL GOING TO TAKE A BATH BEFORE DINNER-SA!
THE REMODELING IN THE BACK IS ALL DONE, SO WE SHOULD ALL GO IN!
びくっ
EVERYONE? EVEN ME?
OKAY!

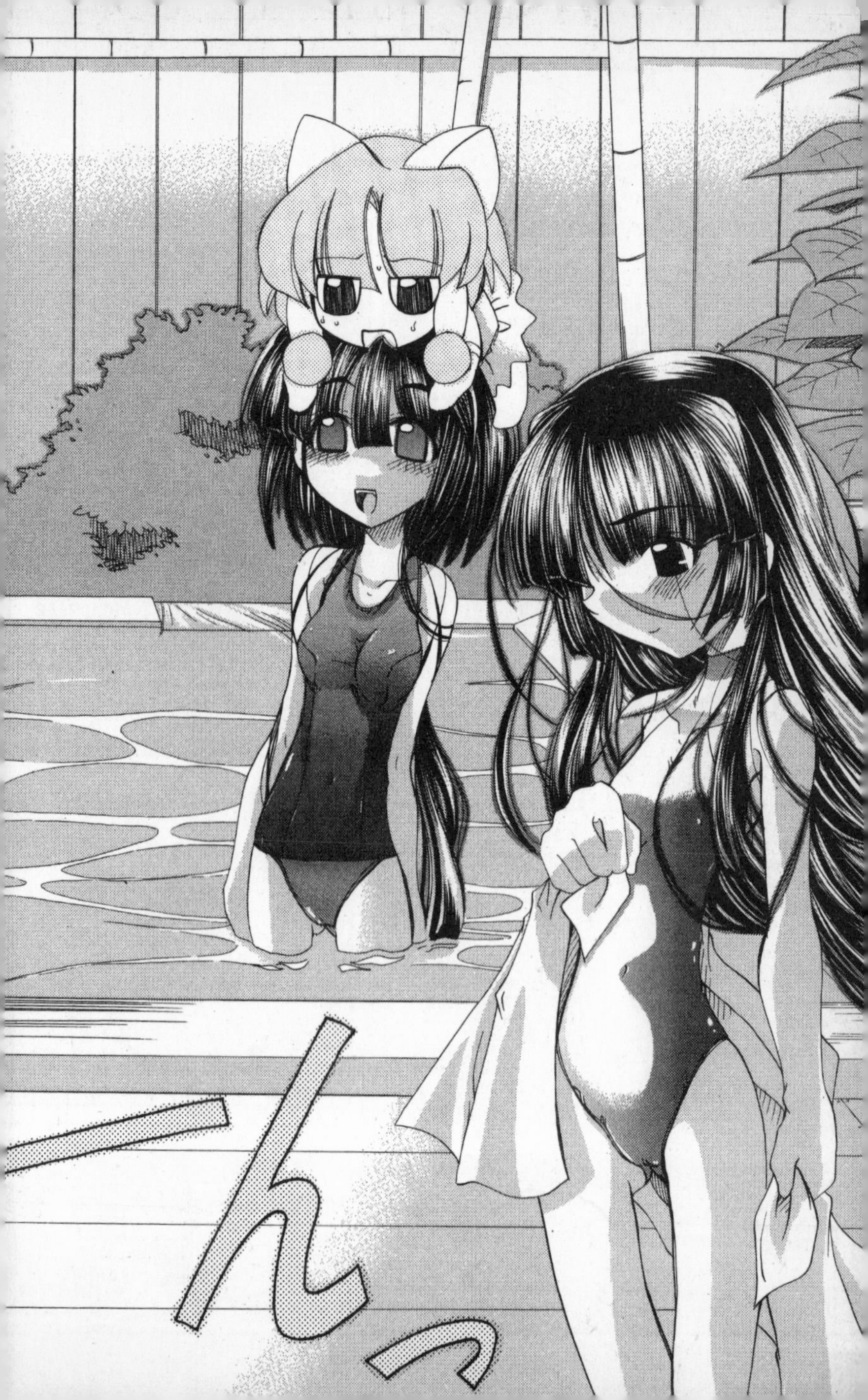
ん～っ

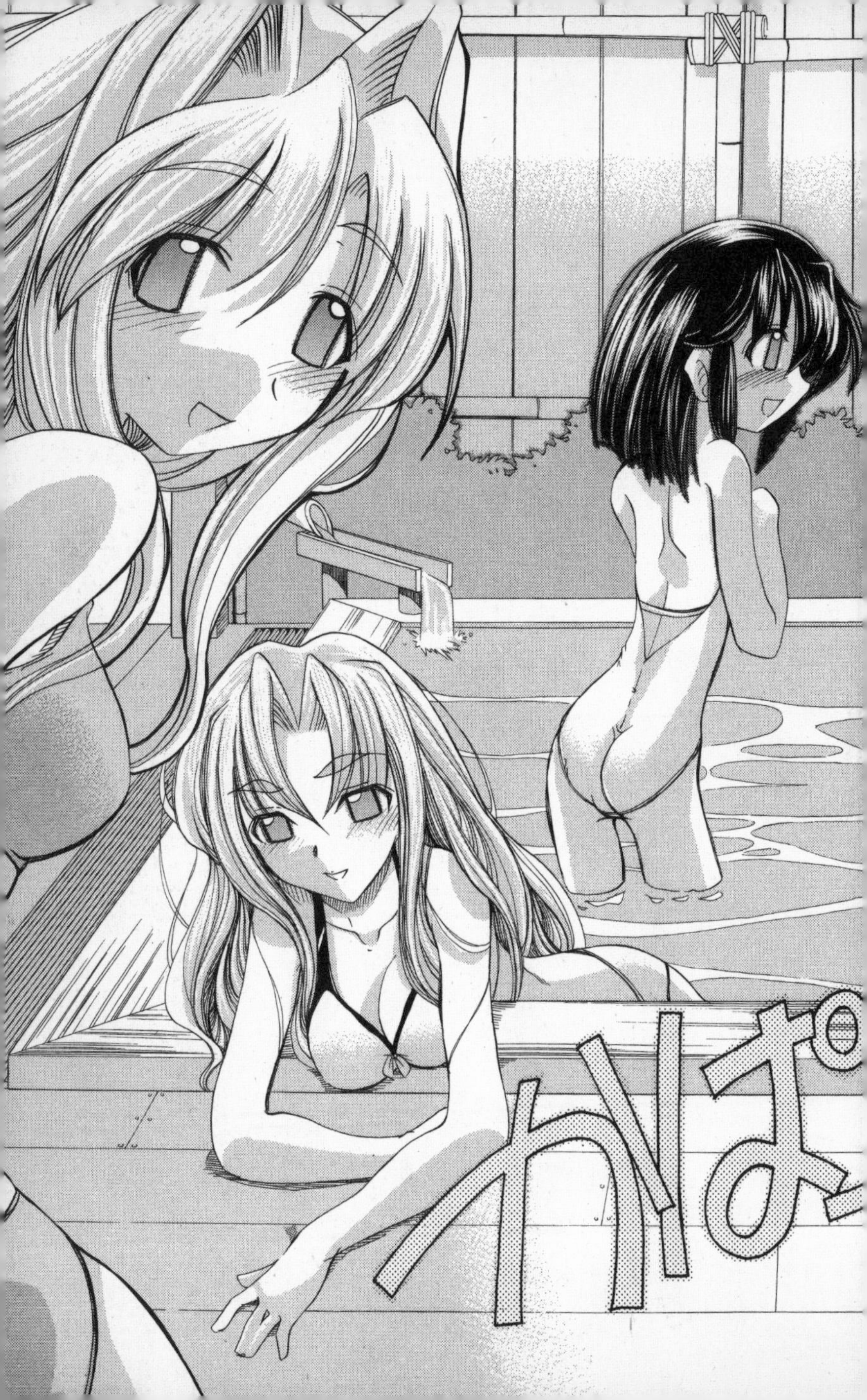

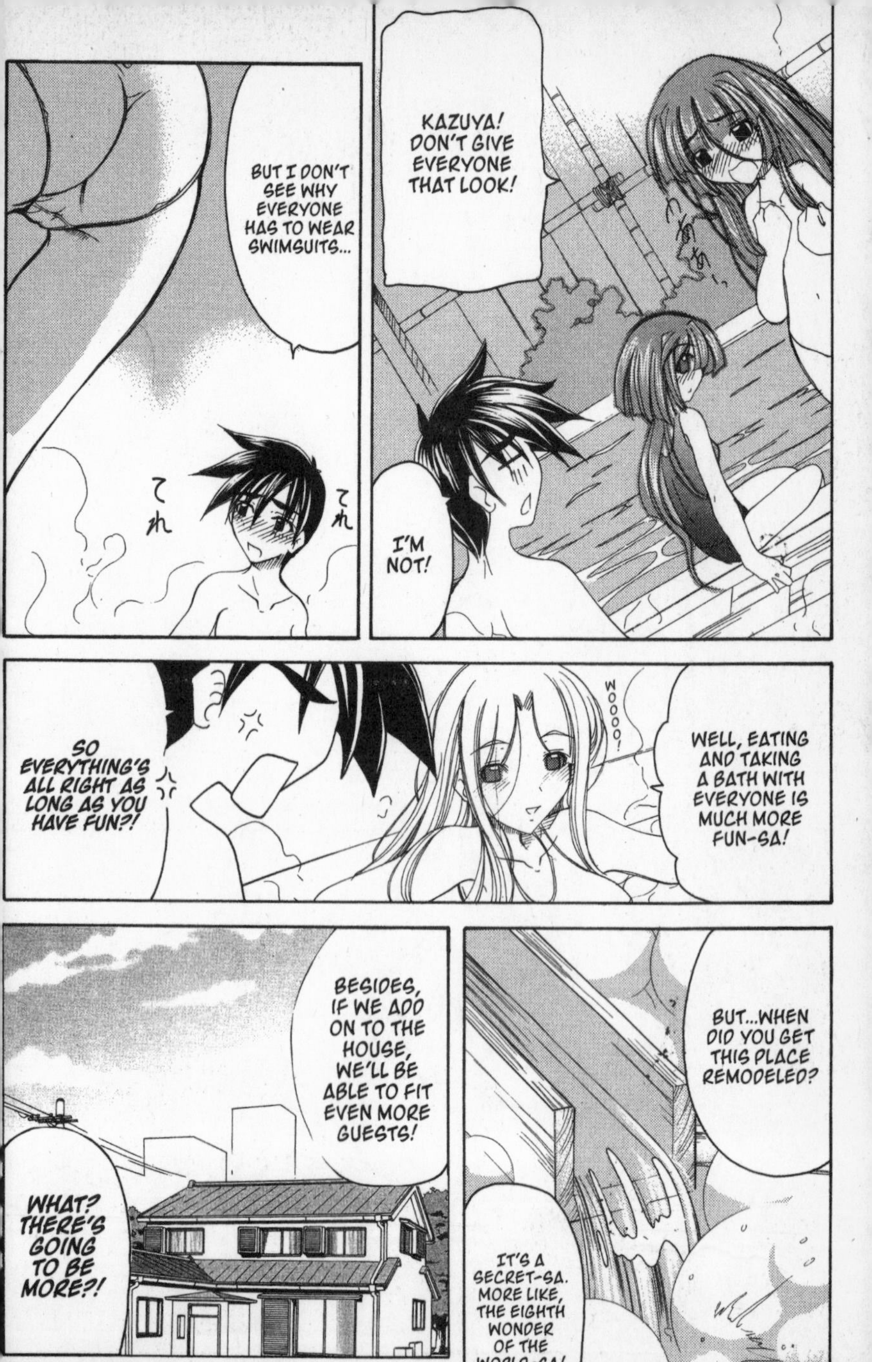
KAZUYA! DON'T GIVE EVERYONE THAT LOOK!
I'M NOT!
BUT I DON'T SEE WHY EVERYONE HAS TO WEAR SWIMSUITS...
てれ
てれ
WELL, EATING AND TAKING A BATH WITH EVERYONE IS MUCH MORE FUN-SA!
WOOOO!
SO EVERYTHING'S ALL RIGHT AS LONG AS YOU HAVE FUN?!
BUT...WHEN DID YOU GET THIS PLACE REMODELED?
IT'S A SECRET-SA. MORE LIKE, THE EIGHTH WONDER OF THE WORLD-SA!
BESIDES, IF WE ADD ON TO THE HOUSE, WE'LL BE ABLE TO FIT EVEN MORE GUESTS!
WHAT? THERE'S GOING TO BE MORE?!

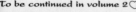

To be continued in volume 2♡

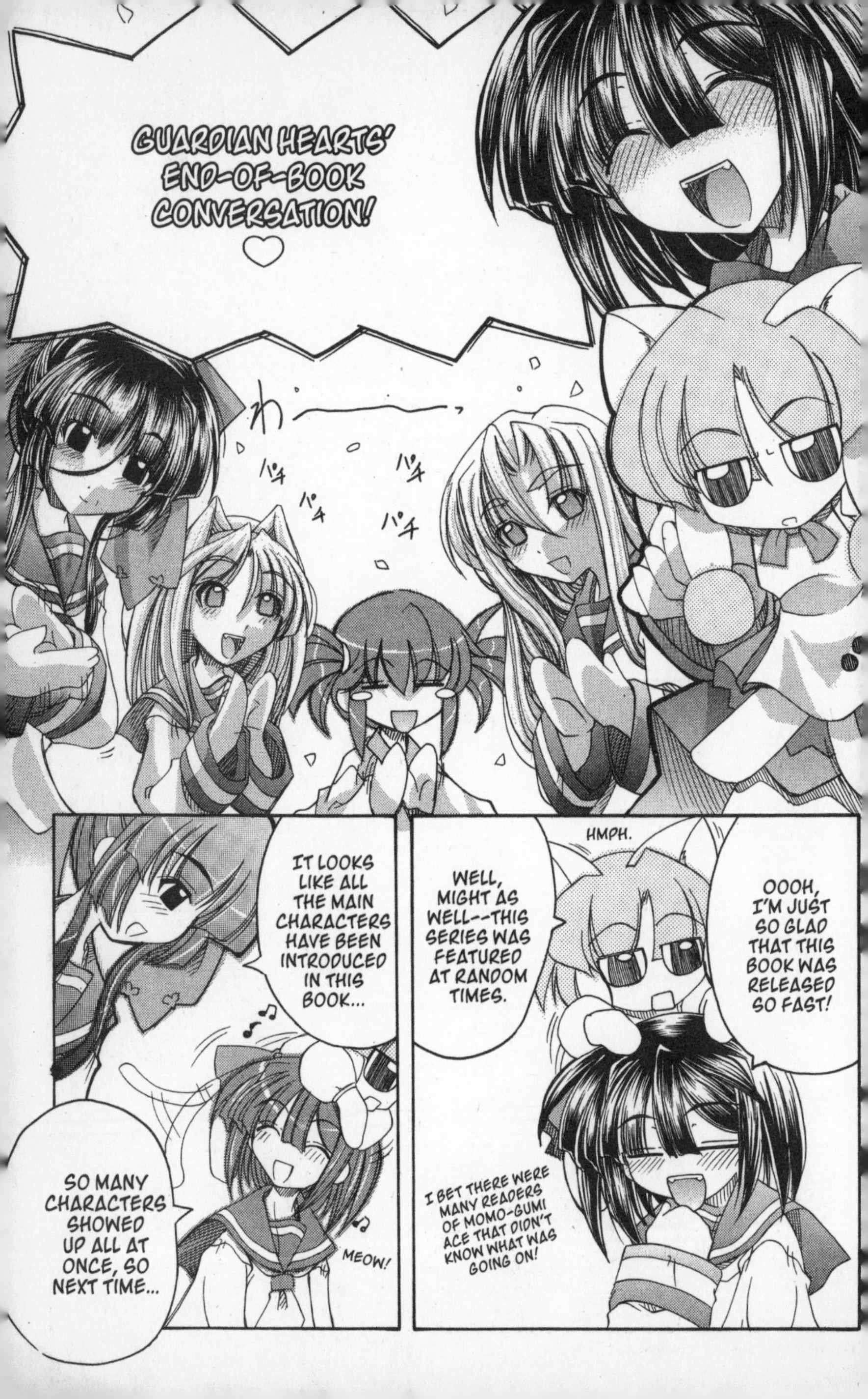
GUARDIAN HEARTS' END-OF-BOOK CONVERSATION!
わーー
パチ
パチ
パチ
パチ
OOOH, I'M JUST SO GLAD THAT THIS BOOK WAS RELEASED SO FAST!
HMPH.
WELL, MIGHT AS WELL--THIS SERIES WAS FEATURED AT RANDOM TIMES.
I BET THERE WERE MANY READERS OF MOMO-GUMI ACE THAT DIDN'T KNOW WHAT WAS GOING ON!
IT LOOKS LIKE ALL THE MAIN CHARACTERS HAVE BEEN INTRODUCED IN THIS BOOK...
SO MANY CHARACTERS SHOWED UP ALL AT ONCE, SO NEXT TIME...
MEOW!

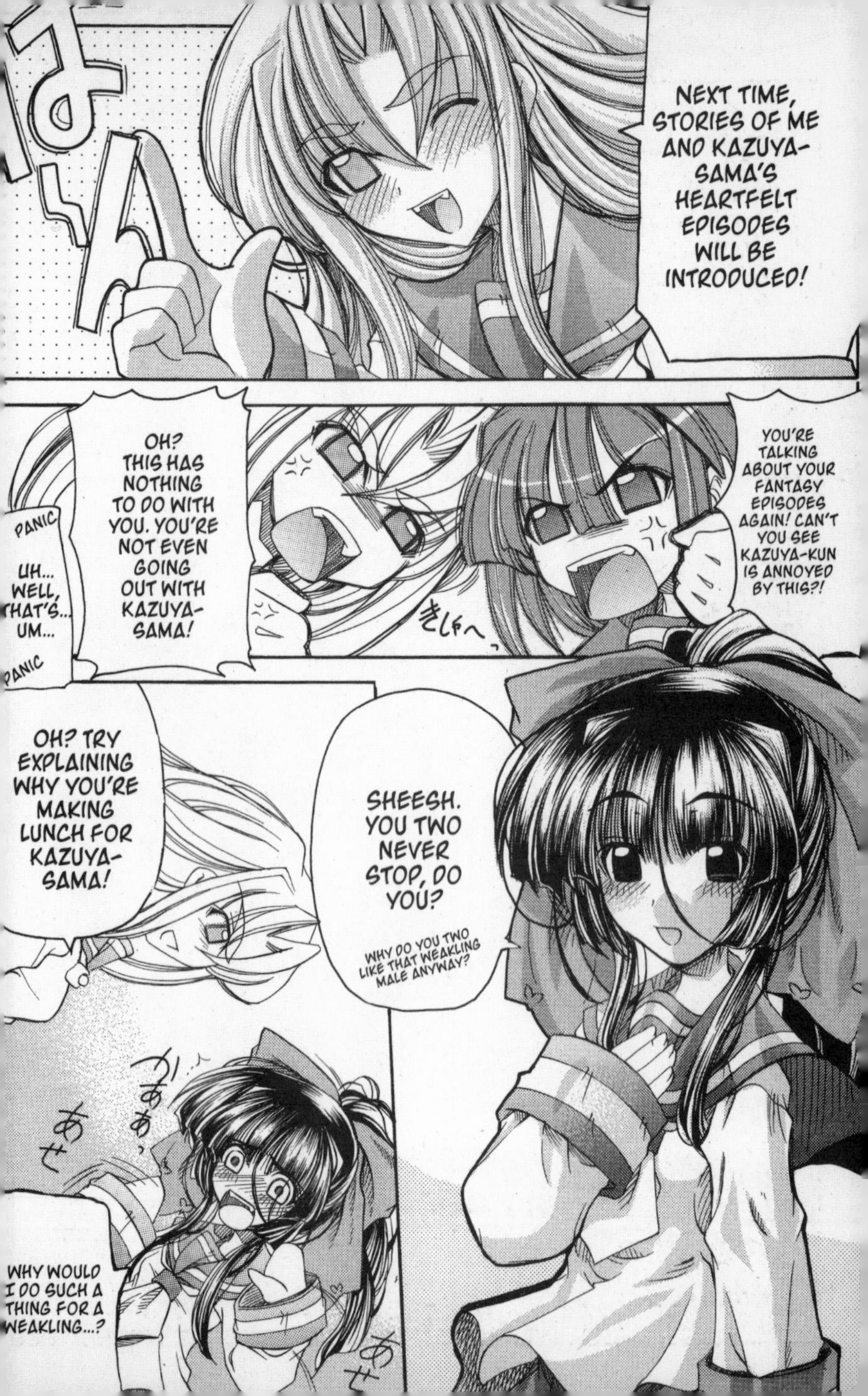
NEXT TIME, STORIES OF ME AND KAZUYA-SAMA'S HEARTFELT EPISODES WILL BE INTRODUCED!
YOU'RE TALKING ABOUT YOUR FANTASY EPISODES AGAIN! CAN'T YOU SEE KAZUYA-KUN IS ANNOYED BY THIS?!
OH? THIS HAS NOTHING TO DO WITH YOU. YOU'RE NOT EVEN GOING OUT WITH KAZUYA-SAMA!
PANIC
UH... WELL, THAT'S... UM...
PANIC
SHEESH. YOU TWO NEVER STOP, DO YOU?
WHY DO YOU TWO LIKE THAT WEAKLING MALE ANYWAY?
OH? TRY EXPLAINING WHY YOU'RE MAKING LUNCH FOR KAZUYA-SAMA!
WHY WOULD I DO SUCH A THING FOR A WEAKLING...?

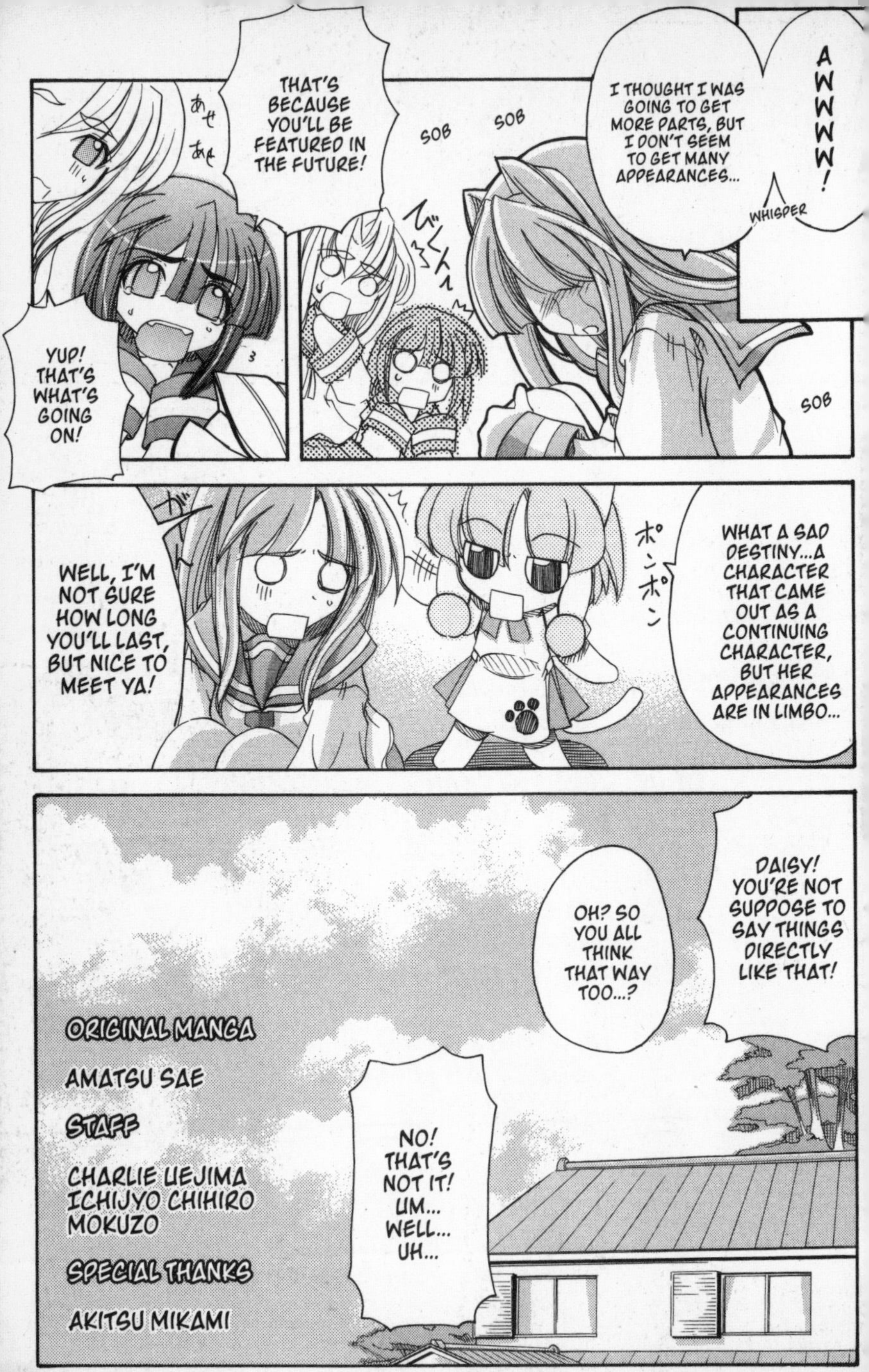
AWWWW!
I THOUGHT I WAS GOING TO GET MORE PARTS, BUT I DON'T SEEM TO GET MANY APPEARANCES...
WHISPER
SOB SOB
SOB
THAT'S BECAUSE YOU'LL BE FEATURED IN THE FUTURE!
あせあせ
YUP! THAT'S WHAT'S GOING ON!
WHAT A SAD DESTINY...A CHARACTER THAT CAME OUT AS A CONTINUING CHARACTER, BUT HER APPEARANCES ARE IN LIMBO...
ポンポン
WELL, I'M NOT SURE HOW LONG YOU'LL LAST, BUT NICE TO MEET YA!
DAISY! YOU'RE NOT SUPPOSE TO SAY THINGS DIRECTLY LIKE THAT!
OH? SO YOU ALL THINK THAT WAY TOO...?
NO! THAT'S NOT IT! UM... WELL... UH...
ORIGINAL MANGA
AMATSU SAE
STAFF
CHARLIE UEJIMA
ICHIJYO CHIHIRO
MOKUZO
SPECIAL THANKS
AKITSU MIKAMI

IN THE NEXT
VOLUME OF

GUARDIAN Hearts

INTRODUCING THE ARCH-ENEMIES OF GAAARTS- *BURN!*
IT'S A SECRET ORGANIZATION WITH THE NEFARIOUS OBJECTIVE OF TAKING OVER THE WORLD!
ONLY GAAARTS STANDS IN THEIR WAY, BUT IT MAY BE TOUGHER THAN EXPECTED WHEN A SPECIAL ASSIGNMENT FOR HINA ATTRACTS SOME UNWANTED ATTENTION FROM BURN!
AND IN THE HEAT OF BATTLE, WE'LL LEARN THAT THERE'S MORE TO HAPLESS KAZUYA THAN FIRST MEETS THE EYE!

ALL THIS AND MORE IN
GUARDIAN HEARTS
VOLUME 2!

STOP!

This is the back of the book. You wouldn't want to spoil a great ending!

This book is printed "manga-style," in the authentic Japanese right-to-left format. Since none of the artwork has been flipped or altered, readers get to experience the story just as the creator intended. You've been asking for it, so TOKYOPOP® delivered: authentic, hot-off-the-press, and far more fun!

DIRECTIONS

1
2
3
4
5
6
7
8
9
10

If this is your first time reading manga-style, here's a quick guide to help you understand how it works.

It's easy... just start in the top right panel and follow the numbers. Have fun, and look for more 100% authentic manga from TOKYOPOP®!

THE MANGA REVOLUTION · LEADING · THE MANGA REVOLUTION · LEADING
漫画革命

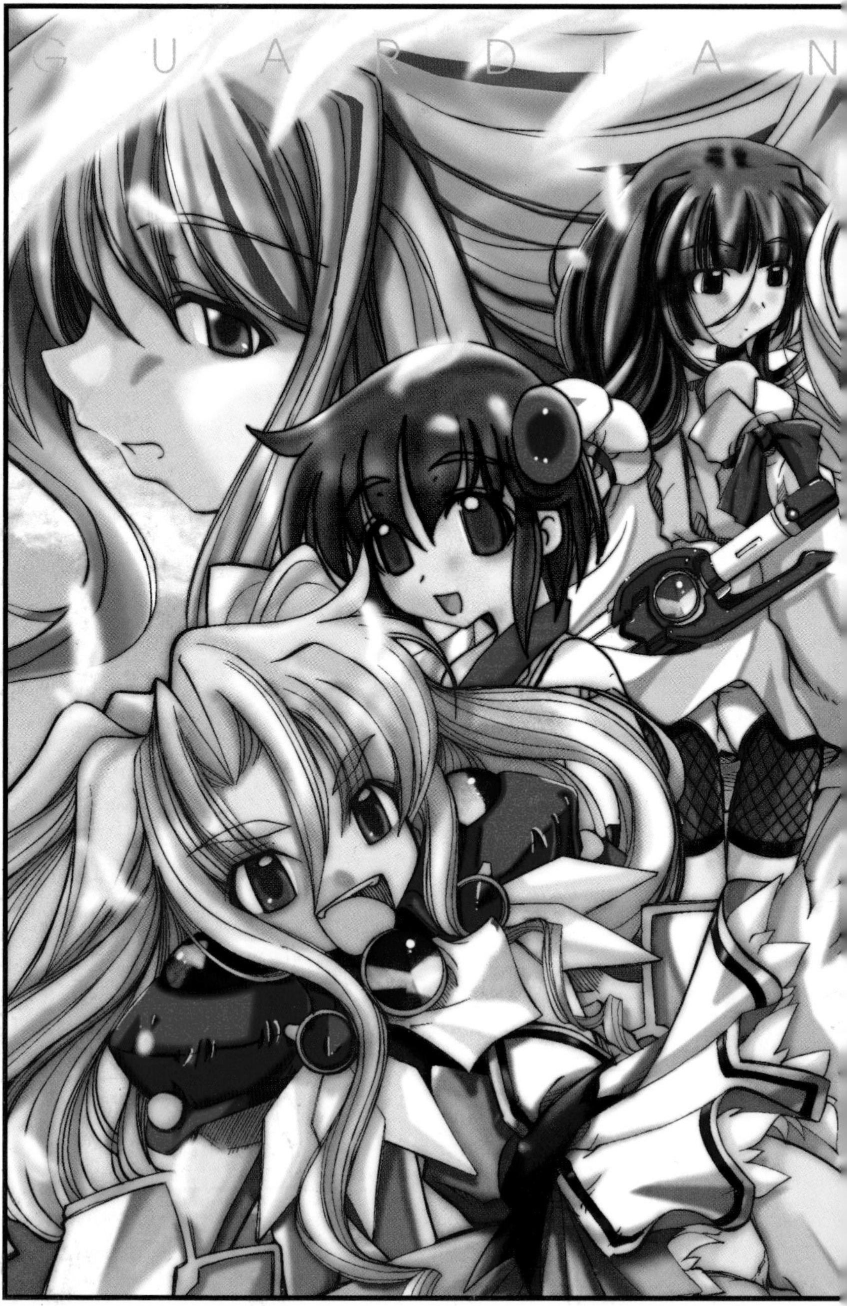
GUARDIAN

Guardian Hearts

C O N T E N T S